What Do Sex and Gender Have to Do with It?

What Do Sex and Gender Have to Do with It?

The Selected Papers of Nancy Kulish

Nancy Kulish

IPBOOKS.net
International Psychoanalytic Books

International Psychoanalytic Books (IPBooks)
New York • http://www.IPBooks.net

What Do Sex and Gender Have to Do with It?: The Selected Papers of Nancy Kulish

Published by IPBooks, Queens, NY
Online at: www.IPBooks.net

Copyright © 2023 Nancy Kulish

ISBN: 978-1-956864-54-0

Introduction: Meet Nancy Kulish

by Arlene Kramer Richards

My first contact with Nancy Kulish was in print. I read her and Deanna Holtzman's paper in *The International Journal of Psychoanalysis* (1998). Their article on the female oedipus complex fascinated me. I am and was gob smacked by its originality and its importance in filling in what Freud had really not even begun to describe about women. What is most amazing to me about her idea is how it has expanded my thinking and that of the entire psychoanalytic community. Rather than one story, the Oedipus story, we now think about each person's own history, own story, own trajectory as it fits into and shapes the present moment in that person's life. As far as I know, Kulish and Holtzman were the first to give detailed support for Karen Horney's proposal that female development was not a simple parallel to male development, but has a different shape and is represented in literature in a different .

Here I want to introduce her to you as an important contributor to psychoanalysis and as a person who uses her own story to illuminate female development. She shows how close attention to the details of character, personality, and social forces of the moment can lead to greater understanding of a particular person and greater capacity to help that person find satisfaction. And she goes beyond that in including the influence of the analyst's own gender in evoking and understanding a patient's communications. I had a telephone conversation with her on November 3, 2023, that I want to share with you. Here it is, edited for brevity:

Arlene: I would like to ask you some questions so that we can appreciate that your work comes from a person, not from a disembodied intellect.

Nancy: Okay.

Arlene: How did you decide to become an analyst?

Nancy: It was a process. I was first interested intellectually when I read Freud in an English literature class in college. That led me to a psychology major. I chose to go to graduate school at the University of Michigan for its great psycho-analytic faculty. A group had come there from England. Nagera, the Novicks, and others. In graduate school I had my first analysis. I had worked for a time in a mental health clinic. The analysis enabled me to choose a good partner, marry and have babies. That was the goal at that time. I then concentrated on raising my family. Once my children went to school, I continued my career.

I was then able to apply for analytic training. I had a second analysis with a training analyst. That was something I had longed for since I was 18 years old and felt that Freud was speaking directly to me.

Arlene: He was a great writer. That was why he got the Goethe prize. He evidently was like that was a person too. Have you read Hilda Doolittle's Homage to Freud? In it Doolittle describes him as first greeting her with "Enter, fair Madame!" His bow, with a flourish, was certainly a personal moment of contact. So, my second question is: What did you think of your own analysis, especially about women's issues as they were understood at that time?

Nancy: My first in graduate school got me to get a good mate. It was a little stiff, formulaic, but the analyst was not experienced so he stuck to the theory. My second was a training analyst so he was experienced, quieter, kinder, a wise man. It was different because of who he was and maybe where I was at the time. He spoke right to the point.

Looking back, the second man was less theory bound. At the end of the first one, I was in the woman's role and that was it. But it seemed a little off, even at the time. That's it. Met the criteria! The second was "Let's see what's inside of you." It was encouraging and empowering. The first was textbook of the time.

Arlene: How has your theory affected your practice?

Nancy: I think theory is not too effective when you fit people into it. Now I try to think of each woman individually. What she's got; what gets in her way; what society wants from her, and what strengths and power she has.

Arlene: How has your practice affected your theory?

Nancy: Theory helped me to wait, listen and learn. More questioning, less certainty, More sense of change. More alive. I feel lucky to be in this era of psychoanalysis with many women and men I can learn with.

Arlene: What would you want young analysts to know about female development and especially being a female analyst?

Nancy: For young women the emphasis on gender has left out the specificity of each woman. I think young women need to know what it means to have a female body. They need to pay attention to their own sense of being a woman and appreciate the complexities of the interplay.

Contents

CHAPTER 1

Gender and Transference:
The Screen of the Phallic Mother

(1986). Int. Rev. Psycho-Anal., (13):393-404

INTRODUCTION

Recently psychoanalytic writers, mostly women, have begun to focus on the question of how gender of the analyst or therapist might affect the transference in psychoanalysis or psychoanalytic psychotherapy. This question has also made its way into the popular literature in the best-selling novel *August* by Judith Rossner (1983). The novel depicts the interfacing lives of a young woman and her female analyst in New York. The story, in which the girl had previously seen two male analysts, gives Rossner the opportunity to comment on the differences in the girl's treatment at the hands of a male versus a female therapist, largely in terms of her feminist concerns with a male's lack of empathy for and power over a female.

Indeed, it may have been at the nudging of feminists that psychoanalysis has turned its attention to the questions of gender-related differences in psychosexual development and how they impact on the psychotherapeutic process. The interest in the subject also reflects a general shift within psychoanalysis in the conceptualizations of transference. The classical view of transference stems from Freud's first writings on the subject. He pictured transference as a fixed disposition within the individual to repeat his or her infantile conflicts with the person of the analyst (Freud 1912), (1915). Later writers such as Blum

1

(1971) and Sandler (1976) have encompassed Freud's later structural theories and emphasis on aggressive as well as libidinal drives into the understanding of transference. Such writers view transference as less fixed and more possibly influenced by present realities within the analytic situation, including the gender of the analyst. Other writers such as Gill (1982) or Langs (1973) have emphasized the importance of the interaction between patient and therapist in the unfolding of the transference. In this interaction, the actuality of the therapist's personality and the patient's view of it help to determine and define the transference. My own view of transference does take as its starting point an unconscious, genetically and internally based disposition, which is influenced by and influences the interpersonal process of which it becomes a dynamic part.

The current interest in gender and transference has generated much excitement and discussion as it touches upon important theoretical and clinical issues, such as the role of reality in the unfolding of transference or the selection of therapist by gender. Yet, a review of the literature on gender and transference (Kulish, 1984) generates many questions but few substantial findings. There is general agreement on several points: one, that gender of the therapist can contribute to major resistances within the transference, especially early in the treatment; two, that gender influences or facilitates positive transferences that may help to launch an analysis; three, that gender shapes or colours the content of the clinical material; and four, that gender may determine the order in which this material emerges. These latter two points were first mentioned by Freud (1931), who suggested that early, pre-oedipal material relating to the mother might make itself known more readily in the transference to female analysts.

Two other intriguing, but more controversial, questions have been raised in the recent literature: The first is that gender of the analyst differentially determines whether the transference takes a 'maternal' or 'paternal' cast. The second concerns the question of strongly erotic or 'eroticized' transferences and how the gender of the analyst may contribute to such manifestations. In both of these questions the concept of 'the phallic mother' has frequently been advanced as an explanation of observed differences. It is my intention here to examine more closely the concept of the phallic mother as it appears in this context. It is not my purpose to focus on the concept in itself, but only to use it to illustrate how gender of the therapist might relate to the transference. It is my feeling that gender can be a major organizing factor both for the patient and for the analyst. A conceptual construction such as 'phallic mother' both conveys gender-related distortions and fantasies which make up transferences, and gender-related biases and blind spots which contribute to countertransferences. Before turning to the discussion of the 'phallic mother' as it relates to gender and transference, however, I will briefly review the usage of the concept of phallic mother more generally within psychoanalysis. Its usage demonstrates how an aspect of theory can serve both as a powerful explanatory device and as a limiting curb to our understanding of ourselves and our patients.

THE CONCEPT OF THE PHALLIC MOTHER

Freud did not use the term phallic mother until late in his writings, although Little Hans' fantasy that his mother possessed a penis is clearly discernible in the material of the case published in 1909. In his writings on fetishism, Freud (1927), (1940) described how the little boy must construct a fantasy of a woman with a phallus to ward off the recognition of the threatening reality of a castrated, penis-less creature, the woman, and the possibility of his own castration. In 1933, Freud referred to Abraham's discussion of the spider as a symbol of the mother. The sight of a spider evokes dread of incestuous wishes toward mother, and horror of the female genital. According to Freud, both little girls and little boys view mother as possessing a penis until the time they discover sexual differences.

Later writers have elaborated on the role of the fantasied phallic mother in defending against the boy's castration anxiety. Bak (1968) described the phallic woman as 'the ubiquitous fantasy in perversions'. Stoller's work (1975) emphasizes the importance of the fantasy for male homosexuals, transvestites and fetishists. In dressing up as a woman, for example, the transvestite acts out this unconscious fantasy of a woman with a penis. Greenacre (1968) also pointed to the underlying castration anxiety and fantasy of the phallic mother in understanding the meaning of the fetish in the male. Both Stoller and Greenacre stress the role of childhood trauma, such as an overly seductive mother, in the reinforcement of the fantasy in such male patients. Helene Deutsch (1965) felt that homosexuality in women also reveals the presence of this fantasy. A lesbian, in taking a masculine role or choosing a masculine lover, may be creating in fantasy such a phallic mother and denying her perception of being castrated.

While the concept has been seen primarily as a denial of castration anxiety of both the girl and the boy, the 'phallic mother' has also been understood as expressing earlier, more infantile fears. Ruth Mack Brunswick (1940) asserted that the concept is a regressive compensatory one. The phallic mother not only possesses a penis, she is 'all powerful'. The idea of a penis is projected back upon the image of the active mother and her breast, from the oral stages.

Roheim (1945), in a fascinating essay on the phallic mother in mythology, focused on the images of witches in central European folklore. The witch with her broomstick, hairy chin, and pointed hat is clearly the woman endowed with a phallus. The common folktale that a witch can be discerned through a hole in a piece of wood betrays the wish that the phallus may be spied through the female's hole or vagina. Thus, Roheim also suggested that the phallic mother defends not only against the threat of castration, but the recognition of the existence of the vagina. At the same time, mythological witches are frequently tied to or identified with images of cows and milk, especially ruined or poisoned milk. The phallic mother is really the oral mother, then, the witch who attacks the source of milk and embodies the infant's aggression against the mother.

Here is the equation: 'penis equals breast'. Other authors (Evans, 1972; (Ewens, 1976; (Greenacre, 1968; (Hermann, 1949) have stressed the pregenital underpinnings of the phallic mother. Chronologically, sexual differences come into focus during the anal phase, so she is also the sadistic anal mother (Chasseguet-Smirgel, 1964).

In a similar vein, Chasseguet-Smirgel (1964) asserted that the image of the omnipotent mother survives in us all. The boy's desire to free himself from her domination and his guilt about his hostility and his triumph over her add power to the fantasy of the phallic mother. The sight of the female genital is frightening, not only because it arouses castration anxiety, but because it confirms the role of the father and his penis in sexual intercourse. The fantasy also expresses the boy's denial of the existence of the adult vagina and the feelings of inadequacy it evokes. The fantasy concerns both fears about differences in the sexes and differences in the generations.

Kubie (1974) explained the fantasy from a unique perspective: as a manifestation of the 'drive to become both sexes', with which, he suggested, everyone struggles. The phallic mother equals the man-woman both male and female patients would wish to become. Kubie believed that the inability to commit oneself to either gender and the desire to identify with both parents spring from a deep tendency of human nature. This wish can be traced in psychopathology, relationships between the sexes, works of art and literature, and in fantasy life.

This brief review of the literature on the concept of the phallic mother shows how it plays a role in many current theoretical controversies: the attack on the notion of the primacy of the phallus and penis envy in female psychosexual development; the meaning and timing of the child's recognition of sexual differences; the role of pre-oedipal versus oedipal factors in the genesis of neurosis; that is, how 'phallic' is the 'phallic mother'? While highlighting these controversies is not my aim, I will attempt to show that our theoretical concepts such as phallic mother, with all the weight that they carry, do shape our processing, understanding, and management of the transference and, particularly as it relates to our gender. The 'phallic mother' has been variously described as a projected image in the transference as maternal, paternal, bisexual, a ban against or an expression of erotic feelings toward the same or opposite sex.

THE MATERNAL VERSUS THE PATERNAL TRANSFERENCE

An obvious influence of therapists' gender on the transference may be its influence on whether the material has a 'maternal' versus 'paternal' cast.

Theoretically, 'maternal' and 'paternal' transferences[1] should be evoked freely by analysts or therapists of both sexes; certainly, we know this to be the case. Nevertheless, Freud (1931) was the first to point out that maternal transferences were less available to and understood by him because of his sex than were paternal transferences. The minuscule bit of empirical data available on the question suggests that in therapies other than analysis, images of therapists correlate with their manifest genders (Goldberg, 1979). The psychoanalytic literature on the subject suggests a puzzling difference, however: that male analysts, since Freud, do report many instances in which they are seen as the mother in the transference, yet virtually no reports by female analysts of *sustained* paternal transferences are available. Even in the novel *August*, this apparent difference is noted in a conversation between a female and male analyst at a cocktail party: "'It's my experience", Seaver said, "that the analyst becomes both the mother and father". "It's not my experience", Lulu said' (Rossner, 1983, p. 38). Does this difference reflect a clinical actuality and if so, why?

In approaching this question, I have been speaking with female analysts from around the country to tap their clinical experiences. Several of these women felt there was no truth to the statement that paternal transferences

---

1 I am uncomfortable with this overly schematic terminology of 'maternal' and 'paternal' transferences, as I view transferences as organized around affects or need-states. For the sake of argument, however, I will stick with this language.

are less common for female analysts and cited their clinical experience in observing paternal transferences. Some suggested that the presumed lack of paternal transferences to female analysts may be a function of referral patterns. Women analysts tend to see fewer men than women, and the men who seek them out, or are referred to them, tend to be more disturbed and hence more prone to pre-oedipal maternal transferences. More of the women analysts, however, used such words as 'more subtle', 'less frequent', 'not sustained', to describe the incidences of paternal transferences to them. In my own clinical experience prior to beginning this research, I had only seen fleeting paternal images.

The difference, if real—fewer or weaker paternal transferences with female analysts—can be explained from the side of the patient, the analyst, or both. From the patient's side, several explanations have been advanced. These revolve mainly around developmental issues. Because early experiences with the mother form the basic matrix from which all object relations spring, maternal transferences are, in general, more prevalent or more central (Greenacre, 1954; Zetzel, 1966). A second argument suggests that our knowledge of 'maleness' comes developmentally later and is differentiated from our knowledge of 'femaleness'. Hence, 'maleness' is tied more to reality and less resistant to breakdown than the concept of 'femaleness'. Thus, paternal or masculine images are more tied to the reality of the therapist's gender and less likely to be superimposed on a female therapist (Zetzel, 1966; Karme, 1979); Mason, 1983).

From the side of the analyst, it is possible that an analyst might have difficulty, in general, in perceiving the transference in terms of images, roles or attitudes related to the opposite sex. This difficulty would, of course, hold true for male analysts as well as female analysts (Stein & Auchincloss, 1984). It may be particularly difficult, however, for women to allow themselves to view or understand the transference in masculine or 'paternal' terms. Several writers have suggested, for example, that women analysts may be inclined to focus too readily on the early maternal material or interpret into the 'dyad' (Bernstein,

1984; Stein & Auchincloss, 1984). Lerner (1974), in a thought-provoking paper about the depreciation of women in society in general and in psychoanalytic theory in particular, concludes that 'the character of the primitive maternal image and women's related fear of their castrating and destructive potential may be such that the female sex has relatively greater difficulty acknowledging and directly expressing aggressive, competitive and ambitious strivings' (p. 551).

Kubie (1974) came to an opposite conclusion about how cultural attitudes may influence the expression of 'the drive to become both sexes'. He felt that in our culture the drive is tolerated or even encouraged in women, but almost totally repressed in men, except in cases of sexual deviation. While Kubie's premise of a primary, unconscious drive to be both sexes is debatable, his notion that the individual expresses or becomes aware of attitudes or attributes relative to both sexes as a function of differing environmental influences is relevant here.

Another explanation of the lack of reported paternal images is that paternal or masculine images in the transference are interpreted in terms of the 'phallic mother'. A search of the clinical literature reveals how a construct such as the 'phallic mother' can obscure the vision of the analyst to other paradigms in the transference. In a case of a male patient presented by Eva Lester (1982), the concept of the phallic mother figured predominantly. Within the transference the patient projected some masculine images, she felt, but a 'consolidating maternal image' arose—a feared phallic mother. In this case and elsewhere (Szmarag, 1982), Lester asserted that in the male patient-female analyst dyad the paternal negative oedipal transference is qualitatively indistinguishable from the maternal one to the phallic mother; that is, she felt that certain paternal images are indistinguishable from maternal ones. In her discussion of Lester's case, Marianne Goldberger (Lester, 1982) pointed out that the manifestations Lester labelled as phallic mother could also be interpreted in terms of the paternal transference. Moreover, Goldberger suggested that phallic mother and penetrating father may not be impossible to distinguish.

Differentiating the 'phallic mother' from images of the father may, indeed, not be simple. As in all other matters, we must be guided by the context in which in the clinical material appears, the accumulated clinical data about the patient, and not the manifest content of the associations. Very little help can be found in the literature on this question.

Bernstein & Warner (1984) summarized several cases of female patients seen by female analysts in which images of the analyst in the transference alternated at times between phallic mother and oedipal father or became condensed into one intrusive figure. Since the cases are not reported in detail, it is not clear how these images were distinguished, except on the obvious grounds of whether pre-oedipal or oedipal concerns were reflected in the material. They suggest that the sexualized homosexual transference which develops initially with certain of their female patients is pre-oedipal, as a defence against deep, early longings for the mother perceived as unavailable. The mother, in such cases, can also appear as phallic. Notably, Bernstein & Warner also observed that female analysts, including themselves, resist seeing themselves in masculine roles in the transference.

Male analysts as well as female encounter the issue of differentiating the penetrating father from the phallic mother in the transference. Shengold (1963), in a rich paper on the sphinx, whom he feels represents the primal parent and the phallic mother, described a clinical case in which he, as analyst, was used as the penetrative phallic mother. Other male writers (Finklestein, 1975; Orgel, 1965), however, described cases replete with genetic and fantasy material about 'phallic mothers' in which they do not report themselves in terms of this role in the transference.

In a clinical paper about a case of a man whose history revealed he had been used as and took on the role of his mother's phallus, Shevin (1963) briefly addressed this issue. In the transference, Shevin described how he became the patient's (phallic) mother for whom the patient performed and with whom the patient was regressively fused. At other times the patient took the role of the mother and treated the analyst as the phallic extension of himself. Later on in the treatment, the patient was able to identify with the analyst and other males by first acting as a phallus for a strong man. Shevin differentiated very similar paternal from maternal images partially on the basis of developmental lines: the analyst in the father role was viewed as more of a whole entity than in the mother role.

Chasseguet-Smirgel (1964) spoke directly to the differences and similarities between the images of the father and the phallic mother. Relationships to the father, for the little girl, often recapitulate the relationship to the mother, as 'penis envy' toward the male carries earlier conflicts toward the mother. In this sense, paternal images are really a double exposure of maternal ones and indistinguishable from them. Yet as it emerges in treatment, she asserts, the transference to the father is more idealized, with triadic dimensions, as compared with the maternal.

Whether or not images of phallic mother versus penetrating father are difficult or impossible to discern in the transference, and whether these or any other criteria for their differentiation can be useful, we cannot make a differentiation if we are not set to do so. It is my thesis that we as well as our patients can become tied up by our manifest sex so that we do not look beyond it. As I said before, until beginning this research, I had experienced only fleeting paternal transferences in my own clinical practice. Since that time, I have begun to see and recognize paternal transferences—some sustained—in many of my cases. The inference here is that my mind has been opened to new understandings and experiences, not that my clinical case load or material has changed.

THE EROTIC OR EROTICIZED TRANSFERENCE

A second suggested difference in the transferences to male and female analysts is in the area of the strongly erotic or the 'eroticized' transference. It is striking that there are virtually no published reports of strongly and sustained erotic or eroticized transferences of male patients toward female analysts, in contrast to the common story of the female falling deeply in 'love' with her male analyst, or into a wildly unmanageable erotic transference. There is much more agreement in the literature and among the female analysts with whom I have spoken that this difference does indeed exist. Several female analysts, however, would contest this assertion by pointing to their clinical experiences with highly erotic transferences. If erotic transferences do occur, however, they are not written about. Again, we must ask what factors—within the patient, or the analyst—might account for this supposed phenomenon, which flies in the face of our theory.

Before answering this question, I should distinguish the 'eroticized' transference from an erotic transference. The eroticized transference, as described in the literature (Blum, 1973); (Rappaport, 1956), is characteristic of the borderline or more disturbed patient. In the eroticized transference, the patient exhibits excessive cravings to be loved by the analyst, often with overt demands for sexual gratification. Eroticized transference is thought to be a manifestation of pregenital issues: underlying hostility, needs for control, and weaknesses in ego functioning. In contrast to the strongly erotic transference characterized by persistent erotic manifestations, the eroticized transference is characterized by the patient losing sight of the 'as-if' quality of the situation. I would also add by way of warning that male and female patients may express similar underlying psychopathology with different outward manifestations. Thus, trying to compare eroticized transferences of male and female patients can become very complicated if not misleading.

From within the patient, there are several inhibiting factors against the development of a strongly erotic transference. First, the incest taboo seems to operate more strongly against mother-son incest than father-daughter incest, against a male's erotic involvement with an older woman than a female's involvement with an older man. Second, the male patient may deeply fear and block the expression of erotic feelings toward a female analyst which may represent merger with the pre-oedipal mother and loss of his masculine identity. Third, the type of male patients sent to or choosing female analysts may be more prone to passivity or to pre-oedipal problems and skew the transferences away from oedipal issues. Finally, the male patient may defend against erotic feelings because of feelings of shame, fear of erections on the couch, and castration anxiety. A common theme in the literature is that the male patient's castration anxiety is stirred by 'the spectre of the phallic mother' (Szmarag, 1982).

Karme (1979) reported on her analysis of a male patient whose brief period of working out negative oedipal feelings in the treatment prompted her to speculate on the differences in oedipal and erotic transferences for male and female analysts. Throughout the analysis, and even during the phase when the patient was dealing with homosexual concerns around his father, Karme felt that she remained in the transference a maternal figure. Further, the fear of her as the phallic mother, she writes, constantly inhibited the patient in directly expressing his erotic feelings toward her in the transference. She asserted that fear of the phallic mother is a major determinant of the negative oedipal complex.

In her case of a male patient, Lester (1982) reported that feared images of the powerful phallic mother overshadowed an erotic oedipal transference. While Lester felt that this fantasy did indeed become a powerful inhibiting force for the patient, she candidly presented her own dream which revealed countertransference against letting the patient express erotic feelings and against presenting herself as an erotic female instead of a nurturing mother.

In a special panel on erotic transference and countertransference between the female therapist and the male patient (Szmarag, 1982), several analysts again raised this spectre of the phallic mother as the impediment to erotic transferences for male patients. Yet it was the consensus of the panel that female therapists 'collude' with their male patients in avoiding a hotly sexual transference.

In an excellent article on countertransference, Lucia Tower (1956) pointed out that erotic countertransferences are in general taboo in psychoanalysis. 'Virtually every writer on the subject of countertransferences, for example, states unequivocally that no form of erotic reaction to a patient is to be toler-ated. This would indicate that temptations in the area are great, and perhaps ubiquitous … Other countertransference manifestations are not routinely condemned. Therefore, I assume that erotic responses to some extent trouble nearly every analyst' (p. 230). I would suggest that erotic countertransference may be especially troubling and subject to inhibition for woman analysts. On the other hand, as we know, erotic countertransferences are more likely acted out overtly by male therapists (Feldman-Summers & Jones, 1984).

CLINICAL MATERIAL

The following brief clinical examples will be presented to illustrate the issues of how the transference may become organized around the gender of the analyst, how maternal and paternal images in the transference may become disguised or confused, and how erotic material may become inhibited in the therapeu-tic interaction. The 'phallic mother' plays various roles in the material, from lurking in the wings to appearing on centre stage.

Vignette 1

A young adolescent girl, Terry, sought treatment because of severe obsessive compulsive rituals. In addition, she was distressed and depressed about current problems with her father. She lived with her mother and step-father, as her parents were divorced when she was a toddler. Her father, who lived out of state, had recently begun to press for her to spend more time with him, which she said she was loath to do. She was very attached and loyal to her very competent and caring mother with whom she also was closely identified.

Because Terry was extremely bright, verbal and introspective, the treatment progressed well. At the end of the second year, however, she became painfully silent and blocked in the sessions. Her discomfort was so great that she said that she should quit. My attempts to interpret the resistance met with rejoinders that she simply had nothing to say; my suggestions as to her possible anger elicited polite denials that she had no reason to 'dislike me'. Knowing this was an obsessive-compulsive girl, I speculated that we had come to an anal struggle between the withholding, stubborn 2-year-old and her mother. I assumed underlying issues over control.

Indeed, she was touchy about times and scheduling. Several months before the impasse, she asked for a time change, which I was unable to meet.

Shortly thereafter, she reported a dream in which her paternal grandmother, from whom she was estranged, appeared transformed: she was wearing tight slacks, high spiked heels, and blonde dyed hair as she tauntingly held out two huge pointed pens.

Here was the cruel, withholding anal/phallic mother, I thought, whom I must have become in the transference. I had this construct in my mind, as I struggled unsuccessfully to understand and break the impasse in the treatment which stretched into several months.

Finally, Terry came into her session and spoke of how she had received a petulant note from her father complaining of her not writing to him. Then came another uncomfortable, long silence. I realized suddenly how blocked out I, too, felt and interpreted the silence as her attempting to push me out of her life as she does her father, that is, in terms of a paternal transference to me. This interpretation was greeted with a rush of words—a relieved, yet anxiety-ridden confession that she had been disturbed with me these last months

14

because she felt that I was being critical of her mother. While these thoughts reflected the projection of Terry's emerging critical feeling toward her mother on to me, they contained a kernel of truth, as I had felt annoyed at the mother's subtle interference in the treatment and possessiveness toward the girl, who was having difficulty with the developmental task of separation in adolescence. Terry felt caught between me and her mother, as she must feel caught between her two parents and by her conflicts in regard to separating from her mother and her fear of oedipal urges toward her father.

The point is that my predilection to process the material in terms of pre-oedipal maternal images and my failure to recognize the paternal transference contributed to and prolonged the impasse we had come to in the treatment.

Vignette 2

A middle-aged woman, Mrs. J, came into treatment with me after two previous therapies with males with whom she had sex. She was immediately caught up in a highly charged eroticized and idealized transference toward me which lasted several years. She was pulled by yearnings to suck on my breasts, or crawl into my vagina; she needed to hold my card inside her brassiere between sessions. Such symptoms revealed her severe difficulties with separation, object constancy, and early trauma. The idealized transference expressed her yearning for a wished-for mother and covered over her rage. Her own mother was a beautiful, extremely narcissistic and ungiving woman who left much of the girl's care to the father. The only time she remembered being touched by the mother was in the administration of enemas as she lay on the cold bathroom floor. After years of treatment, the maternal transference was worked through so that the sexualized narcissistic and oral material subsided and more phallic concerns emerged—in masturbation fantasies, competition and jealousy with me, etc. It is easy to make the transition in the transference to the mother as penetrator, the anal/phallic mother who administered the enemas. Yet, her father, who was the parent who bathed her as a toddler, had her stand in the tub while he sprayed her body with the hose attachment. Both parents apparently were penetrating and sexually exciting to this patient as a child. For patients with such early problems with separation/individuation and/or sexual identity, male and female images are indeed confused and confusing. Does it matter, therefore, and is the question an artificial one, whether we call the images in the transference maternal or paternal? In the above case, I think sorting out paternal from maternal has proved to be important. The patient's initial picture of the mother as all bad and the father as good, while a partial approximation of reality, was a result of defensive 'splitting' and distortion. The image which finally began to emerge in the transference of a sexually seductive father, who himself was ungiving and narcissistic, proved helpful to this patient in un-ravelling her competitiveness and realizing her more genuine loving feelings toward women and her sexual feelings toward men. For example, the patient struggled to understand why she could not have orgasm in intercourse while she could in other ways. That is, to allow herself to experience pleasure with a man via his penis she had to work out in the transference her feelings toward the male and not the phallic mother.

Vignette 3

A young, brilliant scientist, Dr G, came into treatment because his fiancée complained that his anxieties and his preoccupation with work interfered with their relationship. He himself realized that because of his paralyzing conflicts with authority, general anxiety, and sense of inferiority, he inhibited himself from further advancement in his career and from giving fully of himself oth-erwise. These problems appeared to stem from his relationship with his father who was an extremely critical, arbitrary and controlling man. In the first year and a half of his intensive treatment, the patient concentrated on and partially worked through these problems with his father and male figures of authority at work. Correspondingly, the transference over a year and a half took on a consistently paternal cast: he experienced me as a superego, as critical, arbitrary, and controlling, someone he wished to please and yet needed to defy and with whom he competed. These issues were of real importance to the patient and their elucidation brought progress. Yet, the paternal transference also became a resistance. Strikingly, he rarely spoke of women: not his fiancée, who presumably drove him to treatment, and whom he married in the meantime; not his mother whom he described initially as passive, but nice; not even in his dreams which were peopled wholly by males (with only two exceptions—a policewoman and a female barber). Finally, when he remarked that his relations with his boss seem to dictate his moods, I observed that he spoke of nothing else in the treatment.

The next session he reported a dream:

a gun he has been holding accidentally goes off and kills a blond man. All the (male) friends present urge him to escape from the police, who will come to arrest him. He keeps procrastinating and finding impediments to his escape.

Later in his meagre associations, he said that the blond man in the dream is 'a composite', partially reminding him of a competitor at work. His only other association was to the movie *A Passage to India*, in which the character acts as if guilty about a crime of which he is accused and not necessarily guilty. I remembered that the character is a physician and the crime, rape, although Dr G did not say so.

Thus, the first glimpse of manifestly sexual material—possible masturbation conflicts and wet dreams (the gun that went off in his lap)—appeared in a break from the material related to father. Subsequent dreams featured women and triangular interactions. In this case, the paternal transference, not a phallic mother, overshadowed sexual feelings in transference. The patient was not able to admit to himself that he enjoyed coming to the sessions and hence made our scheduling a matter of my coercion and control to which he reacted by complaining, trying to change the time, coming late, and getting me to argue with him, just as he behaved with his bosses in regard to obligations at work.

Vignette 4

Mr. S was a married man who has struggled all his life against strong homosexual impulses. In the course of previous, brief therapies with male therapists, his symptoms receded of themselves, to reappear after termination. In desperation, Mr. S finally decided to seek treatment with a woman, in spite of his manifest terror. Issues of femininity and masculinity, both his and mine, which reflected his deep conflicts about sexual identity, dominated his treatment. In his dreams and fantasies, he produced an unending number of bewildering bisexual images: phallic shaped foods, phallic shaped, yet vaginal containers, such as cars, gloves, shoes, a phallic-shaped 'mummy', white substances he likened to milk and sperm, ambiguously marked rest-rooms, etc. He endowed the woman with a phallus in maternal images of buildings or mountains with peaks or towers, and a cat with claws, or with a hidden phallus, as symbolized by faecal-like objects contained in tunnels and giant tubes. The transference organized itself around such maternal images: first, a cold, rejecting, non-nurturing mother, unappreciative of his needs and his masculinity—the cold, hard mountain; then, the seductive, yet castrating mother who envied his phallus—the cruel cat or a greedy, voluptuous pig. I focused on his feelings of hatred, fear, awe, and jealousy toward me as a woman as they were projected in the transference.

In going over this case, which first stimulated my thoughts as to how gender might influence the transference (Kulish, 1985), I was struck by how the preoccupation with the maternal transferences had made me miss the paternal transference. These potent, compelling images of the mother overshadowed more disguised and buried images of the father. I realized that the patient chose a female therapist, in spite of his fear of women, because of a deeper fear of discovering with intensive work with a male therapist the hate and disappointment he harboured toward his idealized and beloved father. Thus, via the transference, I began to question whether his wish and fear of the penetrating healer was inevitably the 'phallic mother' and to interpret certain negative feelings expressed toward me as referring to his father.

The following dream illustrates this shift, and the patient's sense that I had been missing something:

He is talking to his father who is large and vivid. He only comes up to his chest. His father admonishes him not to use the term 'Daddy'. He answers that it is a term of endearment, not a sign of disrespect. Then his father appears dressed like a clown, with a plastic bra and a peaked hat.

His associations are that 'Daddy' sounds like 'Nancy'. Further, he, like his father, is getting old, which may make him, like his father, an 'intimate' of his mother. The halter-like bra reminds him of blinders.

I ask the patient if he sees me as acting the fool with blinders to something. He replies that may be it is he himself that has the blinders. He goes on to a memory of how his father chastized him as a child for 'swirling' paints together and how controlling his father actually was. In contrast, he tries to let his children have a sense of autonomy. He even let his teen-aged daughter go and visit her boyfriend alone. He agreed, reluctantly, to my observation that beneath his usually glorifying picture of his father were cutting impulses, coming out in the dream and toward me.

19

Thus, both the patient and I were blinded by my manifest sex, as symbolized in the dream by the plastic brassiere.

While fears about the all-powerful mother have inhibited the expression of sexual and positive feelings toward me and women in general, idealized fantasies about men pointed Mr. S toward homosexual objects and obscured murderous and incestuous feelings toward the father. As the 'bad' aspects of himself which he projected on to women were reallotted to men and to himself, he became much more mellow and open toward sexual (perhaps oedipal) feelings toward me.

In this period, seemingly disembodied from the current clinical material and my conscious feelings toward the patient, I experienced on several occasions sexual thoughts which intruded suddenly and surprisingly into my mind. I asked myself whether these intrusions marked a change in the quality of the transference and paralleled the threatening erotic feelings this patient attempted to stamp out throughout the course of his long, difficult treatment. Perhaps this sudden break-through of erotic countertransference resulted from the chronic inhibition of erotic feelings within the psychoanalytic setting, to which female therapists and male patients may be especially prone.

DISCUSSION

It is my contention that therapist's gender does influence the process of psychoanalytic treatment, although this influence may work in unseen subtle ways, and it is, in any case, difficult to isolate. One way in which gender may operate is that it serves as an organizing, limiting factor both for the patient and for the therapist. The reality of gender may set certain limits to the patient's fantasies, just as the form of a Rorschach blot sets limits to the fantasies projected on to it. A good example of this organizing influence is furnished by the theoretical concept of the 'phallic mother'. Such a fantasy is often evoked in the relationship to a female therapist and can become a consolidating transference. Our manifest sex is often one of the few things our patients know about us, and fantasies, curiosities, and feelings revolve around it. The 'phallic mother' owes its ubiquitousness in mythology, dreams, and fantasy to the fact that sexual differences are of such great concern and fascination to us all, throughout the course of our development.

At the same time, the 'phallic mother' is a theoretical construct from psychoanalysis and as such enables the analyst to organize his or her own thoughts. As the confusing array of material emerges in the course of the treatment, we process it through the filter of our own feelings, past and present experiences, and our theoretical expectations which are partially determined by our gender. Thus, gender carries inevitable blind spots, biases, and countertransferences as well as special sensitivities, capacities, and understandings. Gender in interaction with our theoretical, intellectual ideas sets us to understand and react to clinical material in terms of a 'phallic mother' or 'punishing father', being penetrator or penetrated, etc. The patient projects the 'phallic mother' on to the 'blank screen' of the analyst. In another sense, the 'phallic mother' can act as a screen for the analyst's conceptions and misconceptions. The concept of the phallic mother has become institutionalized in psychoanalysis as a barrier to the full exploration of a male patient's erotic fantasies toward a female therapist. Paradoxically it can also stand in the way of a female therapist realizing her masculine role in the transference. At the same time, current emphasis in psychoanalysis on the early mother-child dyad may give males theoretical 'permission' to see themselves in terms of the maternal transference.

Chasseguet-Smirgel (1984) has spoken of both the feminine and the masculine attitudes as crucial to the analyst's functioning. She defines a patient, containing attitude as feminine, and a penetrating curiosity, as masculine. I would suggest that an openness and flexibility to experience oneself in roles or feelings of the opposite sex would help us realize our full potentials as clinicians and human beings as we help our patients realize theirs.

SUMMARY

The question of how an analyst's gender might affect the transference has currently stirred the interest of psychoanalytic writers. Two questions have been raised in the literature: how analyst's gender might determine whether the transference takes a 'maternal' or 'paternal' cast, and how it might contribute to a highly eroticized transference. In both these questions, the concept of the 'phallic mother' has been raised in the explanation of the observed differences. The author critically examines the concept of phallic mother in this context. The concept is reviewed historically to demonstrate how it has reflected changes in psychoanalytic theory. Clinical examples are presented to illustrate how transference can become organized around analyst's gender, how maternal and paternal images in the transference can become confused, and how male patients' erotic fantasies may become inhibited by the female analyst. The fantasy of the phallic mother, which is prominent in the clinical material, is a projection of the patient which can be centred upon the analyst's gender. Phallic mother as a concept can also contribute to gender-related blind spots and countertransferences. It is suggested that such theoretical constructs may become obstructions preventing analysts from perceiving themselves in the opposite-sexed roles within the transference.

REFERENCES

Bak, R. C. (1968). The phallic woman: the ubiquitous fantasy in perversions. *Psychoanal. Study Child* 23:15-16.

Bernstein, A.E. & Warner, G.M. (1984). *Women Treating Women*. New York: Int. Univ. Press.

Bernstein, D. (1984). The Female-Patient, Female-Analyst Dyad Paper presented at the meeting of American Psychological Association, Toronto, 26 August.

Blum, H.P. (1971). On the conception and development of the transference neurosis. *J. Am. Psychoanal. Assoc.* 19:41-53.

——— (1973). The concept of erotized transference. *J. Am. Psychoanal. Assoc.* 21:61-76.

Brunswick, R.M. (1940). The preoedipal phase of the libido development. *Psychoanal. Q.* 9:239–319.

Chasseguet-Smirgel, J. (1964). Feminine guilt and the Oedipus complex. In: *Female Sexuality* ed. Chasseguet-Smirgel. Ann Arbor: Univ. Michigan Press, pp. 94–134.

——— (1974). Perversion, idealization and sublimation *Int. J. Psychoanal.* 5 5:349–363.

——— (1984). The femininity of the analyst in professional practice *Int. J. Psychoanal.* 65:169–178.

Deutsch, H. (1965). *Neurosis and Character Types.* New York: Int. Univ. Press.

Evans, W.M. (1972). The mother: image and reality *Psychoanal. Rev.* 59:183–199.

Ewens, T. (1976). Female sexuality and the role of the phallus *Psychoanal. Rev.* 63:615–637.

Feldman-Summers, S. & Jones, G. (1984). Psychological impacts of sexual contact between therapists or other health care professionals and their clients. *J. Consult. Clin. Psychol.* 52:1054–1061.

Finklestein, L. (1975). Awe and premature ejaculation. *Psychoanal. Q.* 44: 322–352.

Freud, S. (1909). Analysis of a phobia in a five year old boy. *S.E.* 10.

——— (1912). The dynamics of transference. *S.E.* 12.

——— (1915). Observations on transference love. *S.E.* 12.

——— (1927). Fetishism. *S.E.* 21.

——— (1931). Female sexuality. *S.E.* 21.

——— (1933). New introductory lectures. *S.E.* 23.

——— (1940). Splitting of the ego in the process of defence. *S.E.* 23

Gill, M.M. (1982). Analysis of Transference Volume 1 Theory and Technique (*Psychol. Issues, Monogr. 53*). New York: Int. Univ. Press.

Goldberg, J. (1979). Aggression and the female therapist. *Mod. Psychoanal.* 4:*209–222.*

Greenacre, P. (1954). The role of transference: practical considerations in relation to psychoanalytic therapy. In: *Emotional Growth,* Volume 2 New York: Int. Univ. Press, pp. *627–640.*

——— (1968). Perversions: general consideration regarding their genetic and dynamic background In Emotional Growth Volume 1 New York: Int. Univ. Press, pp. *300-314.*

Hermann, I. (1949). The giant mother, the phallic mother, obscenity. *Psychoanal. Rev.36:302–306.*

Karme, L. (1979). The analysis of a male patient by a female analyst: the problem of the negative oedipal transference. *Int. J. Psychoanal.60:253–261.*

Kubie, L. (1974). The drive to become both sexes. *Psychoanal. Q.43:349–426.*

Kulish, N.M. (1984). The effect of the sex of the analyst on transference: A review of the literature. *Bulln. Menninger Clinic* 48:*95–110.*

——— (1985). The effect of the therapist's gender on the transference. *Yearbook Soc. Psychoanal. Psychotherapy* 1:*17–31.*

Langs, R.J. (1973). The patient's view of the therapist: reality or fantasy. *Int. J. Psychoanal .2:411–431.*

Lerner, H.E. (1974). Early origins of envy and devaluation of women: implications for sex-role stereotypes. *Bulln. Menninger Clinic* 38:*538–553.*

Lester, E. (1982). The Female Analyst and the Eroticized Transference Paper presented at the meeting of the American Psychoanalytic Assoc. New York, December.

Mason, S. (1983). Personal Communication, 23 July.

Orgel, S. (1965). On time and timelessness. *J. Am. Psychoanal. Assoc.* 13:*102–121.*

Rappaport, E. (1956). The management of an erotized transference. *Psychoanal. Q.* 25:*515–529.*

Roheim, G. (1945). Aphrodite or the woman with a penis. *Psychoanal. Q.* 14: *350–390.*

Rossner, J. (1983). *August.* Boston: Houghton Mifflin Company.

Sandler, J. (1976). Countertransference and role-responsiveness *Int. J. Psychoanal.*. 3:*43–48.*

Shengold, L. (1963). Parent as sphinx. *J. Am. Psychoanal. Assoc.* 11:*725–751.*

Shevin, F.F. (1963). Countertransference and identity phenomena manifested in the analysis of a case of phallus girl identity. *J. Am. Psychoanal. Assoc.* 11:*331–344.*

Stein, G.J. & Auchincloss, E. (reporters) (1984). The public and the private woman *Bull. Assn. Psychoanal. Med.* 24:*1–19.*

Stoller, R.J. (1975). *Perversion.* New York: Random House.

Szmarag, R. (reporter) (1982). Special panel A: erotic transference and counter-transference between the female therapist and the male patient. *Academy Forum* 26:*11–13.*

Tower, L.E. (1956). Countertransference. *J. Am. Psychoanal. Assoc.* 4:*224–255.*

Zetzel, E.R. (1966). The Doctor-patient relationship in psychiatry. In: *The Capacity for Emotional Growth.* New York: Int. Univ. Press, 1970 pp. *139–155.*

CHAPTER 2:

The Mental Representation of the Clitoris: The Fear of Female Sexuality

(1991). Psychoanal. Inq., (11)(4):511–536

While early psychoanalytic theory made the clitoris the predominant focus of theories of female sexuality, current writers have raised challenges about its role and function in female sexuality and sexual development. Yet it is striking how little has been said about the *mental representations* of the clitoris, insofar as the mental life is the realm with which psychoanalysis deals. It is my purpose in this paper to search for possible representations of the clitoris in dreams, fairy tales, and clinical data from the psychoanalytic situation to see what light, if any, such an exploration may throw on the current questions regarding female sexuality. I also attempt to explore why representations of the clitoris have gone unattended in psychoanalytic writing and in mental life in general.

THE ROLE OF THE CLITORIS IN PSYCHOANALYTIC THEORIES OF FEMALE DEVELOPMENT

Freud's (1905, 1931, 1933) theories about the role of the clitoris in female sexuality can be summarized as follows: Before the discovery of the differences between the sexes, the little girl's sexual development is identical to that of the little boy's. The central erogenous zone for the girl is the clitoris, which is homologous to the penis. Neither she nor the little boy has knowledge of the vagina. In the earlier stages of the phallic-oedipal period, her active or "masculine" strivings are experienced in terms of her clitoris and are aimed at the mother. With the discovery that she has no penis, the girl feels deprived and envious. Feeling inferior, she struggles against her clitoral masturbation and blames her mother for her lack of a penis.

She turns toward her father in an attempt to gain his penis and to obtain a baby, a substitute or equivalent for it. She must therefore give up her clitoris as the main erogenous zone and her mother as main object of her desires. In puberty, when sexuality is reawakened, clitoral, masculine feelings must be repressed and transferred to the vagina, which comes into its own. In intercourse, the role of the clitoris is confined to transmitting the excitation to the adjacent female parts. If this transfer has not occurred in the normal course of development, the woman may suffer from a masculine complex or frigidity.

These ideas were challenged from the beginning. Jones (1927) and Horney (1933) insisted that young children did have knowledge of the vagina. Subsequent writers, citing evidence from both infant and child observation and clinical data from adult analyses, argued against the clitoris being the girl's only erogenous zone. Greenacre (1950), for example, thought that vaginal sensations may be concurrent with or even precede clitoral sensation. She suggested that there is an early hazy vaginal awareness and accompanying body image, with the vagina "borrowing" stimulation from surrounding organs. Clitoral sensations are less frequent but more discrete than vaginal in the prephallic stages. Kleeman (1976) and Chehrazi (1986) also stress an early, pleasurable awareness of both clitoris and vagina before the age of two. Another questionable idea was that sexual excitability must be transferred from the clitoris to the vagina. Freud stated that clitoral masturbation would have to be renounced during the resolution of the oedipal complex and abandoned during adolescence if healthy feminine development was to proceed. Lampl-de Groot (1982) suggested that sexual vaginal excitability is added to, not transferred from, the clitoral during the course of development. Clower (1976) and Harley (1961) observed that clitoral masturbation is commonly observed throughout latency and that it expresses both active and passive sexual aims. Marcus and Francis (1975) added that in regard to masturbation, throughout childhood, the girl's entire genital and anal area may be responsive and that sensations in the vagina, labia, and anus play a part along with those in the clitoris. Marcus and Francis concluded that repression of clitoral sexuality is not necessary for the establishment of "vaginal supremacy," as Freud and earlier theorists such as Deutsch (1930) or Bonaparte (1935) postulated.

Adding strength to these arguments based on clinical data and child observation are data from Masters and Johnson's laboratories (1962). They found that vaginal and clitoral orgasms are indistinguishable physiologically, and that vaginal responsiveness always accompanies clitoral stimulation and vice versa. As Clower (1975) has pointed out, however, physiological responsiveness and psychological experience are not necessarily isomorphic. Women's and girls' reports of differing experiences and sensations with "vaginal" versus "clitoral" orgasm cannot be dismissed. That is, it is very difficult to correlate physiological and anatomical findings with complex psychological phenomena, including phenomenology, body image, and mental representations of the genitals (Marcus & Francis, 1975).

Moreover, Comptom (1983) reminded us that Freud's concept of genital primacy was hardly one of location of orgasm but primarily referred to "cathexis" of zone. In evaluating genital primacy, consideration is given to a transition from autoerotic to object-directed predominance; from separate drives and zones to total genital takeover; from general pleasures to a specifically genital sexual aim. Dickes (1981) argued that the contradictions between Masters and Johnson and Freud are therefore more apparent than real.

Glenn and Kaplan (1968) cogently clarified these observations by pointing out that Freud never used the terms *vaginal* or *clitoral orgasms*. They argued that in order to use these terms we have to distinguish between (1) the physical area stimulated to induce orgasm, (2) the area in which the orgasm is perceived or experienced, and (3) the area in which physiological and anatomical change takes place. Using clinical examples, Glenn and Kaplan demonstrated the many different possibilities of what is meant by "orgasm" in any given case. The careful distinctions they made are generally absent in the literature, which adds confusion to the arguments made.

In general, however, most authors (Eissler, 1977; Lampl-de Groot, 1982; Chehrazi, 1986) agree that exclusive "vaginal" orgasms as opposed to "clitoral" orgasms are not synonymous with mature feminine functioning. Greenacre (1950), for example, described "vaginal" orgasms in schizophrenic women connected with the need to cope with overstimulation. Greenberg and Fisher (1980) cited studies of married women which indicate that preference for clitoral versus vaginal stimulation is not associated with inferior psychological adaptation. Clower (1975) suggested that repression of clitoral sensation and stimulation may, in fact often, accompany frigidity. This observation agrees with my clinical experience with frigid women.

Running throughout the literature is a repeated question: what is the nature of clitoral sexuality and is it "masculine?" Lampl-de Groot (1982) argued that "masculinity" or "activity" associated with clitoral stimulation for the little girl should be considered in terms of *fantasies* not actualities. Thus what the little girl relinquishes in development are her *fantasies* of what it is to be a male, to have a penis, etc., and not necessarily her *active* impulses per se. Similarly, Chehrazi (1986) argued that while early psychoanalytic theory emphasizes that the girl must come to accept her genital inferiority in the course of development, the issue actually is that the girl must struggle with the *fantasy* of genital (clitoral) inferiority. Harley (1961), Gillespie (1969), and Clower (1976) cited their clinical findings that clitoral excitation for the little girl is not necessarily associated with impulses to be like a male, but can accompany fantasies of being in the receptive female position.

In exploring the nature and function of clitoral sensations, Kestenberg (1975) posited an "inner genital" stage which precedes the external genital or phallic stage of development. Under the influences of inner, nonverbalized, and diffuse sexual sensations (from the vagina, uterus, ovaries, anus, prostate, testicles, etc.), both little boys and little girls hope at first to create a baby with the mother. Both boys and girls also tend to transfer inner sensations to the outside of the body in an attempt to concretize and locate them, but because of her anatomy, this need to form an image of the inside genital is much more urgent and manifest in the girl than in the boy. With the onset of the phallic phase, the four-year-old girl ignores inner sensation and masturbates with increasing focus on the clitoris and fantasies of (phallic) power. Thus the cathexis of the clitoris during the phallic stage serves an organizing and defensive function for the girl. Penis envy, in this context, is envy of an organ that can help localize and contain unsettling inner sensations.[1]

In summary, several crucial questions have been raised in regard to psychoanalytic theories about the role of the clitoris in female psychosexual development: Is the clitoris the predominant erotogenic zone for the little girl? What role and function does penis envy play in terms of clitoral sensations and fantasies? Are there distinct types of orgastic experience associated with clitoral and vaginal areas? Finally, is clitoral sexuality to be considered "masculine" or is it an intrinsic part of feminine functioning? I believe that, while clitoral sensations are associated with masculine strivings and the clitoris lends itself to fantasies of women possessing a phallus or phallic power, the issue is much more complex. I propose a different emphasis. I argue that more distinctly female sensations are reflected in the mental representation of the clitoris and that the clitoris is indeed an intrinsic part of normal feminine sexual functioning and development.

---

1 Glover and Mendell (1982) and Chehrazi (1986) argue for replacing the term phallic stage with preoedipal genital or genital stage to reflect the dominance of genitality—clitoral, vaginal, or phallic.

THE MENTAL REPRESENTATION OF THE CLITORIS

Whatever its place in female psychosexual development, we would expect the clitoris to have a discernible mental representation in the mind of the female and the male. Freud's theory certainly gives the clitoris a central role as the leading erotogenic zone for females during early childhood. As such, it should take shape in the mind, unconsciously, even if clitoral fantasies are repressed and clitoral pleasure later set aside. According to Freud such representations would predictably be stamped with phallic imagery in both males and females, especially perhaps in females with "phallic" fixations or problems.

Before proceeding further, I should define what I mean by mental representation. Sidestepping the theoretical problems with the concept of mental representation pointed out by Schimek (1975) and Boesky (1983), I am adopting the definition proposed by Beres and Joseph (1970, p. 2): "A postulated unconscious psychic organization capable of evocation in consciousness as symbol, image, fantasy, thought, affect, or action." That is, a mental representation is unconscious, but we deal only with its conscious derivative, which is usually but not necessarily expressed in verbal terms.

As I have said, the psychoanalytic literature contains very little that might delineate possible mental representations of the clitoris. What has been written has addressed this very issue of how, by and large, the clitoris goes unnamed or ignored. Lerner (1976) called our attention to the fact that the female genital parts are mislabeled and lumped under the name of *vagina*. The little girl is not taught she has a vulva, and when she discovers her clitoris it goes unnamed. This mislabeling, Learner asserted, may be a result of penis envy because the unnamed organ may be perceived as a small and inadequate penis. (It may in fact also result in penis envy.) Ash (1980) made a similar observation that even in most scientific writing the clitoris is mislabeled or not labeled at all. Blau (1943) noted the singular absence of slang or obscene words in English and other languages to denote this organ. He concluded that withholding the name must serve to keep it secret and hidden and that penis envy and castration anxiety may motivate such suppression. He added, in passing, that these defects in language seem to reflect extreme cultural suppression of female sexuality. Austrians do have one slang term for clitoris as a "Jew" which may symbolize an inferior or mutilated penis (Eissler, 1977). In French slang the clitoris delightfully is called *la praline* or "sugared almond" because of the similarity in shape. A dictionary for euphemisms in the English language lists "button" for clitoris (Neaman & Silver, 1983).

One major source for this difficulty in verbal and psychic representation of the parts of the female genital is, as has been described, its lack of visibility and localization for the little girl (Greenacre, 1950; Montgrain, 1983). All parts of the female genitals, including the clitoris, are at first undifferentiated, and bodily sensations are unlocalized, leading to a cloacal concept—that is, of a single body cavity consisting of rectum, vagina, and urethra combined. The cloacal concept persists into adulthood (Freud, 1905; Shopper, 1966). I conclude that a differentiated representation of the vagina from the other inner structures must represent a maturational achievement.

Added to such developmental or cognitive issues are powerful motives to suppress mental representations and imagery of the clitoris. There is ample clinical evidence that for the adult male, the clitoris is associated with castration anxiety. Róheim (1945), in a fascinating article linking the fantasy of the phallic mother with European folklore about the witch, presented clinical material from the analyses of several men who demonstrated such fears. One man, for example, who could never "find the clitoris," unconsciously feared the female's orgasm because he equated it with a phallus. Siegel (1971) described cases of men whose interest in cunnilingus represented an attempt to repair the perceived castration of the woman by making the clitoris seem larger. Feelings of inferiority, penis envy, and the mutilation represented in her lack of a penis also color the little girl's inner experience of her clitoris. In the place of a "stunted penis," then, both sexes would fantasize a hidden inner phallus.

In addition to issues of penis envy, other powerful motivators may exist to keep the clitoris unnamed and unacknowledged. The clitoris is the only organ in the human body that functions purely for pleasure (Baill & Money, 1981). To give the clitoris a name is to give the little girl permission to experience sexual pleasure and to point the way to masturbation. The child considers sexual excitement dangerous and fragmenting. Since she experiences sensations in a place in her body she cannot see, the girl may have special difficulty in developing a sense of control over sexual impulses.

Montgrain (1983) suggested, further, that as the girl struggles to gain control, she wishes for a penis to help achieve an organized inner representation to contain the stimulation. It is more difficult to attain mastery over impulses with the ill-defined representation of the clitoris. For us all perhaps, woman's image is branded in the unconscious as the repository of the repressed and the source of unbridled sexual pleasure. Montgrain reminds us of the myth of the Greek goddess Heras. Her secret was revealed by Tiresea who had lived both as a man and a woman. When asked who had the greater sexual pleasure, Tiresea replied that woman had nine tenths, man one tenth of the pleasure. This myth reveals what history tries to conceal: Feminine sexuality may remain an unknown continent because we do not wish to recognize its intensity (Montgrain, 1983).

Goldstein (1984), discussing the process of sexualization, focused on the mysterious, alluring quality of the sexual woman in fantasy. The girl's inner world associated with her sexuality acquires a fascinating and strange quality partly because it is infused with the image of the cloaca. In separating from the mother, the girl learns to be alluring to her father and to attract his gaze; the boy, in differentiating from the mother, imbues what is feminine with mystery and thus creates a fetish. Similarly, Stoller (1975) stressed the importance of a sense of mystery about the female genitals in the formation of perversions.

Mayer (1985), describing what she calls "female castration anxiety," presented clinical material illustrating the quality of secrecy of female sexuality.

Some women report the need to keep sexual excitement secret and inside themselves. Other women fear losing their *openings* or access to their inner genitals, a fear different from typical castration anxiety in which the fear is of losing the tangible organ. Montgrain (1983) and Chehrazi (1986) presented clinical material that suggests a fear of lack of control over the "hole" and a fantasied need for a firmer and tangible boundary over it are often acted out counterphobically in promiscuous behavior. Both the fear of losing the genital opening or fear of the opening itself, however, add to the fear of female sexuality.

Fraiberg (1972) presented convincing clinical material to demonstrate that fears of overwhelming genital excitement led to the total inhibition of erotic sensation in latency-age girls. These fears were expressed in fantasies of burning crators or of overwhelming waves. Bernstein (Panel, 1976) also argued that the girl's fear of overwhelming orgastic excitement may lead to suppression of early masturbation and vaginal sensations. I would suggest such a fear would lead as well to suppression of awareness of the clitoris, the trigger to such sensations.

FEMALE CIRCUMCISION AND CLITORIDECTOMY

While the clitoris goes unnamed and suppressed in Western societies, it is the focus of various initiation ceremonies in other parts of the world such as Africa, South America, and Australia. In many cultures, genital mutilations are performed on girls: circumcision ("sunna" in Arab countries) in which the labia minora and the tip or part of the clitoris are removed; excision or clitoridectomy in which the labia and the entire clitoris are removed; and infibulation in which after excision both sides of the vulva are sewn up (Barry, 1984). While these practices, often performed without anesthetic, are currently diminishing, they are today still very common (Shaw, 1985), affecting 20 to 70 million women.

Female circumcision is most prevalent in Muslim Africa. Assumed to be an Arabic custom, it has origins that predate Islam in older African puberty rites. The Lydian historian Xanthus, writing for a Greek audience in the fifth century B.C., mentioned clitoridectomies of females by Lydian kings (Hanson, 1989). Assad (1980) traced the custom to ancient Egyptian beliefs in the bisexuality of the Gods. The feminine soul of man was thought to be located in the foreskin and the masculine soul of women in the clitoris. Thus in initiation to adulthood the feminine portion of the male has to be shed as does the male portion of the female.

Assad's careful study of female circumcision in Egypt, which includes in-depth interviews with female respondents, led her to suggest two major functions for the practice. First, it is thought to attenuate and control women's sexual desires and behavior (also see Patai, 1973). Religious leaders sanction it "in view of its effect of attenuating the sexual desire in women and directing it to the desirable moderation" (Assad, 1980, p. 5). Second, as suggested by the ancient Egyptian myth, removal of the clitoris or a portion of it removes the undesirable masculinity from a female and prepares her for her proper feminine role. One respondent illustrated both these functions: "men don't like oversexed women. An uncircumcised woman is put to shame by her husband who calls her 'you with the clitoris.' People say she is like a man. Her organ would prick the man like smallpox. It is shameful ..." (Assad, 1980, p. 13). It is a common belief in such countries that a woman is not a woman until her ugly external genitals are removed.

Lightfoot-Klein's (1989) study of female genital circumcisions in Africa provides compelling evidence that such operations are practiced because they are believed to attenuate or to abolish sexual desire in women. In a six-year journey through the Sudan, Kenya, and Egypt, she interviewed large numbers of women and men concerning their personal experiences and feelings about genital mutilations. While many women report that, in spite of circumcision, they were still able to enjoy sex, countless others told of their resultant experiences of trauma, physical suffering, and inhibited sexual lives.

Anthropologists find diverse meanings and origins in female initiation rites (Bachofen, 1954; Bettelheim, 1954; Delaney et al., 1976), but nevertheless similarities do appear. Female circumcision and clitoridectomies are typically viewed as curbing female sexual desire and addressing counterphobically the castration fears of males and the fears of the "masculine" aggressive side of females held by both sexes.

Lest it be thought that such practices and beliefs are confined to distant societies and times, Spitz (1975) and Barker-Benfield (1975) outlined the history of clitoridectomies performed in the United States, England, and Western Europe in the last centuries and the early part of this century. As late as 1985 female circumcisions have been reported in England and France (Shaw, 1985). The operation was introduced in the 1880s by a prominent London surgeon who was shortly expelled from the obstetrical society. Nevertheless, the operation flourished and was performed on thousands of girls and women as a cure for masturbation, excessive sexuality, and madness. Medical documents give clear evidence that clitoridectomies were advocated explicitly to reduce female sexual impulses and masturbation, both of which were viewed as dangerous, unwanted, and unfeminine.

Marie Bonaparte (Bertin, 1982), who ironically wrote about primitive excision, sought in vain to cure her own frigidity by numerous surgical procedures designed to move her clitoris closer to the opening to the vagina. Harley (1961) has suggested that such extreme measures may symbolically reflect a need to bring together two sides of a conflict between the "masculine" and "feminine" sides of the self. One of my patients reported that she physically experiences her clitoris as totally distant and unreachable from her vagina.

This description of ritual female circumcisions and clitoridectomies illustrates the lengths to which people have gone in denying or disavowing the clitoris by actually excising it.

FEMALES' EXPERIENCE OF SEXUAL EXCITEMENT

In *Three Essays on the Theory of Sexuality,* Freud (1905, p. 220) wrote: "The spontaneous discharges of sexual excitement which occur so often precisely in little girls are expressed in spasms of the clitoris. Frequent erections of that organ make it possible for girls to form a correct judgement, even without any instructions, of the sexual manifestations of the other sex: they merely transfer on to boys the sensations derived from their own sexual processes." While it is true that each sex projects from its own experiences onto the other, each embellishes or overrides that experience, via fantasy, about how it might be to the opposite sex. It would seem that Freud was transferring from his own male experience onto girls. "Spasms" may be an apt description for sensations in the penis, but not necessarily for those in the clitoris. Freud repeatedly described the clitoris as "a real and genuine penis" (Freud, 1908, p. 217), or as a penis that "remains permanently stunted" (Freud, 1909, p. 12n). On the other hand, the clitoris does lend itself readily to girls' *fantasies* of how it might feel to possess a penis.

Let us listen to how a little girl, age three, tried to describe her experiences of sexual excitement to Kestenberg (1975). Dorie stated she had two types of jumping: one a "button" jumping, clearly symbolizing the clitoris. To communicate this feeling, Dorie drew a house which became dominated by concentric circles from which lines emanated radiating outward like rays from the sun. These sensations would not best be described as "spasms," as Freud speculated. A contrasting drawing, which Kestenberg took to represent the little girl's inner genital (vaginal) sensations was of a house with a mother, then a baby in it, framed by rhythmic undulatory patterns intruding inside.

Montgrain (1983, pp. 169–170) speculated about woman's experience:

"It seems to me probable that the essence of woman's sexual pleasure consists of an ever-widening diffusion of sensation in successive waves, throughout her whole body... the limits are... not clearly defined.

In both Kestenberg's and Montgrain's accounts, female sexual experience, clitoral or vaginal, is described in terms of circles or waves, not thrusts or spasms. It seems to me that circular images do come closer to female experience than linear, even for clitoral sensation.[2] Very frequently, little girls can be seen playing twiring or spinning games, more so than little boys. I think such twirling or spinning may represent both an expression of and an attempt to contain sexual excitement and pleasure. The typical little girl's fantasy of being a beautiful ballerina or an ice skater spinning gracefully like a top captures and contains this excitement.

Berman (1989) elucidated the girl's narcissistic and separation conflicts depicted in the fairy tale of *The Red Shoes*. A young girl wishes for magic red shoes which, when worn, make her dance and twirl without being able to stop. He touched upon the significance of the dancing and the ballerina's ultimate death as expressive of punishment for masturbation and of sexuality gone out of control. I would suggest further that the imagery is characteristic of the experience of female excitation—that is, endless spinning.

---

2 From physiology (Baill & Money, 1981), we know that clitoral erection does not occur as quickly as penile, nor is it the first genital response to erotic stimulation, usually being preceded by vaginal lubrication. Furthermore, during intercourse and otherwise, clitoral and vaginal responsiveness occur in conjunction with one another.

REPRESENTATIONS OF THE CLITORIS IN DREAMS, MYTHS, AND FAIRY TALES

The psychoanalytic literature in general, as I have said, has given little mention to mental representations of the clitoris. It is striking, for example, how very little appears about this topic in writings about dreams. "Clitoris" is not listed in the index of *The Interpretation of Dreams* (Freud, 1900) nor, to my knowledge, in the index of caves, purses for the vagina and or uterus; cats, spiders, crabs, jewelry, flowers, gardens, tunnels for the female genitals; fur, woods for public hair, lips for labia. Elsewhere, Freud (1917) wrote that the clitoris is represented in the dreams of women as a phallus, and as such in typically phallic symbols, as a "flying machine" or in dreams of flying, an observation consistent with Freud's interpretation of the clitoris as substitute for penis.

Joseph (1974) reported a dream of a woman in which the clitoris was symbolized by the idea of a private section of a forest. Blau (1943) stated the clitoris is often represented in dreams, but he gave no examples. A colleague recounted a dream of a male patient in which the clitoris was depicted as the button on a radio, that is, something that "turned on" the music. In the context of sexual associations, a female patient of mine recounted a dream that she was running around and around a bright red button.

What are we to conclude from this paucity of material? Surely the clitoris does not completely lack mental representation. Is the clitoris inevitably equated with the stunted, wished-for, lost penis so that it is inevitably represented in dreams as a penis? It is represented symbolically in other ways that have been overlooked or gone unstated by investigators confined by theoretical dispositions to certain perceptions? Does this paucity reflect the general reluctance to look at and to name the clitoris?

Some interesting clues can be gleaned from ancient Greek writers. "Clitoris," according to the most authoritative etymologist (Frish, 1960), is derived from the Greek word "a little hill." The Oxford English Dictionary traces the source to the Greek word "to shut." This meaning seems to reflect the psychological one we have described: a hidden, shut-off spot, a key to sexual secrets. Early Greek medical writers and poets used various terms for the clitoris (Hanson, 1989). The Greek, Soranus, writing about diseases of women in 100 A.D., called the clitoris "nymphe." In a poetic passage, he described the nymphe as "a little fleshy formation which hides itself under the lips like young brides under their veils," (Burguiere et al., 1988, p. 15). From "nymphe" are derived words for maiden, bride, doll. The poet Sappho also used this term. Another term for clitoris was "myrtle berry," which was used by Aristophanes in the fifth century A.D. "Myrtle" is closely related to "Myrrhine," the name of the young wife who teases her sex-starved husband so unmercifully and comically in Aristophanes' comedy *Lysistrata*. Sprinkled throughout Aristophanes' writings are many puns and allusions to myrrh or myrtle, all with sexual overtones intended to amuse his Greek audiences. Another Greek writer, Paulus Aegeneta, described the clitoris under the name "Kaulos," or "stalk," also used for penis. The first to use the term "clitoris"[3] was Rufus in about 150 A.D. (Daremberg & Ruelle, 1879). (Rufus also referred to the clitoris with a verb having the erotic meaning "to touch".) At this time, the early medical writers had, out of a sense of propriety, begun the practice of substituting scientific words for the popular and more colorful terms for sexual parts.

Early Greek writings thus provide evidence that the clitoris was represented not exclusively in phallic imagery, but much more frequently either descriptively—"little hill," "myrtle berry"—or in imagery evocative and appreciative of the sexual female—the seductive, teasing woman or the blushing young bride.

---

3 The Greek traveler Pausania (Graves, 1948, p. 367) of the second century reports on the arcadian city of Clitor, at the head of the river Aroanus, which flows into the Alpheus river. Shrines on the river at Clitor were devoted to Demeter, the barley mother, a symbol of maternal fertility, and to Ilithyia, the "deft spinner," or fate goddess. The image this geographical account conjures up is an anatomical one: the city, the clitoris, standing at the head of the river, or vagina, the source and shrine of fertility and birth.

Psychoanalytic interpretations of fairy tales (Bettelheim, 1977) have yielded rich sexual symbolism. Here too, little or nothing has been written about possible mental representations of the clitoris. If we were to follow the lead supplied by a possible derivation of the word from the Greek "to close," we would look to fairy tales with the themes of locked-up secrets. This theme is illustrated by a vignette supplied by one of my students: A five-year-old girl in play therapy makes a tiny ball out of clay, different from the more phallic-like constructions in her repertoire. "What is that?" asks the young male therapist. "My magic pea," she answers coyly. "Pea?" Yes, like the pea you eat. I put it in my purse and when I'm all alone, I take it out and play with it!" Is the magic pea her clitoris?

If we look for an anatomical analog, "Little Red Riding Hood" comes to mind as a representation of the clitoral hood, both in terms of the color and shape. Bettelheim's (1977) interpretation of that story as a metaphor of the dangers of too young a girl being seduced into sex could be further reduced to more explicitly anatomical meanings.

In terms of its function, the clitoris might be represented as a button. Many children's games and stories involve buttons. There is the old circle game of "Button, Button, Who Has the Button?" Also, a popular child's book tells the story of *Corduroy*, the toy bear (Freeman, 1988) who has lost a button, searches for it among the buttons on a mattress, and is finally rescued by a little girl who sews on the button with the bear on her lap.

I choose, however, to focus on two fairy tales of the brothers Grimm, "Rumpelstiltskin" and "The Three Spinning Fairies" (Lucas et al., 1945).

RUMPELSTILTSKIN AND THE THREE SPINNING FAIRIES

The story "Rumpelstiltskin" can be briefly summarized: A poor miller bragged to the king that his beautiful daughter could spin gold out of straw. The king locked the girl in a chamber of his castle full of straw, gave her a spinning wheel, and ordered her to spin the straw into gold by the next morning or be put to death. He promised to marry her if she succeeded. The poor girl, having no idea how to accomplish this task, was greatly distressed. Suddenly a droll little man appeared through the door and offered to spin the gold for her in return for her necklace. On the second night, the scene was repeated with her giving up her ring. On the third night, the girl had to promise her first-born child to the little man in return for his help. When the baby was born, the gnome suddenly reappeared and demanded she keep her promise. When she pleaded with him to let her keep the baby, he told her she could do so if she could guess his name within three days. The queen's servant had chanced to overhear the gnome, so she was able to discover his name, "Rumpelstiltskin." In his rage at being outwitted, Rumpelstiltskin stamped his feet and tore himself in two.

Freud suggested that the little man represented the penis; the chamber, the vagina, and that the story reflected the girl's envy toward the male, the possessor of the magic phallus, who could impregnate her and make babies (spin gold). Rowley (1951), Heuscher (1974), and Miller (1985) offered similar interpretations. Their arguments that the little man represents the penis are convincing, especially since we are told that the word *Rumpelstiltschen* itself was once used as a vulgar synonym for the penis (Heuscher, 1974).

However, Rinsley and Bergmann (1983) took the analysis of the story a level deeper. They suggest that the gnome, while representing the phallus, is a devalued, diminutive phallus and an androgynous figure. Thus, Rumpelstiltskin can be viewed as the phallic mother: "As it turns out, Rumpelstiltskin ultimately symbolizes the phallic-symbiotic mother from whom the daughter can never separate and individuate, hence preventing her from growing up to become a mature, adult woman" (p. 10). They further suggested that the dwarf represents the clitoris, symbolic of a devalued phallus.

Several arguments can be made for this idea. First, the little man's name is not known: the unnamed organ. The second comes from the symbolism of masturbation in the story. The girl must spin gold on three successive nights. Spinning, like many other activities performed by hand, is a clear representation of masturbation. Here the spinning must be done at night by the solitary girl. The whole story then can be viewed as a masturbation fantasy—the girl's wish for making a baby for the father-king. Moreover, as I have suggested, spinning is a particularly apt metaphor for feminine sexual excitation: It may capture the phenomenology of the experience as well as express the associated fantasies of creative power and generativity.

Most important, "Rumpelstiltskin" is but one version of many similar folk tales found throughout Europe (Yearsley, 1921). In other countries, the visitor has different names. In the earlier Swedish version, three female fairies help the girl by spinning. This is the story of "The Three Spinning Fairies."

In this story, the mother of a lazy girl lies to the queen that her daughter loves spinning. The queen promises the girl her eldest son as husband if she can spin the flax to fill up three rooms. Locked alone for three days, the helpless girl is visited by three ugly looking women who promise to help if invited to her wedding. In secret, the women spin all the flax into the finest yarn. In the happy ending, the fairies reveal at the wedding how they came to be so ugly: The broad foot of the first came from turning the spinning wheel; the large lip of the second, from moistening the thread; the large thumb of the third, from twisting the thread. In horror, the bridegroom declares that his beautiful bride need never spin again and risk becoming so ugly.

The three fairies, made ugly by too much spinning, make clearer the image of the clitoris, swollen by masturbation. Female fairies often appear in fairy tales as spinners: In "Sleeping Beauty" (Lucas et al., 1945), for example, an old woman in a little room in a tower introduces the princess to spinning, which has been forbidden to her. The princess pricks her finger to initiate a curse of being put to sleep for a hundred years. In these tales, spinning is an activity the young girl cannot or should not do. She must be taught or helped by an older woman. The stories thus reflect a girl's conflicts, not only about masturbation, but about partaking of adult sexuality. She wishes and waits for the permission and instruction of the mother before she can take on the adult role.

The three ugly fairies can be traced to the Greek Fates, the Moerae (or Parae for the Romans) (Tripp, 1970). "Fate" was synonymous with "fairy" in the Middle Ages. The Fates, numbering one to three, but usually three, determine the course of a human's life from birth to death. They were early identified as the three daughters of the night. Later they were described as daughters of the all-powerful sky god and the earth goddess. Typically they are depicted as spinners, a metaphor for the allotment of destinies as well as for creativity. They reappear as the three witches in Macbeth who stir the cauldron of fate. The three Fates are Clotho, the Spinner; Aropos, who cuts the thread at death; and Lachesis, the Disposer of Lots. Clearly identified with the Fate Goddess is Ilithyia, the deft spinner and midwife, whose shrine stood at the city of Clitor. It is noteworthy, also, that the Fate Goddesses appear as three; the number is repeated in *The Three Spinning Fairies and Rumpelstitlskin* in the three fairies, the three nights of spinning, and the three days given the queen to guess the name. Three is a sexual symbol not only of the male genitalia but of the female genitalia. Shopper (1966), with convincing clinical data, argued that the number three in a dream represents a developmentally differentiated view of the female genitalia as urethra, vagina, and rectum.

Again we see in these familiar fairies possible symbolic representations of the clitoris. It may be represented, on the one hand, in phallic terms, condensed into a masculine image of a dwarf, a "dwarfed penis." On the other hand, similar figures carry more distinctly feminine meanings connoting female excitation and generativity. I believe that psychoanalytic interpretations of literature or fairy tales are often overdrawn and are used spuriously as proofs. I include this discussion of *Rumpelstiltskin* only to illustrate my point that readings of familiar fantasies in exclusively "masculine" terms can be misleading.

THE MENTAL REPRESENTATION OF THE CLITORIS IN NEUROTIC SYMPTOMS

Freud on several occasions described how repressed and then displaced sensations in the clitoris led to the formation of a neurotic symptom. In explaining Dora's hysterical cough, he (1901) suggested that excitement in the clitoris, in response to an embrace from the infamous Herr K. when she felt his erect penis, was displaced upward and expressed as pressure against the thorax. In "A Case of Paranoia" a female patient felt an unacceptable beat in her clitoris, which she projected outside the body as a perception of a clock ticking. Similarly, a hysterical patient's dream of a knock at the door represented a "knock in her clitoris" (Freud, 1915). In these three cases, it is a sensation from the clitoris—excitement, a beat or a knock—that is translated into another arena. In his brilliant analysis of the common fantasy of "A Child is Being Beaten," Freud (1919) proposed that the fantasy expressed at once punishment for a forbidden incestual wish and a regressive substitute for it. In a later writing, he observed that at the deepest level of the fantasy, the child being beaten or caressed may be "the clitoris itself, so that the statement… will contain a confession of masturbation" (Freud, 1925, p. 254). Here then, the clitoris may be represented as a child, a familiar symbol for the penis as well.

That the clitoris is the object for self-stimulation and exploration for the girl would suggest that it would be central to the symptoms of the obsessive-compulsive female patient. Obsessive-compulsive symptoms are commonly viewed as an elaborate defense against and equivalent for masturbation. A brief clinical case will illustrate the possible connections of representations of the clitoris in the symptoms, the defense against masturbation, and the fear of dangerous sexuality of the female.

Brief Clinical Case

Miss T, a 31-year-old, unmarried woman, was suffering from severe and crippling obsessive-compulsive symptoms about which she could not talk. She entered intensive analytic treatment because she was, in her own words, "stuck in all ways." Miss T described her parents as devoutly religious people who lived a frugal, down-to-earth life. She confessed that throughout her childhood and through early adolescence she had engaged in sex play with a younger brother. Her obsessions and compulsions began shortly after she became seriously involved with a young man when she was 24. Although she said she loved her fiancé, she did not let herself have intercourse with him and finally broke off the engagement without knowing why. Since then her relationships with men remained "platonic."

Miss T denied masturbating until she "read about it" during college. In fact, she could not bring herself even to utter to me the word *masturbate,* or any other sexual terms referring to sexual anatomy or behavior. She felt tremendous guilt about all her sexual thoughts and past sexual behavior. Nor could she describe her compulsions or obsessive thoughts, which she labeled perverse and evil. I did know they involved magical numbers, a fear of spilling liquids, and of touching "things." The thoughts had become entangled with thoughts about me, so to speak of them to me would be to invoke a serious punishment.

For the first three years the patient tried in many ways—silence, teasing, intellectualizing—to induce me to force the thoughts from her and to punish her.

A central part of the transference was the image of me as a temptress and witch who would lead her into evil. She feared that if she let go of her rigid controls, she would go wild sexually. She feared I would "lead her astray," seduce her. She envied and feared my sexuality which she connected with my being sophisticated and Jewish, which to her meant exotic. Images of witches or exotic foreigners came up repeatedly in her dreams. In one dream she associated me with both the male witch played by Jack Nicholson in "The

Witches of Eastwick" as well as one of the three women he seduced and led into witchcraft. She envied daughters whom she fantasied I initiated into sexual knowledge.

After repeated work on the resistance and guilt, which she attempted to externalize, Miss T was finally able to reveal more of her thoughts and relieve herself of the burdens she placed upon herself. In the context of becoming more free to start to date and to think about marriage, she reported a nightmare: "I was in my house and a man was trying to get in. The doorknob was turning.

I ran out the front door, which was open, into the dark street. I was frightened. [pause] Oh! This dream is leading to thoughts that I don't want to talk about....

Sex thoughts, my compulsions.... I can't tell you. Bad. Perverse.... I just can't tell you and I know I should.... Well, I'm going to try. Doorknobs are in my compulsions. And other things. I have to touch them a certain number of times, different magic numbers, or else I'll have to do it over, or else there will be bad punishments. Doorknobs, or switches, or other things.... They are all parts. [Parts?] Yeah, you know ... sex parts. And touching it's like ... can't say it. Oh, this is awful and stupid. Like having sex with yourself [her way of not saying the word *masturbation*]. Like touching sex parts. A doorknob is, ah, the, ah, you know, the cervix? And switches like light switches—they are the part, you know, you touch ... when you have sex with [pause] when—I can't say it—you masturbate. [The clitoris?] Yes. And there are other objects. Like all round objects, like certain lamps are breasts . . ." etc.

At the time, I was surprised by her associations. My own unformulated thoughts about the material went to possible phallic meanings: a doorknob to a phallic protuberance and certainly not to cervix, for example. All the things around her, which she struggled about touching, took on the meaning of the sexual body parts of females. As she later confessed, these parts belonged to women whom she envied and feared—her mother, boss, and me—who had what she did not—husband, bigger breasts, baby.

48

Shortly thereafter, she dreamed of me again: You, Dr. K, were making a big salad with cut-up parts of vegetables. The fancily cut cukes were little penises; the hacked-up tomatoes were "female parts." She came to realize how hatefully jealous she was of her brothers and how her sexual activities with the one brother covered over these feelings. One day as she herself cut up ingredients for a soup, she struggled with thoughts about the various ingredients she was dumping into the pot. She was with difficulty able to begin to clarify her fears about liquids, which had become incorporated into compulsions around not spilling: Spilling referred to loss of control over bowel and urinary functions. Liquids were sexual—seminal fluid, menstrual blood, milk, but finally, as she revealed months later, vaginal secretions with sexual excitement. With shame, she confessed that she masturbated by letting water flow into her vulva from the bathtub faucet.

She came gradually to understand that her whole life was structured as a self-debasing punishment for her guilt-ridden wishes. She had in essence been living the life of an aesetic nun. She herself came to the insight of how her compulsions represented punishment for and substitutes for masturbation—she wished to touch her clitoris and was afraid to let herself become excited.

Miss T viewed sexual excitement and indeed all her desires and drives as dangerous, uncontrollable, and bad, and hence needing literally to be shut off.

On the eve of the first session after a summer break, she reported she was troubled by obsessive thoughts and compulsive rituals. She was compelled to eat some blueberries, and to tell me that she thought of them as my nipples. Also she had to turn a light switch on and off repeatedly. The light switch she thought of as my clitoris. She connected the thoughts with being angry with me. Her associations led to the idea that all women are alike with regard to nipples— Not bigger or littler." "All females' parts—that part—[that is, the clitoris] are the same down there." After a pause, she laughed: "To turn you on would give me the ultimate power, I guess. Big-time power over you!"

The clitoris was represented as a switch, or a button that turns one on to the forbidden sexual impulses and thoughts. Among the forbidden impulses were wishes to castrate and envy of the (brother's) penis, yet she gave no clear evidence that she conceived of the clitoris itself as a male organ. She also had envious wishes to degrade and mutilate the mother's breast and genitals. Predominant in the material was the patient's attempt unconsciously to split up and isolate female sexual parts into a myriad of objects around her so as to take away their power and to disguise from herself the intensity and meaning of her sexual desires. Ultimately, she wanted to avoid the oedipal fantasies into which her aroused sexuality would lead.

The clitoris seems to be reflected in mental imagery and fantasies that go beyond "phallic" or "masculine" conflicts into other areas of female sexuality, more distinctly female areas. In any case, we can conclude that the clitoris is an integral part of the female genitals—only our fantasies make it otherwise.

REFERENCES

Ash, M. (1980). The misnamed female sex organ. In *Women's Sexual Development*, ed. M. Kirkpatrick. New York: Plenum Press, pp. *171–179*.

Assaad, M. B. (1980). Female circumcision in Egypt: Social implications, current research, and prospects for change. *Studies in Family Planning*, 11: *3–16*.

Bachofen, J. J. (1954). *Myth, Religion and Mother Right*. Princeton, N.J.: Princeton Univ. Press.

Baill, C. Money, J. (1981). Physiological aspects of female sexual development: Conception through puberty. In *Women's Sexual Development*, ed. M. Kirkpatrick. New York: Plenum Press, pp. *45–59*.

Barker-Benfield, B. (1975). Sexual surgery in late-nineteenth century American. *Int. J. of Health Services*, 5: *279–298*.

Barry, K. (1984). *Female Sexual Slavery.* New York: New York Univ. Press.

Beres, D. & Joseph, E. D. (1970). The concept of mental representation in psychoanalysis. *Int. J. Psycho-Anal.*, 51: *1–9*.

Berman, L. (1989). A dream of the red shoes: Separation conflict in the phallic narcissistic phase. Unpublished. Presented to the Michigan Psychoanalytic Society, January 14, 1989.

Bertin, C. (1982). *Marie Bonaparte: A Life.* New York: Harcourt Brace Jovanovich.

Bettelheim, B. (1954). *Symbolic Wounds: Puberty Rites & the Envious Male.* Glencoe, IL: Free Press.

——— (1977). *The Uses of Enchantment.* New York: Knopf, pp. *166–183*.

Blau, A. (1943). A philological note on a defect in sex organ nomenclature. *Psychoanal Q.*, 12: *481–485*.

Boesky, D. (1983). The problem of mental representation in self and object theory. *Psychoanal Q.*, 52: *564–583*.

Bonaparte, M. (1935). Passivity, masochism, and femininity. *Int. J. Psycho-Anal.*, 16: *325–333*.

Burguiere, P., Gourevitch, D., & Malinas, Y., ed. (1988). *Soranus, Maldies des Femmes, I.* Paris: Les Bellis Lethres, pp. *14–16*.

Chehrazi, S. (1986). Female psychology. *J. Amer. Psychoanal. Assn.*, 34: *141–162*.

Clower, V. (1975). Significance of masturbation in female sexual development and function. In *Masturbation*, ed. I. M. Marcus & J. Francis. New York: Int. Univ. Press, pp. *107–143*.

——— (1976). Theoretical implications in current views of masturbation in latency age girls. *J. Amer. Psychoanal. Assn.*, 24(Suppl.): *109–126*.

Compton, A. (1983). Current status of the psychoanalytic theory of instinctual drives. *Psychoanal Q.*, 52: *364–401*.

Daremberg, C. & Ruell, C. E., ed. (1879). *Oevres de Rufus d' Ephese.* Paris: Nationale.

Delaney, J., Lupton, M. J., & Toth, E. (1976). *The Curse: A Cultural History of Menstruation.* Chicago: Univ. of Ill. Press.

Deutsch, H. (1930). The significance of masochism in the mental life of women. In *The Psychoanalytic Reader*, ed. R. Fliess. New York: Int. Univ. Press, pp. *165–179.*

Dickes, R. (1981). Sexual myths and misinformation. In *Understanding Human Behavior in Health and Illness*, ed. R. Simons & H. Pardes. Baltimore: Williams & Wilkins.

Eissler, K. R. (1977). Comments on penis envy and orgasm in women. *Psychoanal. St. Child*, 32: *29–84.*

Fraiberg, S. (1972). Some characteristics of genital arousal and discharge in latency girls. *Psychoanal. St. Child*, 27: 439–475.

Freeman, D. (1988). *Corduroy.* New York: Puffin Books.

Freud, S. (1900). The interpretation of dreams. *S.E.*, 4, 5.

——— (1901). Fragment of an analysis of a case of hysteria. *S.E.*, 7.

——— (1905). Three essays on the theory of sexuality. *S.E.*, 7.

——— (1908). On the sexual theories of children. *S.E.*, 9.

——— (1909). Analyses of a phobia in a five-year-old boy. *S.E.*, 10.

——— (1913). The occurrences in dreams of material from fairy tales. *S.E.*, 12.

——— (1915). A case of paranoia running counter to the psychoanalytic theory of the disease. *S.E.*, 14.

——— (1917). Introductory Lectures on Psycho-Analysis, *S.E.*, 16.

——— (1919). A child is being beaten: A contribution to the study of the origin of sexual perversions. *S.E.*, 17.

——— (1925). Some psychical consequences of the anatomical distinction between the sexes. *S.E.*, 19.

——— (1931). Female sexuality. *S.E.*, 21.

——— (1933). New introductory lectures on psycho anal. *S.E.*, 22.

Frish, H. (1960). *Greechiches Etymologisches Worterbuch.* Heidelberg: Carl Winter.

Gillespie, W. H. (1969). Concepts of vaginal orgasm. *Int. J. Psycho-Anal.*, 50: *495–497.*

Glenn, J. & Kaplan, E. H. (1968). Types of orgasm in women: A critical review and redefinition. *J. Amer. Psychoanal. Assn.*, 16: *549–564.*

Glover, J. & Mendell, D. (1982). A suggested developmental sequence for a preoedipal genital phase. In *Early Female Development: Current Psychoanalytic Views*, ed. D. Mendell. New York: S. P. Medical and Scientific Books, pp. *127–174.*

Goldstein, R. (1984). The dark continent and its enigmas. *Int. J. Psycho-Anal.*, 65: *179–189.*

Graves, R. (1948). *The White Goddess.* New York: Noonday Press.

Greenacre, P. (1950). Special problems of early female sexual development. In *Trauma, Growth, and Personality.* New York: Norton, pp. *237–258.*

Greenberg, R. P. & Fisher, S. (1980). Freud's penis-baby equation: Exploratory tests of a controversial theory. *Brit. J. Med. Psychol.*, 53: *333–342.*

Hanson, A. E. (1989). *Greek and Roman Gynecology.* Unpublished. Ann Arbor, MI.

Harley, M. (1961). Masturbation conflicts. In *Adolescents: Psychoanalytic Approach to Problems and Therapy*, ed. L. Schneer. New York: Harper, pp. *51–78.*

Heuscher, J. E. (1974). *Myths and Fairy Tales.* Springfield, IL: Charles C Thomas.

Horney, K. (1933). The denial of the vagina: Contribution to genital anxiety specific to women. *Int. J. Psycho-Anal.*, 14: *57–70.*

Jones, E. (1927). The early development of female sexuality. *Int. J. Psycho-Anal.*, 8: *439–472.*

Joseph, E. D. (1974). An aspect of female frigidity. *J. Amer. Psychoanal. Assn.*, 22: *116–122.*

Kestenberg, J. (1975). *Children and Parents: Psychoanalytic Studies.* New York: Jason Aronson.

Kleeman, J. (1976). Freud's views on early female sexuality in the light of direct child observation. *J. Amer. Psychoanal. Assn.*, 24(Suppl.): *3–27.*

Lampl-de Groot, J. (1982). Thoughts on psychoanalytic views of female psychology, 1927–1977. *Psychoanal Q.*, 51: *1–18.*

Lerner, H. (1976). Parental mislabeling of female genitals as a determinant of penis envy and learning inhibitions in women. *J. Amer. Psychoanal. Assn.*, 24(Suppl.): *269–283.*

Lightfoot-Klein, H. (1989). *Prisoners of Ritual. An Odyssey into Female Genital Circumcision in Africa.* New York: Harrington Park Press.

Lucas, E. V., Crane, L., & Edwards, M. (1945). *Grimm's Fairy Tales.* New York: Grosset & Dunlap.

Marcus, I. M. & Francis, J. J. (1975). Masturbation: A developmental view. In *Masturbation,* ed. I. M. Marcus & J. J. Francis. New York: Int. Univ. Press, pp. *9–51.*

Masters, W. H. & Johnson, V. E. (1962). The sexual response cycle of the human female, III. The Clitoris: Anatomic and clinical considerations. *Western J. Surg.*, 70: *248–257.*

Mayer, E. (1985). Everybody must be just like me. *Int. J. Psycho-Anal.*, 66: *331–347.*

Miller, M. (1985). Poor Rumpelstiltskin. *Psychoanal Q.*, 54: *73–76.*

Montgrain, N. (1983). On the vicissitudes of female sexuality: The difficult path from anatomical destiny to psychic representation. *Int. J. Psycho-Anal.*, 65: *169–186.*

Neaman, J. S. & Silver, C. G. (1983). *Kind Words. A Thesaurus of Euphemisms.* New York: Facts on File Publications.

Oxford English Dictionary (1961). London: Oxford Univ. Press.

Panel (1976). Psychology of Women, E. Galenson, Reporter. *J. Amer. Psychoanal. Assn.*, 24: *141–160.*

Patai, R. (1973). *The Arab Mind.* New York: Scribner.

Rinsley, D. B. & Bergmann, E. (1983). Enchantment and alchemy: The story of Rumpelstiltskin. *Bull. Menninger Clin.*, 47: *1–13*.

Róheim, G. (1945). Aphrodite or the woman with a penis. *Psychoanal Q.*, 14: *350–390*.

Rowley, J. (1951). Rumpelstiltskin. *Int. J. Psycho-Anal.*, 32: *190–195*.

Schimek, J. G. (1975). A critical re-examination of Freud's concept of unconscious mental representation. *Int. R. Psycho-Anal.*, 2: *171–187*.

Shaw, E. (1985). Female circumcision. *American J. of Nursing*, 85: *684–687*.

Shopper, M. (1966). Three as a symbol of the female genital and the role of differentiation. *Psychoanal Q.*, 36: *410–417*.

Siegel, B. (1971). The role of the mouth in the search for the female phallus. *J. Amer. Psychoanal. Assn.*, 19: *310–331*.

Spitz, R. A. (1975). Authority and masturbation: Some remarks on a bibliographical investigation. In *Masturbation: A Developmental View*, ed. I. M. Marcus & J. J. Francis. New York: Int. Univ. Press, pp. *381–409*.

Stoller, R. J. (1975). *Perversion*. New York: Random House.

Tripp, E. (1970). *The Meredian Handbook of Classical Mythology*. New York: New American Library.

Yearsley, M. (1924). *The Folklore of Fairy-Tale*. London: Watts.

CHAPTER 3:

A Phobia of The Couch: A Clinical Study of Psychoanalytic Process.

(1996). Psychoanal. Q., (65):465–494

Conversion from psychotherapy to psychoanalysis and the differences between the two have been the subject of discussion and controversy in recent years. The theoretical and technical questions that have been raised suffer from the lack of detailed clinical accounts that might help to elucidate the processes involved. The author presents a case of a woman whose refusal to use the couch for three years became a central organizing resistance and took on the structure of a phobia. It is argued that the case, rather than a conversion from psychotherapy to psychoanalysis, was one of psychoanalysis from the beginning, with the conflicts about the couch analyzed as are any other resistances.

INTRODUCTION

Psychoanalytic writings about conversion from psychotherapy to psychoanalysis and about the differences between psychoanalytic psychotherapy and psychoanalysis are mired in ambiguities and contradictions. What is not clear is exactly what happens in the process of conversion from psychotherapy to psychoanalysis. For example, what are the resistances in the psychotherapy and how are they worked through? Are resistances in psychoanalysis different and handled technically in a different way? Discussions about the differences between the two modalities often seem reductionistic and misleading, hinging either on superficialities, such as the use of the couch or the frequency of sessions, or on idealistic and artificial generalities about the nature of "true" psychoanalysis. What is missing is detailed, convincing, and clear clinical accounts about what goes on in the psychotherapy, the conversion, and the psychoanalysis to back up the claims made about the differences or the similarities of the processes involved.

The following is an account of the treatment of a woman who sought psychoanalysis, but refused to lie on the couch for the first three years. Her refusal to use the couch was the expression of a major resistance, an organizing point around which fantasies in the transference and countertransference revolved, and a phobic symptom. Although patients frequently are resistant about the couch, especially in the initial weeks of analysis, analysts have not written extensively about the subject, perhaps because such resistances are so commonplace and temporary, as Byerly (1992) has suggested. Most analysts who have addressed the subject (Fenichel, 1941; Glover, 1955; Goldberger, 1995; Greenacre, 1959; Greenson, 1967; Hogan, 1990; Rothstein, 1990; Stone, 1961) have advised flexibility in the technical handling of an initial fear of the couch. An exception is Kernberg (Panel, 1987, pp. 719–721), who has described his insistence that patients follow his recommendations for treatment in order to set the analysis on the correct course from the beginning.

Other writers also have focused on patients' incapacities which interfere with their lying on the couch. Greenacre (1959) pointed to individuals who have too great a regressive potential or who are given to acting out their fantasies repetitively as not being able to go on the couch. Byerly (1992) suggested that inability to use the couch can reflect developmental problems connected with unresolved separation-individuation, masochism, and difficulties with compliance. Jacobs (1990) noted that young adults frequently have difficulties with the couch. Pines (1993) added adolescents and severely traumatized concentration camp victims to the list. It has been a clinical truism, no longer taken for granted, that the couch is contraindicated for borderline patients (Rosenbaum, 1967). Since individuals who fall into all these categories do not necessarily have problems with the couch, these generalizations do not get us very far in understanding the processes involved.

More specifically, vision seemed to play a special role in many of the reported cases. Weissman (1977) described a woman who had major difficulties in lying on the couch. Her unusually strong hunger for visual, face-to-face contact stemmed from early maternal deprivation and separation. Searles (1984) documented the meaning and significance of the analyst's facial expressions to the patient in a series of clinical cases, both in psychoanalysis and psychotherapy, and argued convincingly that vision has an important role in the therapeutic relationship in general.

As for more protracted instances of refusal or inability to lie on the couch, there are only a few reported cases in the psychoanalytic literature. One of these is Weissman's, mentioned above, in which the need for visual contact played such a prominent role. Another was reported by Frank (1992). His patient was a woman who began treatment with a strong fear of lying down, which reappeared intermittently throughout what he considered a successful analysis. While he showed that the symptom was overdetermined, he felt that the significant issue contributing to her fear of the couch was a profound problem in object constancy, which led to a need to keep the analyst in sight. Thus, patients' developmental difficulties are most frequently offered as the explanation for problems with using the couch. This focus draws attention away from the analytic process and from a closer look at the resistances, therapeutic interaction, and technical issues in a given case.

One of the more thoughtful and detailed accounts of a patient who had prolonged difficulty with the couch was given by McLaughlin (1992). During the course of analysis his patient frequently felt troubled in lying down and had to sit up periodically. When she did lie down, she often displayed unusual nonverbal behaviors, such as spreading her legs and holding out her heels.

These behaviors and her fear of the couch were traced to her history of suffering from urinary tract difficulties as a child and having to lie still on her back and in stirrups for long painful procedures. For this patient, as with others with histories of painful, traumatic medical procedures, the couch evoked memories and feelings related concretely to lying down in a passive position.

McAloon (1988) described her countertransference reactions to a provocative patient's refusal over three and a half years to use the couch. During this period, McAloon experienced profound doubts over her own competence and professional identity. She felt she was not a "true analyst" without the use of the couch. The issue of the couch became part of a sadomasochistic interaction in the transference-countertransference. The patient used the couch to control the analyst, whom he experienced as his provocative, exhibitionist mother. In reaction, McAloon felt guilt-ridden, angry, and frustrated. Whenever she felt stymied, she tried to talk the patient into getting onto the couch. In retrospect she concluded that her need to *feel* like an analyst interfered with her ability to *behave* like an analyst.

A similar problem characterized a case of Reiser's (1986), in which the couch mobilized conflicts based on preoedipal issues. The case became stalemated inexplicably until the analyst had the patient sit up. Then the patient was able to explore her memories of early hospitalizations, abandonment, and possible sexual abuse, traumas to which she had reacted by altered states of consciousness. When she lay on the couch, she reexperienced these states and was not able to observe and understand her reactions. Reiser characterized the case as a switch from analysis when the patient was lying on the couch to psychoanalytic psychotherapy when she was sitting up. This characterization strikes me as artificial, based as it was only on the change in the patient's position and not on substantial changes in the analytic work. It is, however, in keeping with the once prevalent notion that any modification in standard psychoanalytic technique meant that the endeavor could no longer be called psychoanalysis (Wohlberg, 1967).

Surprisingly, given its importance to the analytic situation, few of the writers have examined in depth the *meaning* of the couch to the patient and in the analytic relationship. (An exception is McLaughlin, reported above.) Frequently, lying on the couch is thought to have sexual meanings to the patient. Orens (1965), for example, reported the case of a woman who became panicky when she first tried to lie on the couch. He felt her fear was related to the position itself, with the analyst above and behind her. The patient felt powerless and fearful of her fantasies that the analyst would attack her sadistically. Khan (1962) briefly compared the psychology of lying on the couch to the psyche of the dreamer. His ideas are interesting, but not supported by detailed clinical data. Similarly, Bergel (1984), drawing on mythology and anthropology, speculated on the unconscious symbolic meanings of the couch and the positions of analyst and analysand: "Fear or refusal to assume the analytic position on the couch could represent fear of death and change on the deepest levels" (pp. 296-297). These speculations, while intriguing, are far-fetched, and not based on analytic data. Apart from these few cases, there are few detailed clinical reports of the meaning of the couch to the patient.

My case, in which the patient sat up for the first three years of treatment, shares characteristics of cases of conversion from psychotherapy to psychoanalysis in which resistances to analysis are worked through and allow for the switch to be made. I will argue, however, that my case was psychoanalysis from the beginning and that the use of the couch per se is not a defining feature of the psychoanalytic process. My patient also shares many characteristics in common with patients described above— namely, her masochism, her disposition toward acting out and negative therapeutic reactions, and difficulties in self-other differentiation. What is different in this case, however, is how the fear of the couch took center stage and became an organized symptom within the transference.

CASE MATERIAL

When she sought treatment, Ms. S was in her late thirties, married, with two children, a girl of nine and a boy of four. She was employed as an office manager. She sought help because she was troubled by her physically and verbally abusive behavior toward her daughter, Rachel—"possessed by demons," as she put it. She was depressed in general and felt herself to be "nothing but shit." Ms. S reported being incessantly drawn into angry interchanges with Rachel, who was extremely provocative and seemingly masochistic. An example of one of her abusive interchanges with Rachel had occurred several years before. Very jealous, the girl scratched her brother across the cheek. In a rage, Ms. S then scratched Rachel across the cheek and drew blood. A more serious instance of physical abuse occurred during the first Christmas break in Ms. S's treatment.

The patient stated that she had almost total amnesia—a word she used—for her childhood. She dubbed her amnesia "The Black Hole," and this term was particularly pertinent to her feelings about her mother, "a mystery" to her. Ms. S had almost no affective-laden memories of her family and early childhood, but mostly of places, things, isolated scenes. Moreover, denial washed over any negative characteristics of her family or any possible family secrets. The family ethic, preached by her mother, was to put a good face on in public (and in private, as it turned out). Thus, it was months, even years before I learned this account of her history.

The patient's father was an alcoholic, a word she could not apply to him at first.

Frequently, he flew into rages and belittled his family with biting, cruel remarks. Ms. S described him as a raging bear. He had his secrets: there were hints of his troubled business having been destroyed by arson; he owned some businesses in the seedy side of town; the fact that he had a history of syphilis was revealed by his doctors only during an illness several years into the patient's treatment. Yet she experienced him as warm and loving for the most part, and as treating her indulgently as the only girl. He seemed more real and available than the mother, a pretty, genteel lady, who was remote and unemotional. She was given to speaking entirely in clichés and to absolute denial of anything negative in herself or her family. She was frequently critical of the patient, but when confronted, became indignant and threw it back on the patient with a remark like "You're too sensitive."

Most of the patient's memories are of being the onlooker. She characterizes herself as just being the good girl. The patient had two older brothers. Jack, the middle sibling, was "the golden boy," good-looking, smart, a star athlete. He took over the family business and ran it to the ground, even embezzling money from his father. He was also an alcoholic, and his fortunes have steadily declined over the years. Yet he remained the mother's favorite, untarnished in her eyes. Throughout his childhood Henry, the older brother, was tormented by the father for his effeminate mannerisms, apparently evident in early childhood. Henry was "wild and different" and always in trouble. The patient recalled her father pushing a bowl of hot cereal in Henry's face but did not remember any of the other abuses, such as being shoved up against the wall, that Henry and even Jack said they endured. Henry told the patient that he remembered constantly picking on her because he was extremely jealous of her, but the patient recalled very few isolated instances of this, such as being tied up by him in a closet. In one memory the patient was dragged out of bed in the middle of the night by her father, probably drunk, who forced her to show Henry how to do his arithmetic in order to humiliate him. She always felt close to Henry. He took on the role of being an older sister, sometimes mother to her to make up for the mother's inattention and inadequacies. He told the patient what to wear, picked out jewelry for her, even planned her wedding. She met her husband Tom, her first real boyfriend, while in college and married him shortly thereafter.

Two years before she first saw me, Ms. S had been in treatment for about seven months with Dr. T, an analyst whom she liked. Ms. S recalled that in a session when she told Dr. T about the incident of scratching Rachel, she complained of a migraine and inadvertently drew her hand across the side of her face. Dr. T's suggestion that her gesture was connected with feelings of guilt made a lasting impression on her. Because she found their once-a-week meetings difficult, but could not afford to come more frequently, Dr. T recommended that she undertake a low- fee analysis with an analytic candidate. After some delay and ambivalence about following through on his recommendations, she called me. She knew of me through a friend, a mental health professional. She was also "perhaps vaguely aware" that I was connected with the psychoanalytic institute and was an advanced candidate there. The seriousness of her problems and her evident pain impressed me that analysis was needed; Ms. S's clear intelligence and positive response to Dr. T were hopeful signs that she could engage in the process. She readily agreed to begin an analysis on the basis of four times a week as a private patient and with a moderately reduced fee. One month before she first saw me, Ms. S also had arranged for her daughter to begin therapy with a social worker.

EXPLORATION OF THE MEANING OF THE COUCH IN THE SITTING-UP STAGE

The issue of the couch emerged immediately. In the first session after the arrangements had been made, Ms. S sat in the chair and asked, "Is this the same chair?" She had mistakenly thought the chair was dark. Driving to the session she found herself thinking about the couch and how it wouldn't be so easy for her. At first she had thought that using the couch would not be the problem it was for a woman friend of hers who was in treatment. Referring to her friend, she mused, "competitive thing perhaps." Her husband Tom, who had been in analysis, said the couch had a profound impact on him. She asked anxiously, "Do you lose the whole interaction when you lie down?" When I suggested we could talk more about the meaning of the couch for her, she said, "Good! So I don't have to feel like a failure if I don't right away." I agreed there was no great hurry but indicated clearly that I felt the couch would be helpful.

In these early weeks Ms. S gingerly expressed some disappointment with me. I had called her son by the wrong name. I should be more like Dr. T, who would not have made such a mistake. She complained that her mother had not helped her with menstruation. Clearly, she was feeling that I was not helping her either, although she denied it. She did express her feeling that the process was like exposing dirty laundry in public, a taboo in her family. When I interpreted her fear of getting into dirty things in analysis and on the couch, she agreed, and added a memory of her kindergarten teacher's washing her mouth out with soap. It was in this context that the patient revealed that her brother Henry was gay.

Ms. S's conflicts about the couch appeared in the first dream of the analysis, which she reported after about a month:

We were looking at some water down below from a high, high cliff, like watching a movie. A man and I. He said he was afraid to leap, but I said it was O.K. because it was deep not shallow. So he jumped—sitting —and he hit his butt. It was terrible. It wasn't deep … Injured. Like from the movie, Born on the Fourth of July, paralyzed. I was trying to help him, like get to an agency. The movie really affected me. And he had wispy hair, like Jessica Tandy in Driving Miss Daisy looked at the end in the nursing home. To me dreams are feelings, and the feeling here was weird. [How so?] Just so high, steep.

In her few associations the patient referred to Friday's session— "that transference stuff." In that session she had been talking about how she floated into college far from home, a stranger. My interpretation that she felt that way in analysis with me had provoked tears. In answer to my question about the man's sitting position, she replied, "Like sitting here." I said that when she had told me about her emotional reaction to *Driving Miss Daisy*, she had identified with Miss Daisy, disabled and being wheeled around in a wheelchair by a servant. I wondered if the dream expressed her fear of taking the plunge into analysis and being on the couch, and that although I might reassure her it was O.K., she would get hurt. The patient could follow this, but said that, if so, she was "unconscious of it" and added that she had also identified Jessica Tandy with her mother, always the lady. (A few months later she had a dream about me with wispy hair like Jessica Tandy's.) Thus, this opening dream hinted at many of the themes that would emerge in the analysis. Most salient at this point were her feelings of hostility and mistrust toward me, the mother in the transference. A struggle over control and buried competitiveness with me was suggested in the reversal and blurring of roles of helper and helped, servant and mistress.

The dream foreshadowed a major transference-counter-transference interaction between the bad withholding mother and the willful, bad, and disappointing child. In this primarily sadomasochistic interaction, the patient most frequently cast herself as child and me as mother, but at times the roles were reversed. Repeatedly, this paradigm was acted out with Rachel in a confusing interplay of reversals in roles. Typically, the patient would allow or even suggest to Rachel some behavior which was dubbed as demanding, greedy, or bad, then react with rage when the child acted the behavior out. The drama would inevitably end with self-recriminations and guilt on the patient's part.

We came gradually to see that in these enactments the patient often played the role of bad, rejecting mother, but at other times, the greedy, demanding, willful child, or the disappointed, hurt child. At still other times the patient was her sadistic father, the tortured older brother, or the frightened onlooker. Besides the rapid shifts in projections of self and object and the projective identification of induced roles, what made this all so difficult to untangle was the patient's "amnesias." Not only did Ms. S have amnesia for much of her childhood, but she could frequently not recall these incidents between her and Rachel, or what led up to them. The patient's speech in her sessions was filled with small gaps in syntax and content, gaps of which she was apparently unaware. Thus, her words were often incomprehensible. I personally found this aspect of the treatment very difficult. At times I had the fantasy that if the patient would only get on the couch, things would become easier and more comprehensible.

In refusing to get on the couch, the patient acted out a sadomasochistic relationship with me, as she did at times in not paying her bill. Fantasies and interactions about money and the couch were often intertwined. As the analysis proceeded, it became evident that the family's finances were a disaster. There were back taxes, huge credit card debts, and legal difficulties. It was Ms. S who was in charge of managing the family's finances, and she often made major mistakes in balancing the checkbook or ignoring important bills. Tom distanced himself totally from the whole matter. In all of this mess the patient blamed her husband—for passivity, his poor judgment, and for not making enough money.

A major focus in the first three years of treatment was to help her take responsibility for her part in these difficulties, to understand their meaning in her life and as they appeared in the transference-countertransference. For example, she lamented the fact that the IRS was on her back, the utilities were threatened with cut-off, and her poor children were without new sneakers. How could I ask for my money? One consequence of the money difficulties was an attempt to induce guilt and to cast me as the bad mother, the mother who never gave her anything or helped her. As the financial picture became clearer, I learned that the patient's father had always helped her financially and generously—a big sugar daddy. "Daddy" had "loaned" them the down payment for their big house, which they could ill afford to maintain. Indeed, Ms. S had never furnished her house, but there were other reasons for this, as we learned later. The patient jokingly remarked that her family had always said, "Never rely on the kindness of strangers." "But in a sense you do," I replied. Thus, a meaning of the financial acting out was to make me into her "Sugar Daddy," paying for her treatment. I tried to interpret these meanings as I understood them, but the patient resisted understanding the transference. "My feelings about you are a mystery to me," she would lament. She blocked out the fact that such behavior as not paying her bill or not getting on the couch would negatively affect our relationship, or that it had hostile meanings. It seemed that she wished unconsciously to provoke me into forcing her to pay. Indeed, I did finally had to say that her behavior was endangering the treatment, and insist she find a way to pay regularly. She did so, with a few lapses along the way, and finally worked out a scheme to pay me the back balance that had accrued.

Just as she wished me to force her into paying up, she wished me to force her to get on the couch. This fantasy revealed itself early in the second week of the treatment. She reported that her husband asked if I had said anything about the couch. She confessed that she was afraid to bring the subject up, but, "The longer it goes, the harder it gets." She was thinking about Dr. T and "how it would have been if *he* were my analyst. *He* would be more definitive, forceful— but your way is better for me, I think." Thus, the idea of being forced onto the couch had anal connotations as well as phallic, sexual ones; a man would have the power to force her to submit. The patient could readily admit it was a question of control, of "weakness and strength." "Yes, it's there. The trouble is if I feel you want it, I'll never get on the couch." In these sessions she talked of the inequities she experienced between us.

In the first year of treatment the patient reported the following: "Had a dream last night, but I don't remember it, except I realize it had to do with the couch. I was thrust on the couch [she laughs] by someone or something. When I woke up, I felt that would be good. But now that feeling is gone, and I feel I can't again. I am a failure." She had no associations to being thrust on the couch. She went on to tell how Rachel had been better behaved of late, and her report card was improved. The girl had wanted to make her teacher a present, but messed it up and was devastated. The parallel was clear to me in the way the patient told the dream. She wanted to give me the present of going on the couch but then took it back. This type of giving and taking back, of doing and undoing, was to be repeated frequently in the moths and years to come.

Almost a year later, however, she would use the same word, "thrust," in a different context, which I think throws light on an important underlying fantasy.

The patient dreamed she was in a car with her daughter, taking her to a roller-skating rink. The girl was afraid but the patient made her get out of the car; she thrust her out. A similar incident had occurred in reality. The patient associated roller-skating with danger, with the secret, seamy part of town frequented by her father, and with sex. Until the patient's defensive use of externalization was worked through, however, the fuller meanings of the fantasy of being forced could not be explored and appreciated by the patient. I repeatedly interpreted the patient's need to put me in charge of her treatment. I suggested to her that her preoccupation with my wanting her to go on the couch covered her own wishes in that regard.

The Couch and the Need to be Special

Beneath the patient's defiant, stubborn refusal to get on the couch lay many fears and conflicted wishes. Prominent among these was her fear of her intense desires for closeness and to be cared for. In the latter part of the first year the patient had been talking about her Nanny and contrasting her warmth and "soft hands" with her mother's aloofness and coldness. In this context she reported that she had had a dream, interesting, she thought, because it had to do with the couch:

There was the couch, but it wasn't like it was, but like a down quilt, white, soft, inviting. Then I was in the theater, but the seats were out and there was this tapestry rug there. I was watching a projector. The scene was of all the people going up a hill, "down home" people—how corny—music in the background.

Her vague associations were to seeing that a lot of her friends had those fancy quilts (said with tacit envy), a video she watched for her work, and how Rachel's girl scout leader suggested that the girl did not belong in the troop. At that time I took up the wish for me to be her Nanny and her fear of rejection. In the following sessions the patient again brought up "the couch thing," with new insight: "Maybe it's not that I fear the loss of the interaction, but that I'm afraid of not being remote." She admitted that by not paying, she was pretending not to be in analysis. She toyed with the idea of buying an expensive comforter, the price of which just coincided with a month's analytic bill. Then with anger and sadness she related how her mother gave her only *eight* towels as her wedding shower gift, "Why not the standard dozen?" Again a few weeks later she took up "the couch thing," and momentarily admitted that she was feeling closer to me. For the first time in treatment she wept.

In the midst of trying to make sense of her feelings about her mother and beginning to tackle her money problems, the patient had the following dream: "You and me. You were comforting me … this is hard for me … like I was a baby, patting my head. Definitely not like a therapist. Can't put it into words." Later in the session she remembered another part of the dream. "In a long, narrow room with two long, narrow pieces of furniture, like one for each of my children. Or like a couch! But made of plasterboard. Flimsy. Don't know." I said to her that she was afraid of how much she wanted to be close to me, for me to comfort her and hold her like a baby, and that the feelings would overwhelm her when she got on the couch. "Or fall apart, like the furniture in the dream," she added.

Psychological distance from or closeness to me was represented concretely in fantasy by how close she sat to me, as illustrated by a series of dreams. In the context of talking about her conflicts in arranging for a maid who could watch the children and her difficulties in paying her bills, she dreamed: "You were sitting in a chair, which moved forward. As it moved forward, your face changed, became old and fatter, flat, weird. You had hair like Jessica Tandy. What context did that come up in—as mother?" In another dream some months later, the chair had been moved to the other side of the room. In her associations she told how her little boy often just jumped into her lap to cuddle.

The Couch as a Vehicle of Exposure of Forbidden Fantasies

Another fear expressed from the beginning was the idea that lying on the couch would leave her vulnerable, exposed, and on display. In one of her dreams, for example, the couch was an examining table. Early on she expressed her conviction that I would be able to see her and her body more fully if she were lying down rather than seated directly across from me.

Ms. S was afraid of revealing secrets on the couch—family secrets and her own perverse and sexual secrets. She speculated that the couch would help her to get in touch with memories, her "black hole." A series of dreams of rustic buildings, always introduced by the patient as "weird," were linked to secrets. Most of these buildings were long and narrow and at times directly associated with the couch. She reported a dream which came on a night in which her husband had encouraged her to get on the couch: "A group of us are in a line being escorted into a rustic, wooden, box-like building by a man. There was a feeling of something ominous, not quite doom, that's too strong. It was through a process that was mysterious and unknown. The man who was running it was not known but a magician...."

In earlier dreams her conscious identification was with the victim of Nazi attackers. In one such dream a woman's house was broken into by robbers. She associated to her own fears of break-ins, to "thoughts about the couch—it might be a wrong decision," and how Rachel "freaked out" in the middle of the night and ended up sleeping with her. She was afraid something would happen if she got on the couch. Clearly, she was afraid and wished that I would sexually attack her. It was a break-through in the third year of treatment when the patient could acknowledge and take ownership of her identification with the attacker. She could feel that the word "sadistic" applied to her. Much later she would associate rustic buildings with "low life" and the wild sexual side of town her father frequented, and with games she and Henry played which left her tied up or closed in. Thus, the fantasy was that the couch would be the setting for sadomasochistic games.

Another set of representations of the couch in dreams was as various pieces of furniture: other kinds of couches, tables, chairs, a piano. A dining room table had special significance for Ms. S. She had been unable to fix up her house, to furnish it. Her lack of a dining room table was especially upsetting and significant to her. At first she rationalized that it was the lack of money that inhibited her, but we came to understand that a dining room table carried conflicted feminine connotations. She conjured up her mother's beautiful, formal dining room table. Without a dining room table of her own she could not invite people into her house, could not entertain. She wasn't a real grown-up woman or mother. She could see that she just did her house "part way." I added that the same applied to her analysis, not lying down, for example, was doing it part way.

As we came to see, she wished to be a boy, favored by her mother. She could not let herself be a successful female and fix herself up as a woman, get in shape, get a dining room table; and to get on the couch was to display her inadequacies. A central unconscious self-representation was that of a castrated male, the dilapidated, pasteboard couch, or a broken piano. One of her most vivid screen memories was at the age of about seven eagerly awaiting the arrival of a piano that was being shipped from another part of the country. To her horror, the piano had been damaged in shipping; she remembered that the keys fell off. She was devastated, inconsolable.

Ms. S linked getting on the couch to conflicts about playing the piano. Her mother played the piano and encouraged the patient as a child to take lessons. At times, her mother would play duets with her. While the patient enjoyed the piano and showed some musical talent, she was anxious about performing publicly and quit her piano teacher before her senior recital. Thus, playing piano brought her mother's favor and attention and, unconsciously, conflicted identifications with her. Playing the piano also expressed forbidden exhibitionistic fantasies.

In the latter part of the first year of treatment Ms. S made a typical open-ing announcement: she had been thinking more about the couch. The word "embarrassment" came to mind, embarrassment about her body. At her work, she continued, she liked to work behind the scenes, and she shunned the more glamorous jobs, such as public speaking. On Halloween of the same year she expressed her incredulity that children, anyone, could get any pleasure from parading around in a costume. I said that this feeling related to her body, and I linked it to her anxieties about the couch. In response, she related a story about how a superior had complimented her profusely at a meeting. To her surprise she found herself becoming tearful as she told the story. For the first time I could begin to help her to recognize her strong need to be special, to get attention.

These ideas of being special and displaying herself to the mother and their link to the couch come together in a central memory. When she was in the first grade her teacher called the home. The mother answered and relayed the message, in a dispassionate tone, that the teacher had wanted the girl, as one of a select few, to be on a special radio program. Without hesitation, the child refused. The feeling at that moment—"I can't!"—was exactly the feeling she had about the couch. She did not know why, but that was that. This story and the feeling of "I can't!" came to mind whenever she thought of getting on the couch. In an early session she went through a familiar series—first, that she was thinking about the couch, then that she felt like a failure, and that she would be in treatment forever (clearly, a wish).

In the next session she speculated whether her mother preferred her, the good girl, over her brothers. She worried whether or not she would disappoint me (also, clearly a wish, which I repeatedly interpreted). It took her years to acknowledge the wish to shine and perform, which "I can't" concealed, the wish to shine in front of me on the couch, to shine in front of her mother on the piano and her teacher on the radio. Such wishes typically were first voiced in regard to Rachel. In the second year of treatment she reported that Rachel's piano teacher felt that the child had talent. She was able to accept my interpretation that she wished that I would tell her *she* had a talent for analysis. In denying her wish to be special, the patient had to repress the whole situation of how the analysis began and was structured: that I was still in training, that she was getting a reduced fee, and whatever fantasies of being special or not special as a patient that entailed. When questioned about her thoughts about the reduced fee, she expressed the fantasy that I was "just being nice" to her. This wish to be special was another motivation for her to avoid paying the bill and using the couch.

It took still longer for the patient to recognize her anger at her mother for the clear lack of encouragement to excel expressed in the neutral manner she reported the teacher's call. Indeed, the patient realized that she felt that her mother subtly discouraged her in her career and in any attempts she made to better herself as a woman in fixing up her house, etc. In any case, competitive wishes were dangerous and were to be inhibited or punished. In the third year of treatment the patient again announced that she had been thinking about whether or not she'd be able to "do it," i.e., get on the couch, then proceeded to talk about her newly found ability to delight in her daughter's sparkling performance at a dance recital, and then to think that perhaps she herself was not supposed to want to shine. She continued painfully to acknowledge her father's cruelty toward her brothers, how they both were screwed up and unsuccessful, then to recount the memory of the night she showed Henry up with his arithmetic, and finally to express her guilt about being better than both her brothers, but especially Henry, whom she loved. (Not yet acknowledged was her wish to better them.) Following this session she had a severe migraine, which she herself could tie into her reaction to the session and speculate whether it was self-punishment.

The couch was associated with success, or what success meant to the patient. Success meant competing with beautiful women. Thus, she refused to go to the local university, with its emphasis on sororities and social life, "just as I refused the couch," she said noting the analogous feeling. Success meant letting herself get better and hence sometime having to terminate. Success also meant competing with men, or perhaps bettering them, unconsciously castrating them as the hero in *Born on the Fourth of July* was castrated. In her dreams the couch was often represented directly by phallic images, such as cars, her father's big car, the hood of cars, wagons. During one session she had the image of a child's red wagon, like the one her brother Henry had. She had always wanted one, she said, but had never gotten one. Henry's was rusty; the ones she saw now were shiny, maybe plastic. She associated to a TV program with puppets on a long, narrow table. Then she mused, "My wagon here in analysis has stopped." And, of course, she wanted to fix my wagon by complicating, undoing, our analytic work.

The Couch as a Phobic Object

As time went by, more and more of the patient's conflicts seemed to be encapsulated by the fear of the couch. As she herself thoughtfully put it, "The couch is a symbol, isn't it?" The patient had many phobias—of elevators, of heights, of carnival rides; the couch had become another. She likened being thrust on the couch to pushing Rachel to overcome her fear of the roller-skating rink. Again, in a session at the end of the second year, her thoughts went from fear of the couch to her fear of riding a roller coaster, to a memory of a fall on the ice, to playing the piano. Another fear was of jumping off a high board, reminiscent of the initial dream of falling off a cliff. Later that year, she reported being afraid of coming to her session. Then her thoughts went to phobias her daughter seemed to be developing—of being alone upstairs, for example. The patient wondered why she was not more empathic with her daughter; after all, she too had phobias. In the third year she described her fear of driving on ice, of being stranded. I likened this to her fear of the couch, and she agreed. She remembered a feeling of danger associated with the attic in her childhood home. There were long scary stairs like the stairs to my office. She had a scary dream about a mother and a daughter looking for something in an attic. Her statement that the couch was now "like the black hole" summed up her conflicted feelings. In the same session she complained that her husband should help her conquer some of her fears. When I suggested that she wanted me to do the same, she immediately replied her characteristic "no," then wavered, "but…"

As the third year of the treatment was ending and the fourth beginning, Ms. S was showing progress. Steady work on her defensive use of externalization and denial had made her increasingly able to take responsibility for her actions and thoughts. The physical abuse against her daughter had disappeared and the verbal barrages had diminished, even as Ms. S was able to own up to her own sadism and understand its roots in her troubled familial past. She had become a more active participant in her sessions and had taken full responsibility for payment. Still she was not on the couch, and she was avoiding directly talking about sex. She had told me early in the treatment that she was orgasmic, that her first sexual partner was her husband while they were dating, and that she had enjoyed sex. But after their marriage, as the troubles with finances and her difficulties as a mother mounted, their sexual life suffered. There were months of estrangement and no sexual relations. I had persistently interpreted her fear of the couch as related to her fear of talking about her sexual fantasies and of their being realized in analysis.

For example, the patient had two dreams on two successive nights, both vague.

One was about sex; the second about me and some kind of dual relationship. Her associations were how she avoided sex in her relationship with her husband, how she became scared when people try to get close, and how "not doing the couch" was because I wanted her to. She talked anxiously about Rachel's need to get close to a girlfriend and of lying down next to the girl on the bed to comfort her. I interpreted the obvious parallel fears in the transference of getting too close and of a dual relationship, and she agreed. A few months later she again declared she never would do the couch or talk about sex. (She had been able to link this inhibition to her mother's cold prudery and avoidance of the subject.) She complained angrily that her resistance to the couch was worse now. She dreamed she was working for royalty, did something that brought her into disfavor, and was cut in half lengthwise so one could see inside. Her association was to a new law that would ban surrogate mothers. Again I interpreted the fear of being cut open on the couch and her need to flee from the increasing closeness she felt between us. When the third anniversary of the treatment came, the patient lamented that it would go on forever. Shortly after, she dreamed again of long rectangular buildings. Her thoughts went to a friend's question of whether she was on the couch yet.

THE CENTRAL ENACTMENT AROUND THE COUCH

At this time the patient was offered a new job that would mean more pay, but also more responsibility, work, and prestige. She struggled with her ambivalence, acted out by forgetting to call the prospective employers back. It became very clear to her how conflicted she was about letting herself excel and compete, especially with me. For example, she saw the new job as more professional—she would have to wear a suit as I did. Ultimately, she turned the job down, but afterward mourned the lost potential and felt distraught about her self-destructiveness. With new resolve she said she wanted to understand this and overcome it. At this point I asked if it might be time to consider trying the couch. After a bit more work on her fears of success, she decided to do so.

Thus, in the third month of the fourth year of her treatment, in somewhat of an anticlimax, she lay down. As she walked toward the couch she said, "I am very very nervous. As I was driving here I was thinking about the piano recital, about being so scared and so nervous then. You're waiting for your turn, and then when it comes your turn, you go into automatic." Getting on the couch was a performance, a performance for her mother. She said, "I am proud of myself." With the insight that she was referring to the analysis, she went on to describe how after years of thinking her oven did not work properly, she tried cooking dinner in it and the chicken cooked in just the right amount of time. She also was wondering about my feelings about her getting on the couch. "You should think you handled it well and your timing was right. At first it seemed like it was you [who decided the issue], but I think you just took the cue from me."

I see the circumstances of the patient's finally lying down on the couch as the unconscious enactment of a central transference-countertransference paradigm. This was a woman who felt that her mother was cold and ungiving and preferred her brothers. The patient had repeatedly tried to induce me to treat her as special, even as she denied such wishes and recast me as the cold, neutral mother. Yet what could be more special than being a training case who was allowed not to lie on the couch? In spite of my attempts to remain neutral, I finally gave her a gentle shove onto the couch. This shove came in the context of the patient's anguish at her holding herself back from success. The mother had remained neutral when the teacher called to invite her to go on the radio. Unlike the mother, I, in effect, did not remain neutral, but encouraged her to let herself shine. "Taking the cue" from her meant being the loving, engaged mother when the patient was ready to let me be so.

In the following weeks, with new clarity, the negative oedipal transference began to unfold. Her father had become quite ill with cancer. She dreamed of his death and being alone with her mother. She fantasized about "bringing Mother home." She was able to speak angrily of how her mother's attention had always been completely devoted to "Daddy" and to her brothers. To her horror she found herself making jokes about the death of a friend's husband. She recognized her murderous jealousy of her brothers and their favored position by virtue of being males. At the same time she could openly admit that she herself preferred her son to her daughter. She was able to acknowledge masturbating with fantasies which "had to do with" power and control. She accepted her wish to castrate her brothers and to rid herself of all rivals for her mother. She could acknowledge a need to belittle her husband and speculated that she might have had a need to choose a passive man.

She dreamed again of the couch, in the context of talking about her father's sickness and a friend's delivering a baby boy: two babies had been switched at birth. The woman who had the wrong baby, with a birth defect, was lying back on the couch. In the transference she feelingly spoke of the importance I had in her life and could acknowledge that she wanted to please me. Then after she had been on the couch for two months, I went on a short vacation. For the first time she openly expressed some curiosity about me. Enviously, she speculated that I had gone on an ideal trip with my husband. She never got to go away. She tearfully asked, "What good does it do being on the couch?"

I had fantasized that the patient's lying down would make the analysis easier, and, in fact, it seemed to have done so. The material seemed to be more cohesive and understandable. To be sure, this cohesiveness was also a product of the years of work that allowed her to get on the couch. (And, of course, the analysis was not by any means headed for only smooth sailing from that time on.) During those years I sometimes had the feeling that I was nagging the patient about the couch. In going through my notes, however, I was impressed with the evidence that this was not so. If anything, the patient was herself constantly bringing up the matter of the couch. It was used as the medium by which she expressed her feelings.

DISCUSSION

A central transference-countertransference enactment in this case revolved around the patient's conflicted wish to be special to the analyst-mother. Her fear of getting on the couch disguised the wish to be a very special case to me—being in a supervised analysis, yet not being forced to lie on the couch. Her refusal can be viewed descriptively as a resistance, in the most general sense as any interference with the progress of the analysis or defensively as avoidance of underlying fears (Boesky, 1990). The patient repeatedly expressed her fear that not getting on the couch would keep her from "succeeding" in the analysis. It was possible to understand and to work through many of the fantasies involved in this resistance while the patient remained sitting, but it was only after several years and at a particular point in the treatment, which led to a mini-break in my neutrality, that the patient was able to lie down. At that moment my rather mild suggestion that the patient might try to lie down and the patient's response became the unconscious enactment between us of the fantasy of the loving mother- daughter dyad. It became the expression of the love, engagement, and encouragement to be special that the patient had so fiercely warded off yet unconsciously longed for from her cold, detached mother.

It might be argued that the process that led to that moment could be conceptualized simply as a conversion from psychotherapy to psychoanalysis. So-called conversion does bring into focus the question of the distinction between psychoanalytic psychotherapy and psychoanalysis. In the 1950's and 1960's, as psychoanalysis was expanding its techniques and borders to include broader varieties of patients, a debate flourished about whether or not the use of the couch was necessary for a psychoanalytic treatment to be successful or worthy of the name. Wolberg (1967), for example, stated unequivocally that "modification of analytic rules is frequently necessary, but whether we should label such alterations [in which he would include not lying on the couch] as 'psychoanalysis' is another matter" (p. 194). Kubie (1950) asserted that he would not feel secure about an analysis in which the patient had never been able to use the couch. Greenacre (1959), in contrast, stated that there was nothing inherently inimical to analysis in sitting up. Other writers agreed (Kelman, 1954; Robertiello, 1967; Rosenbaum, 1967; Salzman, 1967) and argued that use of the couch should not be taken for granted. Experiments were even undertaken to demonstrate that the couch did or did not make a difference to the flow of free associations (Chessick, 1971; Hall and Closson, 1964).

In a recent discussion of conversion of psychotherapy to psychoanalysis (Panel, 1987) it became evident that no clear distinction could be agreed upon. Gill, one of the panelists, made the distinction between extrinsic criteria, such as the couch or frequency of sessions, and intrinsic criteria, which have more to do with the analytic process, such as resolution of the transference neurosis or restructuring of character. His criteria for the difference between psychoanalysis and psychotherapy rested on attitude or intention; in psychoanalysis the intention is to analyze transference, in psychotherapy, to combat symptoms through the therapeutic relationship. Other panelists, notable Kernberg and Ticho, and members of the audience did not agree with this distinction or with the criteria for making it. Horwitz took a middle ground in stating that the external criteria are necessary but not sufficient for a definition of psychoanalysis.

Elsewhere, Skolnikoff (1990) argued the obvious—that use of the couch does not ensure analytic work. He felt that what distinguishes psychotherapy from psychoanalysis is not form but substance, and that the differences lie on a continuum. Bornstein (1990) argued along similar lines that what distinguishes psychoanalysis from other therapies is "a shared ideal of the systematic integration of all resistances," which strikes me, as do some of the other criteria proposed by others in the literature, as in itself idealistic and also too cognitive. Stolorow (1990) criticized the underlying assumptions in these arguments about the conversion from psychotherapy to psychoanalysis. He argued that the criteria used to define analysis, such as neutrality, uncontaminated transferences, the analyzable patient, etc., are in themselves myths.

In my opinion, implicit in many of the arguments about the distinction between psychoanalysis and psychotherapy are arguments about what is good or ideal analysis versus bad, false analysis. Furthermore, since many therapists approach psychoanalytic psychotherapy with the same goals, myths, and attitudes that analysts, such as Gill, Skolnikoff, or Bornstein, have proposed as the distinctive criteria for psychoanalysis, it would seem that distinctions between the two modalities cannot be made easily on those grounds. It seems to me that many psychotherapies can indeed be considered incomplete analyses, by virtue of the shorter duration, fewer numbers of sessions, absence of the couch, lesser commitment on the part of the patient, or inadequate training of the therapist, but are otherwise indistinguishable in terms of their "intrinsic" characteristics (Levine, 1985).

In a recent article Goldberger (1995) took up these issues and argued that a psychoanalytic treatment can occur without using the couch. She went even further to argue that it is not beneficial to the process to use the couch in all instances. She made a case for not forcing the patient to put unconscious conflicts too quickly into verbal expression, before verbal connections for actions are preconsciously available. Goldberger drew attention to the role of *action* within the analytic setting and its relationship to the use or nonuse of the couch. In my case the role of the patient's *body*, its display, position, and distance from that of the analyst, was also an important factor.

To quote Goldberger, "[T]he couch is intended to facilitate freedom of verbal expression, and in my view it is the latter that is fundamental to the analytic method; the couch does not in itself define psychoanalysis" (p. 40). She stated that what defines the analytic work is the consistent attempt to understand the patient's conflicts in detail. Obviously, I agree and would add that this attempt also involves an effort on the analyst's part to be "neutral," an effort which inevitably fails. I think that the couch helps both analyst and patient immensely in their attempt at understanding the patient's conflicts, but it is no more than a potent tool of the trade. My patient knew that I felt the couch was helpful, but perhaps she sensed that I attached some further importance to it. Like McAloon (1988), a relatively young analyst, I valued the couch as a badge of my analytic identity. This patient with her conflicted needs both to rebel and to be special seized upon that symbol, just as she had refused to play piano, which she knew was important to her mother. Intellectually, and with most of my analytic heart, I felt that it was indeed wise to let her sit and to analyze her behavior, rather than to insist upon her lying down, Yet, unwittingly, a part of me wanted her to lie down, "for her own good" and for that of the analysis—and because I felt it would be easier and better for me.

In this case, Ms. S was engaged in psychoanalysis in terms of both the so-called process criteria and all extrinsic criteria, except, of course, for the use of the couch. Certainly, the couch was omnipresent in the analysis, although the patient did not actually lie on it. In my mind and in hers we agreed to an analysis, though she unconsciously kept her fingers crossed behind her back. Her inability to lie on the couch was from the beginning seen as a symptom by the patient herself. Her agreement to do an analysis, her subsequent refusal and fear of the couch, and her perception that her refusal was a symptom for the two of us to understand constitute a different picture from that of a patient who comes in for psychotherapy, and somewhere in the process analyst and patient decide to begin an analysis. In this sense, then, there is something to Bornstein's (1990) ideas of the mutually shared, conscious goals of patient and analyst that partially define analysis. The meaning of the couch itself, lying on it or not lying on it, as I have demonstrated, became a central arena for the analytic work. The couch clearly had a magical meaning for the patient. Beyond its technical usefulness about which so much has been written, the couch may take on a magical quality for the analyst as well. The magical quality of the couch in both the patient's and the analyst's minds may contribute to the unconsciously shared ideal and idea of what they are doing together.

Each analysis is, of course, different from every other one. In this case I did not insist that the patient lie on the couch (I think that if I had done so, she would have complied) and was convinced that it was better to handle the situation clinically in the way I have described. At the same time, I had to resist an inner, conflicting pressure that it would somehow have been "more correct" to get the patient on the couch sooner. These two attitudes on my part shaped the specific course of this analysis and led to a significant enactment, to which we both contributed (Boesky, 1990). In retrospect, I think that much was gained and, I hope, not much lost by the course that was taken.

REFERENCES

Bergel, E. 1984). Possible unconscious significance of the positions of the analysand and the analyst in psychoanalysis. *Psychiatry*, 47:*23–298.*

Boesky, D. (1990). The psychoanalytic process and its components. *Psychoanal. Q.*, 59:*550–584.*

Bornstein, M.(1990). Psychoanalysis and psychoanalytic psychotherapy: a contemporary perspective. *Presented to the Michigan Psychoanalytic Society.*

Byerly, L. J.(1992). Unresolved separation-individuation, masochism, and difficulty with compliance. *In When the Body Speaks. Psychological Meanings and Kinetic Clues,* ed. S. Kramer. S. Akhtar. Northvale, NJ/London: Aronson, pp. *114–130.*

Chessick, R. D.(1971). Use of the couch in the psychotherapy of borderline patients. *Arch. Gen. Psychiat.*, 25:*306–313.*

Fenichel, O. (1941). *Problems of Psychoanalytic Technique.* New York: *Psychoanal. Q.*, 1969.

Frank, A. (1992). A problem with the couch: incapacities and conflicts. In *When the Body Speaks. Psychological Meanings and Kinetic Clues*, ed. S. Kramer. S. Akhtar. Northvale, NJ/London: Aronson, pp. *89–112.*

Glover, E.(1955). *The Technique of Psychoanalysis.* New York: Int. Univ. Press.

Goldberger, M. (1995). The couch as defense and as potential for enactment. *Psychoanal. Q.*, 64:*23–42.*

Greenacre, P. (1959). Certain technical problems in the transference relationship. *J. Am. Psychoanal. Assoc.*, 7:*484–502.*

Greenson, R. R. (1967). *The Technique and Practice of Psychoanalysis.* New York: Int. Univ. Press.

Hall, R. A. Closson, W. G.(1964). An experimental study of the couch. *J. Nerv. Ment. Dis.*, 138:*474–480.*

Hogan, C. C. (1990). Possible technical modification in the beginning phases of the psychoanalytic treatment of patients with psychosomatic symptoms. In *On Beginning an Analysis,* ed. T. Jacobs. A. Rothstein. Madison, CT: Int. Univ. Press, pp. *229–260.*

Jacobs, T. (1990). On beginning an analysis with a young adult. In On Beginning an Analysis, ed. T. Jacobs. A. Rothstein. Madison, CT: Int. Univ. Press, pp. *83–99.*

Kelman, H. (1954). The use of the analytic couch. *Amer. J. Psychoanal.*, 14: *65–82.*

Khan, M. M. R. (1962). Dream psychology and the evolution of the psychoanalytic situation. *Int. J. Psychoanal.*, 43:*21–31.*

Kubie, L. S. (1950). *Practical and Theoretical Aspects of Psychoanalysis.* New York: Int. Univ. Press.

Levine, H. B. (1985). Psychotherapy as the initial phase of a psychoanalysis. *Int. J. Psychoanal..*, 12:*285–297.*

McAloon, R. E. (1988). The need to feel like an analyst: a study of counter-transference in the case of a patient who refused to use the couch. *Modern Psychoanal.*, 12:65–87.

McLaughlin, J. T. (1992). Nonverbal behaviors in the analytic situation: a search for meaning in nonverbal clues. In *When the Body Speaks. Psychological Meanings and Kinetic Clues*, ed. S. Kramer. S. Akhtar. Northvale, NJ/London: Aronson, pp. 131–161.

Orens, M. H. (1965). Setting a termination date—an impetus to analysis. *J. Am. Psychoanal. Assoc.*, 3:651–665.

Panel (1987). Conversion of psychotherapy to psychoanalysis. C. P. Fisher, Reporter. *J. Am. Psychoanal. Assoc.*, 35:713–726.

Pines, D.(1993). *A Woman's Unconscious Use of Her Body.* London: Virago Press.

Reiser, L. W. (1986). "Lying" and "lying." A case report of a paradoxical reaction to the couch. *Psychoanal. Study Child*, 41:537–559.

Robertiello, R. C. (1967). The couch. *Psychoanal. Rev.*, 54:69–71.

Rosenbaum, S. (1967). Symbolic meaning and theoretical significance of the analytic couch. In *Science and Psychoanalysis, Vol. 11: The Ego,* ed. J. H. Masserman. New York/London: Grune Stratton, pp. 182–191.

Rothstein, A. (1990). On beginning with a reluctant patient. In *On Beginning an Analysis,* ed. T. Jacobs. A. Rothstein. Madison, CT: Int. Univ. Press, pp. 153–162.

Salzman, L. (1967). Discussion of S. Rosenbaum: Symbolic meaning and theoretical significance of the analytic couch. In *Science and Psychoanalysis, Vol. 11: The Ego,* ed. J. H. Masserman. New York/London: Grune Stratton, pp. 197–201.

Searles, H. F. (1984). The role of the analyst's facial expressions in psychoanalysis and psychoanalytic psychotherapy. *Int. Rev. Psychoanal.*, 10: 47–73.

Skolnikoff, A. (1990). The emotional position of the analyst in the shift from psychotherapy to psychoanalysis. *Psychoanal. Inquiry*, 10:107–118.

Stolorow, R. D. (1990). Converting psychotherapy to psychoanalysis: a critique of the underlying assumptions. *Psychoanal. Inquiry*, 10:119–130.

Stone, L. (1961). *The Psychoanalytic Situation. An Examination of Its Development and Essential Nature.* New York: Int. Univ. Press.

Weissman, S. M. (1977). Face to face. The role of vision and the smiling response. *Psychoanal. Study Child*, 32:421–450.

Wolberg, L. R. (1967). Discussion of S. Rosenbaum: Symbolic meaning and theoretical significance of the analytic couch. In *Science and Psychoanalysis, Vol. 11: The Ego*, ed. J. H. Masserman. New York/London: Grune Stratton, pp. *191–197*.

CHAPTER 4:

First Loves and Prime Adventures: Adolescent Expressions in Adult Analyses

(1998). Psychoanal. Q., (67)(4):539–565

Adolescent processes are frequently overlooked in the analyses of adults. The author focuses on the importance and meaning of first loves in the lives of adolescents and demonstrates how these prime experiences reverberate in the analyses of adults. She suggests that adolescent experiences cannot simply or usefully be reduced to preoedipal or oedipal meanings. Explanations for the neglect of adolescent phenomena are offered both historically, in terms of Freud's lack of understanding of adolescence, and clinically, in terms of countertransference and transference. It is argued that the intense affects of adolescence contribute to the resistance to re-experiencing them in treatment.

INTRODUCTION

It was Anna Freud (1958) who forty years ago first noted the lack of attention given to adolescent reconstruction in adult analyses. In a series of papers from the 1960's to the 1980's Lampl-de Groot (1960), Ritvo (1971), Blum (1985), and others commented upon this same lack of attention and speculated about its meanings. It has struck me that adolescent processes are still frequently overlooked by colleagues in their work with adults as well as in psychoanalytic teaching. I have also personally become aware of resistances in dealing with adolescent material during the course of analytic work with my adult patients. Thus, I would like to revisit this question, with particular reference to a current clinical interest of mine, the question of first sexual encounters and first love which typically occur during adolescence. I will emphasize the importance of adolescents' first love experiences and adventures in shaping the rest of their lives. With clinical case material, I will attempt to demonstrate how these prime experiences affect our patients' participation in analysis and how we should not diminish their importance or think of them reductionistically.

THE TASKS OF ADOLESCENCE

Adolescence is a time of major psychological and emotional significance. Bridging childhood and adulthood, it is initiated by the physical event of puberty and ends, variously and ambiguously, with the achievement of emotional, social, and economic independence (Kaplan, 1984). Psychologists and particularly psychoanalysts have long appreciated the psychological struggles and issues of adolescence. In formulating a theory of infantile sexual development which unfolds in stages, Freud did not focus on adolescence. For him adolescence was the culmination of sexual maturity and was only barely mentioned as such in his writings. At the same time, it is a fact that Freud's extraordinary early concepts about hysteria and the unconscious role of sexual conflict were formulated through the study of young adolescent girls, Dora, Katharina, etc. Glenn (1980) asserted that Freud's therapeutic failures and technical errors with his famous adolescent cases reflected his lack of adequate knowledge about the organization of adolescent drive and defense. I would agree with Glenn that Freud did not really understand adolescence.

It would be later psychoanalysts who studied the unique emotional characteristics of adolescence. Anna Freud (1936) gave us a clear description of typical defenses called into play at puberty: asceticism and idealization. Erikson (1950) described a major task of adolescence as the resolution of the conflict between consolidation of identity versus role defusion. Laufer and Laufer (1984) discussed the importance of the adolescent's need to come to terms with new sexual maturity by integrating sexuality into the body image and finding a means of sexual expression and gratification. Novick and Novick (1991) stressed the importance of narcissistic readjustments during adolescence.

A major contribution came from Peter Blos (1979) who described adolescence as "the second individuation process." Blos showed how the adolescent, in struggling to separate psychologically from his or her parental objects, must turn to peers and new love objects as displacements for the earlier ones; thus, the oedipal drama is revisited, revised, and, one hopes, resolved during this process. However, Blos warned that genital maturity stimulates a renewed quest for identity, so that adolescence should not be thought of simply as a replica of the first separation-individuation phase, or of the oedipus complex. Nevertheless, I think that analysts have tended to disregard this admonition over the years and thus characteristically have collapsed and reduced adolescent phenomena into oedipal and preoedipal rubrics.

Adolescence is a developmental phase that is much more than a recapitulation of earlier phases, more than a slender bridge or a mere transition between childhood and adulthood, more than a reawakening of latent sexual impulses and buried conflicts. The advent of sexual maturity puts very powerful impulses into the body and calls for a reconfiguration of the body image and the personality. The adolescent's emotional needs and the cognitive capacity to find a place separate from the immediate family change the whole context of his or her life. As the adolescent goes out to meet the world, the people he or she meets, studies with, works with, and makes love with become lifelong friends, comrades, and often mates, never to be forgotten. All of this is experienced with perhaps the deepest intensity and emotion of one's life. Anna Freud (1958) suggested that it is the affects, the elusive mood swings of adolescence, that are the most difficult to revive and to have re-emerge and be relived in connection with the person of the analyst (p. 143). As Joseph Conrad (1902) wrote: "I remember my youth and the feeling that will never come back any more—the feeling that I could last forever, outlast the sea, the earth, and all men; the deceitful feeling that lures us on to joys, to perils, to love, to vain effort—to death" (p. 176).

In the following clinical material I will focus on the role of and defense against the intense affects of adolescence as they emerge in adult patients.

THE ADOLESCENT EXPERIENCE AND BEGINNING AN ANALYSIS

While psychoanalytic writing has focused on the revival of adolescent experiences in the termination stages, the following will demonstrate how they frequently appear in the initial stages of treatment as well. Mr. S was seventy-one when he embarked on a psychoanalysis. He had been in psychotherapy on several occasions throughout the years with some relief from his chronic feelings of depression and self-worthlessness. He despaired of ever being able to better his conflicted relationship with his wife or to feel better about himself. Psychoanalysis was a last resort; he expressed the hope, without much conviction, that perhaps even at this stage in life he could achieve some measure of happiness. A sophisticated man, Mr. S began his analysis by giving me a clear and rich history of his present situation, past treatments, and early history. After this brief introduction and our establishing that we could work together, Mr. S launched into an account of his experiences as a soldier in World War II. He had enlisted when he was barely eighteen. The only "city boy" in his boot camp of rural southerners, he was subjected to cruel insults and humiliations. Shortly thereafter, he was sent across the ocean to become a part of the invasion of Sicily. He became a bomb demolition expert.

Mr. S's stories were riveting and terrible. He watched his buddies get blown up next to him: his memories were strewn with decapitated heads, bloody limbs, smoke, and terror. He survived, drank rotgut, marched and crawled with the invading forces through Sicily and then into Northern Italy and a freezing winter. He constantly felt frightened and terribly alone. Wounded, he spent time in a hospital unit and then was sent back to the front. As he recounted his experiences, he often cried and seemed laden with unspoken guilt. He told of how he came face to face with an equally terrified German youth, whom he shot and killed at point-blank range. With trepidation and some pride, he showed me poetry and short stories he had written about these experiences as a way "to expiate them." Fishing for compliments and/or reassurance, he worried that this was "all a waste of time," but he needed somehow to tell me everything to get it off his chest.

This content was unusual to hear, and Mr. S was a great storyteller. I realized that I was fascinated and highly entertained. I sensed that this material was a prelude to the interaction to come: a sadomasochistic struggle with me that recapitulated his interactions with his wife and with a seductive, provocative, and narcissistic mother and a critical and belittling father. The content of his war stories laid out his guilt-ridden concerns with castration, sadism, and death. His opening account also had the quality of a little four-year-old boy swaggering before his mother, expecting her admiration and applause. I knew I was being courted, and indeed my heart was being won. This was a little boy in the throes of the oedipal romance: "At last I've found you!" he exclaimed. But the interaction felt even more like an adolescent bragging about his adventures to his girl. In front of me was a young soldier telling me real tales of his adventures and dangers, with real blood and guts. A man no longer young, he needed to demonstrate his virility, conjured up now from his youth. I think it was for all these dynamic reasons—narcissistic, phallic, and oedipal, but especially because Mr. S was venturing on a scary adventure into the unknown with me—that these tales came to his mind at the beginning of his analysis. He was the young adolescent, scared, alone, embarking on a new voyage and looking for an admiring partner to watch, support, and be there for him. I thought the major task technically for me was to be quiet and listen, to comment on his fears and guilt, and let the transference take hold. That is, the patient's adolescent affects, fears, and expectations guided my interventions. In regard to the sadomasochistic and oedipal implications, I remained more or less quiet, knowing that I would be drawn into them in due time.

Patients often experience entering an analytic treatment as adolescent explorers going into virgin territory, as a process of defloration, as a new experience in being opened up by the analyst/deflowerer. The loss of virginity can become a telling metaphor for the beginning of an analysis. For example, a young woman beginning analysis lay on the couch after a brief period of sitting up. She was immediately transported into memories of her beginning menstruation and her first sexual encounters. She recounted how she was afraid of using a tampon, and how she felt her mother was not helpful in preparing her for the experience. Her thoughts went to her first sexual experiences during adolescence. She was anxious, yet curious, and afraid it would hurt. When she lost her virginity she did not know what to expect, and it was messy. She felt ignorant and awkward. The transference meanings were obvious. These adolescent memories conveyed current anxieties: Would the analyst be of help? Would the process be messy? Would the analyst's probes be hurtful to her?

FIRST SEXUAL EXPERIENCES AND FIRST LOVE

In the above example the patient revived a memory of her first intercourse and first menses to express feelings about beginning her analysis. Such experiences are important developmental milestones and typically mark adolescence. Holtzman and Kulish (1997) have found that defloration experiences typically occurring in adolescence are negated, repressed, or dismissed retroactively by adult men and women because of the conflicted meanings attached to such events. As one married woman patient struggling against remembering her first experience of intercourse put it: "It didn't mean anything. It didn't hurt. Well maybe just a little. No, it was nothing. I can't remember ..." For men, fears of castration, sadomasochistic meanings, and oedipal conflicts overshadow memories of being with girls they may have deflowered; for women accompanying feelings are of loss, fear of separation from their mothers, anxieties about genital mutilations, and the sense of crossing over an irreversible threshold. In their resistances against such meanings, patients are joined by their analysts who fail to recognize the significance of such material.

Beyond the actual sexual experiences, with adolescence comes the momentous experience of the first love. The experiences connected with first love, heterosexual or homosexual, dominate memories of adolescence. A recurrent theme in literature, art, and music, the search for the lost adolescent love or first love reverberates psychologically. This search is for the lost object and/or the freshness and the intensity of the experience itself. (These loves, along with our unachieved narcissistic goals, give high school reunions their ambivalently cathected valence: To go or not to go? To chance the encounter: the embarrassments, the shames, the excitements again? To find the lost love of our youth or not?)

In analysis with adults these first loves are revisited time and time again. They frequently occur as unwanted visitors, attachments that the individual cannot shake loose. Many patients are obsessed with their first teenage loves, dream about them, keep them guilty secrets from their current mates as if they were in reality incestuous affairs (and indeed they often are psychically).

Mr. N, a middle-aged accountant, sought analysis because he was not able to get over a depression after being divorced. He was obsessively preoccupied with his ex-wife. She had been his first love whom he met when he was sixteen. In spite of her coldness and lack of enthusiasm for him sexually and romantically, he pursued her and finally married her. His relationship with her was masochistic and submissive. He idolized her and denied the evidence of her unfaithfulness and continued selfish use of him even after the divorce. Much of the analysis became the unraveling of the meanings of this love for the patient, especially as it became revealed in the transference toward me, who in some aspects physically resembled his ex-wife. The following meanings were all present: the use of the analyst as a self-object to soothe narcissistic wounds and rejections from the disappointing mother, images of women as sadistic objects on whom he could unconsciously displace his own perverse sadism through submission, and the wife/analyst as the always unattainable oedipal mother. Yet the adolescent aspect, the intensity of that first passion, remained elusive to interpretation.

I have gained some insight into that intensity from a literary scholar, Dibattista, in her brilliant book, *First Love* (1991). She shows that the yearning for first love and the sadness of the yearning are central to modern literature. According to Dibattista, first affections are the "mysterious necessity that dictate the obsessive themes and original forms which give to modern fiction its distinct and problematic identity" (p. xii). She argues that first love represents a primal form of the modern adventure and leads to the revolutionizing of old customary orders of life. With the advent of first love there is a conscious awareness of a fateful shape to a life's narrative and an estimation of the value of that experience. In her analysis of countless examples of writers, such as Joyce, Hardy, Lawrence, Austen, and Beckett, Dibattista draws heavily on psychoanalytic concepts. She understands first love in terms of Melanie Klein's elucidation of the ambivalent preoedipal attachment to the mother and Freud's insights concerning the conflicts about being first with a loved oedipal object. She cites Freud's ideas that first loves involve traversing the taboo of virginity as well as the incest taboo. "The fateful nature of First Love is Mother Love.... Those who fail to appreciate the significance of *amor matris*, objective and subjective genitive, as the First Love after which all subsequent loves take their image, fail to appreciate not only the significance

96

of birth but the meaning of death" (p. 75). She shows that in literature, often written by men, first love can become the sexual and artistic initiation of the creator who remakes the world to reflect his gratified or frustrated desire, often in the shape of idols or impositions of power. This idea is reflected in my patient, Mr. N, idolizing his ex-wife.

Dibattista's work has helped me to understand that first love cannot be reduced to its preoedipal and oedipal meanings. First love is, she suggests, an adventure organized into a remembered narrative with a beginning and an end and given a transcending meaning. Is it not the adventure that is so characteristically adolescent—the setting off for distant lands, following a star, running away with one's Lancelot? First love, because it is first, shakes the individual and elicits an excess of feeling. Once reflected upon consciously, it becomes a pointed event in one's life, giving it shape and meaning.

What is it about a first-time experience that creates such intense emotions and sets it so permanently in our minds? We remember the rush of affect at our first glimpse of the Rocky Mountains, our first live opera, our first kiss. William James (1902) touched on this question in his ideas about religious conversion. James conceived of the mind in terms of internal groupings of associated ideas or systems, most of which are not at the forefront of awareness. Using the energic metaphors of the era, he described a habitual center of personal energy that can shift suddenly, as in a religious conversion. Such a seemingly sudden mental shift can come after an unconscious incubation and maturing of motives. "But a new perception, a sudden emotional shock, or an occasion which lays bare the organic alteration, will make the whole fabric fall together ..." (p. 197). James observed that "conversion is in its essence a normal adolescent phenomenon, incidental to the passage from the child's small universe to the wider intellectual and spiritual life of maturity" (p. 199). Here James also invoked the notion of a new gestalt that falls into place with a new experience. A first love may bring a new sense of self as a part of a wider inner and outer world.

Thus, for the adolescent in love for the first time, there are intense and deep affects as he or she embarks on an adventure, the self in relationship to the important and novel other. Like fear, Dibattista says, love invests a single lifechanging experience with the need to be repeated in order to be conquered. The affective environment in which first love unfolds is the vivid here and now. Yet paradoxically with the need to be repeated and rediscovered, it imparts a consciousness of time as an irreversible duration. This paradox of the experience of time is a hallmark of adolescence.

A young woman in analysis was obsessed with her first love from her adolescence. She frequently spoke of him, dreamed about him, and felt guilty about her dreams as she felt that in some way she was being disloyal and unfaithful to her husband, whom she loved dearly. Unconsciously, she gave her first son a name very close to that of this first love.[1] Sex with her first love seemed more exciting in retrospect. The memories of him were colored with feelings of regret and loss, even though in most ways she was glad that she had not married this fellow, who sounded to me like an immature cad. She wanted analysis "to cure" her of her preoccupation. There was no doubt that this first love, like most, was an oedipal object, a fill-in for her father. Thus, the regret and sadness carried with it the regret of losing the very first love, Daddy, and not winning him away from her mother. Interpretations of these meanings were accepted and gave some relief from the insistent thoughts and guilt about this man in her mind. Yet, his image remained and haunted her dreams. Finally, at some point I said, "There is something about the first love during adolescence that is so intense and enduring, isn't there?" That somewhat offhand remark seemed to relieve the patient's guilt. We then worked through the psychological meanings of this love in its adolescent context: she met him

---

1 I have observed that this is not rare. Many women, when they leave an early love behind and go on to marry another man and have children, knowingly or unknowingly name their first-born boy after their first love. Sometimes the names are exact or obvious variations—"Edmund" substituting for "Edward," for example.

in a summer job as camp counselor. The relationship bolstered a shaky adolescent femininity even as she strove to keep up with his masculine athletic prowess. That is, we discussed and worked through typical bisexual issues and conflicts of adolescence. In time, she was able to accept, and in fact cherish, the exciting memory of her first boyfriend without feeling it a betrayal to her husband. We might speculate that I, as an oedipal mother in the transference, was implicitly giving the patient the permission to keep her fantasized love in her mind, saying that such wishes and thoughts were okay. And/or was it that I explicitly gave voice to the *adolescent* experience, the intensity of the affect, that helped the patient to accept and integrate it?

ADOLESCENT COUNTERTRANSFERENCE

Let me return to my patient, Mr. N, the accountant who idealized his ex-wife. In his analysis, he was able to work through his ambivalent attachment to his ex-wife and make many strides in other areas of his life. He remarried and had a child whom he adored. He declared that he felt good about himself and his analysis. He began to think about termination and I agreed that we were in the termination stages, but a date had not been set. Pressing for a quick ending, he announced that he had always wanted to finish before his fiftieth birthday—news to me—which was coming up in a month. Utilizing a favorite sports metaphor, he said that he wanted to retire from the game while he was still in his prime. He began to skip appointments as his life was now filled with many more responsibilities and activities. My reply, I thought, was reasoned: to agree that he was approaching the end, but to question the hurry, and to suggest that more time would be needed to understand his feeling about termination. He was still insistent about a quick termination. His behavior could be conceptualized as typical of adolescents (described by Novick and Novick [1991]) who cannot deal with issues of separation, narcissistic disappointments, and strong feelings about mourning and loss, so they engineer a precipitous ending.

In a context in which I was feeling uneasy and vaguely unhappy about the situation, I made an unconscious blunder. I had recently moved to a new office and was not yet settled in. Right before Mr. N's hour, I went down the hall to the rest room and locked myself out of my consulting room. Since I did not have a duplicate key anywhere and the landlord was not on the premises, there was no way in. I met Mr. N in the waiting room, which was open, and told him what had happened. He laughed and forgivingly told me that mistakes can happen and went home.

The next day the patient began to associate with no mention of the events of the day before. He and his wife had had an argument. She was not talking to him and had slept in the other room. I noted to Mr. N that he had made no overt mention of the unusual event of the day before and asked him about his thoughts about it. I pointed out that he had been locked out by his wife and by me. He laughed, "Well, it was funny. I felt bad for you. Why didn't I get angry? It's *your* problem." He laughed again and said, "I don't know what Freud would say about it." I replied that he was suggesting that Freud might say that I should look at what was going on in myself. Just before the session ended, he remembered a dream: he was sitting with a group of older ladies. I came into the room. Someone asked me, "Who are you?" I responded, "I'm his girlfriend," with a feeling of pleasure. He was indifferent to me.

That night I had the following dream: I was looking for, found, and was then ignored by my high school boyfriend, my first love. My personal analysis had taught me that this boyfriend was indeed an oedipal object for me. In thinking about this dream, I realized that far from having a reasoned response, I was feeling rejected and hurt by Mr. N's desire to get out of treatment quickly and his not doing a "proper" ending. Given our corresponding dreams about my boyfriend and his girlfriend, I speculated to myself that there was a piece of the erotic transference (and countertransference) that was left undone, as well. I realized that in my own reactions, which were stirring up my feelings of a lost first love, I too, had been backing away from the situation emotionally. I had been saying and doing the "correct" things but emotionally meeting his defensive retreat with a defensive indifference of my own. We both were suffering as adolescents saying good-bye. With this insight, I interpreted to Mr. N that he was trying to get away from some strong loving feelings toward me and the sadness he had about stopping. I also told Mr. N that I had thought about my mistake, and that I thought it was a kind of signal, my reaction to concern that we were cutting things too short and that we needed more time to complete our work. He was moved by this and agreed to a five-month time frame for termination, after his birthday.

CHOICES

I would now like to turn to another analytic case from some years ago which I think illustrates the constant and repetitive appearance of adolescent material throughout an analysis. I chose the case of this woman deliberately because she was clearly neurotic, fairly well adjusted and functioning, highly motivated and insightful. Because of this, her analysis proceeded relatively smoothly and speedily. I would not characterize her as marked by major adolescent fixations and conflicts, although separation issues in regard to her mother did come into play, particularly in the termination stage of the analysis. In this account I have selectively focused on the adolescent material as it emerged in the analysis.

Ms. C began treatment in her early forties. Married to a politician, she had two daughters. She herself was the daughter of a conservative politician, and both extended families were well known in local political circles. Her obedient nature contrasted with that of her younger brother, the proverbial hellion. An especially bright and pretty child, she was the apple of her mother's eye, apparently a compensation for the mother's self-sacrificing devotion to being the politician's wife. The mother, from strong "Scandinavian stock" held her children to high standards of being Christian, "understanding" of others (which translated into not being angry), and stoical. At the same time, however, she wanted her daughter to be popular and attractive, so Ms. C experienced her as sending mixed messages. During adolescence, the patient felt she was "too close" to her mother, evidenced by her often confessing minor misdeeds via written notes she put under the mother's pillow. Her father was given to stony and disapproving silences when he was angry, although he was clearly devoted to the patient.

In high school, egged on by her mother against the disapproval of the father, the patient entered a local beauty contest and won. She had an intense romance with a sports star but backed away from it. He later left the country for a highly successful career. She looked back on the loss of this boy with deep feelings of regret. Immediately after graduating from college the patient "took the safe route," disregarded her own misgivings, and married a man headed for a career in politics. Her parents covertly disapproved of the match as he was bombastic and less conservative than the father. Wishing for an easier life for her daughter than being a small-time politician's wife, the mother had hoped for a more dazzling and socially prominent match for her beautiful and accomplished daughter. Ms. C was a virgin when she married.

The patient's presenting symptoms were anxiety and phobia. These had surfaced a few months earlier after two events in her life: a hysterectomy which culminated after a string of gynecological difficulties since puberty and the move of her parents out of state to retirement in a sunnier climate. Ms. C's anxiety attacks were associated with the thought of being in large crowds and driving, especially on the expressway. She was becoming increasingly phobic about leaving her house. Also, she had returned to school to obtain a social work degree and had just recently begun to do some counseling. She reported feeling anxious when her clients talked of sex and/or anxiety.

As the sources of her anxiety were explored in the early phases of her treatment, the patient tentatively began to talk about her sexual inhibitions and the longstanding sexual difficulties in her marriage, which had meant months with no sex. She was afraid she was "frigid." Typical of her spunkiness (and perhaps also counterphobically?), she wanted to begin to tackle these difficulties. She called up her husband and told him she wanted to try to have sex. He rushed home on his lunch hour to have intercourse with her and then again later that day. The next day, he abruptly announced that he wanted a divorce regardless of these attempts. The patient was devastated, although the subsequent separation and divorce also brought relief. Fortunately, I was able to see Ms. C as a control case, so that an analysis was possible in spite of her limited finances. In the subsequent months after her divorce, Ms. C seemed to be "hiding out" at home with her children and avoiding any social life. Her phobic symptoms and physical manifestations of anxiety, including a "nervous" stomach, brought to mind a time during her last year in high school, when she became ill with mysterious ailments (including perhaps mononucleosis), which meant she was confined at home for many days at a time.

Being in the mental health field, Ms. C knew the policies pertaining to being a control case. Early in the treatment, fantasies about my supervisor emerged. For instance, in an early fantasy, I was pictured as a "two-headed monster," which I interpreted as one head the analyst, one the supervisor. Encouraged to voice her fantasies, the patient revealed her intense curiosity about the identity of my supervisor who, she was convinced, was a man. She imagined this man to be strict, critical, orthodox, someone under whose dominance I would change from the soft, kind mother pictured initially. The focus on the transference further elucidated material about the relationship between Ms. C's mother and father. The parents frequently argued because the father felt the mother was not "strict enough" with the children. This conflict was particularly strong around matters of dating and sex during the patient's adolescence. In subsequent elaborations of her fantasies the patient voiced the idea that she must be a good patient for me so that I would not "get in trouble with" the father/supervisor.

Ms. C began repeatedly to complain of how she felt the analysis was very difficult, a burden, and at times she broke down into crying and sobbing. These were the first such episodes of affective storms which punctuated the analysis. The ebb and flow of the material, reflective of her initial fantasy of entering analysis as a submission to a huge "Sigmoid," frequently seemed to me to emerge in evacuative spurts. Retrospectively, I wonder if these phenomena could also be considered typical of the affective storms of adolescence.

In the second year of analysis as her reaction formations were breaking down, the phobic symptoms returned and increasingly became focused on the analysis. As Ms. C drove to my office, her anxiety would increase. Her fear was at its peak at the intersection of the expressway where highways merge so that there are many lanes. Her associations were to going out of control and "too many choices!" My interpretation of her fear of going out of control in the analysis allowed her to articulate a deep fear: that I would totally strip her of defenses, of her old values of selflessness and sacrifice, and leave her with nothing to replace these structures. "Too many choices" at this point in the analysis meant giving up the rigid set of rules by which she governed herself, the one right way. This anxiety about choices is a fear which Ms. C and many patients face when they anticipate or experience change in psychoanalysis. Isn't this fear of open possibilities or "too many choices" one of the fears, dilemmas, and challenges of the adolescent, especially in our expanding environment? What to do? What career to pick? Who will be my mate? Where to live? What kind of person am I? Will I follow in my parent's footsteps? The adolescent experience is distinguished by fear of many choices and of internal and external change.[2]

---

2 Recently, another female patient also in the early stages of her analysis, voiced this fear poignantly: things are different. It's weird. What am I doing? Where am I going? I don't feel like I'm me. I have to fill it with something…it's overwhelming. There are too many choices…" to a greater degree than Ms. C, this patient is fixed in an adolescent relationship with her parents

Ritvo (1971) wrote of the increased anxiety during adolescence which derives from the simultaneous emergence of old oedipal and preoedipal fantasies with a concurrent necessity and ability to act upon them. The reappearance of such fantasies, along with a higher level of ego functioning, impels and gives the adolescent means to act upon his or her impulses and desires. Lampl-de Groot (1960) hypothesized that the loosening of ties to paternal objects which is the imperative of adolescence, also results in a loosening of previous superego and ego ideal supports.

Regarding Ms. C and her ego ideals: to the fantasy of being the model patient had been added the idea that I had definite goals for her—perhaps to become a successful career woman like myself. This new fantasy, of course, reflected the actuality that the patient's mother had definite aspirations for her, as well as the idea that as a psychoanalytic candidate I had certain self-serving expectations for her. The idea of analyst as role model to be emulated increasingly became infused with guilt-ridden feelings of jealousy and competition. These feelings were an amalgam of oedipal, competitive wishes that mark an adolescent girl's comparisons and identifications with her mother.

For Ms. C after the divorce, anticipation of dating and moving to a new house brought fears about sexual freedom and loss of control. For example, she talked of her fear that her teenaged daughter would "get into trouble" on her senior trip to Florida. I suggested that she was projecting her own fears about loss of control over sexual impulses onto the girl, out of mother's sight. The patient was able to see the parallel between her writing notes to her mother and her daily "confessions" to me and to understand how she used the externalized image of confessor as a self-control. This is a typical adolescent strategy, to externalize one side of a conflict onto a parent and fight the battle on an external field. Subsequently, she recovered buried memories of sexual

---

and with me, wanting to please, compelled to rebel, often childishly, and unable to feel free to make her own choices.

pleasures early in her marriage. She admitted to the power she felt over boys and men when during adolescence and early adulthood, she let herself feel attractive and alluring. Ms. C realized that she had inhibited and repressed her sexuality for years out of guilt over an extramarital affair early in her marriage.

The advent of her older daughter's departure for college and Ms. C's subsequent acute depression brought to light the following fantasy. She recounted her own leaving for college. Her self-sacrificing mother sewed and bought her fancy new outfits. Ms. C arrived at her freshman dorm dressed in a tailored navy blue suit, matching heels, and white gloves, causing a sensation. When her parents bade her goodbye, they told her not to return home until Thanksgiving. She felt the message was clear that she was dispatched to succeed, to catch a good husband, and to live out her mother's fantasies, a variant of a madame/prostitution fantasy which was to emerge more clearly later in the analysis. She was now able to realize how she, too, lived through her teenage daughter as, for example, she became intensely preoccupied with the girl's love life and boyfriend while she herself hid from the world. These guilt-ridden conflicts over sex were played out repeatedly in the patient's transference fantasies that I was living through her sexuality and was sending her out "with too many choices" for evil. She recalled an essay she wrote during high school called "Freedom versus License." Together we now were able to understand the onset of her symptoms, which followed her hysterectomy and her parents' retirement, as an unconscious reaction to her loss of external restraints to her sexual desires. (That is, she no longer needed to fear becoming pregnant, and her parents, her watchdogs, were gone.) We also understood how the move to her own house and the departure of her daughter reawakened frightening fantasies of sexual freedom from her youth. The patient began expressing thinly disguised fears about me as a "hands on" coach—an image in a dream set in high school—to help her overcome her sexual problems. Such wishes seemed to be a sexualized version of the adolescent girl's common need to get instruction and guidance from her mother about how to be an adult woman and how to deal with sex.

As Ms. C began to "come out of her cave," there were drastic changes in her demeanor during the sessions and in her life. She announced she had been losing weight on a diet and had begun exercising. She went after and landed a new, higher paying and promising job in the world of business. Shortly after, she called an attractive older man she had met some months before and began to date him. She had sex and was delighted to find she enjoyed it. Ms. C began to act politely dismissive of any comment by me. The patient agreed with my suggestion that she was acting as if she felt I would interfere with her course of improvement. Yes, she must do this for herself. Like a toddler or an adolescent in the throes of the struggle for autonomy and individuation, she was afraid newfound pleasures and achievements would be taken away. Afraid to look at the relationship with her lover critically, she projected her doubts onto me. She was convinced that I, like an adolescent's parent, disapproved of him. New elaboration of her fantasies of being a control patient were expressed. She remembered how disapproving ladies in the community reported her teenage flirtations to her father. Similarly, she fantasized that I would report her sexual wrongdoings to my supervisor and to the Institute.

In the summer of the third year of analysis in the midst of talking about my upcoming vacation plans and her own plans which were disappointing, Ms. C announced that she wanted to talk of termination. When I interpreted this in terms of resistance, the patient became furious. "This proves I am all messed up." (Her relationship with the boyfriend had also just broken up, and she worried that she was to blame.) Interpretation of her feelings of deficiency and of being criticized and that her independence had been rebuffed seemed to mollify the patient only temporarily. She repeatedly tried to engage me in struggles over separation as she did her mother during adolescence. For example, after she missed an analytic appointment to have her hair cut, she became very angry while I tried to explore the meanings of this behavior. I interpreted to Ms. C how she tried to set up an external struggle between herself and me to avoid understanding her internal struggle over coming to her session.

She continued to battle. Finally, I took my supervisor's suggestion and simply asked the patient her thoughts about whether she was ready to terminate or not. She answered that progress had been made, but there was still much to do. That is to say, when I overtly granted and acknowledged her autonomy, as one needs to do with an adolescent struggling to become an adult, she responded positively and maturely.

Dressed in a new navy blue suit, Ms. C made a dramatic arrival at a session. She acknowledged a fantasy of "coming out" of her cocoon, her new edition of her arrival at college. She was going to visit a health care organization for her work. She talked about how she would have to check out the situation and to sell a contract that involved managed care. I said that in some sense she was checking herself out in terms of what was left to do in analysis. Perhaps "managed care" referred to her analysis and her questions about how long it should go on. She agreed. "There is some separation now, and it stirs up feelings. I can feel myself becoming tearful. It will be hard on the road. If you are the person in the red car [referring to a previous dream in which she was followed by a woman driving a red car], I pull away from you. I'm on my own. A strong feeling of moving away. I can remember tremendous dependency on you." Like an adolescent, she was trying to get "it all together" for herself.

A year later when a date was set for termination, the patient had another dream which took us back to choices: "I was on a trip, driving a scooter, on expressways, on roads. I was having to read maps and directions on the way because I didn't know where I was going. It was night. There were several hallway intersections, like in an old hospital or like in schools. At one intersection there was a podium, and I was stopped there. A woman politician and old people in wheelchairs passed by. Kids my daughter's age there. Like in a college union. One boy said, 'She's only about twenty-eight years old.' Behind him is a mirror. I look in the mirror and I see I hadn't brushed out my hair perfectly.

"I think it's another leaving. This one requires that I expend the energy to go. I do a reasonably good job in reading the map, or directions. It's kind of what I've learned about myself. For example, I think to myself, 'When you have this certain kind of reaction, think!' I do have to pay attention to myself. The hall reminds me of choices, not being sure where you'll get to. The podium was like where you'd sign in, or teachers or politicians have podiums. The elderly in wheelchairs are where I was. I kept myself immobile and dependent. I knew women politicians who really devoted themselves to something. I knew that I would never choose that route for myself. I did think I should do something that helped out my fellow man. A piece of me that I got from my dad. She, the politician, would like center stage. Narcissistic. I was in the union, like in college. There were young men there. It's some kind of fantasy that as I am aging there are wishes to stay younger. Did I have my daughter, no, I didn't at twenty-eight. I was twenty-seven. Oh, I saw a client last night, she was twenty-eight. She married her high school sweetheart and got an abortion even after she was married. She has been punishing herself since by denying her sexuality. I see that, because I did the same thing. In the dream I am not perfect. Hair not perfectly brushed out. I am who I am."

I said that the dream expressed the wish she could go back and relive those years that she had given up her sexuality. I asked if she thought the narcissistic woman politician represented me? She pondered. "Well, I see you as making decisions about your life, and following through on them. Don't know about the narcissistic. There remains in me a conflict about what I want to do. It is a dream about choices. The choice to be a social worker came from my past, and I need now to figure out my own life. I chose that at that time. Given choices now, I'd like to do something else. Give up this giving profession to do something like travel. My daughter came home last night. I said I was really glad to see her, but that K [new and serious boyfriend] was coming over, so she got the message that she couldn't stay overnight. I asked myself, 'Do nice mommies do this?' I don't know where I'm going. But I don't get lost. I do have confidence that I can do my own scooter...."

We see here that the patient, as she is terminating her analysis, is mulling over, with mixed feelings, choices she made for herself largely during adolescence— her choice of mate, not her first love, her career. She runs through in her mind her identifications with her "do-good" father, her sacrificing mother, with me, identifications of which she is now aware and trying to modify. She has a newfound sense of freedom and autonomy.

It is a paradox of adolescence that it seems to offer so many choices, which the adolescent often does not feel free or brave enough to take. First love, characteristically experienced not as a free choice but as a compulsion that must be followed, exemplifies one of the paradoxes of adolescence.

ADOLESCENT PHENOMENA IN ADULT PATIENTS

The major tasks of adolescence can be summarized as the integration of sexuality into the self, the psychological separation from the parents, and the development of an adult identity within the larger social context. Child analysts have used these insights to work analytically with adolescents and have applied them also to their work with adults. Novick (1990), for example, suggested that his work with adolescents has sensitized him to the importance of the need to establish a firm working alliance, to appreciate nonverbal communication, to pay attention to reality and to interpersonal relationships, and to follow the vicissitudes of narcissism.

The most attention to the presence of adolescent phenomena in adult work has come in its relation to termination. Novick and Novick (1991) wrote about the lessons to be learned in adult termination by an appreciation of how adolescents typically or frequently terminate prematurely or resist a true termination. Key to dealing with these resistances in adults may come from understanding the difficulty they may share with adolescents in giving up fantasies of omnipotence and omnipotent self-images which interfere with a mature termination. Recall how Mr. N, the accountant, struggled to cut short his termination in order to preserve the narcissistic image of himself as "in his prime." Similarly, Burgner (1988) pointed to barriers to termination that adolescents erect. Her excellent clinical material illustrates how adolescent patients attempt to keep a union with the analyst by creating continued perverse excitements in the transference. Perverse phenomena put to similar uses in the transference with adult patients have become the focus of current psychoanalytic writings (see Coen, 1992).

Other analysts have likened the entire termination phase in adult analysis to adolescence; in both there must be a coming to terms with separation from parental figures, in both there must be mourning for these and other losses, in both there should be a consolidation of identity. Dewald (1982), for example, described how in termination the psychological task for the patient is the working through of loss and separation from the analyst, both in transference and in the "real" relationship. There is a re-enactment in termination of prior separation experiences. The patient also has to accept limitations in the outcome of the treatment, a kind of mourning process. Erlich (1988) pointed out that Freud's (1937) pessimistic tone in "Analysis Terminable and Interminable" is that of a parent of an adolescent asking how well or badly have I prepared my child/analysand for life? Erlich suggested that this concerned relatedness on the analyst's part may constitute a powerful signal of approaching termination.

Hurn (1970) made a significant contribution to this topic by writing about what he called the "adolescent transference" in adults. He observed that in adolescence there is frequently a shift in the psychic balance toward an adaptation to reality. This shift can also be observed in the adolescent transference during termination with adult patients. Failure to recognize these transferences leads to the error of treating the patient like an adolescent, that is, in a dismissive or parental manner, rather than as an adult in need of analysis of his or her adolescent conflicts and transferences. In adolescence the changing realities of the self and a growing maturity and autonomy must be accepted and integrated by the adolescent and the parent; by analogy this acknowledgment is necessary for patient and analyst in termination. When I treated Ms. C as an adult and asked her what she thought of her rebellious insistence on terminating, she was able to step aside from her adolescent-like acting out and analyze it. Both Hurn and Dewald suggested that the adolescent transferences can pull for changes in technique but urged an adherence to regular analytic practices.

There has not been much written about adolescent phenomena in adult analyses outside of the termination phase. In a lecture which touched on the subject of the adolescent process in the analyses of adults, Blos (1989) spoke of the "cherished but largely lost causes" of a derailed or never completely traversed adolescence which are rediscovered in the analysis of the adult (p. 9). Peter Blos, Jr. (1990), elaborated on similar ideas about adolescent fixation in adult psychopathology. It is incorrect, he asserted, to reduce all such manifestations to infantile fixations. He presented a case in which two experiences contributed to his patient's fixations, an adoption kept secret from her and only reconstructed in analysis, and an undiagnosed adrenogenital syndrome which, until it was discovered during analysis, interfered with some aspects of her female physical development. Medication was prescribed which brought about immediate and dramatic physical changes. Thus Peter Blos, Jr., was able to observe and analyze this adult woman's responses to bodily changes normally experienced during puberty and early adolescence. He speculated about the resistance to reconstruction of adolescent experience seen in analysts and patients alike. There is a need to repress the sexual onslaught experienced by the adolescent and to divert attention to the reconstruction of infantile (and I would say less intense) sexuality. Such a need to repress the memories and reliving of intensity of the sexual onslaught during adolescence was present in the re-enactment of my locking Mr. N and myself out of my office before his termination.

Several other psychoanalysts have focused on reconstruction of adolescent experiences in adult analyses. Feigelson (1976) suggested that the focused attention of the analyst on childhood experiences often excludes appreciation of adolescent transference repetitions when they occur. Goettsche (1986) argued that there is a barrier to reconstruction of adolescent experiences in adult analyses because adolescence is "too close" for comfort for analyst and patient alike, that in some ways it is easier to deal with a more distant childhood. At the same time, his emphasis that adolescent reconstruction is a vehicle for understanding and working through infantile conflicts and for strengthening the therapeutic alliance detracts from the idea that adolescent phenomena are important in and of themselves.

The reconstructions in many of these cases in the literature are of traumatic experiences in adolescence. One dramatic case is furnished by Blum (1985). His patient was traumatized during adolescence due to persecution stemming from anti-Semitism. Three previous analyses had not undone a massive defense against the affective re-experiencing of this whole period of the patient's life. In Peter Blos, Jr.'s case, a dramatic adolescent fixation was the result in part of a physical abnormality. But as my case of Ms. C illustrates, adolescent material that emerges in the analytic process is not fruitfully conceptualized as pathological or the result of significant trauma during adolescence. My point is that adolescent phenomena in general, not necessarily categorized as major fixations or trauma, are frequent components of the analytic process with adults. Often they are missed, reduced to earlier underpinnings and interpreted as such.

Why this is so is an open question. Part of it is, as I have suggested, historical and theoretical: Freud's misunderstanding and underappreciation of the emotional importance of adolescence. Many of the above writers (Blos, Jr., 1990; Novick, 1990; Ritvo, 1971) and others (Deutsch, 1967; Isay, 1975; Jacobson, 1964) have suggested that analysts' own narcissistic and sexual conflicts, revisited in adolescent patients and adolescent phenomena make them skittish and unconsciously reluctant to face them in adult patients. I think that

113

it is also the pain and the intensity of adolescence that we all would like to put behind us and to minimize. How often do we hear ourselves and our friends say, "I would not like to live that period over again!" It is this that prompts us to be insensitive, to squelch and minimize the passions and power of an adolescent's first love and call it "puppy love;" to patronize and mock the adolescent's earnest and often life-changing idealism and purposes; to distance ourselves from his/her exuberance and ardor by disapproval and rigidity. First love and the adventure of embarking on one's own path stir in us all unforgettable, yet painful passions. The experiences are often remembered and recounted, but the uncomfortable affects and unconscious reverberations are not so easily accessible. These conflicted and highly charged experiences are rich potentials to be tapped in any person's analysis and will help to facilitate growth, the hallmark of adolescence.

REFERENCES

Blos, P. (1979). *The Adolescent Passage: Developmental Issues. New* York: Int. Univ. Press.

——— (1989). The place of the adolescent process in the analysis of the adult. *Psychoanal. St. Child*, 44: *3–18.*

Blos, P., Jr. (1990). Adolescent fixation in adult psychopathology. In *Child and Adolescent Analysis: Its Significance for Clinical Work with Adults*, ed. S. Dowling. New York: Int. Univ. Press, pp. *67–79.*

Blum, H.P. (1985). Superego formation, adolescent transformation, and the adult neurosis. *J. Amer. Psychoanal. Assn.*, 33: *887–909.*

Burgner, M. (1988). Analytic work with adolescents: terminable and interminable. *Int. J. Psycho–Anal.*, 69: *179–187.*

Coen, S. J. (1992). *The Misuse of Persons: Analyzing Pathological Dependency.* Hillsdale, NJ/London: Analytic Press.

Conrad, J. (1902). *Youth: A narrative. In The Collected Stories of Joseph Conrad,* ed. S. Hynes. Hopewell, NJ: Ecco Press, 1991, pp. *151–180.*

Deutsch, H. (1967). *Selected Problems of Adolescence.* New York: Int. Univ. Press.

Dewald, P. A. (1982). The clinical importance of the termination phase. *Psychoanal. Inq.,* 2: *441–461.*

Dibattista, M. (1991). *First Love.* Chicago: Univ. of Chicago Press.

Erikson, E. H. (1950). *Childhood and Society.* Second Edition. New York: Norton, 1963.

Erlich, H. S. (1988). The terminability of adolescence and psychoanalysis. *Psychoanal. St. Child,* 43: *199–211.*

Feigelson, C. I. (1976). Reconstruction of adolescence (and early latency) in the analysis of an adult woman. *Psychoanal. St. Child,* 31: *225–236.*

Freud, A. (1936). *The Ego and the Mechanisms of Defense. The Writings of Anna Freud, Vol.* 2. New York: Int. Univ. Press, 1966.

——— (1958). Adolescence. In *The Writings of Anna Freud, Vol. 5.* New York: Int. Univ. Press, 1969, pp. *136–166.*

Freud, S. (1937). Analysis terminable and interminable. *S.E.,* 23.

Glenn, J. (1980). Freud's adolescent patients: Katharina, Dora and the 'Homosexual Woman.' In *Freud and His Patients, Vol. II,* ed. M. Kanzer & J. Glenn. New York/London: Aronson, pp. *23–47.*

Goettsche, R. L. (1986). Reconstruction of adolescence in adult analysis. *Psychoanal. St. Child,* 41: *357–377.*

Holtzman, D. & Kulish, N. (1997). *Nevermore: The Hymen and the Loss of Virginity.* Northvale, NJ/London: Aronson.

Hurn, H. T. (1970). Adolescent transference: a problem of the terminal phase of analysis. *J. Amer. Psychoanal. Assn.,* 18: *342–357.*

Isay, R. A. (1975). The influence of the primal scene on the sexual behavior of an early adolescent. *J. Amer. Psychoanal. Assn.,* 23: *535–553.*

Jacobson, E. (1964). *The Self and the Object World.* New York: Int. Univ. Press.

James, W. (1902). *The Varieties of Religious Experience.* New Hyde Park, NY: University Books, 1963.

Kaplan, L. J. (1984). *Adolescence: The Farewell to Childhood.* New York/London: Simon & Schuster.

Lampl-de Groot, J. (1960). On adolescence. *Psychoanal. St. Child*, 15: *95–103.*

Laufer, M. & Laufer, M. E. (1984)). *Adolescence and Developmental Breakdown: A Psychoanalytic View.* New Haven/London: Yale Univ. Press.

Mahler, M. S., Pine, F. & Bergman, A. (1975). *The Psychological Birth of the Human Infant: Symbiosis and Individuation.* New York: Basic Books.

Novick, J. (1990). The significance of adolescent analysis for clinical work with adults. In *Child and Adolescent Analysis: Its Significance for Clinical Work with Adults*, ed. S. Dowling. Madison, CT: Int. Univ. Press, pp. *81–94.*

——— & Novick, K. K. (1991). Deciding on termination: the relevance of child and adolescent analytic experience to work with adults. In *Saying Goodbye: A Casebook of Termination in Child and Adolescent Analysis and Therapy*, ed. A. G. Schmukler. Hillsdale, NJ/London: Analytic Press, pp. *285–303.*

Ritvo, S. (1971). Late adolescence: developmental and clinical considerations. *Psychoanal. St. Child*, 26: *241–263.*

CHAPTER 5:

Primary Femininity Clinical Advances and Theoretical Ambiguities

(2000). J. Amer. Psychoanal. Assn., (48)(4):1355-1379

This paper examines the use of the term "primary femininity" in current psychoanalytic thinking. The concept of primary femininity arose in reaction to early theories about female sexuality and development; based on a model of male development, these presented problems when applied to females. The author attempts to demonstrate the clinical advances that have resulted from the idea of primary femininity. At the same time, she argues that the idea has been used to carry widely differing meanings, and has reflected many writers' differing frames of reference, which range from gender identity through biological traits, object relations, genital anxieties, and bisexuality. Like the terms it originally was intended to replace or augment, it has come to be used reductionistically or loosely. The author warns against its misuse and argues that primary femininity is not a unitary concept, but rather encompasses a related group of ideas about the female body and mind.

The concept of "primary femininity" has been heralded as an advance in the reexamination of psychoanalytic views of women and of female psychosexual development. Early views of female development, which were modeled upon development in the male, conceived of femininity essentially as a secondary reaction to an original masculinity. Ideas about primary femininity were advanced as antidotes to what was perceived as the phallocentrism of these theories. The concept of primary femininity has contributed substantially to the psychoanalytic understanding of females, yet I believe that it harbors new conceptual problems of its own. Not a unified or clear concept at all, it has been used in widely differing and sometimes ill-defined ways, and from many different frames of reference. It has been used in conjunction with concepts as varied as gender identity, innate biological traits, early object relationships, aspects of the self, and types of anxieties. The terms "primary" and "femininity" themselves both pose problems, raising questions about what is primary, as opposed to secondary, and also about what is meant by "feminine." Thorny clinical questions persist about how to apply these newer ideas and how to integrate them with older ideas about penis envy and castration. Like some of the theoretical formulations it was meant to replace, "primary femininity" is now frequently used in a reductionistic or shorthand manner, as a mere label replacing understanding and covering a lack of clarity.

In this paper I will attempt to demonstrate these definitional and conceptual problems with the idea of primary femininity. I will begin with a brief history of its origin, then selectively review the theoretical and clinical inconsistencies in the ways it is currently used. Finally, I will call for caution in its application, and suggest that it may have outlived its usefulness, except as a crude guide in our efforts to explore and revamp our theories of female sexuality and female psychosexual development. Just as many of our early theories of psychosexual development rested upon concepts of primary masculinity, so ideas of primary femininity have, implicitly or explicitly, influenced a broad range of contemporary psychoanalytic writings about female development. I will, however, focus primarily on those writings in which the concept of primary femininity is used explicitly.

It is my opinion that there is no such entity as "primary femininity" per se, any more than "primary masculinity" is a single entity. I think it would be preferable to separate the different areas subsumed under the term *primary femininity*— female gender identity, body image, object choice, representations of femininity, identifications with the maternal object, and psychosexual developmental phases—and try to articulate more clearly the early contributions from inborn biology, developing object relations, and societal influence to each of these, both clinically and in developmental theory and research. In the area of gender identity, Elise's recent suggestion (1997) that we think in terms of "a primary sense of femaleness" rather than "primary femininity" has brought needed clarification.

ORIGIN OF THE CONCEPT OF PRIMARY FEMININITY

The idea of a primary femininity was proposed by psychoanalysts in opposition to Freud's original theories of female psychosexual development, which were founded on notions of a primary masculinity. For Freud, the development of the little boy and the little girl were identical at first, as captured by his now infamous words, "the little girl is a little man" (Freud 1933, p. 118). He asserted that until the age of three or four neither the girl nor the boy has any knowledge of sexual differences or of the existence of the vagina (Freud 1925). Both the girl and the boy go through a preoedipal "phallic stage," with phallic, masculine sexual aims focused on the mother. The little girl's sexual sensations are concentrated in the clitoris, which was conceptualized as analogous to the penis. Moreover, Freud (1905) stated that libido itself was "masculine" (p. 219). Thus, the girl's sexuality begins as masculine and her future development depends on a reaction to, or a renunciation of, the original primary masculinity. Penis envy, her reaction to her lack of an adequate organ, initiates both the triangulation of her object relations and the turn toward oedipal interests, and forms as well the motivational basis for the wish for a baby. In Freud's account, the course of feminine development toward heterosexuality and motherhood was extremely convoluted. These formulations did not include ways to think about how a positive sense of self as female, of agency over sexual pleasure, or of pride in the female body might develop, or develop easily. (For a thorough discussion of the question of agency over female desire, see Hoffman 1996.)

From the start, contemporaries of Freud challenged his theory on the grounds that it lacked such concepts of primary femininity. Both Horney and Jones mounted early and serious, and to my mind compelling, challenges to Freud's ideas; these unfortunately were not heeded, in part because of the political climate in psychoanalysis at the time (Fliegel 1973). Horney (1924, 1933) did not use the term *primary femininity*, but advanced the idea in her argument that a little girl's sense of being inferior was not primary, but acquired and culturally reinforced. She (1926) also argued that a girl's reproductive urges did not necessarily stem from the compensatory substitution of a baby for a missing penis, but rather from identification with her mother, an idea which, we shall see, re-emerges in contemporary concepts of primary femininity (Tyson and Tyson 1990). Horney and others such as Jones (1927, 1933) and later Greenacre (1950) insisted that the girl does have early knowledge of her own vagina, although this is often repressed. In these early writings first appears the idea of a primary quality of femininity: early feelings about the female body that do not carry with them meanings of inferiority.

Jones (1933) also questioned the phallic phase in girls, which he felt was secondary and defensive. He posited that there was a primary femininity for girls—"the earliest stage of their development is essentially feminine" (p. 31)—and he believed in an inborn bisexuality. As described by Jones, this primary (heterosexual) femininity took the form of early, inborn, oedipal impulses that impelled girls toward their fathers and brought genital fears of penetration. Thus, for Jones, penis envy did not provide the girl's impetus into the oedipal phase. Jones's psychobiological notions reflected Kleinian notions of innate oedipal fantasies and inborn sexual knowledge.

PRIMARY FEMININITY AS GENDER IDENTITY

While the idea of primary femininity originally came up in the context of early formulations of psychosexual drive development, the term was first used in an entirely different context: the study of the development of core gender identity. The implications of primary femininity as gender identity have been far-reaching and clinically useful. At the same time, this broad applicability has often been accompanied by theoretical looseness. Even though gender identity is primarily a sociopsychological concept, writings about primary femininity as gender identity often slip into simple "essentialist" or biological types of explanations, which seem unwarranted and reductionistic. Primary femininity is often advanced as a kind of protofemininity, an inborn state of femaleness, that forms the core of a primary gender identity.

The term *primary femininity* was originally used by Stoller (1968) in his studies of the development of core gender identity and its disorders. First, he attempted to counter Freud's notions about the primacy of masculinity, which had rested in part on a nineteenth-century view of embryology. In Freud's time it was thought that the sexual organs were originally male, and that the female organs differentiate from this original form later in fetal development. Hence, masculine sexuality was seen as the primary state. Stoller (1976) pointed out that modern embryology tells us the opposite: with the secretion of testosterone, male sexual organs differentiate from an original female configuration. In that sense, it is femininity that is "primary": at least if one is going to use that kind of teleological reasoning. Stoller then argued that femininity for both females and males was primary in another sense as well, in that the first object of identification for the infant is female, the mother.

Stoller (1975) also applied this concept of primary femininity to the psychology and the psychopathology of males. Here the concept of primary femininity is a particular kind or state of object relatedness. Like Greenson (1968), Stoller suggested that boys have the difficult task of disidentifying from their mothers in establishing their gender identities and sense of masculinity. That is why, he thought, more men than women are transsexual, or manifest other gender identity disturbances.

Stoller's work on core gender identity also reflected ideas of primary femininity. "Core gender identity" refers to the most basic sense of being a male or a female, which is now known to be set early, at about eighteen months. Stoller (1968, 1972, 1976) argued from a large body of research that different sources contribute to gender identity: inborn biology, sexual assignment, parental attitudes, learning and conditioning, and the body ego. He hypothesized that core gender identity is largely a matter of learning, based on parental assignment and developing out of the conflict-free sphere of the ego. In this view, the first conviction a girl has of herself as a female is free of conflict. Stoller did attend to the role of conflict and defense, however. For example, he wrote (1972) that the repudiation of femininity in men and the girl's wish for a penis are to be conceptualized as defensive maneuvers, not the biological bedrock that Freud imagined. Although he used entirely different frames of reference, Stoller's views of primary femininity, and of a secondarily defensive masculinity, resemble those of Horney and Jones.

Many have questioned Stoller's ideas. As Birksted-Breen (1996) has pointed out, the notion of a non-conflictual primary femininity is not accepted by many British and French psychoanalysts, for whom there is *no* area of cognition that is free of ambiguity, conflict, and unconscious fantasy. Person and Ovesey (1983) criticized Stoller's views along different lines. Stoller's notion is that primary femininity is a protofemininity from which both males and females must disidentify and separate. Person and Ovesey questioned whether the early undifferentiated "symbiotic" state is one that confers gendered behavior or identity. That is, why should having been merged with mother during infancy in terms of self and object confer on the infant a cognitive sense of femininity? They also argued that transsexualism is not necessarily nonconflictual. According to Stoller, primary femininity is an early state from which transsexuals never move; for Person and Ovesey, it is a complicated, partially defensive construction: a result of fantasies of merger used defensively against the fear of separation.

I share the doubts of such writers as Person and Ovesey that initial lack of separation from the mother imparts a primary sense of femininity. There is a difference between separation and disidentification, and between a lack of separation and identification. I see development of gender identity and the development of differentiation of self and object as two related, but different, lines of development.[1]

Coming from the perspectives of sociology and object relations, Chodorow's early writings (1978) about gender differences resemble Stoller's ideas of a kind of primary femininity in the development of the sense of self and gender identity. Although Chodorow did not use the term *primary femininity* as such— and in fact has recently placed herself in opposition to the "primary femininity theorists" who define femininity in terms of "an inevitable developmental bodily-based primary cathexis of the female genitals and/or fears of injury" (1996, p. 219)—her ideas about gendered differences based on early maternal identifications (or disidentifications) imply concepts of primary femininity in the establishment of gender identity. Both Stoller and Chodorow stressed that the implications for the developing child are different, according to whether the need to separate involves a same-sexed or a different-sexed object. Chodorow speculated that some clinically and sociologically observed differences between males and females reflect differences in their respective

---

1 In contrast, Fast's (1979) formulations about the development of gender identity do not rest on ideas of a primary femininity. Fast asserts that gender identity is first undifferentiated. The young child gradually learns and takes in what a given family or society presents as "masculine" or "feminine," and must come to grips with the narcissistic blows inherent in this process. As with Stoller, this is a learning process, although not necessarily without conflict, and in the context of enfolding object relations. Fast states succinctly that if biology has a contribution, it is minimal, usually in the same direction as the biological sex of the individual, and able to be overridden by environmental influences. Thus, for Fast there is not a primary femininity or a primary masculinity in terms of gender identity, but a primary undifferentiated state.

developments based on how separation proceeds in boys and girls, given that the primary caretaker is typically the mother. She deduced that females, because they must first separate from the same-sexed object, experience themselves as less separate than do males; and conversely that males, in separating from the opposite-sexed object, strive more for a sense of independence than do females. Women, more than men, will be more open to and preoccupied with the very relational issues that go into mothering. In contrast to boys, girls need to identify with their mothers or want to be like their mothers, and usually are encouraged in this.

Criticized for overgeneralizing and "essentializing," Chodorow has modified these positions. In her most recent writings (1994) she has taken a strong stance against universalizing about femininity and masculinity, and suggested that we should think in terms of "femininities and masculinities." I agree that Chodorow's early work can be criticized for overgeneralization. Nevertheless, her point about the possible differential effects of separation from a same versus a different-sexed parent is a powerful one, and it was a major contribution to psychoanalytic thinking about feminine development.

Chodorow's, and before her Stoller's, ideas about the gendered asymmetry in object relations have had broad influence. Similar ideas about asymmetry in the development of males and females have been applied to many different areas: clinical psychoanalysis (Miller 1982; Silverman 1987), philosophy of science (Keller 1985), literature (Foley 1994), feminism (Benjamin 1988), and psychological research (Gilligan 1982), to name only a few. The most poetic expression of these kinds of ideas can be found in the work of the French philosopher/psychoanalyst Irigaray (1994): "Woman's subjective identity is not at all the same as man's. She does not have to distance herself from her mother as he does—by a *yes* and especially a *no*, a *near* or a *far*, an *inside* opposed to an *outside*—to discover her sex" (p. 18; emphasis Irigaray's).

Theories that conflate separation of self from object with structuralization of gender identity are problematic. Many broad conceptual leaps are made:

from objective behavioral data to unconscious processes and inferred abstract concepts such as individuation; from specific singular observations to universal declarations about the differences between women and men. In this context primary femininity no longer refers to a basic sense of being female—a phenomenological concept belonging to the self system—but instead to ideas about early identifications that shape the relationship between self and other. In some places it takes on an undefinable essence, an almost cellular female quality. Although Stoller made it very clear that his idea of primary femininity was a psychological "bedrock" and not a biological one, in some writings the term is used in ways that evoke Freud's ideas of embryologically basic masculinity.

Greenberg (1993, p. 520) quotes Rosbrow-Reich as suggesting that "a sense of primary femininity develops in the preverbal stages of early infancy as gender identity is imprinted upon the child during this period of intimate bodily closeness with the mother." Here primary femininity is a kind of imprinting upon the psyche, like a cloning of the mother's femininity onto the infant's identity. This is what I mean by the overly concrete ideas of primary femininity as gender identity, and an example of how they may be conflated with object relations.

It should be pointed out that this entire line of investigation (of gender identity and primary femininity) has taken psychoanalysis into an area outside of Freud's scope of interest and investigation. Freud was not interested in gender identity per se. His notion that the girl was in all respects "a little man" pertained to the area of sexual development—of libidinal aims and fluctuations—and not to this more cognitive concept. Surely, if Freud had thought of it, he would not have claimed that the little girls around him *identified* themselves as little boys. Criticisms of Freud, as Compton (1983) has pointed out, are more pertinent if they focus on his ideas about *libidinal* development in girls, and not on concepts that came after his time and that overstep his area of investigation.

When applied clinically, however, ideas about primary femininity as gender identity or core gender identity have been interesting and useful. For example, a clinically astute use of these concepts can be found in the work of Welldon (1988), who applied Chodorow's reproduction of mothering to a study of the reproduction of perverse mothering. Welldon explored the psychopathological expressions mothering can take in perversions or prostitution. Welldon's examination of the dynamics of motherhood falls within the framework of primary femininity as it relates to core gender development: "The female core gender-identity includes a preoedipal identification with mother which becomes well established by the second year of life, when body awareness and internal representations have become distinct and therefore differentiation between the sexes has been acknowledged. The wish for a baby has become by then part of the 'primary femininity'" (pp. 44-45).

Many of the writers who have applied the concept of primary femininity as core gender identity most judiciously have been child and adolescent analysts, who tend naturally to use these concepts in less static and more process-oriented contexts. Tyson and Tyson's broad writings (1990) on development stressed ideas of primary femininity in the sense of core gender identity and gender identity. In a panel on female sexuality (Grossman 1994), Phyllis Tyson, echoing Stoller, stated that if there is a bedrock of femaleness, it is primary femininity, or core gender identity. The latter precedes identifications, which become embroiled in conflicts in latter development. Elsewhere Tyson (1982) traced a line of development of gender identity for the girl as it is influenced by, and interacts with, object relationships, drives, changing ego capacities, and superego developments. She stressed that the girl's sense of herself as feminine depends on the quality of the mother-child relationship and on the mother's sense of her own femininity. Such concepts of primary femininity as gender identity have been put to good use clinically, as in Tyson's own clinical examples, or those of other child analysts (Yanof 1986).

The conceptual problems, as I see them, come with the theoretical gyrations around the *ideas* of primary femininity, more than in clinical applications, which stick closer to observation. I am in essential agreement with a recent article by Elise (1997), who clearly pointed out that the concept of primary femininity has brought important advances in our understanding of the psychology of women, as well as accompanying contradictions and problematic assumptions. She argued that the term imparts the erroneous idea that *femininity* is primary, derived in a preordained way from the female body, and that gender identity and heterosexuality are also inherently linked. She proposed that we use the phrase "primary sense of femaleness" instead of "primary femininity." This proposed shift would focus our explorations in the right direction—toward studying the multiple influences on the little girl's development of a positive sense of being female—and at the same time diminish the misleading and faulty conceptual ties to ideas of bedrock determinism.

However, the problems with the concept extend farther than Elise takes them, and would not all be solved by this substitution. "Primary femininity" has not been confined to studies of gender identity or the "primary sense of femaleness" (the area stressed by Elise), but has appeared in numerous other contexts and frames of reference, which I will outline below. These meanings are burdened by the same conceptual issues clarified by Elise with regard to gender identity, as well as by other clinical and theoretical dilemmas on which she did not focus.

PRIMARY FEMININITY AS FEMALE GENITAL ANXIETY

A second major context in which "primary femininity" appears is the topic of female genital anxieties: that is, anxieties related to fears of damages or loss to *female* bodily parts, as opposed to envy of and fantasies about loss of *male* attributes. The current psychoanalytic inquiry into female genital anxieties follows the line of critical reaction to Freud's early formations about women that I traced back to Horney and Jones above. Both Jones and Horney wrote about the fantasies and fears of genital damage from penetration aroused in the little girl by what she perceives as her father's huge and dangerous penis. Ideas about female genital anxieties have their roots in the arguments that girls are aware of their own genitals, and that their ideas about themselves are not confined to being penis-less. There has been a shift in theoretical and clinical interest from girls' and women's beliefs about what they lack genitally, to their fears about losing or damaging what they already possess.

A major contributor to the literature on female genital anxieties has been Arlene Kramer Richards (1996), who explicitly puts her ideas in the context of primary femininity (p. 261). Expanding on Bernstein's classification of three female genital anxieties (1990)—fear of access, fear of penetration, and fear of diffusivity—Richards emphasized the flexing of the perineal musculature in the development of female genital awareness and sensation. The contraction of these sphincter muscles in toilet training results in a spreading sexual excitement that is experienced as genital. Richards also described a primary fear of castration in women, which she saw in terms of a loss of pleasure from, or function of, the female genital apparatus. Richards asserted that girls fear that their capacity for sexual excitement may be subject to loss as punishment for forbidden oedipal wishes. These ideas have commonalities with Kestenberg's (1968, 1982) theories about the centrality of inner genital sensations for girls. Richards's use of the term primary femininity suggests the meaning of primary as early and basic: "All of this is to say that the sensory experience a little girl has of her genital may not be one she can put into words, but it is deep, going back to her earliest life. It is permanent as the result of flexing and relaxing the sphincters and surrounding musculature, and it is valued as it gives a great deal of pleasure. (1996, p. 279)

In her influential work, Mayer (1985) proposed another primary feminine genital anxiety, which she called the "female castration anxiety." This female anxiety involves the feared loss or closing of the genital opening, and allied fears of the loss of openness as a trait of the personality. Mayer argued that a little girl's primary femininity—that is, her knowledge of her uniqueness, her body, and her genitalia—inform her feminine identity and can contribute to a valued sense of herself. The little girl's fantasy that "everybody must be just like me" is an aspect of the early narcissistic investment of the self. Mayer's contributions have led many analysts and analytic therapists to focus clinically and usefully on their female patients' conflicted yet *positive* feelings about their femininity. A random sampling of the clinical papers in this journal's recent (1996) supplement on the psychology of women reveals how pervasively Mayer's ideas have shaped current clinical understanding of women's conflicts and fantasies about their bodies. In her stress on the idea that the girl cherishes her own body and genitals and fears for their loss, Mayer has made a most significant contribution to a transformed perspective on clinical analytic work with women and girls.

In elaborating these ideas further, Mayer (1995) compared female castration anxiety with traditional phallic castration anxiety as it manifests itself in girls. The girl values her feminine parts, and she fears losing them; hence she experiences signal anxiety at the anticipatory threat of such a loss. On the other hand, the little girl can also envy males for their prized penises and feel that she is inferior or lacking. The sense of loss makes for a sense of depression over the phallus that she fantasizes she had once, and then lost. This traditional phallic castration anxiety is signaled by the presence of depression. Mayer made another major suggestion, namely that these two types of anxieties, the traditional phallic castration anxiety and the newly conceptualized female castration anxiety, are organized along two separate lines of development.

This interesting attempt to integrate the radical new ideas about female development with the older ones raises problems, however. First, it does not always seem possible to differentiate the two types of castration anxiety in women by differing affects: that is, anxiety at the fear of losing female functions ("female castration anxiety") and depression at the idea of loss of the phallus ("phallic castration anxiety"). (Mayer is careful to say that this division is only a generality, and that these affects *tend* to be organized within these two complexes in this way.) Many women feel *depressed* at the fantasy of having lost aspects of their femininity or their own female genitals, as well as at the loss of the imagined phallus. In many cases women feel depressed, inferior, or lacking in comparison with other *females*, not just "superior" males. Many women feel dejected that other women have bigger or more beautiful breasts, and this concern is not always a displacement from penis envy. One of my patients was convinced that her vagina, in comparison to other women's, was misshapen, ugly, and inadequate. As is often the case, guilt over masturbation as a child contributed to these feelings of mutilation and loss. Sometimes the masturbation and masturbation fantasies express the wish for a penis and/or the fantasy of punishment by the loss of a penis once possessed. At other times, however, a girl's fantasy is that she has damaged or mutilated her own female genitals by her masturbation or other sexual misdeeds.

On the other hand, anxiety in a woman does not necessarily signal the threatened loss of a feminine part or attribute. Women frequently anticipate with fear the loss of a fantasized phallus, or an inner phallus. It could be argued that such a fantasy is already evidence of, and a defensive reparation for, loss and depression; but in any case, anxiety and loss are intermingled in its content. I am reminded of an obsessive-compulsive teenage girl I once saw who feared she would lose her intelligence if she did not obey her compulsions. It was clear from her dreams and her symptoms that her intelligence was her phallic power. She felt that wearing pink was not intelligent, and some of her compulsions had to do with avoiding objects of a pink color. Her fear of losing her intelligence was "castration anxiety," linked to guilt about sadomasochistically tinged fantasies and masturbation urges.

Secondly, I find it difficult to think of phallic castration anxieties and female genital anxieties as separate lines of development. Olesker (1998), using both child observational data and analytic material from women and girls, also argued against a separate line of development for female genital anxiety. There are dangers and disadvantages to dividing these phenomena along gendered lines.

First, posing a phallic castration line of development takes us straight back to the early psychoanalytic theory of psychosexual development for the girl, with its intrinsic empirical problems and phallocentric biases. Such problems cannot be addressed simply by conceptualizing a feminine line of development alongside the contested one. Furthermore, there is another possible danger in this separation: it seems to me that this idea could be boiled down to a "feminine" line of development that corresponds to the side of the girl that is happily female, and a "masculine" line of development that corresponds to the side of the girl that is not happy, and wishes to be male. Psychoanalysis has struggled with, and been completely tangled up in, the dialectics of masculine and feminine (and active and passive, and sadism and masochism) from the beginning. Masculine versus feminine lines of development, or masculine versus feminine genital anxieties, bring us back to this dialectic. On the other hand, the idea of an autonomous woman's voice, submerged beneath patriarchally given law, as delineated by the feminist writer and scholar Gilligan (1982), has much appeal. Such ideas fit congenially with the idea of two lines of development, "masculine" and "feminine."[2]

Lax (1995) used the concepts of "primary" and "secondary" genital anxieties in a somewhat different sense than the above writers. For her, primary genital anxiety, an early phenomenon, is the fear of losing the genitals the little girl possesses. Secondary genital anxieties, which can be equated with phallic castration feelings, come subsequent to the girl's discovery that she lacks a penis. Such feelings of penis envy and devaluation of the self are directed onto the

---

2 Others such as Goldberger (1993) have voiced their concerns about using the term "castration" to apply to female phenomena. I, too, think that the term "castration anxiety" should not be used with women unless there is clear evidence of a fantasy of losing an imagined phallus. Mayer has acknowledged the argument, made by many psychoanalysts, that the term is misleading and misused with regard to women. Like many of our psychoanalytic terms, it can be used reflexively, allowing us in the clinical situation to blur over the phenomena to which it is attached. I prefer the term genital anxiety, which I think is more generally accurate (or less inaccurate), and which allows room to understand specifically what the anxiety might be. Moreover, "castration anxiety" does not cover the range of genital anxieties experienced by men, either.

131

mother as loved but disappointing object during the end of the negative oedipal phase. Thus, "primary" and "secondary" refer to developmental chronology. Lax's descriptions of secondary genital anxieties sound like Jones's secondary phallic stage and Horney's idea of a secondary and defensive stage characterized by feeling of inferiority and penis envy. In contrast to Mayer who proposed separate lines of development for two seemingly different kinds of anxieties, Lax proposes anxieties characteristic of sequential subphases of development. Again, I wonder whether, at our current state of knowledge, and without much more research, we can make the general statement that anxieties of differing contents come from differing subphases of development. Only on a carefully restricted case-by-case basis might we be able to infer with more confidence if one set of conflicts and fantasies precedes or follows another developmentally. When working with adults it is not possible to reconstruct with certainty when a particular genital anxiety comes from an earlier developmental level than another. Whether one type of anxiety or fantasy covers another defensively is not self-evident; it calls for complex clinical inference. This latter point was also made by Shaw (1995).

Thus, these (and most) accounts of female genital anxieties struggle with the question of how such anxieties fit, clinically and theoretically, with traditional ideas about penis envy. Authors who try to fit newer ideas in with familiar theories meet with mixed success.

Another issue concerns the distinction between fantasy about the body and bodily sensations. It is important to keep in mind that primary and secondary female genital anxiety refer to *fantasies* and feelings girls have about their genitals, and not to genital sensations themselves. At times the literature seems to conflate primary genital anxiety with a "primary" and given set of bodily sensations. If we add to this argument Kubie's (1974) notion that we all want to be both sexes, and Fast's (1979) related proposal that we all grapple with a narcissistic sorting out of what we can and cannot be in the course of development, I conclude that "masculine" and "feminine" fantasies, wishes, and anxieties about the body and the genitals coexist and commingle in both sexes. I think that even penis envy is a *feminine* genital anxiety or conflict-laden affect, and should not be classified as masculine. It is a feeling females have as part of the course of female development. Penis envy and feelings of inferiority as a female very frequently are used defensively, and often cover over other kinds of anxieties about *feminine* sexuality. Many women fear and experience their "feminine" sexual impulses as too intense, potentially uncontrollable, or bad. This is so in women with anal fixations in particular (Kulish 1991; Richards 1992). Shaw (1995) has addressed this issue. Presenting illustrative clinical material, she concluded that the attempt to separate masculine versus feminine genital anxieties is conceptually ambiguous and clinically artificial, and that the fantasy formations are complementary.

In summary, do our newer concepts about female genital anxieties, derived from ideas about primary femininity, have clinical validity? What is to be gained by viewing clinical material from women in these new lights? Do female genital anxieties exist side by side with penis envy and castration anxiety? Are the two "types" of anxieties, if that categorization is correct, to be conceptualized as defenses against each other? Which and what to interpret first? Is one developmentally later than the other? In spite of some thorny theoretical questions, the current psychoanalytic literature is replete with examples of how clinicians have put these ideas about female genital anxieties to very good use (Birksted-Breen 1996; Evert 1991; Kalinich 1993; Olesker 1998; Renik 1992; Shaw 1995; Wilkinson 1993). My sense is that those who write about female genital anxieties have adhered more closely to the clinical situation, and have therefore avoided some of the pitfalls of biologizing or essentializing that have plagued some of those writing about primary femininity as gender identity.

PRIMARY FEMININITY AS AN ASPECT OF BISEXUALITY

Still other meanings beyond these two major categories have been associated with concepts of primary femininity. In some writings, particularly earlier ones, primary femininity is pictured as one side of an inborn bisexuality, as in a fascinating study of George Sand by Deutsch (1928). Deutsch speculated that Sand's troubled background did not allow her to develop her "femininity" and thus fostered her "masculinity." Deutsch wrote: "Masculine and feminine evolved out a primordial original unity that survives as a bisexual constitution in everyone…. Thus, there are always male components in women and female components in men" (p. 446). Similarly, Parens (1980) described a basic inborn bisexuality and neutral genital libido, from which "heterosexual libido deriving from primary masculinity and primary femininity" differentiates (p. 110).

Elise (1997) discussed the compatibility of concepts of bisexuality with concepts of primary femininity as gender identity. According to many psychoanalysts, Phyllis Tyson (1982, 1989) for one, primary femininity—in the sense of gender identity, which is a culturally derived and learned experience—does not seem to allow for an inborn bisexuality. Elise argued that an early sense of femaleness, a description that she prefers to primary femininity, can and does develop alongside of bisexual identifications, which do not necessarily rest on constitutional factors. Furthermore, she pointed out that the fantasy of unlimited gender potential would be a different experience for each sex. I would emphasize that there is more than one way of conceiving bisexuality, just as there are differing concepts of femininity and masculinity, primary or otherwise. Bisexuality has many referents: from inborn biological predispositions and factors to inborn psychological predispositions to conscious and unconscious fantasies of being both sexes to bisexual identifications, the mix of self-representations that define or make up "feminine" or "masculine" aspects of the self. These different referents need to be specified and clarified.

PRIMARY FEMININITY AS A SPECIFIC
PSYCHOSEXUAL STAGE

Concepts of primary femininity have led to ideas about renaming or revising the traditional psychosexual stages of development, particularly the phallic phase. Many psychoanalysts, including myself, question the appropriateness of a normative developmental stage for girls that is named for and dominated by conflicts, sensations, and defenses that relate exclusively to the male organ. Thus, instead of a primary masculine or phallic phase which all children must traverse, some have suggested that we might think in terms of a "primary feminine" phase, or an early "genital" phase.

A step in this direction is Edgcumbe and Burgner's (1975) suggestion that the phase be more aptly called the "phallic-narcissistic." They stressed that it is characterized by psychically narcissistic fantasies and reactions. In emphasizing the narcissistic aspects of this stage, and deemphasizing the phallic aspects traditionally proposed to characterize both sexes, they anticipated Fast's (1979) ideas of the "narcissistic sorting-out" that accompanies gender identity development.

Kestenberg (1982) proposed a new genital stage, "the inner genital stage." She suggested that there are inner genital sensations, with characteristic patterns of rhythm, discharge, and defense for males and for females. These are prominent in a prephallic stage, from the ages of two and a half to four years. She asserted that women's identities are strongly based on this inner genital core and on the vicissitudes of inner sensations throughout development.

More traditionally, Roiphe and Galenson (1981) proposed an early genital phase concomitant with the rapprochement phase, at sixteen to twenty-four months. This phase, which they do not elevate to a delineated stage, includes manipulation of genitals, sexual curiosity, and a generally heightened genital awareness. According to their research, these early phenomena mingle with anal-urinary and phallic urges. Both Kestenberg's and Roiphe and Galenson's

135

suggested sexual phases of development are nongender-specific, and allow some room for the development within them of a "primary" femininity. Although they have been criticized as constrained by traditional rubrics and biases, Roiphe and Galenson's hypotheses about these early sexual manifestations fit coherently within the developmental framework of the standard psychosexual stages. In contrast, Kestenberg's proposed inner genital stage seems to be tacked onto the classical psychosexual sequence in an unintegrated way.

More radical is the suggestion by Glover and Mendell (1982) that psychoanalysis replace the "phallic" stage with a "pre-oedipal genital" or "genital" stage. The dominant zone in this stage is the actual genital: in the case of the girl, the genital is the female genital, and the characteristic affect is penetration anxiety. Others, including Chehrazi (1986), Parens (1990), Tyson (1994), and Dorsey (1996) have made similar proposals. These have grown in many instances out of ideas associated with primary femininity, but have in general fallen on deaf ears. I agree that a more generic name would be desirable, and more in keeping with contemporary psychoanalytic thinking about female development.

CONCLUSION

As I have attempted to demonstrate, the term *primary femininity* has been used in many ways. It takes on different meanings and applications depending on author and context, and covers a hodgepodge of concepts. It can have specific bodily referents: an early awareness of the existence of the vagina, and of vaginal sensations or more general inner genital sensations.[3] It can mean an inborn

---

3 Interestingly, as Balsam (1996) has pointed out that the female body as a whole, and, particularly the body of the (pregnant) mother, as on object of identification for the girl has been neglected as a topic of psychoanalytic interest. The body-to-body comparisons that a little girl makes with her mother must contribute to her primary sense of herself as a female.

biological disposition toward heterosexuality in the female of the species, as in Jones. Sometimes there are added connotations that such inborn or early experiences are pleasurable, non-defensive, and without conflict. In other contemporary usages primary femininity is related to unpleasure, to female genital anxieties. Other connotations address the cognitive and interpersonal areas. In one prevalent meaning it refers to core gender identity, or more broadly to the sense of being female. Some meanings imply a mode of object-relatedness, a closeness between infant and mother that defines a primary state of identity. These many frames of references range from the specifically biological to the highly abstract, from the sociological to the fantasied, from the observable to the inferred, from the conscious to the unconscious. In addition, newer concepts of primary femininity are sometimes loosely mixed with traditional familiar concepts; often these juxtapositions do not fit, as in the attempts to add in a new genital psychosexual stage within the classical developmental paradigm.

In addition to the problems of definition and of varying and inconsistent usage, there are theoretical issues with regard to both the "primary" and the "femininity" aspects of the concept. In her recent paper, Elise (1997) has cogently argued that both terms in the phrase *primary femininity* are in need of definition and clarification. To start with, it is not clear what is meant by "primary." Does "primary" simply mean first chronologically? As I have shown, this is its meaning for some writers, as in Lax's construction of the sequence of development of primary gender anxieties. Other writers imply, sometimes explicitly and sometimes not, that they mean something different or more; they mean primary in the sense of basic, or core. For others, such as Horney and Jones, primary means primary to a secondary defensive organization. Thus, core gender identity means chronologically first, set in the earliest stages of development, and also "core" in the sense of central and organizing to the whole personality. Primary can imply that which is unconsciously and topographically bedrock: that is, what is "the deepest" in the unconscious. For example, in a work by Herman (1989) we find a kind of celebration of primary femininity as bedrock (replacing Freud's repudiation of femininity as bedrock): "Is there or is there not in the experience of women, however buried and obscured by cultural and other factors, a concept of primary femininity, present from infancy to slowly ripen and mature to full exultation of its potency in time?" (p. 18).

These are differences with clinical implications. In line with much contemporary psychoanalytic thinking, Grossman and Kaplan (1988) argue against treating any psychoanalytical constellation as primary. They point out that Freud's position was that nothing about sexuality should be taken at face value. They argued that psychoanalytically there is no concept of the primary. Therefore, it follows that there is no primary femininity or masculinity. That is to say, nothing should be considered primary and without antecedent, especially in terms of the psychoanalytic method of inquiry in the clinical situation. I agree that within the psychoanalytic treatment situation the attitude of taking any fantasy, behavior, or expression as primary forestalls analytic inquiry and exploration. Those of us who have argued against taking feelings of penis envy, feminine inferiority, or masochism as primary or "bedrock" see similar problems with ideas of *primary* feminine genital anxieties.

Perhaps a bigger problem comes with the "femininity" side. The question of what femininity means gets into many of the thorniest philosophical and scientific issues raging in contemporary psychoanalytic discourse: questions of causality and evidence, the challenges of intersubjectivity and postmodernism, the efficacy of the single-case method in building a general theory, the relationship of psychoanalysis to other disciplines, the dilemma of reconciling the theoretical differences within psychoanalysis. Some of the literature on primary femininity, however, seems to skip over these issues too blithely.

A central concern is the issue of "essentialist" versus "constructivist" views about gender. Many who write about primary femininity take an essentialist viewpoint, stating that there are essential feminine characteristics—an essential femininity, however this may be influenced by biology, anatomy, neonatal hormones, brain chemistry, environment, object relations, and parental and societal attitudes—or interactions among these. Elise (1997) demonstrated that the concept of primary femininity is often used in such a manner as to convey the impression that femininity is innate, and linked to innate heterosexuality and the desirability of same-sex identification.

I will bow to Chodorow's (1994) excellent critique of this issue (which includes a critique of her own earlier position). She argued that psychoanalytic thinking on gender and sexuality has tended to subsume individuality and difference in the interest of universalist theories. She warned us to distinguish between subjective and observed gender, and to attend to the relationship between individual uniqueness and commonality. She offered one universal observation to which she holds: that every individual constructs a gender and a sexual subjectivity. Chodorow pointed out that many primary femininity theorists fall into the mistake of making universalistic claims about women, and of implying they can describe the core experience or essence of femininity or masculinity (p. 217).

Psychoanalytic thinking tends not to be sufficiently cognizant of the inextricable linguistic and cultural biases in our theorizing. Many contemporary writers on primary femininity began their work with a critique making just this point as it applies to traditional theories about women. Yet they sometimes fail to see that they may slip into similar errors, and leave themselves open to the same criticisms they themselves have leveled. The traditional theories had an inherent phallocentric bias and assumption of male superiority. Unfortunately, newer writings turn the tables and subtly suggest that what society and culture take for granted as intrinsically feminine is not inferior, but may be superior. For example, beginning with the presumption that women's identities are more organized around the need for affiliations, Miller (1976), calling for a new psychology of women, wrote that "this psychic starting point contains the possibilities for an entirely different and more advanced approach of living and functioning" (p. 83). From another frame of reference, Sherfey (1966), in opposition to Marie Bonaparte's early writings, claimed that the female is more, not less, endowed with libido than the male, in that she is "insatiable."

The nature/nurture controversy is an old and fruitless one, but its shadow falls across the writings about primary femininity. Recently Robbins (1996) intrepidly took up this issue in an essay on the origins of gender differences. He stressed the role of culture and its interaction with biology in the development of gender identity. Neurobiological scientists who investigate gender-related differences in the structure of the brain and in hormonal activities warn about the danger of taking a narrow view, or coming to set conclusions, in interpreting their findings. For example, a review of the research on sex differences in brain organization (Springer and Deutsch 1993) ends by posing a series of questions, which I think would guide psychoanalysts well: Are the differences between males and females real? What is the adaptive advantage of such differences? How does brain organization relate to other patterns of higher mental function? How is brain organization affected by maturation? How do differences in child-rearing practices affect brain asymmetries?

I do not mean by all this to say that I think that the concepts that fall under the umbrella of 'primary femininity' have not advanced our understanding of female sexuality and development. I believe that they have, in spite of the contradictions, inexactitudes, and dilemmas I have found within them. The concepts embraced by this term have proved useful clinically and theoretically, but they need to be clarified and worked out much more carefully and rigorously. Clinically, they have provided us with powerful ways of understanding our female patients that were not possible with our older theories. The danger is that we may repeat the mistakes of the past and not ask the next question, "Where do we go from here?"

REFERENCES

Balsam, R. (1996). The pregnant mother and the body image of the daughter. *J. Amer. Psychoanal. Assn.* 14:401-427.

Benjamin, J. (1988). *The Bonds of Love: Psychoanalysis, Feminism and the Problem of Domination.* New York: Pantheon.

Bernstein, D. (1990). Female Genital Anxieties, Conflicts and Typical Mastery Modes *Int. J. Psycho-Anal.* 71:151–165.

Birksted-Breen, D. (1996). Unconscious Representation of Femininity *J. Amer. Psychoanal. Assn.* 44:*119–132.*

Chehrazi, S. (1986). Female Psychology: A Review *J. Amer. Psychoanal. Assn.* 34: *141–162.*

Chodorow, N. (1978). *The Reproduction of Mothering: Psychoanalysis and the Sociology of Gender.* Berkeley: University of California Press.

——— (1994). *Femininities, Masculinities, Sexualities.* Lexington: University Press of Kentucky.

Chodorow, N. J. (1996). Theoretical Gender and Clinical Gender: Epistemological Reflections on The Psychology of Women. *J. Amer. Psychoanal. Assn.* 44:*215–238.*

Compton, A. (1983). The Current Status of the Psychoanalytic Theory of Instinctual Drives—II: The Relation of the Drive Concept to Structures, Regulatory Principles, and Objects. *Psychoanal Q.* 52:*402–426.*

Deutsch, H. (1982). George Sand: A Woman's Destiny *Int. R. Psycho-Anal.* 9: *447–460.*

Dorsey, D. (1996). Castration Anxiety or Feminine Genital Anxiety? *J. Amer. Psychoanal. Assn.* 44:283–302.

Edgcumbe, R. and Burgner, M. (1975). The Phallic-Narcissistic Phase—A Differentiation Between Preoedipal and Oedipal Aspects of Phallic Development. *Psychoanal. .Study Child* 30:*161–180.*

Elise, D. (1997). Primary femininity, bisexuality, and the female ego ideal: A reexamination of female development theory. *Psychoanal. Q.46:489–517.*

Evert, E. C. (1991). Sexual Integration in Female Adolescence—Anne Frank's Diary as a Study in Healthy Development. *Psychoanal. Study Child. 46:109–124.*

Fast, I. (1979). Developments in Gender Identity: Gender Differentiation in Girls. *Int. J. Psycho-Anal. 60:443–453.*

Fliegel, Z. O. (1973). Feminine Psychosexual Development in Freudian Theory—A Historical Reconstruction. *Psychoanal Q. 42:385–408.*

Foley, H.P. (1994). The Homeric Hymn to Demeter. Princeton: Princeton University Press.

Freud, S. (1925). Some psychical consequences of the anatomical distinction between the sexes. *Standard Edition 19:243–258.*

——— (1933). Femininity. *Standard Edition 22:112–135.*

——— (1937). Analysis terminable and interminable. *Standard Edition 23: 211–253.*

Gilligan, D. (1982). *In a Different Voice.* Cambridge: Harvard University Press.

Glover, L., & Mendell, D. (1982). A suggested developmental sequence for a preoedipal genital phase. In *Early Female Development,* ed. D. Mendell. New York: S.P. Medical and Scientific Books, pp. *127–174.*

Goldberger, M. (1993). Paper presented at the Colloquium on Female Sexuality, Friends of the Michigan Psychoanalytic Institute, Bloomfield Hills.

Greenacre, P. (1950). Special Problems of Early Female Sexual Development. *Psychoanal. Study Child 5:122–138.*

Greenberg, M. (1993). Meeting of the Psychoanalytic Society of New England, East. *Psychoanal Q. 62:519–520.*

Greenson, R. R. (1968). Dis-Identifying from Mother: Its Special Importance for the Boy. *Int. J. Psycho-Anal. 49:370–374.*

Grossman, L. and Renik, O. (1994). Contemporary Theories of Female Sexuality: Clinical Applications. *J. Amer. Psychoanal. Assn.4 2:233–241.*

Grossman, W., & Kaplan, D. (1988). Three commentaries on gender in Freud's thought: A prologue on the psychoanalytic theory of sexuality. In *Fantasy, Myth, and Reality: Essays in honor of Jacob A. Arlow, M.D.,* ed. H.P. Blum, Y. Kramer, A.K. Richards, & A.D. Richards. Madison, CT: International Universities Press, pp. *339–370.*

Herman, N. (1989). Too Long a Child: The Mother-Daughter Dyad. London: Free Association Books.

Hoffman, L. (1996). Freud And Feminine Subjectivity *J. Amer. Psychoanal. Assn.* 44:*23–44*

Horney, K. (1924). On the Genesis of the Castration Complex in Women. *Int. J. Psycho-Anal.* 5:*50–65.*

——— (1926). The flight from womanhood. *Int. J. Psycho-Anal.* 12:*360–374.*

——— (1933). The Denial of the Vagina—A Contribution to the Problem of the Genital Anxieties Specific to Women. *Int. J. Psycho-Anal.* 14:*57–70.*

Iragaray, L. (1994). *Thinking the Difference.* New York: Routledge.

Jones, E. (1927). The Early Development of Female Sexuality *Int. J. Psycho-Anal* .8: *459–472.*

——— (1933). The Phallic Phase *Int. J. Psycho-Anal.* 14:*1–33.*

Kalinich, L. J. (1993). On the Sense of Absence: A Perspective on Womanly Issues Psychoanal Q. 62:206–228.

Keller, E.F. (1985). Reflections on Gender and Science. New Haven: Yale University Press.

Kestenberg, J.S. (1968). Outside and Inside, Male and Female *J. Amer. Psychoanal. Assn.* 16:457–520.

——— (1982). The Inner genital phase: Prephallic and preodipal. In Early Female Development, ed. D. Mendell. New York: S.P. Medical and Scientific Books, pp. *71–126.*

Kubie, L.S. (1974). The Drive to Become Both Sexes *Psychoanal Q.* 43: *349–426.*

Kulish, N. (1991). The Mental Representation of the Clitoris: The Fear of Female Sexuality Psychoanal. Inq. 11:*511–536.*

Lax, R. F. (1994). Aspects of Primary and Secondary Genital Feelings and Anxieties in Girls During the Preoedipal and Early Oedipal Phases *Psychoanal Q.* 63:271–296

Mayer, E.L. (1985). 'Everybody Must be Just Like Me': Observations on Female Castration Anxiety Int. J. Psycho-Anal. 66:331–347.

———. (1995). The Phallic Castration Complex and Primary Femininity: Paired Developmental Lines Toward Female Gender Identity *.J. Amer. Psychoanal. Assn.*43:17–38.

Miller, J.B. (1976). *Toward a New Psychology of Women.* Boston: Beacon Press.

———.(1982). Conflict and psychological development: Women in the family. In *The Woman Patient,* ed. M.T. Notman & C.C. Nadelson. Vol. III. New York: Plenum, pp. *287–299.*

Olesker, W. (1998). Female Genital Anxieties: Views from the Nursery and the Couch. *Psychoanal Q.* 67:

Parens, H. (1980). An Exploration of the Relations of Instinctual Drives and the Symbiosis/separation-Individuation. Process *J. Amer. Psychoanal. Assn.* 28 *89–114*

——— (1990). On the Girl's Psychosexual Development: Reconsiderations Suggested from Direct Observation. *J. Amer. Psychoanal. Assn.* 38:*743–772.*

Person, E., & Ovesey, L. (1983). Psychoanalytic theories of gender identity. *J. Amer. Psychoanal. Assn.* 11:*203–226.*

Renik, O. (1992). A Case of Premenstrual Distress: Bisexual Determinants of a Woman's Fantasy of Damage to her Genital. *J. Amer. Psychoanal. Assn.* 40: *195–210.*

Richards, A.K. (1992). The Influence of Sphincter Control and Genital Sensation on Body Image and Gender Identity in Women. *Psychoanal Q.*61:*331–351.*

——— (1996). Primary Femininity and Female Genital Anxiety. *J. Amer. Psychoanal. Assn.*44:*261–281.*

Robbins, M. (1996). Nature, Nurture, And Core Gender Identity. *J. Amer.* Psychoanal. Assn. 44:93–117.

Roiphe, H., & Galenson, E. (1968). Some suggested revisions concerning early female development. *J. Amer. Psychoanal. Assn* .21(suppl.):*29–57.*

——— & ——— (1981). *Infantile Origins of Sexual Identity.* New York: International University Press.

Shaw, R. (1995). Female genital anxieties: An integration of new and old ideas. *Journal of Clinical Psychoanalysis* 4:*315–329.*

Sherfey, M. J. (1966). The Evolution and Nature of Female Sexuality in Relation to Psychoanalytic Theory. *Amer. Psychoanal. Assn* .14:*28–125.*

Silverman, D.K. (1987). What Are Little Girls Made Of? *Psychoanal. Psychol.*4:*315–334.*

Springer, S., & Deutsch, G. (1993). *Left Brain Right Brain.* New York: W. H. Freeman.

Stoller, R. J. (1968). The Sense of Femaleness. *Psychoanal Q.*.37:*42–55.*

Stoller, R. (1972). The "bedrock" of masculinity and femininity: Bisexuality. In *Psychoanalysis and Women,* ed. J.B. Miller. New York: Penguin, 1973.

——— (1975). Sex and Gender, vol. 2: The Transsexual Experiment. New York: Aronson, 1976.

——— (1976). Primary Femininity. J. Amer. Psychoanal. Assn. 24:59–78

Tyson, P. (1982). A Developmental Line of Gender Identity, Gender Role, and Choice of Love Object. *J. Amer. Psychoanal. Assn.* 30:*61–86.*

———. (1989). Infantile sexuality, gender identity, and obstacles to oedipal progression. *J. Amer. Psychoanal. Assn.* 37:*1050–1069.*

———(1994). Bedrock and Beyond: An Examination of the Clinical Utility of Contemporary Theories of Female Psychology. *J. Amer. Psychoanal. Assn.* 42:447–467.

——— & Tyson, R. (1990). *Gender development: Girls. In Psychoanalytic Theories of Development: An Integration.* New Haven: Yale University Press, pp. *258–276.*

Welldon, E. V. (1988). *Mother Madonna Whore*. New York: Guilford Press.

Wilkinson, S.M. (1993). The Female Genital Dress-Rehearsal: A Prospective Process at the Oedipal Threshold. *Int. J. Psycho-Anal. 74:313–330.*

Yanof, J. A. (1986). The Specter of Genetic Illness and its Effects on Development. *Psychoanal. Study Child 41:561–582.*

CHAPTER 6

Female Sexuality: The Pleasure of Secrets and The Secret of Pleasure

(2002). Psychoanal. Study Child, (57):151–176

Why are secrets so fascinating and pleasurable, especially for little girls? A review of the psychoanalytic literature suggests that the ability to keep a secret represents an important developmental step. This paper proposes that secrets are integral features of female sexuality and that the sharing of secrets is important in how females relate to each other throughout development. It examines the role of sharing secrets in the psychoanalytic process and presents case material of female patients who cherished secrets and for whom the novel *The Secret Garden was a favorite during childhood.*

A few years ago, I stole away from a professional meeting to dash through a beautiful John Singer Sargent exhibition that was touring the country. One large painting, *The Daughters of Edward Darley Biot,* stopped me in my tracks. Four girls, dressed in the prim dresses and starched pinafores of the 1880s, appear to have been caught in a moment of doing nothing. One sitting in the foreground had her eyes averted; another had her hands behind her back; the two in the background were partially obscured by shadows. Their slyly innocent expressions were strange, somehow hinting that they concealed a shared secret. I realized that Sargent had captured an important part of my childhood world. I remembered how it was for a little girl, to have and to share a special secret with a best friend or a small select circle of other girls.

I don't think that I was alone in this; it seems to me that all children, especially little girls, love secrets. A favorite book of mine was *The Secret Garden* by Frances Hodgson Burnett, written in 1911; it is still a favorite of thousands of children. I began to think, as a psychoanalyst, about why is it is that secrets are so fascinating.

A review of the psychoanalytic literature on secrets suggested one possible answer: that the ability to keep a secret represents an important developmental step for children in establishing a sense of separation from adults. But I still wondered why *females* especially might treasure secrets. I have come to believe that secrets are integral features of female sexuality and that sharing secrets is important in how females relate to each other.

In this paper I review the psychoanalytic literature on secrets, discuss the role of secrets in female sexuality and development, and finally, examine briefly the role of sharing secrets in the psychoanalytic process. I present clinical material from the analyses of three adult women who cherished and held on to secrets—sexual secrets. All three also loved *The Secret Garden*.

Psychoanalytic theory and technique from the beginning have been concerned with secrets: unearthing them, interpreting them, and helping patients with them. Our interest has usually been with the darker side—dangerous secrets, guilt-ridden secrets, murderous secrets, incestuous secrets, family secrets. But here I forgo the shady side of secrets, to focus on the pleasurable. It is my thesis that for many women and girls, sexual pleasure must be kept secret, and that it involves for them both the pleasure of secrets and the secret of pleasure.

PSYCHOANALYTIC UNDERSTANDINGS OF SECRETS

From the vast psychoanalytic literature about secrets, I will attempt to distill only what seems pertinent to the questions I have raised here. It is probably safe to say that the whole development of psychoanalysis was stimulated by

Freud's sublimated need to discover the answer to his own family's secrets and the secrets of nature and of sexuality (Barron et al., 1991).

Psychoanalysts view the ability to have a secret as a developmental achievement. Tied to the development of the sense of self, the ability to have a secret implies a sense of inner versus outer space, an established boundary between self and other (Hoyt, 1978; Margolis, 1974; Meares, 1992; Meares and Anderson, 1993).[1] This capacity comes into being around the age of two. It is only when children begin to realize that there are aspects of themselves that they know and others do not—that is to say, *secrets* —that they can feel separate and independent (Margolis, 1966, p. 518). A newly acquired sense of autonomy and independence give the toddler the capacity to say "no" and the choice of whether or not to share and tell thoughts and memories, which are now recognized as inner possessions. A toddler who has gone off to nursery school for the first time may refuse to tell mommy anything about the experience; it has become a proud and secret possession. Greenacre (1960) likened the secret to the fetish; both are transitional objects bridging the gap between object and self, defending against separation anxiety, and ensuring bodily integrity. The newly acquired capacity for secrets is insecure and incomplete, as young children often feel that their parents can read their thoughts.

Hoyt (1978) has said that the child's first lie breaks the tyranny of parental omniscience. Secrets give power. According to Hoyt and many other psychoanalytic writers, the basic dynamic of the secret is anal, giving it up or holding it in. The word "secret" is related to "secretion" (Gross, 1951; Jacobs, 1980). Toilet functions become the basis for the earliest communications around secrets. Perhaps it is this developmental link that gives secrets their inevitable tension: there is always a pull to tell a secret and an opposing pull to keep it (Margolis, 1974).

---

1 Hoyt (1978) points out that the Latin origin of the word "secret" is "secernere," meaning to pull apart, to separate.

In a fascinating pair of papers, Meares (1988, 1992) examined interpersonal interactions with the help of these developmental notions about the importance of the attainment of the concept of secrecy. He argued that knowing that one's thoughts are not accessible to others is the basis of social exchange. In the psychoanalytic situation, an intimate play-like space in which thoughts and secrets are displayed and shared is created between patient and therapist. For people who have not achieved this capacity to share secrets the interplay between inner and outer cannot occur, so they live in non-intimate space, and participation in the psychoanalytic endeavor is very difficult.

The contemporary emphasis on transference/countertransference and intersubjective space leads to a different view of secrets. Secrets may be shared, as in Meares's writings described above, or co-created in unconscious collusion, as in Boesky's (1990) concept of co-created resistance. Caruth (1985) has written that the analyst must listen to her own secrets—her inner responses, feelings, and fantasies about the patient—in order to understand the psychoanalytic situation, and decide whether or not to disclose them in some fashion.

SECRETS AND WOMEN: BODILY SECRETS

There is a ubiquitous tendency to link powerful secrets with women and their sexuality. Innumerable myths and fairy tales across many cultures allude to the hidden secrets held by women. For example, there are the various incarnations of the three female fates, such as the three witches in *Macbeth* dispensing their mysterious predictions. There are the Eleusinian Mysteries, the secret rites to the Goddess Demeter, which were practiced throughout the ancient Greek world to celebrate females' fertility and sexuality (Foley, 1994). Women are depicted as mysterious, and while males often view them with dread, women themselves derive pleasure from their secrets.

150

In "The Taboo of Virginity" (1918), Freud noted the connection between secretiveness and eroticism in female sexuality. He seemed to take this connection as self-evident. To me it is not. So, I will look further abroad for some possible answers, starting with Anne Frank (1993 [1947]), whose diary has taught us all so much about the blossoming of an adolescent girl's sexuality.[2] In the following passage, Anne's body is developing into a woman's:

> *I think that what is happening to me is so wonderful, and not only what can be seen on my body, but all that is taking place inside. I never discuss myself or any of these things with anybody; that is why I have to talk to myself about them. Each time I have a period—and that has only been three times—I have the feeling that in spite of all the pain, unpleasantness and nastiness, I have a sweet secret, and that is why, although it is nothing but a nuisance to me in a way, I always long for the time that I shall feel that secret with me again (p. 130).*

In another passage she expresses her growing sexual feelings toward Peter, her first love:

> *I believe that it's spring within me, I feel spring is awakening, I feel it in my whole body and soul. It is an effort to behave normally…. I only know that I am longing (p. 151).*

In these passages the girl's pleasure in her femininity is obvious, but it is a secret pleasure, a "sweet secret," and the very secret is pleasurable in itself.

---

2 Interestingly, Freud wrote in the preface to another journal, a young girl's diary, by Frau Von Hug-Hellmuth, published in 1919: "the diary is a little gem…. The secret of sexual life begins to dawn on her indistinctly and then takes complete possession of the child's mind…. In the consciousness of her secret knowledge, she at first suffers hurt, but little by little overcomes it" (p. 341).

Part of the secret is an increased positive awareness of the inside of her body, an awareness that is crucial to progressive development for adolescent girls (Dalsimer, 1982). Second, even though Anne has a secret that she feels she must keep inside herself, she is compelled to share it with her diary. I will say more later about the importance of keeping diaries for girls.

Anne Frank tells us that her body contains wonderful secrets. I believe that the configuration and functions of the female body convey powerful, secret-bearing meanings. It is a fact that a woman's body contains sexual openings and that unseen powers lie within its cavities. Within a woman's body lie the secret of giving life and the potential to produce an actual baby (Balsam, 1996).

Women's sexual arousal can be kept hidden and secret within the body. This invisibility lends a woman power; she does not have to "show her hand." The penis betrays its secrets. Perhaps this is the very reason that the penis is not always envied or its lack bemoaned by women. Little girls can masturbate secretly and indirectly, sometimes even not registering the secret to themselves.[3] I am aware, of course, that in a very real sense it has been necessary throughout the ages and across cultures for women to keep their sexual urges secret. When a woman is seen as the property of father and husband, whose honor depends on her chastity, it was, and still is, too often a matter of life and death for her that her sexuality be bound, veiled, hidden.[4]

---

3 I do not mean to imply that men do not have interior sexual feelings for men (see Fogel, 1998), but only that the nature of sexual arousal and pleasure for women has a more secret interiority.

4 Carson (1990), a classical scholar, has written extensively about attitudes in the ancient world toward women and their bodies. Women were perceived as creatures formless by their very natures, who could not or would not maintain their own boundaries and who had tendencies to let themselves go in emotion or appetite. According to Plutarch, for example, "a good woman does not exceed the boundary of her household.... Neither the body nor the speech of a "chaste and sensible" woman is "for the public." Her feelings, character and disposition must be kept hidden. Euripides distinguishes the hidden nature of women's virtue from the public nature of man's: 'the quest for virtue is a great thing: / for women it is a secret quest concerned with love, / but for men, the good order innate in each nature / multiplies to make the city thrive.' a fragment of Sophocles warns women to keep their own shame closely concealed: "cooperate, restrain yourselves in silence: women have an obligation to cover up womanly shame"

From a psychoanalytic perspective, Person (2000) has discussed the power of the weak as a resource left to women. Secrecy is one weapon of such power. In this sense, I will admit that woman's pleasure in secrecy may be making a virtue of a necessity.

I have suggested that most little girls like the fact that they are made the way they are, and that they have the capacity for secret pleasures (Kulish, 1991). Mayer (1985) asserted that a little girl has a narcissistic investment in her body the way it is, in its openness, cavities, holes: she values what she *has* (p. 342). Mayer (1995) also elucidated "female castration anxiety"—that is to say, the female's fear of losing what she values about her own body and its genitals—in contrast to the traditional "penis envy"—anxiety about a missing masculine attribute. "Women are at some level deeply anxious about their own capacities to be feminine; and they ultimately report versions of a fantasy that the capacity to be genitally open … can be endangered, can be lost" (p. 331).

Mayer's ideas have been a valuable contribution to contemporary psychoanalytic understandings of women. An appreciation of the psychology of secrets, however, may have something to add to these notions. I think that it is neither her "hole" nor her "openness" per se that a woman fears to lose. Rather, I think that a woman values the ability to open and to close, to give or not give access, to share her sexual secrets or not. That is, women value not necessarily the thing, the "opening," but rather the capacity to open or not. "Openness" as a character trait is valued, but with the implication of choice, fluidity, and control.

Little girls during the anal stage have not yet sorted out sexual sensations from other bodily sensations (Barnett, 1966; Oliner, 1982; Richards, 1992). Much has been written about how little girls at this age therefore experience their sexual sensations as confusing, undelineated, and in need of control.

(pp. 156-157). The French scholar Sissa (1990) wrote that an unmarried woman in ancient Greece was rigorously forbidden to have an overt sexual life; 'its necessary conditions are dissimulation and secrecy' (p. 347)

Barnett (1966) argues that because the sphincter does not control the vagina, unlike other internal orifices and cavities, the girl does not easily achieve a sense of mastery over its opening and closing. Similarly, Bernstein (1990) conceptualized typical female genital anxieties in terms of fears of diffusivity, penetration, and access. These fears reflect the idea that to the little girl her sexual sensations may seem diffuse, hard to locate within her body, mysterious. I agree that the sense of diffusivity and vulnerability are common female genital anxieties, but I think that this very quality also may carry positive valences. The hiddenness and secretness of their sexual feelings may give girls a sense of power in the ability to keep a secret and to choose to share it or not.

Another link between power and secrecy for women lies in the intensity and power of their sexual feelings. Fears of loss of control often cause little girls to fear the intensity of their sexual impulses. This intensity can become a secret from themselves as well as from others. Men also fear the intensity of female desire, perhaps even more than women do. In an insightful essay, Elise (2000) examines the many reasons, cultural and psychological, that both men and women might wish to hide female desire. Elise suggests that there are specific forms of male and female genital defense. "The male embellishes his sex; the female secretes hers" (p. 136). Elise thinks as I do that a woman may gain power from hiding her sexual desire: "A paradox ensues: woman is kept 'phallically' powerful by appearing not to be so. Everyone has a stake in believing the dissimulation, the masquerade" (p. 137). Elise posits central dynamic for "why women may not want to want": girls need to cover painful early erotic experiences of wanting and not getting the mother.

I have written that the denial and removal of the clitoris reflect the fear of the strength of female desire is also very much a part of the psychology of women as well as of men (Kulish, 1991). Ritual female mutilations and excisions of the clitoris have been practiced in many parts of the world for thousands of years, in the quite conscious belief that the way to keep women's sexuality in line is to cut it out. In addition to being literally excised, the clitoris has gone unnamed in many languages and cultures, perhaps a reflection of the fact that it is the only organ in the body that seems to function solely for pleasure. To name something is to gain power over it, hence, to give it a name is to give girls permission to have sexual desires and to masturbate.[5]

DEVELOPMENTAL SECRETS

Through all stages of development, the need for secrets is tied up with the girl's relationship with her mother. As is suggested in the foregoing discussion, developments during the anal stage give girls added motivation to keep their sexual feelings secret. Secrecy is necessary as a fragile autonomy is being established over the body and bodily functions. Chasseguet-Smirgel (1970) has described how a girl's typical anal struggles with her mother color her fantasies and feelings about her sexuality. Sexual fantasies often must be kept secret from the mother because of their fusion with dangerous anal sadistic impulses.

During the oedipal stage, more reasons are added for sexual secrets. As the girl becomes aware of sexual impulses toward her father, she comes into competition with her mother. This thrusts her into a major conflict of loyalty, between her sexual attraction to her father and her love for, and dependency on, her mother. Because the mother is typically the major caregiver in most families and societies, sexually competitive feelings are perceived as a threat to continued safety and nurturing care. The girl feels, therefore, that she must hide her sexual feelings from her mother. Sexuality, which is seen as belonging to the mother, must be inhibited and driven underground. In my clinical experience, I have observed that women thus experience their sexuality as part of a separate and often secret psychic world.

---

5 The clitoris has also been denied its rightful place in psychoanalytic theory of female development. It was conceptualized as a stunted penis, an enfeebled masculine organ, not as an articulated part of female sexuality.

The myth of Persephone depicts such an underworld, a nether world, separated from the world above. Holtzman and I (1998, 2000) propose that the female's dilemma in the triangular period be called the Persephone Complex rather than the Oedipus Complex because the tale of Persephone better captures the girl's typical conflicts over loyalty and entry into the adult sexual world. The myth tells the story of the maiden, Persephone, who is abducted by Hades, God of the Underworld. Persephone's mother, Demeter, Goddess of Vegetation, searches for her and in her grief and fury causes famine to scorch the earth until a compromise is reached: Persephone is to stay part of the year (summer) with her mother in the world above; for the rest of the year, she is Hades' mate and queen of the world below. Clinical material demonstrates how very frequently this idea of separate worlds—one sexual with a man and one non-sexual with the mother—appears in women's fantasies. The sexual world —the "underworld" is portrayed as more exciting, murky, and mysterious (Holtzman and Kulish, 2000).

Dahl (1989) also emphasizes the need for keeping secrets from the mother as a component of the Oedipus complex. She suggests that the common fantasy of the witch/mother configuration hides two secrets: secret sexual yearnings for the mother, which are disguised by loathing; and the secret that the girl loves her father and in so doing betrays her mother. The girl's oedipal rivalry is projected onto the figure of the vengeful witch.

While there is a need to keep secrets from the mother, there is an equally strong pull to share them. Sharing secrets is part of the closeness between mothers and daughters, among girls, and among women. In latency secrets may help to consolidate gender identity. During this time, boys and girls divide into separate groups for play. These groups often are organized around shared secrets, not to be told to the other sex. During adolescence, girls look to their mothers to hand down to them the secrets of successful womanhood: beauty secrets, secrets for alluring men, secret family recipes, etc. The story "The Secret

Phrase," by Jessamyn West, beautifully illustrates this idea that mothers hold the keys to womanhood:

> *Some day her mother would tell her the secret phrase, the magic sentence—something the other girls already knew. Then the boys would notice her.... "But no one," she mourned, "ever looks at me." ... It's because Mother hasn't told me yet. Something the other girls know. Sometimes she'll tell me—some beautiful word I've been waiting a long time to hear. Then I'll be like a lamp lighted, a flower bloomed (pp. 54-55).*

Adolescent girls search for answers to the secrets of womanhood from other girls. They share with one another their secret "crushes," the details of their first experiments with sex, tips on how to put on make-up or how to be more "popular." An important boyfriend, the girl's first love, may become a new confidant, eclipsing the place of former best friends of the same sex. It is this first love who may hear the girl's cherished dreams for the future or secret troubles in the family.

Gilligan and her colleagues have tracked the common crises girls experience at puberty arguing that the girl's sense of self becomes submerged in the press of strong needs to get along with others. Thus, she often loses her "voice" (Gilligan, 1991). "'Cover up,' girls are told as they reach adolescence, daily, in innumerable ways. Cover your body, cover your feelings, cover your relationships, cover your knowing, cover your voice, and perhaps above all, cover desire. And the walls that keep memory from seeping through these covers may be the wall with the sign which labels body, feelings, relationships, knowing, and voice and desire as bad" (pp. 22–23). This may be true, but secrets are not always experienced as "bad," as I have been arguing. In addition, the sharing of secrets during adolescence helps to forge intimate relationships between friends and loves of the same or opposite sex and helps to consolidate a sense of femininity.

When they get together, women share confidences and secrets as they have done with their best friends since they were little girls and adolescents. (This is not to say that little boys do not like secrets, too; witness their secret rings, codes, hideouts, etc.) The sharing of secrets binds groups of individuals together into sisterhoods or brotherhoods, leaving others out. One very common transference in the female-to-female dyad is the wish to have the analyst/mother initiate the patient into adult womanhood, to share the secrets of how to be a woman or how to be successful at a career and yet remain "feminine." A corresponding pitfall in the countertransference is to try to enact this imparting of secrets, perhaps in an unconscious attempt to be a better or more powerful mother than the patient's mother—or the analyst's—was.

To return to the diary of Anne Frank, Anne found it important and pleasurable to have secrets and to tell no one; at the same time, she told the secrets to her diary. Many adolescent girls keep diaries. It has been suggested that the diary is the unseen other, perhaps a self-object, perhaps the mother with whom the girl is unconsciously talking while at the same time maintaining her separation. (Other famous diaries, such as that of Anais Nin, seem to be aimed at the father, often a lost or absent one.) I would argue that to have a secret paradoxically implies the existence of an other to whom one is or is not telling it. As we have said, the capacity to have and to share a secret depends on a separated sense of self.

THE SECRET GARDEN

This idea of a sequestered secret world of female sexuality can often be discerned in children's stories and myths of hidden rooms or caves holding fabulous treasures: "Rumpelstiltskin" and "Ali Baba and the Forty Thieves" are examples, as is *The Secret Garden*. According to Peller (1958), such themes in children's stories reflect "universal daydreams," which account for the success of these stories. She asserts that in the stories more popular with girls, the secrets concern the heroine and her body personally, as for example in the story of the "little mermaid" and the secret sacrifice of her tongue, by which she can become human and remain near her beloved prince. Secrets figure prominently in boys' stories too, but there they usually are shared by an entire group of boys.

In *The Secret Garden*, a nine-year-old little girl, Mary, has been sent to live with her uncle at the imposing and gloomy Misselthwaite Manor on the English moors. Her parents have both died in colonial India during a cholera epidemic. Mary had been neglected by both parents and raised by servants. She was a disagreeable child, spoiled, ill tempered, and without loving attachments to others. At Misselthwaite she is put in the care of warm and down-to-earth English servants who do not indulge her. The manor is full of many secrets, which Mary slowly begins to discover. The uncle is embittered and deeply depressed by the death of his lovely young wife. His sickly son, Colin, is hidden away in the mansion, neglected by his father, who does not want to be reminded of his lost wife. He is haunted as well by the fear that his son will become a hunchback, like himself.

Colin's character is much like Mary's; he is narcissistic and imperious, and the two children understand each other. Mary comes upon another secret: an overgrown, mysteriously beautiful garden that has been hidden and locked for the ten years since the young mother was accidentally killed by a falling branch. With the help of Dickon, a local boy whom she lets in on the secret, Mary works in the garden to help bring the flowers into bloom. Eventually the two let Colin into the secret, and they furtively convey him to the garden so that he can enjoy its regenerative powers. The garden, over the spring and summer months, becomes full of blossoming flowers, nesting birds, and baby animals. Mary and Colin blossom too; they change from sickly and unhappy children, lacking in human warmth, to happy and healthy individuals. The story ends happily. The uncle is brought out of his depression when he discovers the change in Mary and his son, who can now walk.

The Secret Garden is a tale of regeneration on many levels. Psychoanalysts have seen it as such, and as a metaphor for psychotherapy. According to Pedder (1977), the secret garden, a needed space in which life can grow, is like the potential space that Winnicott (1974) understood to be necessary in the therapeutic relationship. Almond (1990), too, perceives the story as a demonstration of the therapeutic process. In her excellent analysis, she examines the metaphoric meanings of the story and its appeal to pre-pubertal girls. She states that the book deals with the development of sexuality and femininity: "The garden is a sexual metaphor in many ways. It may represent the female genital, a hidden place that must be opened up and planted. It is also a place where feminine roles can be learned and rehearsed. The themes of reproduction and nurturance permeate the scenes that take place within its walls" (p. 493). The following passage illustrates this idea:

> *The seeds Dickon and Mary had planted grew as if fairies had tended them. Satiny poppies of all tints danced in the breeze by the score, gaily defying flowers which had lived in the garden for years and which it might be confessed seemed rather to wonder how such new people had got there. And the roses—the roses! Rising out of the grass, tangled round the sun-dial, wreathing the tree trunks and hanging from their branches, climbing up the walls and spreading over them with long garlands falling in cascades—they came alive day by day, hour by hour. Fair fresh leaves, and buds—and buds—tiny at first but swelling and working magic until they burst and uncurled into cups of scent, delicately spilling themselves over their brims and filling the garden air (p. 236).*

Reading this, we appreciate both the loveliness of the writing and its depiction of a lush feminine fertility.

Orgel (1975) has briefly noted the oedipal significance of the story, which Almond does not stress. He had a female patient who loved *The Secret Garden.*

Orgel felt that the story expressed the patient's fantasy that her father, who died when she was four, would return. These interpretations greatly illuminate the meanings of the book and help to explain its appeal. But above all I think the reader's pleasure in the story comes from the *pleasure* of the little girl's secret. As Ann M. Martin wrote in her introduction to my copy of *The Secret Garden*, "I didn't want to leave. I wanted to visit that house on the moor. I wanted to work in the garden with Mary and Dickon, talk to the robin, and have secrets from the grown-ups. But most of all I wanted to stand up and chant (maybe even shout), 'The Magic is in me!' … as Colin chants, 'The Magic is in me —it's in every one of us.'" It is that magical power of secrets that draws us to this story.

CLINICAL EXAMPLES

The following examples concern three young women, of different backgrounds and dynamics, all of whom kept their sexual pleasure a secret from themselves and others. I will present process material from each case to highlight the meanings of secrets in their psychic lives.

Case 1

Ms. B., a 30-year-old young woman, struggled with two conflicting sides of herself. Her "masculine" side, as she called it, included her love of sports and physical labor, and her profession as a lawyer. The other side, she felt, was the more "feminine" and creative. Her parents had discouraged her artistic endeavors and ambitions as impractical.

Her "feminine" side was also expressed in her love of gardening and her hope to have many children some day. She came into analysis feeling depressed and unfulfilled. Her mother was controlling and ungiving; Ms. B adored her father whom she saw as more loving, although she resented his weakness and seeming inability to stand up to the mother, both for himself and on her behalf.

Her interest in growing things was the opening theme of her analysis. She had noticed some rather bedraggled plants in my waiting room and expressed the worry that I might be like her mother: not nourishing. Thus, we were immediately into her negative maternal transference. The patient was open and introspective, however, and these issues were worked through enough for us to establish a good working relationship. The transference evolved into a more idealized one; she expressed the longing that I could help her straighten out her issues of femininity. She saw me, in contrast to her mother, as someone who could be both feminine and strong. She came to understand that she attributed the masculine, "phallic" power in the family to her mother, a source of confusion for her. She began to reveal some bodily concerns; she felt that her masturbation as a child had damaged her genitals and was responsible for whatever signs of physical weakness she could discern in herself.

With some progress on these issues in the first year of analysis, she was able to make a big change in her life. Despite her parents' disapproval, she gave up her secure and well-paying job to pursue a career as an artist. In the context of a showing of her artwork, she talked about how difficult it had been for her mother to accept her separateness. In the midst of this she remembered her love of the book *The Secret Garden*:

> *In my family, separations are never easy. Like, my mother and aunt won't telephone when they're angry about something. OH! I went to see the movie The Secret Garden this weekend. It was my favorite story as a child. It was neat watching it, thinking why I read it. The idea of people not being there for me, and the influence on how much I love gardening. And how the relationship between the girl and this boy grew in her garden. And the beauty in there. There was also beauty in the growth of the*

boy, Colin. My grandmother gave me the book. She was always there for me. It was she who got me my first set of oils. I called her and told her I saw The Secret Garden and that it was my favorite book. I never told her that. I read it and read it and read it. And then the other thing about it, the important thing, was that there was this secret garden; and the girl had her own space, and she got away from the withered, unhappy, crazy, adult world.

Here *The Secret Garden* represented a sought-after sense of separateness and safety for the self. As a child the patient had gone out alone into her backyard to get this sense of space and peace. She remembered lying on the grass and staring up at the leaves in the trees. But secrets were linked to forbidden sexual pleasures as well.

Two years passed. Ms. B. made a happy marriage and became pregnant. She began talking about sexual concerns not dealt with before. In the session I will report, she began by describing her campaign to clean up and re-do her house before the baby's birth.

I suggested, "You want to have your house literally, and maybe symbolically, in order."

Patient: "Oh, like my body."

Analyst: "Your body, yourself, your house."

After a thoughtful pause, Ms. B reported that her relationship with her mother had improved. In recent conversations her mother had shared her own experiences with a hired nurse after her babies were born. The patient felt somewhat critical of her mother for hiring a nurse, but said: "I don't want to be too hard on her. And all this sexual stuff that we've been talking about … I was thinking about that, and reaching to it. About how I worried about being caught at masturbation. Hiding it from my mother."

When I asked her thoughts about this, she replied,

It seems so classic—my mom got so angry a lot. I only have that one experience with my father getting angry, at the chocolate-covered cherry. [This was a highly charged memory. Her father had brought home a special present of chocolate-covered cherries when she was five. She bit into one, and the filling squirted on him, making him angry.] And the time I kissed him on the lips, and he got kind of angry, I think. I don't remember much being attracted to him. Although once he was wearing thin pj's and I remember trying to see through them.... Ah ... Fantasies ... And feeling I was doing something wrong all the time with my masturbation.

I said, "Do you mean you felt guilty about the masturbation or the fantasies that went with it?"

The patient, in a different, somewhat strained tone: "I don't remember what they were."

In retrospect, it appears that she might have experienced me as intrusive and prying, like the controlling critical mother in the transference, but at the time I did not recognize this enactment. The patient's denial following my question suggests that in this context she needed to keep her fantasies secret from me.

She then switched to thoughts about the prohibition of masturbation:

I asked my mom about masturbation that one time. And she said I probably shouldn't do it anymore. In nursery school there was this boy. I liked him. I was stimulated a lot at that time. Masturbated a lot. One day I was chosen to be leader for the day. I didn't know what to do, how to be a teacher. But there was an excitement about being the leader. Pride in it. I like to think about those memories. They're positive. Like camp. Accomplishments. And I feel so good about them. But with my mother I had to cover everything up. I was supposed to play second fiddle. Masturbation was something I did on my own, a secret, and I liked it.

The session ended with the patient's declaring, "Being pregnant. It's something I do. Me, and nobody else!"

In the weeks following this session, she had frequent dreams of summer camp, which she had loved. There had been a sense of freedom there, and some sexual experimentation. In one dream was the idea of "tricking." The patient did not associate to the usual meaning of tricking: "Tricking. That reminds me of my status in comparison to my mother. I remember going out the window onto our roof and smoking. It was my greatest pleasure. My secret spot. A sense of freedom related to camp stuff, too."

Here "secret spot" referred to a place, a secret garden to which she could escape. It also meant a place in her mind where she could be free to find and express herself, separate from her mother or others. It obviously referred to the body and her genitals as well—the "secret spot" in which she could find pleasure. Being pregnant brought her into the competitive arena with her mother and at the same time stimulated sexual conflicts from childhood. The sexual secrets that she needed to keep included her masturbation itself, and, more importantly, the fantasies that accompanied it. Her associations to the little boy she liked in kindergarten, playing "second fiddle," and the early, sexually tinged memories of her father suggest that her tacit masturbation fantasies concerned oedipal wishes and rivalry with her mother. She kept secret her sexual pleasure itself, as well as the pleasure she took in her inner mental life. Within the transference to me, now experienced as the rival, threatening mother, she had renewed reason to hide her sexual fantasies and pleasures.

Shortly before she terminated her analysis Ms. B had an important showing of her paintings, which was held in a public arena. She expressed the wish that I visit the show, as I had never seen her work. I did so and was deeply moved and impressed. There were beautiful, bright, and boldly sensual paintings of gardens and flowers, done in an abstract style. Now she chose to share with me (and the public) her passion-filled fantasies, no longer secret.

Case 2

Mrs. A began analysis as a phobic, sexually inhibited woman who had spent years in a sexless marriage. She came from a strictly religious home. Her father was stern and strict; her mother more permissive, but competitive with her. An important screen memory at age three was of gleefully dressing up in her mother's clothes and painting herself with mother's make-up. When she paraded in front of her father, the child was devastated by his response. Demanding that she take off her finery, he pronounced: "No daughter of mine will be a slut!"

In adolescence, as she struggled to separate from her mother, she had alternated between somewhat rebellious behavior, such as flirting with boys, and an anxious reliance on her mother for guidance. When she was about thirteen, she had a nighttime ritual of slipping notes under her mother's pillow on which she would write secret "confessions." Looking back, Mrs. A realized that these "secrets" were totally innocuous confessions of minor misdeeds, such as skipping a chore or being a little late. We understood them retrospectively as a defensive maneuver to get around her superego; that is, she would confess little sins in order to prompt an instant pardon from her mother. The slips were offered up as small tokens to appease her conscience. I think that these nightly confessions were akin to the diary-keeping of young adolescent girls. In this instance, however, the patient had not separated enough from her mother to keep her thoughts totally secret from her and locked in a diary.

Shortly after she began treatment Mrs. A's marriage ended. Years followed in which she hid out at home alone. Early on she talked of her resentment toward the men in her life and her jealousy of their power and freedom. She wallowed in her sense of inferiority to men and was quite willing to talk about "penis envy." As she began to understand and overcome her phobias, she began to show some interest in changing her lonely, but safe, existence.

She came into one session bemoaning her fear of entering the dating scene.

166

She declared that she felt she was walking around with a scarlet letter "U" for "Uptight" on her chest. I remarked that the scarlet letter was not "U," but "A" for "Adultery." This infuriated her, but in subsequent sessions she struggled with new revelations and insights.

She recounted with great difficulty the tale of an adulterous affair she had had early in her marriage, over which she had long suffered in secret. Next, she began to talk about her daughter, who was born some time after the affair and who had a birth defect. In reality she knew the child was her husband's, but she recalled that at the time she had harbored painful fantasies that the baby was the fruit of her affair.

In one session Mrs. A reported that she had gone to a parent-teacher conference and had been aware of feeling defensive and anxious. As she talked in the session, she realized that she felt that her daughter was the embodiment of her sin and that the child's deficit was her punishment, her scarlet letter. She broke down sobbing in an agony of guilt and pain. In subsequent sessions, she also came to see that she felt her painful and humiliating gynecological difficulties were also punishments for this sexual misdeed, as well as for earlier ones in childhood. She unconsciously felt that she had had to punish herself for the affair by cutting off her sexual feelings forever. "*It wouldn't have been so bad if I hadn't enjoyed it!*" she cried.

She summarized her growing understanding: "So underneath I'm not uptight but interested?" She began to remember how she felt very pretty when she was younger. She loved being the center of men's interest. She confessed that she enjoyed the feeling of power her sexual attractiveness and her sexuality gave her over men. She said, "I think I feel this anxiety about what I suspect I might be. I might be a *very sexual woman.*" She went on to talk of her fears of "going hog wild" if she were to release her inhibitions. Perhaps she would become promiscuous, a prostitute, turn to kinky sex, etc. Thus, inhibition and a feeling of inferiority served as a defense against her sexuality, which frightened her by its intensity, its anal-like, out-of-control meanings, and its oedipal, incestuous associations. Experiences such as her father's calling her a slut provided the background for this little-girl feeling that her sexual impulses were unacceptable and bad. She felt inferior as a female and envious of her brothers. Nevertheless, the "penis envy" covered over other, and presumably more basic, fears that she had about the wildness and intensity of her female sexual desires.

After this she dreamed of going around and around on a ferris wheel in an amusement park she had enjoyed visiting as a pubescent girl. Her associations led to ideas of long-lost pleasures, which I interpreted as buried sexual feelings. As she approached the end of her analysis, Mrs. A told me that she was contemplating ordering some new books. One was *The Joy of Sex*; the other she described as "a new book full of woman's fantasies," referring to Nancy Friday's contemporary work entitled *The Secret Garden*. That night she had a long dream. In it is a male stranger with whom she had a long-forgotten sexual relationship in the past. She is outside, and it is hot and dry. She starts watering the lawn, which is suddenly covered with brilliant flowers. "The flowers, they were in all different stages of growth. I guess that equals my growth. I like flowers. If I were a princess, I'd always have cut flowers around. And lots of flowers in gardens."

She dreams of gardens of flowers and forgotten love as she is getting in touch with her repressed—secret—sexual longings and pleasures. A neglected garden is rejuvenated, as in *The Secret Garden*. The basic secret in this case was the secret of intense sexual pleasure, consciously felt to be sinful. Remember the patient's words, "It would not have been so had if I had not enjoyed it." The secret of adultery covered another, the secret of pleasure and the sense of power her sexuality gave her over men.

Case 3

Mrs. S.'s entire life, personality, and analysis were dominated by secrets. A teacher in her thirties, she was married with no children. She had come into treatment on the recommendation of her psychiatrist. Medication had provided some relief for her long-standing depression and her tormenting obsessive thoughts. She announced that she was very much interested in the idea of exploring and trying to understand her problems.

The following history emerged slowly in the treatment. Mrs. S came from a prominent family in which appearances were important. She and her siblings were well dressed and well behaved, and were expected to do very well in the private schools to which they were sent. They were paraded with shining faces and immaculate clothes to church every Sunday. They were told that they were better than other people and that their background made them special. Until her analysis was under way, Mrs. S had bought into this myth and believed that hers was indeed a very happy and superior family. However, although this was never acknowledged, both parents were alcoholics who fought bitterly with each other. The older children were especially teasing and unkind toward the younger ones. Her mother became increasingly unable to care for her, and both parents eventually died of complications of alcoholism. Another shameful secret that Mrs. S divulged was that she too had abused alcohol and other drugs and had been sexually promiscuous when she was a teenager and young adult. In the present, she was sexually inhibited and found sex with her husband distasteful.

Besides the family alcoholism, Mrs. S revealed with great shame that an older brother had molested her from the time she was about seven until the age of about nine. A further family secret erupted in her adulthood when her father was accused of sexual abuse by several of her nieces. This accusation, which Mrs. S tried hard to deny, later reverberated in the analysis in the form

169

of wondering whether he might have abused her as well when she was very young, perhaps before the age of three.

Digging for hidden treasure had been a passion for the patient since she was a little girl. As a very young child she began almost compulsively to dig in the earth, hoping to find something buried, she knew not what. She also hid things, all kinds of things, in nooks and crannies—little toys within the bodies of other toy animals, bits of pretty ribbon or pebbles tucked away in pockets. Like many little girls, she loved tiny containers that held her specially treasured possessions and discoveries. She had always loved gardening, and this pleasure grew into an adult passion. She had a best girlfriend with whom she shared secrets and played out games about mysteries. She, too, loved reading and especially the book *The Secret Garden.*

In a delightful paper, Fraiberg (1954) suggested multiple symbolic meanings of buried treasure in myths and children's tales. Buried treasures or secrets could represent an embryo or fetus, a hidden phallus, or solving the puzzle of procreation. I found with Mrs. S that the need to dig had many of these meanings: oral, anal, phallic, and genital.

Mrs. S also had another passionate hobby: genealogy. She spent many hours researching her family history on both sides and constructing a family tree. She was surprised to find that her parents had told her many fictions. Their background was neither aristocratic nor especially heroic but, as one might expect, ordinary, with ordinary problems.

It is not surprising that with these predilections for exploring and digging, Mrs. S would be drawn to psychoanalysis. It is also not surprising that the process of unearthing her personal history was not free from conflict or anxiety. As we have seen, secrets exert at the same time a pull to be revealed and also a pull to be concealed. In a very real sense, the course of Mrs. S's analysis could be described as a tension between these pulls. The following excerpts from some sessions provide a flavor of this struggle, as well as of the sexual meaning of certain secrets to this woman. There was hardly a session in which material about secrets did not appear.

The following dream occurred in the first year of analysis, as Mrs. S was struggling to answer for herself the question of whether she had been sexually violated:

I had the worst night's sleep ever, or yet. This is getting terrible. Fragments of dreams. One I made myself remember. Where did this thing start and end? It involved violence. Somebody's son was being charged with something sexual, criminal sexual conduct.... I got involved as an outsider. Also, a father involved. Then I was sitting at a table with two women fiddling with clay. The woman on my right was talking about how she had been physically abused by a man. [The patient sits to my right.] The other was someone who worked with domestic violence and was helping her. While she was talking I made two rings for myself and told how a boyfriend in college had physically abused me. One ring was being molded into a mouse. The other was for my finger. I wanted to roll jewels and tiny little shiny things into it. That reminds me of course of my toy mouse that I sewed inside my stuffed dog. I said to myself, I have to remember that dream.

A secret. Related to violence? Keeping my mouse safe. The son in the dream, would that be my brother? The father—would that be my dad?

I don't know why rings. Shiny jewels. You have to hollow out the center. Well, that has to do with sex. To make it prettier, nicer, not ugly.

I commented that in the dream Mrs. S seemed to be expressing the wish that she were an outsider to the sexual abuse or violence that was going on in a family—Mrs. S. nodded—and that she wished that she would be safe, and not be hurt.

171

Yes, that I'd be safe. I wanted to protect the mouse, like I wish my mother had protected me. I had thought about my mother yesterday after here. It is painful to say that she wasn't a warm mother.... Yesterday you asked about maybe did I want to be closer to you. It was hard for me to see that. It's hard for me to acknowledge any attachment toward anybody except toward animals. It's not safe. Like Monday you were sick. OK, I might have some worries about that. But more what if you changed.

(She had been talking earlier about how her mother had deteriorated over the years.)

I said, "So it's not safe here. Like with your mother, I might not protect you." She nodded apprehensively.

Here the patient was struggling with dangerous and frightening secrets.

At the same time, though, the hiding and keeping of the secrets offered some solace and safety. The difficult process of sharing secrets with the analyst, depicted in the dream—two women, sitting and talking while fiddling with clay —provided relief.

A year later in the treatment brought a shift toward more pleasure in the secrets and the beginning of a more positive, albeit still conflicted, view of her femininity and sexuality. The patient had gotten a good new job, which she enjoyed and did well at. She began a session talking excitedly about it. Then she began musing:

I was thinking about treasures, and jewelry, and candy, how I group them together. Colorful, tempting, forbidden. Things I wanted—my mother's necklace, cotton candy. I kept everything in boxes ... a box of balsa wood. I felt it was so neat. Little tins I had too. I still have that urge. I saved everything. I even had a pencil lead collection for the little pieces of lead that came off the pencils when the kids sharpened their pencils. [She laughed.] It was so intriguing in my little box. I would make a collection

172

of containers. There must be something to it. I don't know—an outside and an inside. Special. You don't know what's in the box, what's inside, unless you open it up. Then there could be a beautiful, enameled container with a dog's rotten tooth that could be inside, or tiny little seashells. You don't know.

I asked, "Fantasies about what might be inside yourself, your body?" "Yes," she said thoughtfully, and went on:

A feminine symbol, I think. There could be anything from something pretty or colorful to something ugly. There was something secretive about these boxes. Some kind of comfort in opening my little boxes. A hiding place only I would know and then I could dig it up. A fascination really. Wanting, wanting. That's what it's about, some more little boxes with the inside nobody sees.

It's kind of the same thing as existing if nobody sees you. If you can't see in then there's really space. I'm fascinated by that and always was. The space must be a feminine symbol, but my uterus isn't as nice as all these little boxes. [Why?] "Fleshy, ugly, bloody. Though, as a kid, I was fascinated about the inside of an egg, that there was an air sac. [Wanting to know, to have?] That's it!

The patient went on to describe the origins of her interest in science and philosophy: "I can see how it's all fascinating. And I still am fascinated by how seeds sprout... but even now with my interests, I feel more like a child than an adult."

A year later Mrs. S was speaking of her emerging wish for a baby and how she had always felt she had to keep such wishes hidden from her mother. Then she said, "I wanted to tell you about how I saw this beautiful garden on my trip. The garden was perfect. There were little figurines hidden, rabbits, here and there. Going there made something come alive in me, like warmth and closeness might actually be possible." She paused briefly, then, tentatively, said, "I guess there is a wish to be sensual, along with warmth and softness. But I see how guarded, afraid of feelings, I am."

Like Mary in *The Secret Garden*, Mrs. S was finding regeneration, sensuality, and the possibility of human connectedness in the thought of a beautiful garden that she has discovered within herself. She tells us clearly that secret gardens are feminine, fertile, and rich with pleasures.

DISCUSSION AND CONCLUSION

All three of these women, especially the latter two, were inhibited sexually. All three had difficulties with self-expression in general. All three perceived assertiveness as masculine. Thus, acquiring a sense of agency over sexuality and a positive feeling about femininity was complicated and difficult for them. All three women were aware of and more comfortable with an image of themselves as inhibited and sexless rather than passionate and assertive. By that stance they defended against pleasure in their feminine selves and in their sexuality. The experience of sexual pleasure had to be kept secret, and the secret itself became a hidden source of pleasure, of unconscious control over self, and of power over others. In my experience, many female patients share these dynamics.

At the end of his life Freud (1937) concluded that elucidating penis envy was the endpoint in the analyses of women. Yet we have seen in these cases that penis envy or a "masculine protest" was used defensively and covered over intense fears about the strength of feminine desire and sexual pleasure. Current psychoanalytic thinking does not conceive of the analytic endeavor as an archeological dig, with any given complex of ideas as bedrock. The mind is no longer considered a neatly layered set of unconscious complexes, each a defense against the one below. Contemporary analytic technique can be better captured by ecological metaphors of interaction, context, and balance. These three cases illustrate that the aim and focus of action in therapy are not simply to divine the content of a secret but, more importantly, the process of sharing it.

Feminine sexual pleasure often must be kept secret because it is associated with danger or because it is forbidden. My point is that keeping sexual secrets is also a source of pleasure for women. In contrast to the early psychoanalytic theories about females, which conceived of female psychology as organized around the sense of a lack, or as a masculinity that needed to be relinquished, contemporary psychoanalytic thinking has stressed that females value their bodies, their femaleness, and their sexual capacities. I am old-fashioned enough to continue to believe that bodies are important, that feminine identity is not constructed by societal expectations alone but also by the meanings the individual female gives to her body, with its secret cavities, mysterious powers, and awe-inspiring creative potentials. These powerful bodily secrets are cherished and valued by females. Sharing secrets binds women with each other and gives them deep comfort.

We might be able to trace a developmental line for secrets, with different meanings, contents, and ways of being handled at each stage of development. At the stage of separation/individuation the ability to distinguish inner from outer space, and hence a rudimentary sense of inner secrets forms. During the anal phase, negotiations over bodily exchanges between mother and toddler become secrets to be withheld or shared. Moving into the oedipal phase, the child discovers sexual secrets and embraces within herself secret fantasies and pleasures. During the latency or school-age years, secrets shared among little girls help in the consolidation of gender identity. Adolescence intensifies the power of sexual secrets and the need to share them to solidify a sense of gender identity as a mature sexual woman. Throughout, secrets are important interpersonal transactions for girls with their mothers and other females. The developmental lines may also be different for boys and girls. I would speculate that boys' secrets might have different contents, meanings, and interpersonal functions than those of girls.

175

"We are experiencing major cultural changes these days in attitudes toward female sexuality. Women in this society certainly are allowed much more sexual freedom than in the past. Pop culture allows the display of images of women lustily pursuing sexual pleasure. Will the need for and pleasure in secrets in women and girls fade with these changes in contemporary culture? As Person (2000) suggests, changes in cultural attitudes are slow to filter down to the individual mind. Given the powerful influence of the body and the common recurring and secret-promoting psychodynamics within families and between mother and daughters that promote secrets, I wonder. In the meantime, *The Secret Garden* continues to delight millions.

REFERENCES

Almond B. (1990). The secret garden: A therapeutic metaphor. *Psychoanal. St. Child*, 45:*218–241*.

Assad, M. B. (1980). Female circumcision in Egypt: Social implications, current research, and prospects for change. *Studies in Family Planning*, 11:*3–16*.

Balsam, R. (1996). The pregnant mother and the body image of the daughter. *JAPA*. 44/suppl.:*401–427*.

Barnett, M. (1966). Vaginal awareness in the infancy and childhood of girls. *JAPA*14:*129–140*.

Barron, J. W., Beaumont, R., Goldsmith, G. N., Good, M. I., Pyles, R. L., Rizzuto, A., Smith, H. F. (1991). Sigmund Freud: the secrets of nature and the nature of secrets. *Int. J. Psycho-Anal.*18:*143–163*.

Bernstein, D. (1990). Female genital anxieties, conflicts, and typical mastery modes. *Int. J. Psycho-Anal.*71:*151–165*.

Boesky, D. (1990). The psychoanalytic process and its components. *Psychoanal.*

Burnett, F. H. (1999). *The Secret Garden*. New York: Scholastic. Original (1911) New York: Dell.

Carson, A. (1990). Putting her in her place: woman, dirt and desire. In *Before Sexuality,* eds. D. M. Halperin, J. J. Winkler, & F. I. Zeitlin. Princeton: Princeton U. Press, pp. *135–169.*

Caruth, A. (1985). Secret bearer or secret bearer: Countertransference and the gossiping therapist. *Contemp. Psychoanal.,* 21:*548–561.*

Chasseguet-Smirgel, J. (1970). Feminine guilt and the Oedipus complex. In *Female Sexuality: New Psychoanalytic Views,* ed. J. Chasseguet-Smirgel. Ann Arbor: University of Michigan Press, Pp. *94–134.*

Dahl, E. K. (1989). Daughters and mothers: Oedipal aspects of the witchmother. *Psychoanal. St. Child,* 44:*267–280.*

Dalsimer, K. (1982). Female adolescent development: A study of The Diary of Anne Frank. *Psychoanal. St. Child,* 37:*487–522.*

Elise, D. (2000). Woman and desire: why women may not want to want. *Stud. Gend. Sex.,* 1:*125–145.*

Fogel, G. I. (1998). Interiority and inner genital space in men: What else men can lose in castration. *Psychoanal. Q.*67:*662–697.*

Foley, H. P. (1994). *The Homeric Hymn to Demeter.* Princeton: Princeton University Press.

Fraiberg, S. (1954). Tales of the discovery of the secret treasure. *Psychoanal. St. Child,* 9:*218–241.*

Frank, A. (1993 [1947]). *The Diary of a Young Girl.* New York: Bantam Books.

Freud, S. (1918). The taboo of virginity.*S.E.,* 11:*191–208.*

——— (1919). Letter to Dr. Hermaine Von Hug-Hellmuth.*S.E.,* 14:*341.*

——— (1937). Analysis terminable and interminable.*S.E.,* 23:*211–253.*

Gilligan, C. (1991). *Women, Girls, and Psychotherapy: Reframing Resistance.* New York: Haworth.

Greenacre, P. (1960). Further notes on fetishism. *Psychoanal. St. Child,* 15:*191–207.*

Gross, A. (1951). The secret. *Bull. Mennin. Clinic.,* 15:*37–44.*

Holtzman, D., & Kulish, N. (2000). The feminization of the female oedipal complex, Part 1: separation issues. *JAPA*, 48:*1413–1437*.

Hoyt, M. (1978). Secrets in psychotherapy: Theoretical and practical considerations. *Int. Rev. Psycho-Anal.5:231–241*.

Jacobs, T. (1980). Secrets, alliances, and family fictions: Some psychoanalytic observations. *JAPA*, 28:*21–41*.

Kilmurray, E., & Ormond, R. (1999). *John Singer Sargent*. Washington, D.C.: National Gallery of Art.

Kulish, N. (1991). The mental representation of the clitoris: The fear of female sexuality. *Psychoanal. Inq.*, 11:*511–536*.

——— & Holtzman, D. (1998). Persephone, the loss of virginity and the female oedipal complex. *Int. J. Psycho-Anal.79*: pp. *57–71*.

Lightfoot-Klein, H. (1989). Prisoners of Ritual. An Odyssey into Female Genital Circumcision in Africa. New York: Harrington Park Press.

Margolis, G. (1966). Secrecy and identity. *Int. J. Psycho-Anal.47:517–522*.

——— (1974). The psychology of keeping secrets. *Int. Rev. Psycho-Anal.*1: *291–296*.

Mayer, E. (1985). Everybody must be just like me. *Int. J. Psycho-Anal.66: 331–348*.

——— (1995). The phallic castration complex and primary femininity: Paired developmental lines toward female gender identity. *JAPA*, 43:*17–38*.

Meares, R. (1988). The secret, lies and the paranoid process. *Contemp. Psychoanal .24:650–666*.

——— (1992). Transference and the play space: Towards a new basic metaphor. *Contemp. Psychoanal.28:32–49*.

——— & Anderson, J. (19 93). Intimate space: On the developmental significance of exchange. *Contemp. Psychoanal.29:595–612*.

Oliner, M. M. (1982). The anal phase. In Early Female Development. Current Psychoanalytic Views, ed. D. Mendell. New York: Spectrum, pp. *25–60*.

Orgel, S. (1975). Split object choice. *Psychoanal. Q.44:266–288*.

Pedder, J. (1977). The role of space and location in psychotherapy, play and theatre. *Int. Rev. Psycho-Anal.4:215–223*.

Peller, L. (1958). Reading and daydreams in latency, boy-girl differences. *JAPA*, 6:*57–70*.

Person, E. S. (2000). Issues of power and aggression in women. Paper presented at the Dec. meetings of the American Psychoanalytic Association, New York.

Richards, A. K. (1992). The influence of sphincter control and genital sensation on body image and gender identity in women. *Psychoanal. Q*.61:*331–351*.

Rustin, M. (1985). The social organization of secrets: towards a sociology of psychoanalysis. *Int. Rev. Psycho-Anal.*12:*143–158*.

Sissa, G. (1990). Maidenhood without maidenhead: the female body in ancient Greece. In *Before Sexuality,* eds. D. M. Halperin, J. J. Winkler, & F. I. Zeitlin. Princeton: Princeton Univ. Press, Pp. *337–364*.

West, J. (1953). The secret phrase. In *I'm On My Way Running,* eds. L. Reese, J. Wilkinson, & P. S. Koppelman (1983). New York: Avon, pp. *52–57*.

Winnicott, D. W. (1974). *Playing and Reality.* Harmondsworth: Penguin.

CHAPTER 7:

Frida Kahlo and Object Choice: A Daughter the Rest of Her Life

(2006). Psychoanal. Inq., (26)(1):7–31

I argue that the entry into the triangular "oedipal" situation for girls does not necessitate a change in object, as Freud proposed, but an addition of object. My argument rests on different strands in contemporary psychoanalytic thinking: an appreciation of the complexity of internal objects, a reconsideration of the concept of bisexuality, an understanding of the role of multiple identifications in gender identity and object choice, and a reexamination of the triangular situation for girls. I focus on the life of Frida Kahlo—as revealed in biographies, journals, and art—to elucidate the layering of internal object choices. I conclude that object choice—heterosexual, homosexual, or bisexual—represents a composite or compromise formation.

When a man marries he gets him a wife, but a daughter's a daughter the rest of her life." Although this saying refers to familial relationships and the idea that a girl remains close to her mother even after she marries, it reflects the intrapsychic world as well. It implies that a daughter remains more tied to her mother internally than does a son. Indeed, psychoanalytic formulations of female development have contained such ideas that girls have more difficulty separating from their mothers and reaching sexual maturity.

According to Freud's (1908) early formulations of female development, the path into the triangular "oedipal" phase for the girl is a tortured one, starting from an inborn masculinity to a hard-won femininity. Freud believed that to find her way into the "normal" Oedipal Complex and hetero-sexuality three changes must occur for the girl: of sexual organ, aim, and object. She must abandon pleasures from the "masculine" clitoris; she must convert a phallic, masculine orientation to a more passive feminine one; and finally, she must renounce her original sexual object, the mother, for the father. What drives this development is the girl's discovery of sexual difference and her envy of the penis. In his 1916 "Some Character Types Met with in Psychoanalytic Work," Freud delineated the psychological consequences of the girl's penis envy: wounded narcissism, a lasting sense of inferiority, character traits of persistent jealousy, and deep resentment against her mother. I will argue that the entry into the triangular oedipal situation for girls does not necessitate a change in object, as Freud proposed, but an addition of object. That is, girls retain their desires toward their mothers, and they add other objects—male or female. This point is often missed, because libidinal attachments that girls hold toward their mothers are very often embedded and camouflaged in their attitudes and orientation toward male objects. This idea of multiple layers of internal objects or the complexity of object choice is stressed by contemporary psychoanalytic approaches.

REVIEW OF THE LITERATURE

Over the years, many psychoanalytic writers have questioned the sequence of female psychosexual development as originally laid down by Freud. In reviewing the literature, I will briefly address only those arguments that I believe have relevance for the issue of change of object. Among the important considerations are the timing of the discovery of sexual differences, the role of penis envy, the understanding of the importance of maternal identifications, considerations of bisexuality, and the nature of the female triangular situation.

Starting from the false premise that little girls' original sexuality was masculine, Freud had to find explanations for their eventual femininity and entry into the oedipal phase. His logic, in keeping with clinical observations of female envy toward men, provided an internally logical, step-by-step sequence. The first step in this progression was the girl's discovery of her "castration," her subsequent sense of lack and penis envy, resulting in her turning away from her mother in anger and disappointment and toward the father to gain compensation for her missing penis via the promise of a baby. Thus, castration impelled her into the oedipal situation but left her there. Being already "castrated," she lacked the motivation to resolve the oedipal conflicts compared with the boy. The boy's castration anxiety was formulated as what motivated him to give up his incestuous wishes, identify with his rival, the father, and move out of the oedipal phase.

A long series of psychoanalytic works, based on clinical and observational research, has challenged this sequence as erroneous and skewed (Chehrazi, 1986). To begin with, the timing of children's discovery of sexual difference is much earlier than Freud thought—eighteen months not three or four years of age (Kleeman, 1976). Thus, the discovery of the sexual difference that was thought to trigger the chain of events leading to triangulation would occur several years before the oedipal phase was thought to commence. Secondly, the role of penis envy in girl's development has been extensively rethought and reformulated. Although subsequent analysts have observed penis envy clinically, they have, from the beginning, disagreed about its primacy and its role in change of object and initiation of the Oedipus Complex. Early on, Horney (1924) asserted that the girl's inferiority complex and penis envy were secondary and culturally based. Through the years, many others have offered rich clinical understandings of the role of penis envy, which puts it in a different perspective vis à vis the developmental sequence for the girl (Lerner, 1976).

Most clinicians have linked penis envy to problems the girl might have with her mother and conceptualize it not as inevitable or a necessary cog in a stepwise schema but as a passing experience in childhood. Penis envy will become prominent or fixed if there are particular forces within the family constellation, such as the birth of a baby brother, favoritism toward males, or problems in the mother-daughter relationship that reinforce it. Chasseguet-Smirgel (1970), for instance, focused on the anal-sadistic struggles between mother and daughter that nourish the girl's fantasy of mother's castrating, controlling powers and defensive idealization and envy of the paternal phallus. Frenkel (1996), in an article expressly dealing with object choice in women, presented clinical material of women and girls that demonstrated that penis envy was pathological and did not contribute to a shift in object choice to father. It is commonly agreed now that in "normal" development, the psychological consequences of penis envy that Freud originally described would more likely impede triangular development than advance it. In an influential article, Grossman and Stewart (1976) emphasized the need to analyze the meanings and functions of penis envy, when it is observed, rather than taking it as "bedrock."

Others also have questioned the inevitability of the sequence described by Freud, and further elaborated by Nagera (1975), which pictured the girl as going through a period, the so-called "negative oedipal" phase preceding the "positive oedipal" phase; that is, of first the loving mother as a phallic boy might before she turns to her father. According to Anna Freud (1965, p. 196), the negative Oedipus Complex represents a normal "homosexual" phase in the life of both boys and girls. Edgecumbe and colleagues (1976) doubted whether a negative oedipal phase is a necessary step in normal female development. In their clinical research, they found that what is described as a negative oedipal constellation may actually be considered an arrest at, or regression to, the preoedipal phallic narcissistic level characterized by dyadic object relationships.

The Kleinians, and those closely influenced by them, have offered different theories about the impetus for the male and female child's entry into the oedipal drama (Britton, et al., 1989). For them, the oedipal situation rests on a primitive unconscious awareness of the primal scene, known to the child much earlier than posited by Freud. Thus, there was no need to put forward a complicated explanation of how the girl finds her way into the oedipal situation. According to Klein (1928), primitive oedipal fantasies colored by oral sadism make their appearance in the first two years of life as a consequence of frustration by the mother. The acuteness of the ambivalence, the predominance of oral trends, and the uncertain choice of the love object characterize the Kleinian conceptualization of the very early stage of the Oedipal Complex. Segal (1974) noted the rudimentary dawning of oedipal dynamics as the infant becomes aware of the important link that exists between the father and mother. In a Kleinian tradition, Jones (1933) described very young girls' fearful fantasies of rape by their fathers, giving evidence of their projected oedipal desires.

Conversely, many analytic traditions still cling closely to essential aspects of Freud's ideas about the course of female development. Like Freud, Lacanians give primacy to the concept of a change in object. The French Lacanian analyst, Hamon (2000), posed the question, "Why do women love men and not their mothers?" The question itself reveals a theoretical assumption: that is, that girls start out with their mothers as primary objects so that there is a need to explain how they end up desiring their fathers. Hamon traced the contributions of all the early psychoanalytic pioneers to the question of the change in object for the girl and evaluated them through the lens and language of Lacanian theory. A central, defining issue for Hamon is how each theorist deals with the girl's "castration." According to Hamon, the necessary change of object, which she takes as a given, occurs through the girl's recognition of the mother's and her own castration, her acknowledgement of the father as the bearer of the "Phallus," and submission to his "Law." I question the necessity, in the first place, of such explanations for change of object, and, in the second place, for an insistence on the role of castration in the forward movement of female development.

CONTEMPORARY UNDERSTANDINGS OF OBJECT CHOICE

I now would like to draw on several different strands in contemporary psycho-analytic thinking that add further substance to the argument that object choice in females cannot be understood as a simple matter of a change from mother to father. These trends come from many sources: first, the appreciation of the complexity and multilayering of internal objects; second, the reconsideration of the concept of bisexuality; third, the role of multiple identifications in gender identity and object choice; and fourth, a reexamination of the triangular situation for girls.

The Complexity of Internal Objects

Through the intimate study of the minds of their patients in the process of psychoanalysis, psychoanalysts have come to understand the complexity of internal object representations. Arlow (1980), with his usual clarity, reminded us of this:

> *From a psychological point of view the individual's concept of a person is a conglomerate of many earlier object representations. This coher-ent organized concept may be dissolved regressively into its antecedent object representations [p. 118]. ... The concept of the object, as well as the concept of the self and even of the superego, may undergo regressive dissolutions into their antecedent identifications.*
>
> *This may be observed in dreams and in psychopathology [pp. 121–122].*

Thus, the final point in any individual's choice of love object—male or female—is not the entire story. Pertinent to the subject of change of object, according to this line of thought, the girl's sexual object choice of father may be built up of many earlier object representations, including maternal ones.

Young-Bruehl (2003) illuminated this complexity with clinical examples. Like Arlow, she suggested that everyone carries over varied representations of beloved familial figures into their love objects. She described four processes of transferential object choices in everyday life that contribute to the many and varied permutations of object choice:

Part objects: Part objects can stand for a whole object. If the part object happens to be gendered, such as a breast, then the whole object will correspondingly be gendered.

Split or doubled objects: Split or doubled objects are those objects onto which an individual places and separates desires once directed toward a single object. These doubled sets of objects can be male and female.

Composite objects: Composite objects blend parts, traits, and characteristics from at least two sources. These original sources can be objects of both genders.

Layered composite objects: Composite objects that are layered, for example, manifest and latent, may be male at one level and female at the other.

As Young-Bruehl stated, these fundamental processes, which can become manifest as male versus female, show up in object choice in the most varied combinations and are socially supported in complex ways (pp. 204–205).

Many contemporary writers have struggled with the question of what determines the end choice of object. Is object choice fixed in early childhood? Is it determined by biology or shaped by the environment? For Freud, object choice in women was the final outcome of a torturous set of circumstances.

Problems in development could "fix" a female in a male orientation and a homosexual object choice (1931), whereas biological influences—an inborn "masculine" disposition in a girl—also could be at play (1920, pp. 169–172).

Kirkpatrick (2003) argued that sexual orientation is a "multivariate sequential determinism" and is more flexible in women. She asserted that female homosexuality does not appear to be influenced by biological factors. She pointed out that a specific gene for male homosexuality has not been found either, but rather character traits, influenced by biology, might enhance that possibility. In other words, object choice, especially for women, does not appear to be a once-and-for-all, preordained situation.

Fischer (2002) observed that the idea that the girl retains her ties to her mother as she turns toward her father can help to explain the comfort that girls and women appear to have with their bisexual inclinations as well as the emergence of homosexuality in midlife. Making another salient point, which she put succinctly: "Ties to each parent develop in tandem, not sequentially" (p. 278).

Bisexuality

As in indicated earlier, the current controversies about the "causes" for homosexuality intersect with ideas of bisexuality that have resurfaced in psychoanalytic discourse. As Young-Bruehl (2003) pointed out in a recent review of the subject, the term "bisexual" has changed meanings over time in psychoanalytic thinking. Beginning with Freud's biological bisexuality, meanings then shifted to the idea of heterosexuals or homosexuals as types of people defined by their object choices, as in Kinsey's (1948) categorizations, and now lead to a current emphasis on object choices and behaviors, which are known to be diverse, changeable, and strongly influenced by environmental factors. Young-Bruehl reviewed the research on the biological domain and concluded that none of the research has yet yielded anything that resembles a causal explanation for homosexuality or heterosexuality but that biological factors do appear to have an influence on object choice in unspecified, indirect ways. Most researchers would also now concur that gender identity and object choice/sexual preference are not related in a simple, linear way.

Gender Identity and Object Choice

Contemporary conceptualizations of the complexity of gender identity inspire parallel careful approaches to the understanding of object choice. Balsam (2001), for example, proposed that mature gender identity in women is made up of an integrated blend of male and female identifications and bodily representations. She decried the older polarized view of female development as repudiation and overcoming masculinity. Elise (1998) adds another important voice in this discourse. She proposed that we use the term "early sense of femaleness" rather than primary femininity to keep us from reductionistic or overly simplistic thinking about female gender identity (1997). According to Elise, an early sense of a gendered self co-exists with the unconscious fantasy of potential unlimited by gender. Thus, she, like Fast (1979), would add the concept of an initial unlimited gender matrix to the Freudian bisexual matrix. She described how the individual has the possibility to reconcile—or to deny— masculinity and femininity within the self in a variety of ways. These varied somatic and cross-sex mental representations are difficult to identify beneath the surface manifestations of object representations. Thus, both Young-Bruehl and Elise have suggested that object choices are not what they appear to be on the manifest level and are composed of many conscious and unconscious layers, including bisexual components.

The Triangular Situation and Loss of Virginity

The current reformulations about female development and psychology have neglected the female triangular situation until most recently. Among the issues now being scrutinized are the idea of change of object and the girl's transition into triadic object relationships from the earlier maternal dyad.

Penis envy as the prime motivation for the girl's entry into the triadic relationship also has been questioned. Other motivations have been postulated, as outlined earlier: innate propensity to experience the primal scene (Klein, 1928), innate biological pressures, and a bisexuality from which society and family shape and guide girls typically to their fathers and lead to a suppression/repression of homosexual impulses (Butler, 1995). Whatever the explanation, penis envy is not seen by most contemporary American psychoanalysts as a satisfactory or observable explanation for girls' transition into triadic relationships. Wilkinson (1993), for example, spoke of a dress rehearsal for the triangular situation, as little girls try out blossoming sexual fantasies via masturbation first. Wilkerson followed the work of Ogden (1987) who emphasized the need for a transitional experience for the daughter to participate in an erotic relationship with another, without giving up the mother as subjective object. The girl loves the father in the mother, which is to say, the father's representation in the mother's mind. The mother, in this way, allows herself to be loved as a transitional object or substitute for the father.

Others, such as Abelin (1971) and Brown (2002), have added an account based on separation-individuation and have posited that triangulation has an earlier sequence, with the father breaking into the original dyad for both sexes and becoming a "third" for the infant. Brown (2002) proposed that there is a separate developmental line for triadic relationships. Following the Kleinian concepts, he accepts the idea of an early stage of triangularity and conflicted relations that is characterized by an early awareness and development of inner representations of the parental couple. To interpolate from these kinds of thinking, there is not a necessity, theoretically, of a change of object for the girl at the oedipal period. Instead, even in what has been called the preoedipal period, there exist primitive internal representations of father and mother. Lax (2003) added another twist to the explanation of the girl's turn to the father. She stressed the importance of the father's active role in seducing or drawing the girl to him. This is another motivational pull into heterosexuality of the triangular period for the girl.

By the same token, if castration does not get girls into the triadic situation, it does not account for their getting out of it. As Freud (1933) saw it, girls are without the motivation to develop strong superegos, which he tied to oedipal resolution and identification with the opposite parent. Although a discussion of superego development is beyond the scope of this article, I would like to say that what the early theory did not take into account or have at its disposal were the concepts of gender identity formation and of other motivations for the development of the superego, that is, ongoing identifications, throughout childhood, based on love or fear of its loss rather than fear of castration. In a contemporary reevaluation of theories of superego development, Lichtenberg (2004) presented evidence that development of morality is a gradual process that entails continual additions and revisions of values and standards throughout infancy, childhood, and adulthood.

Holtzman and Kulish (2000) have argued that the girl's entry into the triangular situation differs from that originally depicted by Freud. Holtzman and Kulish take into account the pattern of little girl's typical object relationships, in comparison to the little boy's, at that period of development. These speculations derive from the work of other psychoanalytic thinkers, such as Chodorow (1978), Person (1982), Burch (1997), and Reencola (2002). Such arguments take, as their starting point, the fact that girls separate from the same-sexed object has ramifications for their further development in the triadic situation. In contrast to little boys, girls' rivals in the positive oedipal situation are of the same sex: their mothers. In the typical family constellation, girls, like boys, are very dependent on their mothers for nurture and care. Their rivalrous feelings toward their mothers are especially dangerous to their security and present a major dilemma. Hence, girls must find a way to move toward their fathers and balance those impulses with their feelings toward their mothers. Girls add rather than replace a sexual object. The situation also means that girls are particularly sensitive to issues of intimacy and to interpersonal relationships. Such arguments provide explanations for research that finds that girls' interests and values lead them more often into interpersonal domains rather than the typical abstract or spatial-motoric preoccupations of boys.

Because my colleague and I see the triangular situation for the girl as one of balancing loyalties and relationships, we (Kulish and Holtzman, 1998; Holtzman and Kulish, 2000) have called for the use of the term "Persephone Complex" rather than the oxymoron, "Female Oedipal Complex." We have proposed that he myth of Persephone and Demeter is a better fit for naming the female triangular situation—it tells the story of a girl's separation from her mother, her introduction into the adult world of sexuality, and her eventual reunion with her mother with a compromise that allows her to keep her new-found position with a man. The gods work out a compromise so that Persephone can spend part of the time with her mother and part of the time with her new husband. This story emphasizes what we have found to be true for girls, which is that they typically do not wish to leave their mothers behind as they progress through their adult development.

Burch (1997) also argued for the applicability of Persephone myth: "... the male's entry into the story ends the exclusive nature of the mother-daughter bond; henceforth the daughter's existence moves back and forth between mother and (symbolic) father. Her dilemma is that of a divided psyche, oscillating between two worlds (p. 20). ... The Demeter-Persephone narrative invites us to question whether female development is qualitatively different from male development. ... it shifts the emphasis to the task of managing complex relationships—how to continue in relationship with more than one loved person without losing the self" (p. 22). Put a little differently, the dilemma of how to preserve a relationship with more than one loved person without losing the other person is a typical conflict in the female experience.

When women and girls first enter the world of adult heterosexuality, what is on their minds is their mothers (Holtzman and Kulish, 1997). Feelings of loss and regret for a lost childhood and separation from mother are common accompaniments of this initiation of loss of virginity. This clinical finding adds support for the idea that for the girl in her entry into adult sexuality, there is an addition of object, not a change of or a renunciation of object. She holds onto her mother as she finds a new kind of relationship with a man (or another woman).

Other current writers make salient points about how girls typically give up or suppress their erotic feelings for their mothers in the course of their development. Wyre and Wells (1989) have described maternal erotic transferences, which they contend are often incompletely explored in psychoanalytic therapies. These transferences illuminate conflicted early erotic and sensual feelings, oedipal and preoedipal, of the girl toward her mother.

CASE EXAMPLES

To summarize, an individual's object choice represents a composite or compromise, whether or not it results from a heterosexual, homosexual, or bisexual orientation. The little girl, in loving her "Daddy," does not give up her "Mommy." She tries to retain both in some fashion. In the case of a woman's heterosexual object choice, she typically remains close to her mother and identifies with her. Her choice of husband may very well be a compromise—the manifest picture being father-male, but an impression of the mother lies underneath. Similarly, the man's choice of an oedipal object, mother, may contain or mask the preoedipal facets. In people who are bisexual in their object choices,

193

switching from male to female loves, this amalgam is deconstructed. Cases of a paternal object choice that masks or contains the maternal object are very familiar and frequent to most analysts.

I will present two such examples, a woman's object choice of a partner that is clearly an amalgam and a woman who seemingly tried to balance both oedipal objects.

A Case of a Composite Object Choice—Frida Kahlo

As an example of these arguments, I will offer the life of Frida Kahlo, the extraordinary Mexican artist, who has been the subject of a recent popular film *Frida* (Taymor, 2002) and a continuing source of interest for artists and art historians, feminists, and psychoanalysts. This choice to illustrates my point may seem perplexing, because Frida Kahlo appeared tied not to her mother but to her father and to her husband, the famous muralist, Diego Rivera. Nevertheless, it is for this very reason that I think a closer examination of her relationships—as revealed in her life, writings, and art—will help to elucidate the complexity and layering of her internal object choices. Although we do not have psychoanalytic data, we are fortunate in the case of Frida Kahlo to have access to many very personal and intimate writings, notebooks, and letters and to her fanciful and self-revelatory art, from which we can draw some reasonable inferences about her fantasy life. To read her diaries from the last tragic years of her life when her physical and mental health were deteriorating is to have an opening into her mind at that time.

The recent film *Frida* (Taymor, 2002) depicts the life of this extra ordinary woman—"a vital force" according to Fuentes, in a forward to her diaries (Kahlo, 1995).

The narrative of the film highlights her love story. After the opening shots in Kahlo's famous blue house, the film begins with a sequence showing Frida as a young girl, part of a mischievous group of adolescents (the "Cachuchas"), spying on the famous Diego Rivera having sex with one of his beautiful models. This sequence, with its primal scene impact, lays out a characterization of Diego, the great artist and womanizer; Frida, his fearless, gutsy admirer; and the future shape of their complicated, passionate, and stormy relationship. It can be taken as a paradigm of their passionate, but often sadomasochistic, relationship, bristling with jealousies and the threat of betrayal.

Kahlo's early childhood and the last tragic years before her death help to illuminate her character. To do this, I have drawn on many sources—documentaries, biographies, artistic critiques, her diary from the last 10 years of her life, and psychoanalytic writings about her. Kahlo's father was born in Germany to Hungarian Jewish parents. A head injury at 18 years old cut short a promising scholarly career and left him with epilepsy and seizures, from which he suffered all his life. He immigrated to Mexico where he became a photographer. A somewhat melancholic, bitter man, he was described as never feeling quite at ease in his adopted land. Frida clearly adored her father and identified with him and with his artistic interests. Her 1951 *Portrait of My Father* stands as testimony to her deep love for her father. She, in turn, was his favorite. Frida's mother also was of mixed ethnic origins—Indian on the paternal side and a granddaughter of a Spanish general.

Frida gathered the diverse pieces in her background and subsumed them in a love of Mexico and the mantle of her Mexican identity. She fashioned her image literally in her colorful peasant costumes, in her carefully constructed interiors of her home, and in her political embrace of Mexican nationalism and socialism. For Kahlo, this mixed ethnicity did not, as it does so often, contribute to disquiet and disharmony psychologically but rather to unquiet and dynamism. I read in her psyche not fusion or closure to aspects of the self but a mélange of contradictory elements; her art reflects this quality. Although she herself refused to be classified as a surrealist, her art contains a surrealistic and idiosyncratic mix of fantasy and realism, autobiographical and social referents, Mexican folk art, and contemporary artistic trends (Zamora, 1990; Lindauer, 1999). Frida Kahlo could tolerate disparity and paradox; in fact, she embraced it and made the most of it. I am also thinking of Kahlo's bisexual identifications, with which she appeared comfortable. As has been well documented, she had affairs with men and women, reflective of her free spirit and the Bohemian, intellectual milieu in which she moved.

Because her mother became ill shortly after Frida's birth, the infant was suckled by an Indian wet nurse. Her mother was 31 years old when Frida was born; as she approached middle age, she also began to suffer from "seizures" so that the older sisters were largely responsible for Frida's care. Frida made much of being nourished by an indigenous woman's milk and painted the wet nurse as a mythic embodiment of her Mexican heritage, as, for example, in her 1937 painting *My Nurse and I* and the 1949 painting *The Love Embrace of the Universe, the Earth {Mexico}, Me, Diego and Mr. Xolotl.* With poetic license and typical flourish, Frida, the dedicated communist, put her birth date as corresponding with the Mexican revolution, which it did not.

Some writers and psychoanalysts have speculated that this factor of her mother's unavailability laid a psychic foundation in Frida of a yearning for love and nurture and a vulnerability to loneliness. Siltala (1998), for example, traced the ambiguous and paradoxical image of the mother, infused with contrasting shadings of softness and hardness, in Kahlo's art. She hypothesized that because of the early difficulties with her mother, Kahlo's internal representation of her was diffused with anger and disappointment. Thus, through the medium of her art, she repeatedly tried to mend an image of a damaged mother. Frida's mother died in 1932 at the same time that Frida was completing the painting *My Birth.* In this painting, the mother lies on the bed, with a sheet pulled over her head, as one covers a dead body. On the wall above the bed is a painting within a painting, of the sorrowful Madonna, pierced by swords, covered with blood, a weeping Virgin of Sorrows.

Kahlo often appropriated this religious imagery of the "Mater Dolorosa" tradition in Mexican art, which gives value to expression of maternal pain. Many of Kahlo's works concerned the mother-child relationship, fertility, and birth.

For instance, *My Nurse and I* depicted an idealized image of a strong Mexican woman—the nurse who suckled her. In Kahlo's own words, she painted a picture "From her nipples falls milk as from the sky …" (Herrera p. 220). Yet, as Sitala points out, the nurse appears as an icon whose face is a stone mask and there is no eye contact. "The empty space—the being without—comes alongside the good experience, to be received and endured in a tension of soft and hard" (1998, p. 149).

This ambivalence toward the mother runs throughout Kahlo's life and work. It would have been difficult to please her religious, stern mother, being the girl Frida, was by nature, probably nonconforming and high spirited. It is quite plausible that Frida and her sisters would feel anxious about their mother's approval or love; she had the two older half-sisters by the father's first marriage sent away to a convent when she married him, and she banished another sister from the family for several years in displeasure. The 2002 film depicts the differences between Frida and her mother in the daughter's disdain for her mother's religion and for the conventional and expected feminine role.

Although Frida constantly strove to be a mother herself, she could not easily identify with or please her mother. Nevertheless, she was devastated by her mother's death. Her biographer reports that a portrait of Frida taken at this time shows "a darkness in her eyes, the unmistakable darkness of sorrow" (Herrera, 2002, p. 156).

In addition to the conflicted identifications with her mother, we can point to the abiding influence of another early trauma. At the age of six, Frida came down with polio. Sources describe her as at once being transformed from a happy, plump child to a somber thin soul. She was to spend nine months confined to her room and was left with a withered leg, which added to the continuing

197

medical complications after her later bus accident. Because of her disfigured leg and limp from the polio, she became the object of cruel teasing by neighborhood children.

At the time of her illness, Frida developed an imaginary friend, who appears in the self-portrait *The Two Fridas*. I quote from her diary:

On the window of my old room ... I used to breathe on one of the top panes. And with my finger I would draw a door. ... Through that door I would come out, in my imagination, and hurriedly, with immense happiness, I would cross all the plain I could see until I reached a dairy called Pinzon. I entered by the O of Pinzon and I went down into the interior of the earth, where my imaginary friend was always waiting for me....I do know that she was gay—she laughed a lot. She was agile and she danced as if she were weightless. I told her my secret problems [Kahlo, 1995, pp. 245–246].

Here we see the loneliness and depression of this little girl in her forced isolation, perhaps reviving the separation from her mother's breasts—she goes to a dairy that supplies milk. With this fantasy, she undoes her aloneness and her being crippled. Perhaps we can view this as a precursor of the mirrored self-images that appear and reappear in her artwork and perhaps in her choice of female sexual partners later on. What is also impressive is the child's creativity and will to master trauma by her own imagination. We see the beginnings of the efforts to invent a new, happier, and graceful persona, reinvented throughout her life. Later, when Frida put on her long Mexican costumes she repeated this story—making a statement about her Mexican identity, displaying her gaiety and her love of bright colors, and, most importantly, hiding her withered leg. She was described as laboring to make herself walk without a visible limp, gliding as it were.

Then came the horrendous life-altering accident, on top of the earlier physical trauma. A trolley plowed into the flimsy wooden bus in which Frida, then aged 17 and a student in Mexico City, and her boyfriend, Alejandro Gomez Arias, were riding. Frida was impaled by a steel rod that penetrated her pelvis and came out her vagina. Quite concretely, she was raped and left for dead by this steel rod. Her spinal column was broken in three places; her leg in eleven; her pelvis in three. Her collarbone, ribs, and foot were broken or crushed.

Throughout her life, she suffered more than thirty operations, procedures, bone grafts, infections, numerous hospitalizations, plaster corsets, braces, tractions, constant back and leg pain, and finally amputation of her toes and then her bad leg, not to mention numerous miscarriages and abortions. Many of these painful medical procedures were not helpful and probably made matters worse.

A major sorrow for Frida was her inability to have a child. In spite of the physical jeopardy pregnancy and childbirth would mean for her, she repeatedly tried to become pregnant and suffered countless miscarriages and medically necessary abortions. Her preoccupation with childbirth and her sorrow over her inability to bear children runs throughout her work. For example, the famous painting *Henry Ford Hospital*, which helped to establish Kahlo as a revolutionary voice for female experience, depicted, with graphic force, the agony of her miscarriage in 1932. She wrote of her deep yearning to have Diego's baby in a letter to her doctor shortly after the miscarriage, "I had such hope to have a little Dieguito who would cry a lot" (Herrera, 2002, p. 143). She told a critic that three concerns impelled her to make art: a vivid memory of her own blood flowing during her childhood accident; her thoughts about birth, death, and the thread of life; and her desire to be a mother (Herrera, 2002, p. 319).

We might wonder why Kahlo was so intent on having a baby. Clinicians know that very often, when a girl has difficulties in identifying with her mother and the mother's role, she rejects the idea of becoming a mother herself.

Certainly, this was not the case with Frida. Her strong identification with the role of mother can be discerned not only in her relentless wish for a child but also in her lifelong love of children and animals and the joy she took in teaching.

Frida's intense need for having a child may also have reflected her worries about her adequacy as a female. Her early illness, her broken body, perhaps buried rivalry with a dominant mother and many sisters, a wandering husband, all called for a proof, by way of giving birth to a child, that she was a well-functioning woman.

Kahlo first began to draw from her sickbed as a child, although until the accident she had planned to go to medical school. In her art, Frida Kahlo was able to depict perhaps better than anyone the experience of her physical and emotional pain and of her female body and sexuality. Surely, as the movie and her biographies suggest, painting helped her to manage and master her pain, helplessness, and rage. As her biographer Herrera (2002) stated, "by looking at her wounded self in her paintings, Frida could sustain the illusion of being the strong, objective onlooker to her own misfortune" (p. 347). (I am not suggesting, nor do I think, that creativity can be explained as some kind of sublimation of trauma or as a mechanism of mastery over inner psychic conflicts, although any given creative individual can use her talents in these ways, as did Kahlo.)

Frida was quoted as saying that the "second great accident" in her life was Diego Rivera. When she married him, Diego Rivera was 43 years old and was Mexico's most famous artist. She was 22 years old. An infamous womanizer, Diego had had two long-term unions and countless affairs. The turbulence of their marriage is attested to by the fact that it was punctuated by a divorce and remarriage.

Frida was deeply in love with Diego, and his constant womanizing and love affairs caused her great pain. He was charismatic and was attractive to and attracted by many beautiful women. With his large ego and appetites, he could not refrain from infidelities. Frida depicted her pain about his infidelities in many of her self-portraits—a deer pierced by arrows, a self-representation with a bleeding and literally broken heart, or a self-portrait bearing a tear- stained face. After discovering Diego making love with her sister, Frida was devastated. As shown in the film *Frida* (Taymor, 2002), in her anguish and rage at his betrayal of her, she cut off her long beautiful hair that Diego loved and later painted the image of her self dressed in a man's suit—*Self Portrait with Cropped Hair*(1940). In this complex gesture, she cropped off a symbol of her vulnerable femaleness—a "castration" of her femaleness, appropriated "maleness," and took highly visible and angry vengeance on Diego. In cropping her hair, she also may have been asserting her rage at not attaining an ideal beauty or being woman enough to keep her man and bear children. The affair with her sister was especially painful, a betrayal by him and by the sister immediately younger who replaced her with her mother.

Her contemporaries, biographers, letters, diary, and her paintings all attest to her deep attachment and love for Diego. Some critics have asserted that the film *Frida* (Taymor, 2002) paid too much attention to the romance and to Diego. That may be true, but they might as well complain that Frida herself paid too much attention to Diego. I don't think Frida's love for Diego is so hard to understand, although her mother called their marriage "the mating of a dove with an elephant." Diego was the center of the universe for her and the love of her life, clearly an erotic love, as evidenced by erotic passages about Diego in her diary. In her self-portraits, such as *Diego and I* (1949), she painted Diego's face on the center of her forehead, a statement of his central importance and influence to her as an embedded introjection.

On his part, Diego found a soul mate: a woman whose art he respected. He bragged to everyone that she had a piece in the Louvre. (Diego never gained that distinction.) She shared his politics and love for Mexico. She understood him and took care of him. She loved him fiercely but could not be pushed around and from all accounts, in spite of her disabilities, or perhaps because of them, had a burning sexuality and unique attractiveness.

201

Kahlo herself had many affairs with powerful and famous men throughout her life—Trotsky, the sculptor Noguchi, the photographer, Nicholas Muray, and others, but none of these really captured her love. This seemingly free love was in many ways part of the scene of intelligencia in which they moved. However, her biographers and friends felt that many of the affairs were initiated in response to and as a way to cope with her feelings of rejection, jealousy, and the narcissistic wounds generated by Diego's affairs.

Although the macho Diego supposedly believed in free love for himself, he could not tolerate his wife's heterosexual affairs, which she hid from him, but her relations with women apparently did not threaten him. She appeared to prefer men until late in her life, when her physical frailty made heterosexual intercourse difficult (Herrera, 2002, p. 199).[1]

We might speculate that there was another strong motive for her affairs; it appears plausible that, given her physical traumas and her triangular conflicts within her family, Frida constantly needed to strive to prove herself as an attractive woman. It is also plausible that Kahlo, in her relationships with women—and she had many close female friends—had undertones of her earlier search for mirrored self-images, her unmet needs for affection from her mother, as well as her competitive and comradely relationships with her sisters. She moved easily from friendship to sexual encounter and back to friendship with men and women. Her powerful sexual appetite and sensuality permeate her art.

If we explain her turning to affairs with women in terms of "unmet maternal needs," we assume a hierarchical layering in choice of objects. That is, unsatisfied needs become a residue that does not allow for a complete "change in object" from mother to father. Preoedipal conflicts, as evidenced

---

1 Frida's bisexuality showed itself early. In a portrait of the family taken during her adolescence, the ever-rebellious Frida, assumes a mannish posture and wears a man's three-piece suit and tie. Her first homosexual liaison occurred during her last year at the national preparatory school and caused a trauma. She presumably was seduced by an older woman "school teacher" (Herrera, 2002, p. 43).

by bisexuality and a seemingly troubled relationship with her mother, would heighten and color her later object choice and make it difficult for her to give up her mother as primary object. Conversely, we might take another view of Kahlo's shifting love affairs from men to women to men. It can be explained more simply by the idea that, quite naturally, internal love objects are composites, mixtures, and additions, not one dimensional. If we view female development in terms of an addition of object, then Kahlo's apparent shift between male and female objects need not be seen in a negative light. Indeed, as we noted earlier, many contemporary writers have noted that women appear less constrained than do men in shifting genders of sexual object choice (Kirkpatrick, 2003) Frida Kahlo's more open psychology may allow us a view into what societal mores and individual repression have sealed over—the bisexuality in object choice and identifications that are ubiquitous.

This being said, it is important to remember that all her lovers and friends realized that they were second to Diego and could not compete with his place in her heart. One of her lovers, Nicholas Muray, wrote to Frida after she left New York for Mexico, "I knew NY only filled the bill as a temporary substitute and I hope you found your haven intact on your return. Of the three of us there was only two of you. I always felt that. Your tears told me that when you heard his voice" (Herrera, 2002, p. 269).

Diego represented for Frida many things: father and oedipal object, for he was old enough to be her father; child, for she babied him and took care of him emotionally and physically; and mother, for he fulfilled the wished-for place of the unavailable mother. The ambivalence and this yearning Frida felt toward her mother were folded into her attitudes toward Rivera. A maternal symbiotic-like meaning can be discerned in her note to Diego in her journal: "My blood is the miracle that travels in the veins of the air from my heart to yours" (Kahlo, 1995, p. 215). In another place in her journal, she wrote "Every moment, he is my child. My newborn babe, every little while, every day, of my own self" (Kahlo, 1995, p. 205). Clearly, Diego also represented a narcissistic object for her.

Certainly, the two were comrades, colleagues, and friends—intellectual and artistic equals who shared the same politics and worldviews. In the film *Frida,* there is a symbolic scene in which Frida first calls Diego down from the scaffolding to her level to look at her portfolio. They had a good time with each other, that is, when they weren't making each other miserable. Diego could be a cad, narcissistic and childish, but he loved Frida above all others. He wrote, "Too late now I realized that the most wonderful part of my life had been my love for Frida" (Rivera, 1960, pp. 285-286). Observers said he became an old man all at once when she died.

In her diary, Frida movingly summed up his meanings for her: "Diego beginning, Diego, builder, Diego, my child, Diego, my boyfriend, Diego, painter, Diego, my lover, Diego, 'my husband,' Diego, my friend, Diego, my mother, Diego, my father, Diego, my son Diego = me = Universe. Diversity within unity" (Kahlo, 1995, p. 235).

Diego certainly was an oedipal object—old enough to be her father, a teacher and powerful figure, and always not quite attainable. That, I think, was part of his appeal to her. That he was an androgynous figure in other ways meant that to her he represented mother as well. Frida loved his soft, vulnerable quality and his fat man's breasts. Herrera quotes her commenting on this quality:

> Of his chest it must be said that if he had disembarked on the island governed by Sappo, he would not have been executed by the female warriors. The sensitivity of his marvelous breast would have made him admissible. Even so, his virility, specific and strange, makes him desirable also in the dominions of empresses avid for masculine love [1995, p. 370].

The aspect of Diego as mother on the one hand and child on the other is portrayed in her painting, *The Love Embrace of the Universe, the Earth Diego Me and Senior Xolotl* (1949). Frida is seated on the lap of a huge, pre-Columbian idol of a goddess. A nude baby Diego is on her lap, equal in size to her. A third eye of "supervisibility," as Kahlo wrote, is in the middle of his forehead, indicating her idealizing attitude toward him. It is striking to me that Diego's stony expression resembles that of the goddess. These three figures are set in a fantastic, organic matrix of vivid mountains and plants, desert, and jungles. Thus, Frida is caught up in an interlocking set of love embraces, one inside the other, like Russian dolls. It is as if a cosmic matrix joins and sustains her and her spouse.

Years later in her diary, as she lay ill and approaching death, she scribbled to Diego:

> Only one mountain can know the core of another mountain. Your presence floats for a moment or two as if wrapping my whole being in an anxious waiting for the morning. ... For my Diego the silent life giver of worlds, what is most important is the nonillusion. Morning breaks, the friendly reds, the big blues, hands full of leaves, noisy birds, fingers in the hair, pigeons' nests—a rare understanding of human struggle simplicity of the senseless song the folly of the wind in my heart ... sweet [chocolate] of ancient Mexico [1995, pp. 216–217].

I believe that this creative, brilliant woman's freedom of expressiveness and comfort with ambiguity and paradox allowed her to communicate overtly in her words, life choices, and art what is latent in most other people. In such artistic people, who offer us their fantasies for our viewing, we can deconstruct what is carefully and tightly packed in others. What is tightly packed in others—the multilayering, or multifaceted, make-up of their internal object representations—is distinctly depicted in her art, writings, and life. To be true to Frida Kahlo, we could never speak of a "renunciation" of anything. Her psychic embrace of possibilities cannot be captured by the idea of a change from maternal love object to paternal love object, but rather an addition of object.

A Case of Mrs. L—Conflict About the Addition of an Object

Mrs. L was in her early forties and had been married for 18 years with two adolescent children. Mrs. L. came for a consultation, because she suffered from anxiety attacks and obsessive thoughts. She dated her symptoms of anxiety to right after the birth of her second child, a boy, who she felt completed their family. She could not rid herself of what appeared to be inexplicable ideas that she had made a mistake in marrying her husband and should leave him. What ran through her head were the questions that perhaps somewhere there was somebody else she should have married, although she could not imagine being married to anyone else. She could make no sense of these symptoms, because she loved her husband. She felt she and her husband were compatible, had good times together, could communicate well, and had good sex. The symptoms diminished in psychotherapy. As we discussed her marriage, it became apparent to us both that there really was not significant dissatisfaction with her husband or her marriage. Mrs. L. quickly realized that the symptoms must represent something else, something less apparent. A point to start our explorations was suggested when the anxiety symptoms flared up again after she got together for lunch with an old girlfriend who had been her best friend in high school. She recalled for me the story of her romance and marriage. She had married her husband after a quick courtship, one month after her high school sweetheart married this best friend. After she graduated and went off to college, the boyfriend began a technical school. Mrs. L would come home on some weekends to see him. Her best girlfriend went to another college in yet another town. Suddenly she discovered—she did not remember how—that on the weekends in which she didn't come home, he was going to see her girlfriend and that the two had had secret romance brewing for some time.

When the patient discovered this double betrayal, she was very upset but especially at the thought that her girlfriend would no longer be her friend. She launched an insistent campaign to keep her friendship. She drove to the other college to implore her that they remain friends. It was around the same time that she met her husband, who was several years older. At their wedding, she wanted to invite the girlfriend and ex-boyfriend, but her husband put his foot down against this. Nevertheless, she has remained friends with the girlfriend who is still married to the ex-boyfriend. Thus, it was suggestive that it was the lunch with the girlfriend stimulated the flare-up in symptoms. Mrs. L stated her belief that her husband was a much better match for her than the boyfriend would have been. In fact, her husband adored her. Perhaps this was her only complaint: his devotion made her feel guilty and unworthy, given her obsessive thoughts.

Her history was unremarkable. She felt loved by both parents and was successful in school and with her peers. She had an older brother, whom she looked up to. Her father, a very good looking and a natty dresser, was very conscious of his appearance and proud of his good-looking children. During adolescence, she dressed in the baggy and campy clothes that were characteristic of the era. She recounted how her brother gave her a pair of high-heeled shoes for her sixteenth birthday. He said, "Here, you'd look really good dressing in more sexy feminine attire." From that time, as she remembers it, she wore the high heels to school with skirts and felt very good about herself. My hunch was that her older brother was a paternal figure for her, as is often the case. In this instance, his interest in her looks and sexiness was charged with oedipal significance and served as a positive stimulus in the development of a feminine identity.

The story of her boyfriend and her subsequent marriage certainly provide triangular oedipal themes ("negative" and "positive")—the proverbial love triangle and betrayal. What is striking, however, is that the primary concern was with losing her girlfriend as much as or more than her boyfriend.

This concern appears evocative of what I have argued is characteristic of the triangular situation of the little girl. As she is driven by sexual feelings toward her father and becomes jealous of her mother, she is caught in a dilemma. She is jealous of her rival, the mother. She really does not want to kill off her mother; she is afraid of losing her and needs her. She is also jealous of the father and does not want to lose her place with her mother. The Persephone myth captures this dilemma well, for it tells the tale of a girl caught in a loyalty conflict between mother and father (personified by Demeter and Hades). Thus, as the little girl, nurtured by a close, dyadic loving relationship with her mother, enters the triangular situation, she does not change sexual objects, she adds one.

At the end of adolescence Mrs. L was caught up in a persephonal conflict. She wanted to keep her relationships with women and also have a relationship with a man for herself. It is also apparent that Mrs. L's object choice of an older man was incestuous, probably having paternal and brotherly components. Her older brother, who, with his gift of the high-heeled slippers, was a kind of fairy godmother and Prince Charming, rolled into one.

In the transference, which in this short-term treatment could not be explored in any depth, Mrs. L appeared to relate to me as a mentor or older sisterly guide. In retrospect, I suspect that she may unconsciously have put me in the position of her older brother. What she came to understand was that she married her husband on the rebound, to deal with wounded pride, for "the wrong reasons," as she put it. Nevertheless, she was convinced that he was a good and appropriate choice for her. In our discussions of the events of her adolescent romance, she assumed that her behavior made sense, and it was absolutely natural to want to keep her girlfriend. She acknowledged her feelings of betrayal, but the loss of the girlfriend was more of a potential hurt. We lightly touched on the "oedipal" or "persephonal" dynamics in her choice of her husband. In fact, whenever we discussed her reasons for her choice of her husband, her thoughts would stray to her father. Thus, she gained some understanding that her obsessive thoughts about the man "she should have married" might relate to her father. Mrs. L. left treatment satisfied with her life and with her symptoms under control.

CONCLUSION

In their everyday clinical work, psychoanalysts know and practice this: that the internal object world is multilayered and dynamically complex. The psychoanalytic theory of female psychosexual development, in its insistence on the idea of the girl's change of object from mother to father, rather than addition of object, has stood separately from this accumulated wisdom and experience. It has also ignored the common wisdom in the saying with which I started—that "a daughter's a daughter the rest of her life."

REFERENCES

Abelin, E. (1971). The role of the father in the separation-individuation process. In: *Separation-Individuation, ed.* J. McDevitt & C. Settlage. New York: International Universities Press, pp. *229-252.*

Arlow, J. (1980). Object concept and object choice, *Psychoanal. Q.,* 49: *109-133.*

Balsam, R. (2001). Integrating male and female elements in a woman' gender identity, *J. Amer. Psychoanal. Assn.,* 49: *1335-1361.*

Britton, R., Feldman, M., & O'Shaughnessy, E. (1989). *The Oedipus Complex Today.* London: Karnak.

Brown, L. J. (2002). The early oedipal situation: Developmental, theoretical, and clinical implications, *Psychoanal. Q.,* 71: *273-300.*

Burch, B. (199). *Other Women.* New York: Columbia University Press.

Butler, J. (1995).Melancholy gender-refused identification, *Psychoanal. Dial.,* 5: *165-180.*

Chasseguet-Smirgel, J. (1970). Feminine guilt and the Oedipus complex. In: Female Sexuality: New Psychoanalytic Views, ed. J. Chassguet-Smirgel. Ann Arbor: University of Michigan Press, pp. *94-134.*

Chehrazi, S. (1986). Female psychology: A review, *J. Amer. Psychoanal. Assn.*, 34: *141-162.*

Chodorow, N. (1978). *The Reproduction of Mothering: Psychoanalysis and the Sociology of Gender.* Berkeley: University of California Press.

Edgecumbe, R., Lunberg, S., Markowitz, R. & Salo, F. (1976).Some comments on the concept of the negative oedipal phase in girls, *Psychoanal. St. Child,* 31: *35-61.* New Haven, CT: Yale University Press.

Elise, D. (1997). Primary femininity, bisexuality, and the female ego ideal: A reexamination of female developmental theory, *Psychoanal. Q.,* 66: *489-517.*

Elise, D. (1998). Gender repertoire: Body, mind, and bisexuality, *Psychoanal. Dial.,* 8: *353-371.*

Fast, I. (1979). Developments in gender identity: gender differentiation in girls, *Int. J. Psycho-Anal.,* 60: *443-45.*

Fischer, R. S. (2002).Lesbianism: Some developmental and psychodynamic considerations, *Psychoanal. Inq.,* 22: *278-295.*

Frenkel, R. S. (1996). A reconsideration of object choice in women: Phallus or fallacy, *J. Amer. Psychoanal. Assn.,* 44S: *133-156.*

Freud, A. (1965). *Normality and Pathology in Childhood: Assessments of Development.* New York: International Universities Press.

Freud, S. (1908). On the sexual theories of children. *Standard Edition,* 9: *205-226,* London: Hogarth Press, 1959.

———(1916). Some character types met with in psychoanalytic work.*Standard Edition,* 14: *309-333,* London: Hogarth Press, 1957.

205-226, London: Hogarth Press, 1959.

——— (1920). A case of homosexuality in a woman. *Standard Edition,* 18: *145-172,* London: Hogarth Press, 1955.

——— (1931). Female sexuality. *Standard Edition,* 21: *221-243,* London: Hogarth Press, 1961.

———. (1933). Femininity. *Standard Edition,* 22: *112-135,* London: Hogarth Press, 1964.

Grossman, W. & Stewart, W. (1976). Penis envy: From childhood wish to developmental metaphor, *J. Amer. Psychoanal. Assn.*, 24 (Suppl.): *193-213*.

Hamon, M. (2000). Why do Women Love Men and Not Their Mothers? New York: Other Press.

Herrera, H. (2002). *Frida: A Biography of Frida Kahlo.* New York: HarperCollins.

Holtzman, D. & Kulish, N. (1997). *Nevermore: The Hymen and the Loss of Virginity.* Northvale, NJ: Jason Aronson, 1997.

Holtzman, D. & Kulish, N. (2000). The feminization of the female oedipal complex. Part 1: A reconsideration of the significance of separation issues, *J. Amer. Psychoanal. Assn.*, 48: *1413-1437*.

Horney, K. (1924). On the genesis of the castration complex in women. *Int. J. Psycho-Anal.*, 5: *50-65*.

Jones, E. (1933). The phallic phase. *Int. J. Psycho-Anal.*, 14: *1-13*.

Kahlo, F. (1995). The Diary of Frida Kahlo: An Intimate Self-Portrait. New York: Abradale Press.

Kinsey, A. (1948). Sexual Behavior in the Human Male. Philadelphia: Saunders.

Kirkpatrick, M. (2003).T he nature and nurture of gender, *Psychoanal. Inq.*, 23: *58-571*.

Kleeman, J. (1976). Freud's views on early female sexuality in the light of direct child observation, *J. Amer. Psychoanal. Assn.*, 24 (Suppl.): *2-29*.

Klein, M. (1928). Early stages of the Oedipus conflict. In: Love, Guilt and Reparation and Other Works: The Writings of Melanie Klein, Vol. 1. London: Hogarth Press, 1975, pp. *186-198*.

Kulish, N. & Holtzman, D. (1998).Persephone, the loss of virginity and the female oedipal complex, *Int. J. Psycho-Anal.*, 79: *57-71*.

Lax, R. (2003). The daughter's seduction by her father, *J. Amer. Psychoanal. Assn.*, 51: *1305-1309*.

Lerner, H. (1976). Parental mislabeling of female genitals as a determinant of penis envy and learning inhibitions in women, *J. Amer. Psychoanal. Assn.*, 24 (Suppl.): *269-283.*

Lichtenberg, J. D. (2004). Commentary on the superego—A vital or supplanted concept, *Psychoanal. Inq.*, 24: *328-339.*

Lindauer, M. A. (1999). *Devouring Frida: The Art History and Popular Celebrity of Frida Kahlo.* Middletown, CT: Wesleyan University Press.

Nagera, H. (1975). *Female Sexuality and the Oedipus Complex.* New York: Aronson

Ogden, T. (198). The transitional oedipal relationship in female development, *Int. J. Psycho-Anal.*, 68: *485-498.*

Person, E. (1982). Women working: Fears of failure deviance and success, *J. Am.Acad. Psychoanal. Dyn. Psychiatr.*10: *67-84.*

Reencola, E. M. (2002). *The Veiled Female Core.* New York: Other Press.

Rivera, D. (1960). My Art, My Life: An Autobiography. New York: Citadel.

Segal, H. (1974). *Introduction to the Work of Melanie Klein.* New York: Basic Books.

Siltala, P. (1998). I made a picture of my life—As life from the picture. The life of the body in the pictures and writings of Frida Kahlo, *Int. Forum Psychoanal.*, 7:*133-155.*

Taymor, J. (Director) (2002). *Frida* [Motion picture] United States: Miramax

Wilkinson, S. (1993).The female genital dress-rehearsal: A prospective process at the oedipal threshold, *Int. J. Psycho-Anal.*, 74: *313-330.*

Wrye, H. & Wells, J. (1989). The maternal erotic transference, *Int. J. Psycho-Anal.*, 70: *673-684.*

Young-Bruehl, E. (2003). *Where Do We Fall When We Fall in Love.* New York: Other Press

Zamora, M. (1990). *Frida Kahlo: The Brush of Anguish.* San Francisco, CA: Chronicle Books

CHAPTER 8

Clinical Implications of Contemporary Gender Theory

(2010). J. Amer. Psychoanal. Assn., (58)(2):231–258

The current intellectual scene in psychoanalysis is marked by vigorous theoretical controversies about gender. The ideas being debated have important implications for clinical work, which have not been thoroughly explicated or integrated into common practice. These implications include the following: gender can accrue idiosyncratic meanings; gender identity is considered fluid and rigidity of gender identity deemed problematic; gender related conflicts are typically described as *divergent;* analysis of superego conflicts related to gender becomes particularly important; and, finally, gender related biases are seen as inevitable and must be taken into account in the clinical situation. A detailed clinical example illustrates the application of these ideas. While the more dramatic cases related to gender have been more frequent subjects of study, conflicts about gender are everyday occurrences for our patients and deserve further attention.

The current intellectual scene in psychoanalysis is marked by fascinating and vigorous theoretical controversies over gender, with feminists and gender theorists, as well as clinicians of all stripes, joining in the dialogue. The ideas emerging from this discourse have important implications for clinical work, and are increasingly finding their way into psychoanalytic practice. At the same time, because our assumptions about gender, both in psychoanalytic theory and in society at large, are changing so rapidly, the clinical ground for working with gender-related problems is shifting. Both theoretically and clinically, there are no longer—and perhaps there never were—clear-cut and uniformly recognizable guideposts in approaching issues related to gender. In this paper I will review the current psychoanalytic thinking about gender, outline what I see as its major implications for clinical practice, and then illustrate these ideas with clinical material. My goal is to illustrate how I have struggled with these challenges and ambiguities, and tried to integrate some of these new ideas into my clinical work.

I believe that conflicts about gender are everyday occurrences for our patients—probably as frequent as conflicts about libido, aggression, dependency, or narcissism. However, it is the more drastic, flamboyant, or controversial cases—of "gender disorder," of transgender, of cross-dressing, of individuals who feel they are prisoners in the wrong-sexed bodies—that have caught our attention. Certainly, in these cases the gender issues stand out in strong relief, making their examination inescapable and in a sense easier. One might question whether we can generalize from these more conspicuous cases to more subtle ones, or whether these cases are exemplary or relatively unusual. One certainly might question whether we can use such cases to build theories about gender development. A research study group on gender in which I participated asked why for some individuals gender assumes a distorted and exaggerated role in the subjective sense of self. The group concluded that in the cases studied gender served many functions and that gender disturbances were never primary, but rather were secondary to various difficulties in integration, cohesiveness, separateness, depression, and problems with aggression and rivalry. In these individuals, gender frequently played an important role, in various ways, in their family backgrounds (Olesker 2003).

SELECTIVE REVIEW OF THE LITERATURE

Contemporary thinking about gender can be organized into five major areas, all interrelated: (1) the social construction of gender; (2) the complexity and fluidity of gender; (3) the separation of gender and object choice; (4) normality vs. marginality; (5) embodiment. Several other issues could also be addressed, but I have chosen to focus on those I find most relevant to the clinical material I will present.

The Social Construction of Gender

In a groundbreaking and well-known paper, Fast (1978) proposed that gender identity develops though a process of differentiation. Children at first know no limits to their gender; the sense of gender is boundless or undifferentiated. Through a process of learning, largely within the family, children gradually distinguish what constitutes maleness or femaleness. (Fast acknowledges that inborn factors can and do influence gender.) This developmental process of differentiation entails narcissistic disappointments as the child comes to grips with the fact that he or she cannot be everything. Current gender theorists (Bassin 2000) have begun to quarrel with Fast's theory, not happy with the idea of "renunciation" implied in the child's having to limit the boundlessness of its gender possibilities. Still, Fast's clear and seemingly simple conceptualization helped turn psychoanalytic thinking about gender theory in a new direction. Before Fast, concepts of gender had been framed in terms of Freud's concepts of psychosexual development (1925): that is, his account of how the young child's discovery of the anatomical differences between the sexes—and the resulting castration anxiety or penis envy—influences male and female development, conflicts, and personality.

215

Freud did not use the terms *gender* or *gender identity,* or operate in those frames of reference, but generations of psychoanalytic theorists have grappled with the questions about gender that his original ideas on psycho-sexual development raised. These questions include: (1) The nature/nurture question: that is, are characteristics of gender inborn or environmentally induced? Is anatomy indeed destiny? (2) Are there gender-linked characteristics? (See Schäfer 1974.) (3) Does femininity really arise from an inborn masculinity, achieved through the series of renunciations, of aim, object, and organ, as Freud proposed? I will not reopen these questions here. By now they are old stomping grounds for psychoanalytic debate and, though they still haunt us, are hopefully beginning to be put to rest.[1]

Starting from the idea that gender is socially constructed, many gender theorists, such as Foucault (1978) and Butler (1990), question the basic premises and terminology of gender. For such theorists, the terms *masculinity* and *femininity,* or *male* and *female,* have no real or fixed meanings, but are always defined by context and culture. Layton (2000) argues that gender inequality is the result of a culturally induced and changeable splitting of the world into two categories. Masculinity and femininity are defined by each other, by what the other is not (see also Benjamin 1998) and have no intrinsic meaning. Dimen (1991) agrees: "at the heart of gender is not 'masculinity' or 'femininity' but the difference between them" (p. 335).

---

1 The idea of primary femininity was advanced as an antidote to the perceived phallocentrism of the early theories. Not a unified or clear concept at all, primary femininity has been used differently in various frames of reference. Both of the component terms of this concept—primary and femininity—are problematic (Elise 1997; Kulish 2000).

The Complexity, Multiplicity, And Fluidity Of Gender

Contemporary conceptualizations of gender identity stress its fluidity and complexity (Elise 2000b). Harris (2005) argues that gender is socially instructed, is mediated by family and society, and emerges in the context of personal interactions between self and others. She coined the idea that gender is "softly assembled"—that is, that gender is not hardwired, with a predictable unfolding from a given starting point, the way inborn sexual variables may be. Rather, the gender "package" in different people has different patterns and different contents; it follows multiple pathways to unfixed outcomes, serves various psychic and social functions, and is influenced by a large number of variables, intrapersonal and interpersonal, conscious and unconscious. The idea of "assembly" emphasizes process rather than structure. For a possible model for the psychic development of self and gender, Harris turns to contemporary chaos theory resting on nonlinear dynamic systems, in which outcomes cannot be predicted from initial conditions.[2] The clinical applications of chaos theory to psychoanalytic theory and practice have at this point been demonstrated only sketchily.

In her arguments Harris puts aside the stalwart psychoanalytic model of developmental lines, which, she asserts, provides too rigid and absolute a blueprint for human development. Corbett (2001b) warns us to think of developmental lines as metaphor not fact. If we keep this caution in mind, I think, we need not be so quick to throw out the concept, which can provide useful guidelines for child development, if not applied in a rigid, lock-step manner, like a yardstick

---

2 Coburn (2000) describes the characteristics of a nonlinear system: its developmental trajectory is determined by mutually organizing components of that system and their continually changing configurations. "the results of a system's nonlinear, dynamic process tend to violate the traditional expectations inherent in the notion of teleological, epigenetic progression" (p. 753).

Attempting to expand concepts of gender, Benjamin (1996) argues that psychoanalytic theories of oedipal development leave us with too narrow an idea of gender identifications. Oedipal logic, she says, is a logic of binary opposites—a seamless identification with the same-sexed parent, and a sexual object choice of the other, an either/or logic. She describes the "post-oedipal" development of gender as not so dichotomized, ideally allowing for a sense of self that can accommodate multisidedness: "Differentiation in the oedipal phase is not the final achievement that often has been supposed by psychoanalytic theory" (p. 33). (I think that in fact most psychoanalytic theorists today do not subscribe to the fixed view described by Benjamin.)

Young-Bruehl (2003) is another who questions old categorizations, instead favoring complexity and fluidity: "ours is an era in which much psychoanalytic interest is focused on phenomena that call the categories Woman and Man, Masculinity and Femininity, directly into question as categories... Historians working in the relatively new subdiscipline history of sexuality have shown the many ways in which even physiological and anatomical differences between the sexes, once thought to be matters of objective knowledge, are always interpreted" (p. 158).

These changing ideas of gender have in recent years been illustrated with rich clinical accounts. For example, Balsam (2001) proposes that mature gender identity in women is made up of an integrated and complex blend of male and female identifications and bodily representations. She convincingly illustrates this complexity of gender representations as expressed in her patients' fantasies and body images and as played out clinically in their transferences. Similarly, Yanof (2000), in a compelling case of a little girl in analysis, traces her patient's feelings and fantasies about gender over the course of a five-year treatment. The case illustrates how multiple meanings become attached to gender and how gender functions as a solution to shifting conflicts. In agreement with Harris, Yanof concludes that gender development is not linear, but rather more chaotic and complex, based on interactions between biology and environment and subject to continual reorganization.

Diamond (2004a,b, 2006), in a series of clinical papers about male development, argues against the prevailing idea that a boy must "disidentify" with his mother to achieve masculinity, and shows how gender identity can be reworked over the course of men's lives. He is one of many psychoanalysts (Ross 1986; Elise 2001; Fogel 1998, 2006; Reichbart 2006) writing about masculinity who have tried to "unpack" the rigid phallic modes and ideals embraced by their male patients and embedded in psychoanalytic theories. Fogel (1998) widens the meaning of castration anxiety in men by identifying an interior bodily genitality, split off from experience, that he deems "feminine." All these clinical accounts make evident that gender fluidity is itself not constant; even in a given individual, gender identity seems fixed at one time and, at another time and in a different context, more fluid.

Gender and Object Choice

Contemporary psychoanalytic writers agree that it is important to distinguish between gender (and gender identity) and object choice (Tyson 1982). In a brilliant set of essays, Chodorow (1994) makes the argument that both heterosexuality and homosexuality should be viewed as compromise formations and that "normal" heterosexuality cannot be taken as a given that need not be questioned, whereas homosexuality is automatically questioned. Chodorow asks us to unpack the tight connection between gender identity and object choice. She attacks assumptions that psychoanalysts have heretofore taken for granted: that identification with one parent necessary leads to erotic desire for the other. "How," she wonders, "do we reconcile a complex and varied view of the multiplicity of sexualities and the problematic nature of conceptions of normality and abnormality with a dichotomous, unreflected-upon, traditional view of gender and gender role or an appeal to an undefined 'masculinity' and 'femininity.' ... [For example] developing homosexual boys are 'feminized,' as if it is only by being feminine that someone could desire a male..." (p. 60).

Thus, on the contemporary scene both heterosexuality and homosexuality are to be questioned, but the *origin* of homosexuality is not "relevant." This approach is put most clearly by Corbett (2001b): "The overwhelming majority of my gay patients approach their sexuality with a certain inevitability that does not brook questions of specific origin or legitimization. Through this assertion, I do not mean to imply that I do not set out with my patients to understand—to the degree that we can—in what manner their sexuality has developed. But our efforts in this regard are guided by the question 'How homosexuality?' (With what meaning and to what effect?) as opposed to what I consider to be the ill-conceived etiologic project of 'Why homosexuality?'" (p. 325).

In these discussions the concept of bisexuality is often evoked. Butler (1995), another influential gender theorist, weaves concepts of bisexuality into her theories about object choice. She posits a bisexual base in the individual from which society and family shape and guide children to a sexual object choice of the opposite sex and to a suppression/repression of homosexual impulses. She bases her arguments on her understanding of Freud's "Mourning and Melancholia" (1917) and his theories of psychosexual development, in which heterosexuality is attained at the end of a complicated and difficult developmental pathway. She then elaborates her idea that this laborious and uncertain accomplishment of a tenuous state of heterosexuality wards off a repudiated homosexuality. The situation leaves an eternally unmourned and unmournable state of being that is covered over by same-sex identifications and a conventional and socially sanctioned hetero-sexuality. In a critique of these ideas, Balsam (2007), argues that Butler downplays the fate of ambivalence and internal aggression so crucial to Freud's theory of melancholy.

The concept of an original bisexuality, which is part of Butler's thesis, is endorsed by a long string of psychoanalysts, though they have conceptualized it in a variety of ways. Parens (1980), a child analyst, describes a basic inborn bisexuality and neutral genital libido out of which "heterosexual libido deriving from primary masculinity and primary femininity" differentiates (p. 110). Layton (2000) argues that bisexual *behavior* should be recognized as an acceptable sexual solution independent of heterosexuality and homosexuality.

Normality vs. Marginality

Contemporary theories of gender challenge traditional guideposts and assumptions about what is normal vs. pathological gender. Corbett (1997, 2001a, b) argues forcefully that traditional developmental models of gender were dominated by a normative logic of centrality, with limited accounting for the necessity of marginality. The homosexual or "invert" was at the margin. This logic has been replaced by a "queer ethic", which declares that all manner of things are "fabulous," aims to expand mental freedom, and gains its meaning and energy by its oppositional relation to the norm. For Corbett, the sign of health is mental freedom. At the same time, he warns that both polarities—coherence and similarity vs. difference and ambiguity—have associated problems. He argues that gender can have a regulatory effect, constraining a person by its embedded social stereotypes and rules about roles. While dissimilarity and incoherence may be celebrated, he believes that the significance of (and I think the *need for*) similarity and coherence must also be taken into account. Patients suffer from non-integration and depersonalization and the pain of being a nonconforming subject faced with the "strong arm of culture." Cautiously and wisely, he concludes that "we must champion paradox, but not idealize it" (1997, p. 270).

Consider how "gender diffusion" or categories of "transgender" are thought about in the contemporary theoretical literature, in which there is a call for acceptance of all varieties of sexuality and gender-related behavior. Take for example, Benjamin's plea "in defense of gender ambiguity" (1996). We are listening to a new series of voices from the edge, from the intersex and trans-gendered communities, which demand acceptance and call for our giving up traditional binary categories of gender and "normality."

Corbett (2001b) admonishes clinicians for mistaking gender normality for health. He and many others argue that gender is not an entity, but functions in multiple and overdetermined ways as surface, performance, and psychic solution. Psychoanalysts, he feels, have positioned themselves as gender border guards, with one size to fit all. He points to the transgendered subjects who have had no voice in the dialogue and are labeled deviant. Of course, lurking behind these arguments is the long, and unfortunate, history of psychoanalysts trying to "cure" homosexuals of their homosexuality (Goldberg 2001).

Another take on the normality/abnormality question comes from Crawford (1996), a self-psychologist who puts strong emphasis on gender in the clinical situation. For her, too, it is gender identity itself (a tightly packaged one) that poses a trauma, a narcissistic one. The socialization process mandates rigid enforcement of what is acceptably masculine or feminine and make self-resti-tution impossible (Ulman and Brothers 1988). The process leads to a sense of inadequacy, of incompleteness, and basic lack of trust in the self and others, all of which become her focus clinically. Like Corbett, she would focus on "freedom" as the goal for gender-related problems.

Gender Biases

There has been much discussion of the gender biases of therapists, frequently with writers of different vantage points hurling insults about biases back and forth over theoretical divides. Layton (1998) contends that "all self-disclosures and interpretations are loaded with content that reflects one's gender and sexual positioning" (p. 738). Some analysts feel they can escape such biases by focusing on the patient's psychic reality. Kaplan (1990), for example, argues that a critical or philosophical exploration of the ideals of femininity and masculinity—laid down by the social order—has never been the purview of clinical psychoanalysis, but belongs more specifically to applied psychoanalysis and other disciplines. The analyst's role is to explore the patient's use of repression in conflicts around social values vs. internal unconscious urges. Kaplan acknowledges that psychoanalysts over the years have been misled by gender stereotypes, especially theoretically, but he holds—more optimistically than I do—that keeping the focus on the patient's conflicts about masculinity and femininity can keep the clinical process free of such bias. In the clinical situation, he believes, the social reality of gender is always a resistance, as adherence to one set of social values closes out consideration of another, and masks unconscious conflicts. In this discussion, Kaplan offers an interesting perspective on the development of conformity and the narcissism of difference and similarity.

A few analysts (Greenberg 2006; Hirsh 1993; Mitchell 1996) have written openly and movingly on their gender-related biases in clinical cases.

To me, these accounts offer the most useful approaches to coming to grips, clinically, with such biases.

Embodiment

Closely related to the issue of social construction of gender is the issue of embodiment. Many contemporary theorists are leery of concepts about bodily influences on gender, anxious to stay clear of old reifications and old saws like "anatomy is destiny." Since the prevailing idea is that gender is articulated and mediated in the interpersonal communicative sphere, such theorists are more trusting of, and more comfortable with, relational and intersubjective clinical approaches (Harris 2005). One can sense this discomfort in Dimen's introduction to a colloquium on gender and the body (1996). She begins by noting that in postmodern thought the body has become a "linguistic cultural co-production" (p. 386). Contemporary inquiry focuses on *embodiment* rather than *constitution,* on how patient and analyst communicate with one another, and how an individual uses the body to represent or communicate a fantasy, dissociated feelings, or unverbalizable thoughts. (For an interesting clinical example of how the body is used to represent fluctuations in a person's sense of gender, see Elise 1998.)

In this sense, then, the body is a variable and individualized subject matter for representations of gender. For Diamond (2006), "destiny is what we make of our anatomy" (p. 1103). He tries to bridge the polarities between social constructionism and biological essentialism by offering a more complicated and ambiguous understanding of gender, constructed fundamentally out of early identifications with each parent, but leaving open the possibility of influence by biological variables. Stimmel (2000), Elise (2000a), and Layton (2000) join in this dialogue by arguing, from somewhat different positions around the pole of constructionism (as against essentialism), that bisexuality takes its meaning from the meaning ascribed to it by a given individual, and not from necessarily intrinsic biological givens.

CLINICAL APPLICATIONS

These contemporary understandings of gender have important implications for clinical practice.

If gender is multilayered, complex, and fluid, and if its meanings change over time and in different contexts, and are not fixed by innate imperatives, it can become attached to, or entangled with, an unlimited range of thoughts and fantasies in a given individual. It can accrue idiosyncratic meanings. These entanglements may need to be addressed explicitly in the clinical situation. In many ways, until recent explorations, gender has been held to be immune from the concept of overdetermination.

If gender is socially constructed, or to the extent that it is, clinicians must become aware of the gender-related biases and countertransferences, and the deeply embedded assumptions about gender, that interfere with or cloud our judgments and assessments. Many psychoanalysts (I am one of them) assume that these attitudes are inevitable and cannot be avoided.

Underlying assumptions about what is psychopathological in the realm of gender and gender identity have shifted. A hundred years ago, psychoanalysis was complacently unaware of its socially based perceptions of what constitutes "normality" in the area of gender (Schäfer 1974). If a person deviated from socially accepted norms in certain ways, then these drew attention as symptoms or problems. Moreover, the pendulum has shifted in other areas as well; fluidity or even instability in gender identity is now considered more "healthy" and constancy or rigidity more "unhealthy." In much of contemporary thinking, in fact, rigidity in gender identifications or identity is a frequent though unacknowledged sign of pathology.

Gender-related conflicts cannot always be conceptualized in familiar drive vs. defense terms. Gender-related conflicts may be more readily described and understood in Kris's terms (1985), as *divergent rather than convergent.* In divergent conflicts two forces pull in opposite directions, as in a fantasy of being independent and "masculine" and, at the same time, pampered and "feminine." In convergent conflicts, which are more familiar, two forces, say a drive and a defense, are aimed at a single object (e.g., hating and at the same time being dependent on one's mother).

The analysis of the superego or what has come to be known as "ego ideals" may be especially cogent in the treatment of gender-related conflicts. Patients often feel in conflict around values or ideals surrounding masculinity or femininity that cannot be met.

CLINICAL EXAMPLES

Following are two clinical vignettes and a longer case study demonstrating the varied ways in which ideas of masculinity or femininity may fit into the self-concept, take on narcissistic meanings, serve defensive functions, and infiltrate unconscious fantasies. The clinical material is meant to illustrate the social construction of gender, its incertitude, and its relation to object choice.

Case 1

For some time' I supervised a psychoanalytic candidate, a serious and responsible young man, who was struggling to balance his many roles and responsibilities. He was married with two young children, and was very actively involved with his family. He also held down a demanding position at a local university, had a clinical practice, and was in psychoanalytic training. His control case was a young man around his own age, and like him married with two young children. But the similarities seemed to stop there. Before he began his analysis, the patient had quit a full-time job in computers to set up a free-lance design business. His wife's family had money, though she worked as an adjunct professor for very little pay. Her trust fund, in essence, supported them and his low-fee analysis.

The patient suffered from depression and anxiety, and from a general dissatisfaction with himself. He spent hours and hours obsessively constructing and perfecting his projects, anxiously ruminating about his occasional jobs, and periodically masturbating to internet porn. He did take good care of his children, for whose care he was largely responsible. In his sessions he ruminated at length in an intellectualized monotone. Needless to say, he drove his analyst crazy. And I could sympathize.

This patient had been devastated by his parents' divorce when he was five years old. His father had left his mother to marry another woman, with whom he had already fathered a baby, and eventually left the state. The patient was left to take care of his childish and overly seductive mother.

Underneath his intellectualization, we discerned a father hunger in this man. We speculated that he had an angry need to defeat his father and his analyst by defeating himself and backing away from his competitive oedipal triumph. We pointed to his anxiety and clear anguish and conflicts around masculinity. For him, being a good dad meant never separating from his children. His idea of "masculinity" was all mixed with selfishness and sexual unfaithfulness.

My supervisee and I sometimes asked ourselves the following question: What if this patient were a woman? A more or less stay-at-home mother, supported by her spouse, doing work she had always wanted to do at home and beginning to make money at it? Would we look at her situation, would we pathologize it, in the same way? Probably not. But neither the candidate nor I could rid ourselves of our gender-related standards.

And neither, we argued to ourselves, could the patient, who grew up in the same society and was in conflict with his own internalized standards. For the time being we decided, uneasily, that our formulation was right, that we had untangled our own values and conflicts from those of the patient. But I also think it was important and useful that we thought this through, together, and that we continued to think it through as the analysis and supervision continued.

Case 2

When she began her analysis, Mrs. A., a forty-year-old businesswoman, was anxious and resistant. She seemed sensitive to separations, though she could not, or would not, talk about her reactions to them and missed a lot of sessions

227

herself. In analysis she worried that she was getting nowhere and also that she could not express herself well. I was struck by how Mrs. A. referred to her father as "Les" and to his family not as "my grandmother" or "my aunt," but as "Les's mother" or "Les's sister." I speculate that this reflected the bitterness and distance of her mother toward Les. Shortly after the patient's birth, Les abruptly left the mother for another woman.

One day toward the beginning of the analysis, Mrs. A. came early to a session. She recounted that to pass the time, she had walked around in the vicinity of my office and encountered a mail carrier. "When I was growing up," she remembered, "I had wanted to be a mail carrier. I haven't thought about that in a really long time. I grew up in such a sterile environment that to be a mail carrier seemed like something that was a lofty goal. My step-dad was a factory worker; my mom worked as a salesclerk or at the bar. On my [biological] paternal side, Les's mother did go to two years of college, and Les's father owned a small business. On my mother's side I was the first to go to college. Later my [maternal] uncle did go to college. One evening he and I were talking philosophy and I got excited and told my mother about how neat it was to be talking to him. She slapped me across the face and said, 'You think you're so goddamn good, you're just like Les. He would use a fifty-cent word for anything.' I guess I equated wanting to be intelligent with being crazy, and maybe masculine, like Les. If my report card would be good, my stepdad said, 'We don't want an all-A student.' I was not allowed to read, like for pleasure. They said that meant I was just like Les."

I remarked, "So to do well means you were masculine and crazy, or abandoned." This simple remark seemed to calm her anxiety and gave me a basis for approaching her resistance in this early phase of the analysis. Here "masculine" had idiosyncratic meanings—"too" smart and also someone to reject to reject before being rejected.

This vignette demonstrates the elasticity of gender—how meanings can accrue to it like Velcro. "Masculine" had accrued the meanings, idiosyncratic and particular to this woman's background, of bad, smart, crazy—bringing rejection one way or another. In treatment, the meanings, often unconscious, can be unpacked and unstuck, and thus free anxiety and open disavowed aspects of the self. It is an instance of the everyday kind of conflicts around gender that we encounter in our patients.

Case 3: Christina

I will draw more extensive process material from a case in which the issues about gender were predominant. Christina came from a family that made much of gender. Additionally, the issues about gender are especially clear because the patient was very self-aware and self-searching.

Christina was a woman in her early forties who sought treatment for a rather severe reactive depression. Some months before, she had discovered that her long-standing female partner had betrayed her with another woman. The subsequent separation left her lost and aimless, and forced her to return to the area where her family lived. An artist, she soon found a job as a teacher at a local magnet art and technical school. When I first began seeing her, Christina was involved with a man she had met at her athletic club, who wanted to marry her. She considered him a good friend and found him sexually attractive, but felt they were too different to get married, as he did not share her intellectual interests and she was leery of his tendency toward alcohol abuse.

Christina came from a traditional Italian Catholic family, one of eight siblings. Her father, an autoworker, drank too much; her mother was a home-maker. Christina described her father as cold and cruel. His sharp, sarcastic, and demeaning tongue was feared by all the children, but he was especially hard on Christina, who never toed the family line. He made no bones about the fact that he preferred males, but his sons were not spared his wrath.

Christina had no conscious early sexual memories, except for some sexual play with a brother in the bathtub, but she wondered about possible sexual abuse of some sort. In the analysis we reconstructed an experience at age three in which the father spanked her, nude, over his lap. Her sense was that her father was probably sexually aroused, and perhaps had an erection.

Christina's mother was more accessible, but always backed up the father and defended him. She treated her daughters as a unit when they were girls, wanting to dress them alike in frilly outfits for church or, when they were adults, wanting to have an all-female day of shopping. Christina resisted her mother's attempts to dress her in dresses and hats and preferred the company of her brothers. She was especially close to her brother, a year older, who was her parents' favorite, the "golden boy" who excelled at sports. The family tolerated Christina's tomboyishness until grade school, when her brothers turned their backs on her; in her adolescence the pressure to be "more feminine" became even more intense. Her sisters all followed very traditionally feminine, even "hyperfeminine," pursuits such as modeling. Christina took solace in her exceptional athletic abilities, which put her through college and earned her much acclaim. Later her talent in art won her a prestigious graduate fellowship abroad.

In general, Christina felt that in order to have her own identity, she had to distance herself physically and psychologically from her family, and from their unwavering rituals and demands for conformity.

Christina took readily to my suggestion of analysis. A sense of her distress at that time led me to be especially careful not to proceed too quickly or assuredly. She was a self-reflective person and comfortable with fantasy and dreams, but much of her history was repressed. "I don't do narrative," she said. In the early months of treatment she would bring in her artwork, which she would use to show me her fantasies and memories. Before she began analysis, she would come into the office and lay her prints down on the couch, waiting for me to respond to them. I didn't say much—I didn't know what to say, except to ask her to tell me about the pieces and to remark on their striking effects. Her art was beautiful and powerful. At this stage of her analysis, she was making collages of layered objects—razorblades, spools of thread, baseball mitts, leaves, hands—in jarring but strangely pleasing arrays. This aspect of her treatment, which related to issues of creativity and how it relates to verbalization, is especially fascinating, but demands more focused attention in its own right.

As you can infer from this brief history, Christina could be called bisexual in at least two meanings of the term. She was bisexual in object choice, in the sense that either a female or a male partner was okay with her; she was more sexually attracted to males, but preferred females emotionally. In terms of her gender identity, Christina had never been happy being female; she had wished she were, and tried to be, a boy. This discontent, which mixed in with her depression, was a primary focus of her treatment. She could not identify comfortably with either parent—not with her father, whom she saw as a mean bully, or with her mother, who was his handmaiden. In the course of the analysis, however, we uncovered many unconscious identifications and disidentifications with both mother and father, and along with them conflicted fantasies, conscious and unconscious, about femininity and masculinity. (I make no attempt here to define these terms; I am referring to what the *patient*, idiosyncratically, meant by femininity and masculinity.) From this dense and ultimately successful analysis I am going to pick and choose moments to show how we worked through this interwoven material about gender.

The following is from a session early in the analysis. Christina complained of hot flashes. (Her signs of menopause added to her depression, as we came to understand in the course of the analysis; it meant to her the waning of her body and its athletic abilities and, at a deeper lever, the reality that she would never have babies.) She referred to a dream she had had two nights before, and commented that if she were a boy she wouldn't have the fears and worries that she did. "Many times I feel asexual. I don't have either identity. It's uncomfortable to float there. In that dream my mother was working on something on her lap, like cross-stitching. That makes me think of the time when I went to my mother about something I was upset about and she said, 'Don't worry. Let's do cross-stitching.'"

In retrospect, I wonder to myself whether cross-stitching perhaps had another unconscious meaning—"cross-dressing"—but at the time I linked this to the feelings she frequently expressed about my silence.

"It brings up the feeling that I'm not there for you. Not a safe harbor."

"You're right. I'm waiting for the repercussions from you. To show emotional honesty was not allowed at my house. Certain expressions were disallowed. We had to adopt a formal false language. In English, you couldn't call my mother 'she.' You had to refer to her as 'mother' or you could get whopped by the side of the head [by the father]."

At this point in the analysis, the transference alternated rapidly between a disappointing mother who could offer no words of comfort, but only traditional gender-related diversions, and a harsh critical father sitting behind her, who might "whop her by the side her head." At this time, I could not appreciate or associate to the many layered meanings of "lap," which later emerged in the analysis—lap was linked to her father, the bodily site of his abuse of her, and to her longed-for mother's lap, which appeared repeatedly in dreams and images of me, sitting in an armchair, inaccessible, and to her own lap and the sexual feelings harbored there. Later in the analysis she confessed shamefully that she once masturbated as a child by putting a little kitten in her lap.

Three months later, she spoke of liking her female internist, how much memory a new computer had, how some married friends seemed to be getting along well, and her wish to work with glowing light in her art. She referred to a dream we had worked on in the session before, in which she—dressed as a tomboy and innocent—was hiding in the attic, scared. An adult male, perhaps a sculptor, was looking for her. She remembered actually dressing like that and wanting to be ten forever.

I pointed out that it is not unusual for kids to want to be ten forever: "They can still play, and there is not yet adult sexuality. In the dream you were dressed as a tomboy, and that suggests that you needed to be a tomboy as a way to hide out from a scary adult male and from sexuality. Of course, being a tomboy also meant you could be the kind of person you wanted to be, play the games you wanted to play."

"That's true. With the sculptor in the dream there was interest and fear."

I stated that she was very conflicted about sexuality and said, "As you begin to try to sort it all out, as a young adolescent, in this dream, or here, things are not clear about where you are: Do you want to be sexual, and with a man or a woman?" I concluded, "There were mixed-up feelings about it all, and there still are."

"I agree. It's extremely helpful, figuring out the origins and meanings of my responses. My parents played stuff out with me too, which made it worse."

At this point early in the analysis, I was beginning to comment on her conflicts about sexuality and gender. Perhaps there was a tilt in my phrasing, which many contemporary gender theorists would sharply criticize, toward suggesting that she needed to make a binary choice; perhaps she unconsciously thought that I, like her parents, was "playing something out with her." What I was trying to respond to and understand, however, was her fear of sex. At this point I did not comment on the obvious transference implications, of which she was clearly aware—her liking her female doctor, or how much memory I had. She also perceived me as the scary male sculptor in the dream, who might mold her into something else or handle her sensually and erotically. Such homoerotic, heterosexual, preoedipal transferences were explored in much depth in the course of the analysis. Her obvious appreciation and penchant for our analytic work was gratifying.

In the months that followed, many complex and shifting identifications emerged. For example, she designed a business card with a geisha image, dark hair cut straight and short. Her associations were to the Nancy comic strip she liked during childhood, and to the submissive role of women in her family. She linked this with a growing awareness of identification with another Nancy, me: "I'm more curious about you. We have sort of similar temperaments. Both have allergies. We both like helping. Just like the little girl puppet. ... At some point I gave up wearing dresses. I played with my brother and his friends. Yet I had a crush on this little boy when I was five. I did have crushes on boys. Then in junior high I joined the soft-ball group. My parents tried to pressure me to be something else. ... I'll never repay the debt of what softball did for me, and what the woman coach did for me. She was not a lesbian." She had begun to cry. (The reference to the coach not being lesbian is important. Christina told me how many of the coaches she had had over the years had crossed boundaries with the woman athletes, and how she found this abhorrent.)

I said, "In looking at me and thinking that we have the same temperament, the question is, what kind of woman am I, and what kind of woman are you, will you be?" Note that the identification with me at this point was as another handmaiden (a geisha) but had another component—the spunky cartoon character of Nancy.

A month later she returned to these themes in the transference, which was heating up: "I had a dream. I'm making love to an Asian man. [She laughs.] He has amazing skin. We are lying side to side, head to foot. He is caressing my buttocks. I pleasure myself. I have this long clitoris, almost like a penis. [This image reminded me of the practice Christina had confessed earlier in the analysis of masturbating by pulling her labia and pretending she had a penis.] Then he's above me. I have a desire to be part of this amazing skin. I've said I was repulsed by my mother's skin, which actually was so soft. Yesterday I asked what it means to be phallic. It means to have power. My mother belongs to The Mothers with Penises Club [laughs]."

I explicitly commented on the bisexual images in the dream—her dreams were full of bisexual images—and then asked, "Aren't you saying it would be nice to get it *all* from one person—from me?"

Agreeing, Christina laughed and said, "Isn't that what heaven's for?"

Thus, narcissistic, gender-related, and sexual conflicts are represented and repaired through concrete bodily fantasies.

So far we can view an amalgam of conflicted and complex identifications and love-objects: Christina as a boy like her bothers; Christina who had crushes on little boys; Christina as a little puppet, a geisha; Christina as a self that can pleasure itself; Christina with both a penis and a clitoris; Christina identifying with a phallic mother; Christina longing for the soft skin of a mother or of a male lover; Christina being chased by a threatening but somehow alluring male; Christina helped by a non-lesbian coach; Christina crushed by a lesbian lover. Her wish to be all and to get all puts us in mind of Fast's formulations about young children's narcissistic wishes around gender. It also very clearly illustrates what contemporary gender theorists like Harris and Young-Bruehl posit: that gender serves to solve internal psychic problems and that gendered identifications and meanings are multiple, layered, and shifting. Here Christina's sense of her gendered self is fluid and unfixed, with pieces of brothers, sisters, mother, and father in the mix. So too is her fantasized love object—a male who has what she defines as feminine characteristics (e.g., soft skin). As sexual subject, Christina has bisexual power—both male and female genitalia. Thus, she need not feel vulnerable to potentially painful and disappointing longings for the other, or devalued experiences of self.

The middle phase of the analysis was marked by themes carrying primal scene meanings in which the patient quickly and often confusingly oscillated in her identifications and desires, wanting to be or have the father, then the mother, both being unacceptable, frightening, and unattainable; then later by periods of more sustained homoerotic transference that might be characterized as "negative oedipal." That is, Christina yearned for my love, often in highly erotic terms, and felt jealous of the males she imagined as her rivals, just as she had always felt that her father and brothers came first in her mother's heart. Her jealousy of her brothers and father was intense and aroused much guilt. We were able to understand how she fantasized that to be a male would help her achieve that love. She also wished for her mother's nurturance and care, wishes that she had disavowed until they became activated in the interaction with me. She summarized these insights: "I did want her attention, but I rejected her completely. There was a big conflict." We speculated that wanting to be a boy pulled together a lot of fantasies; besides gaining her mother's love, it represented a wish to gain acceptance from her father. In all of this, I was often thrown by the shifting sands and searched for more coherence. I think this was both a projective identification of Christina's confusion (perhaps reflecting primal scene-like experiences) and search for coherence, and my own personal need quite apart from hers.

A few months later she began to allow herself more open homoerotic feelings toward me. In one session she began by talking about a series of situations in which men were always in charge. Then she reported a series of dreams. In one was a naked beauty contest, in which a male was in charge, with women who were "visually stimulating." They had different colors of genital hair—blond, red, or reddish-blond—but one also had hair on her abdomen, "like on a man's body": that was the one for her. She associated to a movie starring the redhaired actress Julianne Moore. She admitted having such thoughts about me, but felt it was "taboo" for her as a woman to look at women.

Following is a session about a year later, which shows considerable working through of these ideas and less oscillation between identifications.

"Well, you are going away. Anywhere special or just a break? I'm not teaching that class at night. Been given a double message about whether I need to or not. I got a letter from my mother saying she came across a box of my trophies from my challenging years. So maybe I would want to come get them. Ha!"

In answer to my query if she would go to get her trophies, Christina said, "Yes, it's worth it to me. She has to lure me with a toy, though. She doesn't have enough self-esteem. It's disappointing ultimately."

"We have to leave this and go to my dreams. I remember how badly I wanted to be a boy. Like how I pulled one of my lips [i.e., labia]. Pain and pleasure all mixed—screwed up. In this dream I'm kind of in and out of it. All boys … a couple of exercise bikes. Friday night I ate at a Vietnamese restaurant. An Asian man was there kind of flirting with me. So there was an Asian man in the dream, with some tying going on—of legs…red yarn being wrapped around sexually … I don't know. It was sexually exciting. More men, boys come into the room, like a sauna. I'm thinking of my brothers. I think I can't participate. They'll be doing things sexually with each other. I was left out. … See what happens when you go away? He's getting manipulated by a hand under water. Creamy white stuff like ejaculate on the surface."

She continued: "First of all you'll be going away a long time. I don't want you to… I saw the movie *Pleasantville* yesterday. It's about a mother-son relationship. They get their color when they find their passion… I bought myself a purse. [Typically she carried a backpack.] A huge symbol! I can't be too feminine."

Note that the reference to the movie *Pleasantville,* in which the mother and son find their passion, is a clue to the countertransference in this period. There were times when I unconsciously pulled back from the patient's erotic longings —by changing the subject, by focusing on her conflicts around gender identity, by confusedly losing sight of the transference—not, I think, because of their ~~homoerotic~~ contents, but because of their intensity.

"What's the connection with my going away and this talk about wanting to be male, or not too feminine?"

"If you go, I'd kill myself?"

"If you were a male, maybe you'd be going with me?"

"Certainly your husband will be going with you."

I pointed out how much of what she was talking about expressed the feeling of being excluded by me, her brothers, her mother—she wanted her mother to say directly she wanted to see her.

She agreed and said, "Yes, and I get what you've said. My mother left me in the tub. If I were a boy this wouldn't happen to me." In a more forgiving tone she mused, "Mother's letter—it *is* a way of communicating," but then, more bitterly, "It's little wonder if that's what passed for love in my family, I have been so crippled. What's the use?"

In this vein, some months later, the patient mused, "There's a seductive thing turned around here. I thought I was like my mother and I was competitive for my father, but this is the other way around, isn't it? *She,* not my father, was the desired one for me. It's one more way that I couldn't win though, isn't it? I couldn't get my father, and I couldn't get my mother. I was always competing for Daddy too; I think I was the one who looked like my mother. But what is natural is this—I watch my little niece with my brother, and she is coy and flirtatious and it's lovely. I think that's the way it is with little girls and their dads." Here she recognizes her dilemma of having sexual yearnings for both father and mother, neither of whom could reciprocate with appropriate affection. She longs for, in imagination, what she (and culture) labels "normal"—the positive oedipal situation between little girls and their fathers.

Beginning in the fourth year of analysis, the patient began to approach some deeply conflicted, shameful wishes to be more "feminine." She linked them to the shameful position of females, as she perceived it, in relation to males: "The tie between the victim and her abuser. The currency of my parent's relationship. Mutual shame and service. I can see how I reject everything to do with my mother, anything. That idea of feminine beauty; it affected me and her relationship with me. A lot of who I was—I felt it was killed. Feeling good about who I was as a person and with my sexuality." That is, she felt that in order to be accepted she had to accept a false femininity, the kind of femininity that was prescribed by her family and, at the same time, to give up important aspects of herself that were unacceptable to them, aspects labeled masculine—athleticism, being adventuresome.

In our analytic work she painfully had to acknowledge other "masculine" aspects of herself—identifications with her father, the aggressor, that is, her sadism and cold anger. For instance, in one session after describing the power plays at her school among her fellow teachers and how she situated herself in the dynamic, she observed: "My father. Being like him. I will have the power, and then I won't get hurt. Is that what this is about? I can't think or say my father and love in the same sentence. Dad was a dictator. Like with the Jews in Europe who collaborated with the Nazis. When the Nazis come knocking at the door to say 'Turn in so-and-so or we'll kill you'—that makes them collaborators. Although then they'll come back in three months and get you anyway. But my mother was the real collaborator. In order to make my mother happy and get her approval you had to try to please my dad."

In the last year or year and a half of analysis, the sessions became very intense and painful, as they were filled with Christina's now more openly expressed yearnings for me to be "the one" she was searching for to love and to love her —her very significant other. She had figured out that she and I shared interests in common—art, cinema, literature, psychology. I had all she might want. At the same time, she knew this was impossible, and reflected her never-to-be fulfilled wishes toward both her parents. The last months of analysis were marked by her mourning for what would never be, within the transference and her family. At the same time, an acceptance of herself and the possibility of a better, more hopeful future emerged.

Christina came to understand that in her rage about her mother's rejection of her, her lack of support and empathy, she rejected all things about her mother —all things she perceived as "feminine."

"It's just amazing how strong my feelings of rejection toward her are. I was looking at this stuff in some stores. I went shopping the other day. I need some pants and there were some cool summer dresses I was looking at, so I tried on a black cool dress, like loose, plain and sleeveless. I can't even go there ... I look in the mirror and I see my mother. I can't be that, I can't!"

I commented, "You can't because you reject her, and reject wanting something from her."

"My mother, who was beautiful, had a black dress like that. I remember. I look like my mother. ... Black dresses are like whores, too."

The following session is taken from the week of termination. More comfort within the transference and increased ability to work out her feelings herself were accompanied by changes in her feelings about gender.

Christina began: "Spring is in the air and I got a book on gardening. Listen to this dream: I had a small sewing machine. I would really like one. I couldn't use it because it had no thread. Then somebody found the thread. Reminds me that actually in class the kids found a solution to a problem in an art project we were working on. In the dream, the thread was in basic colors, and then they found all the colors. This is a great dream. I've used that thread imagery in a lot of my work, but sewing, threads, I have rejected all of that from my mother. We talked about that. Now, it's an indication of accepting that and it equals knowledge of all the colors, a sense of completion there. It's related to here, completion from you." This attitude toward herself and her sense of femaleness contrasts with the earlier fantasy of cross-stitch, cross-dress. Her gender identity is more integrated—full of many colors, and not a clashing two-tone of masculinity/ femininity.

I spoke of the sense of choice and creativity, to feel free to choose to be what kind of woman to be. Like she had been talking recently about what to wear.

"Yes, just yesterday I went shopping and there are huge sales. I need a robe. My robe is like a man's—plaid—it's ugly. I was looking for an identity; it has to be just right, though. I know what I have in mind. A few months ago I found one. It was too much money. It was silk with an exotic Asian print. Maybe I'll go back and get it. ... The kids helped in the project and it's good I can depend on them."

The frequent Asian references reflect Christina's special liking for things Asian.

Her parents had a small "oriental" black table in the house, clearly a special object, handed down from a distant but admired relative on the father's side.

240

Christina considered it an "art" object and more sophisticated than anything else in the household. Here then was an object that carried condensed meanings with maternal/paternal and feminine/masculine connotations.

When she terminated treatment, Christina was much happier in general, and specifically within herself in regard to feelings about gender. She was more content with herself as a woman, more free to accept aspects, behaviors, and desires she (and society) deemed "feminine"; she also accepted with less guilt the aspects and identifications she deemed "masculine." Her art had changed too. Still powerful and beautiful, it now was less jarring, the compositions no longer fragmented, and with brighter, more vibrant colors. She had worked through a long period in the analysis of giving up and mourning the fantasy that her special person would be the analyst. At that point, she was looking for, but had not yet found, a mate—the someone with whom she could share love, sex, and life. She had decided that it would be easier and she would prefer that the someone be a male; but if a woman came up, she would keep that option open.

DISCUSSION

I believe that these clinical examples, and this last most particularly, demonstrate contemporary ideas about the fluidity and complexity of gender. I have tried to show that conflicts about gender are common, everyday occurrences, acquiring idiosyncratic meanings and functions, yet mirroring shared cultural beliefs.

For Christina, gender had become entangled with meanings and fantasies about power, acceptance, and lovability. Analysis revealed her fantasy of obtaining magical power through a bisexual love object. She felt she could not get the unconditional love she yearned for—by either being male or being female, which left her uneasy and unhappy about her own gender. I have included examples in which I addressed these fantasies and conflicts explicitly in the clinical situation and tried to demonstrate how the attached meanings changed over the course of our work. Following the process material, we can see how gender was at one time or another fluid or fixed, linked or unlinked to sexuality.

I tried to keep in mind my own gender-related biases and countertransferences as I worked with Christina's conflicts around gender, to separate mine from hers. As I

look back on this material now, I can detect in the transference the patient's fears that I would try to seduce her into femininity, as her mother had, or beat and bully her into heterosexuality, as her father had. I think that she did intuit a bias in me to "make her feminine," and I ask myself if I shared her conviction that heterosexuality might be an easier lifestyle for her and pushed her in that direction. Perhaps. But I really think that I felt that if she could find that true soul mate, of either gender, I would be happy for her. I could always appreciate and admire the expanding creative potential in this woman that reflected the multifaceted identifications and aspects of herself.

I think that all individuals have multiple identifications with both males and females, although in most people these may be less visible and more seamlessly integrated within their personalities than they were in Christina. My experience has also led me to believe that especially creative individuals like Christina seem to have more comfort with and more access to bisexual fantasies and multigendered identifications than other people (Kulish 2006). At the same time, she was not comfortable with the incoherent and inconsistent sense of herself and her sexual identity. In any case, Christina's background of painful rejections at the hands of both parents, which were explicitly linked with gender, contributed to her gender-related conflicts.

CONCLUSION

Contemporary gender theorists have tried to move us away from binary catego-ries of gender and constricted ideas of normality. For them, gender pathology is more closely tied to conformity to societal norms and constrictions than to intrapsychic conflict—a culturally inflicted malady, if you will. In my first example, my supervisee and I asked ourselves if we were attributing such "pa-thology" to his patient. Indeed, countless people suffer from over-rigidity in the meanings and values they ascribe to gender and that govern their lives: men who cannot let themselves acknowledge fear, or to be vulnerable and cry, or to earn less than their wives (Reichbart 2006); women who cannot let themselves experience anger lest they not be "nice," or who force themselves at great cost to meet societal, familial, or internalized standards of beauty (Lieberman 2000).

3At the same time, I do not feel that the dictum "anything goes" makes for psychic happiness or "health." People need some sense of continuity and cohesiveness of self—and, I think, of gender. I certainly thought it was better for Christina to accept and like herself as a female than it was to stay "floating," asexual, with no sexual identity, as she was when she began treatment.

Those who decry the old certainties can in turn create new rigidities and closedmindedness. For example, it is not politically correct in today's climate to try to understand and unravel object choice; that is, to question the "origin" of homosexuality, when heterosexuality is taken as the norm. But I believe that the "whys" of any object choice—homosexual or heterosexual—are important areas of investigation in a psychoanalytic inquiry. Christina is a case in point: she was interested in why she chose one sex object over another, in terms of sex and "gender," as well as its likeness and difference vis-a-vis loved and hated, fantasized and remembered aspects of her mother, father, sisters, brothers, and members of her extended family. The investigation of these meanings and the background of these choices and identifications proved both illuminating and ultimately helpful to her. Ideally, we should be able to approach and utilize such

243

clinical evidence—and evidence from other sources—without preconceived notions in any one direction. So I make a plea for tolerance: I think we need to be open-minded not only clinically, but also scientifically. We need to accumulate more scientific and clinical evidence about gender.

It is not possible, I believe, to rid oneself of one's gender-related biases. What I have tried to do, in working analytically with my patients, is to try to become aware of them as I focus on the patient's psychic reality and affects. Whether we admit it or are aware of it or not, I think we all have some notions of "health" and "non-health," even if they are not guided by social norms or statistical bell-shaped curves. Corbett argues that psychoanalytic theories of gender should accept and have a place for marginality, but at the same time not idealize it. I find this argument compelling but would add to it that psychoanalysis should *investigate* the margins and the center as well.

Contemporary gender theory both elucidates and decries our need for certainty about gender and for the comfort of binary categories. As I have tried to apply the contemporary gender theories to my clinical work, I am well aware of and struggle with that paradox.

REFERENCES

Balsam, R. (2001). Integrating male and female elements in a woman's gender identity. *J. Amer. Psychoanal. Assn.*49: 335–1360.

——— (2007). Toward less fixed internal transformations of gender: Commentary on "Melancholy femininity and obsessive-compulsive masculinity: Sex differences in melancholy gender," by Meg Jay. *Studies in Gender & Sexuality* 8:137–147.

Bassin, D. (2000). On the problems with keeping differences where they belong. *Studies in Gender & Sexuality* 1:69–77.

Benjamin, J. (1996). In defense of gender ambiguity. *Gender & Psychoanalysis* 1:*27–43*.

Benjamin, J. (1998). In the Shadow of the Other. New York: Routledge.

Butler, J. (1990). Gender Trouble. New York: Routledge.

——— (1995). Melancholy gender—refused identification. *Psychoanal. Dial.* 5:*165–180*.

Chodorow, N.J. (1994). *Femininities, Masculinities, Sexualities.* Lexington: University of Kentucky Press.

Coburn, W.J. (2000). The organizing forces of contemporary psychoanalysis. *Psychoanal. Psychol.* 17:*750–770*.

Corbett, K. (1997). It is time to distinguish gender from health: Reflections on Lothstein's "Pantyhose fetishism and self-cohesion: A paraphilic solution?" *Gender & Psychoanalysis* 2:259–271.

——— (2001a). Faggot = loser. *Studies in Gender & Sexuality* 2:3–28.

——— (2001b). More life: Centrality and marginality in human development. *Psychoanal. Dial.* 11:*313–355*.

Crawford, J. (1996). The severed self: Gender as trauma. *Progr. Self Psychol.* 12:*269–283*.

Diamond, M.J. (2004a). Accessing the multitude within: A psychoanalytic perspective on the transformation of masculinity at mid-life. *Int. J. Psycho-Anal.* 8 5:*45–64*.

——— (2004b). The shaping of masculinity: Revisioning boys turning away from their mothers to construct male gender identity. *Int. J. PsychoAnal* . 85:*359–380*.

——— (2006). Masculinity unraveled: The roots of male gender identity and the shifting of male ego ideals throughout life. *J. Amer. Psychoanal. Assn.* 54:*1099–1130*.

Dimen, M. (1991). Deconstructing difference: Gender, splitting, and transitional space. *Psychoanal. Dial.* 1:*335–352*.

——— (1996). Bodytalk. *Gender & Psychoanalysis* 1:*385–401*.

Elise, D. (1997) Primary femininity, bisexuality, and the female ego ideal: A reexamination of female developmental theory. *Psychoanal. Q.* 66:489–517.

——— (1998). Gender repertoire: Body, mind and bisexuality. *Psychoanal. Dial.* 8:353–371.

———(2000a). "Bye-bye" to bisexuality? Response to Lynne Layton. *Studies in Gender & Sexuality* 1:61–68.

——— (2000b). Generating gender: Response to Harris. *Studies in Gender & Sexuality* 1:157–165.

———(2001). Unlawful entry: Male fears of psychic penetration. *Psychoanal. Dial.* 11:499–531.

Fast, I. (1978). Developments in gender identity: The original matrix. *Int. Rev. Psycho–Anal.* 5:265–273.

Fogel, G.I. (1998). Inferiority and inner genital space in men: What else can be lost in castration. *Psychoanal. Q.* 67:662–697.

——— (2006). Riddles of masculinity: Gender, bisexuality, and thirdness. *J. Amer. Psychoanal. Assn.* 54:1139–1163.

Foucault, M. (1978). *The History of Sexuality.* New York: Random House.

Freud, S. (1917). Mourning and melancholia. *Standard Edition 14:237–258.*

——— (1925). Some psychical consequences of the anatomical distinction between the sexes. *Standard Edition 19:241–263.*

Goldberg, A. (2001). Depathologizing homosexuality. *J. Amer. Psychoanal. Assn.* 49:1109–1114.

Greenberg, J. (2006). "What daimon made you do this?" Thoughts on desire in the consulting room. Paper presented to Michigan Psychoanalytic Society, April.

Harris, A. (2005). *Gender as Soft Assembly.* Analytic Press, Hillsdale, NJ.

Hirsh, I. (1993). Countertransference enactment and some issues related to external factors in the analyst's life. *Psychoanal. Dial.* 3:343–366.

Kaplan, D.M. (1990). Some theoretical and technical aspects of gender and social reality in clinical psychoanalysis. *Psychoanal. St. Child4* 5:3–24.

Kris, A. (1985). Resistance in convergent and in divergent conflicts. *Psychoanal. Q.* 54:*537–568*.

Kulish, N. (2000). Primary femininity: Advances and ambiguities. *J. Amer. Psychoanal. Assn.* 48:*1355–1379*.

———. (2006). Frida Kahlo and object choice: A daughter the rest of her life. *Psychoanal. Inq.* 26:*7–32*.

Layton, L. (1998). What's disclosed in self-disclosures? Gender, sexuality, and the analyst's subjectivity: Commentary on paper by Samuel Gerson. *Psychoanal. Dial.* 8:*731–739*.

——— (2000). The psychopolitics of bisexuality. *Studies in Gender & Psychoanalysis* 1:*41–60*.

Lieberman, J.S. (2000). *Body Talk.* Northvale, NJ: Aronson.

Mitchell, S. (1996). Gender and sexual orientation in the age of postmodernism: The plight of the perplexed clinician. *Gender & Psychoanalysis* 1:*45–73*.

Olesker, W. (2003). Gender and its clinical manifestations. *Psychoanal. St. Child* 58:*3–18*.

Parens, H. (1980). An exploration of the relations of instinctual drives and the symbiosis/separation-individuation process. *J. Amer. Psychoanal. Assn.*28:*89–113*.

Reichbart, R. (2006). On men crying. *J. Amer. Psychoanal. Assn.* 54:*1068–1098*.

Ross, J.M. (1986). Beyond the phallic illusion: Notes on man's heterosexuality. In *The Psychology of Men,* ed. G.I. Fogel, F.M. Lane, & R.S. Liebert. New York: Basic Books, pp. *49–70*.

Schäfer, R. (1974). Problems in Freud's psychology of women. *J. Amer. Psychoanal. Assn.* 22:*459–485*.

Stimmel, B. (2000). The baby with the bath water: Response to Lynne Layton. *Studies in Gender & Sexuality* 1:*79–84*.

Tyson, P. (1982). A developmental line of gender identity, gender role, and choice of love object. *J. Amer. Psychoanal. Assn.* 30:*61–86*.

Ulman, R., & Brothers, D. (1988). *The Shattered Self.* Hillsdale, NJ: Analytic Press.

Yanof, J.A. (2000). Barbie and the tree of life: The multiple functions of gender in development. *J. Amer. Psychoanal. Assn.* 48:*1439–1465*.

Young-Bruehl, E. (2003). *Where Do We Fall When We Fall in Love?* New York: Other Press.

CHAPTER 9:

Obstacles to Oedipal Passion

(2011). Psychoanal. Q., (80)(1):3–32

Many new theoretical and technical developments have extended our understandings of triangular conflicts in the psychoanalytic setting. Yet until recently psychoanalysis has lacked theoretical concepts for passion and, most particularly, for oedipal passion. Contemporary psychoanalytic understandings of the nature of oedipal passion help explain why it is both difficult to articulate and why it continues to be "forgotten." The author argues that individual resistances to oedipal passions reappear and are reinforced in collective theories that distance us from oedipal issues. She presents two clinical cases that illustrate enactments around, and resistances to, oedipal passions within both analyst and patient.

REEXAMINING THE OEDIPAL COMPLEX

When I first began to think about this topic—the Oedipus complex and obstacles to love and passion—a memory of one of my favorite early psychoanalytic teachers popped into my mind. Frank Parcells was a crusty, wonderful character, full of pithy wisdom on the nature of life and psychoanalysis. As he walked out the door after our last class in Basic Concepts, he remarked nonchalantly: "Don't ever forget, your patients will fall in love with you—let's hope you can accept that and be worthy of it."

Another memory, this one from several years earlier while I was still a graduate student: My father, spotting the name of the author of the book I was reading *(The Psychoanalytic Theory of Neurosis)*, was surprised to discover that his cousin from the old country, Otto Fenichel, wasn't such a nobody, as he had always thought, but was in fact a rather famous psychiatrist. He demanded to see the book for himself, and, over the next two days he read straight through it without comment. At the end, he asked only one question: "Humph, so do you believe in this oedipal stuff?"

Well, yes, obviously, I did, I do. But it is one thing to read about the Oedipus complex in Fenichel's text; it was quite another to confront it in the person of my father and his obvious rivalry with his cousin, who was taking up my passionate interest, let alone having to admit in real time to him that I believed in (and obviously experienced) such "stuff." I believe that the emotional constellations we call oedipal conflicts lie at the heart of much of our clinical work, manifesting themselves often as obstacles to loving. And I have come to appreciate that Dr. Parcells was right in his warning that to be "worthy" of our patients' love makes some demands on us—namely, that we recognize and understand our own oedipal issues.

Over a quarter century ago, Grunberger (1980) warned that analysts' unresolved oedipal conflicts often interfere with their ability to help their patients resolve *their* oedipal conflicts. He emphasized that analysts are particularly vulnerable to the narcissistic aspects of the complex. Twenty years earlier, in a groundbreaking paper, Searles (1959) had reported romantic and erotic desires toward all his patients, which usually occurred late in analysis. Searles argued that in a successful psychoanalysis, the participants analyst and patient—need to renounce (and by implication, to become aware of) incestuous goals. He felt that such renunciation rests on recognition of separateness and acknowledgment of mutual love and respect.

Drawing attention to how current psychoanalytic theories have turned away from sexuality, Green (1995) challenged the field by asking, "Has sexuality anything to do with psychoanalysis?" And more recently, Fonagy (2008), in his plenary address to the American Psychoanalytic Association, observed the dramatic decline in psychoanalytic articles with direct references to sexuality: "The major theories of psychoanalysis today place the crux of their clinical accounts elsewhere—principally in the domain of emotional relationships" (p. 14). Even here, Fonagy is lamenting that the field has turned away from sexuality, not specifically from the oedipal complex.

The oedipal complex has undergone much reexamination and reformulation since it was first proposed, and there is still lively debate about its role in psychic life and in psychoanalysis. Freud himself warned us that resistances to its recognition were inevitable; he spoke of the "horror of incest" (1912-1913, p. 1), and wrestled with his own countertransferences to the passionate, difficult transferences of young female patients such as Dora. Over the years, other "horrors" have been articulated—"erotic horror" of the experience of intense sexual desires in the immediacy of the therapeutic dyad (Kumin 1985–1986) and the homoerotic sides of triangular conflicts, which are especially difficult for both patients and analysts to handle (Wrye 1993; Wrye and Wells 1989).

Many of the reformulations about the oedipal complex have enhanced our ability to understand and work clinically with our patients' oedipal issues. From self psychology has come an increased appreciation of the narcissistic conflicts and injuries associated with the oedipal situation (Rothstein 1979). Kleinian contributions (Bollas 1996; Feldman 1990; Steiner 1989) have demonstrated how conflicts connected to the triangular situation, especially the early experience of the primal scene, are reflected in modes of thinking, often interfering with higher-order cognitive functioning. Interpersonalists and intersubjectivists (e.g., Davies 1994; Hirsch 1994) have highlighted parents' participation in the oedipal situation and analysts' participation in their patients' oedipal transferences. Anthropologists constantly remind us of the powerful influences of culture, evident in the myriad forms that the oedipal myth takes (Gu 2006; Pollock 1986). Gender theorists have offered alternative views that take the developmental experience of females more accurately into account (Benjamin 1998; Chodorow 1976; Harris 2005).

Yet serious theoretical problems still entangle us. One is how to delineate a three-person theoretical and clinical picture at a time when we are still looking for balance on the shifting ground between one- and two- person psychologies. Many theorists, primarily Kleinians, have struggled to conceptualize a third party or position within the analytic interaction itself. This position is characterized by a way of thinking in which a participant can stand outside the dyadic interaction to observe and to understand what is going on. This capacity parallels the child's observing position in the early primal scene. The ability to reflect upon and to accept triangularity and its reality marks the attainment of oedipal development. For Benjamin (2004), this capacity begins in the early nonverbal experience of sharing and creating a pattern of relating between mother and infant. Such experiences foreshadow patterns that are co- created in the analytic situation between analyst and patient.

I find these formulations about the kind of thinking, a kind of thirdness, that develops in the analytic situation intriguing and clinically applicable. Indeed, part of the developmental readiness to enter into triadic relationships is marked by the cognitive capacity to deal metaphorically with complexity and with three dimensions. The idea of a co-created thirdness in the therapeutic field, as articulated by theorists like Britton (1989), captures a mental capacity or phenomenon in the cognitive, imaginative sphere.

In the clinical situation, the way in which Kleinians and others work with the concept of thirdness bridges the cognitive, symbolic sphere of mentalization to the emotional field. In interpreting what interferes with a patient's ability to take an observing position, the analyst confronts the patient's strongly charged fantasies and fears, such as the fear of internal dissolution in moving away from the original dyad (Perelberg 2009). But when so-called thirdness is achieved, is this state of mind as it appears in the analytic field equivalent to a fully alive oedipal engagement, or does it simply signal the *capacity for,* or a cognitive dimension of, triangularity?

To my mind, ideas of a co-created thirdness fall short in bringing to life figures within the oedipal triangular drama as they might appear on the analytic stage in the transference-countertransference. That is, the idea of an analytic third and the conceptualization of an enacted triangular drama in the analytic relationship reflect different explanatory frames of reference and different levels of abstraction. The passionate encounter and playing out of oedipal fantasies and conflicts within the transference-countertransference takes place at the experiential, affective level, described and understood through many conceptual lenses.

PSYCHOANALYTIC IDEAS ABOUT PASSION

So how can we talk about passionate oedipal encounters in the therapeutic situation? Does psychoanalysis have a ready vocabulary for *passion?* I have in mind the definition of the word found in *Webster's International Dictionary* (1976): "a violent, intense, or overwhelming emotion," or "enthusiasm for one's object of interest" (p. 1651). (Interestingly, these are not the first of Webster's definitions, which is "suffering on the cross.") But to begin with, one major issue—as Hoffman (1999) has pointed out—is that psychoanalytic theory has long lacked a vocabulary for female passion. Without one, we have no way to articulate intense or positive feelings that a girl or woman may have as a sexual female; we have words only for a renunciation of conjectured inborn masculinity.[1]

---

1 Under the umbrella of the term primary femininity, contemporary psychoanalysts are now finding ways to address this conceptual lack and to conceptualize a female's positive sense of her body, sexual pleasures, and passions. (See, for example: Elise 1997, 2000; Kulish 1991, 2000; Marcus 2004; Martinez 2001; Mayer 1995; Palacio 1996; Richards 1996; and Tyson 1994.)

This omission dovetails with deeply built-in societal expectations and anxieties. The prohibition against female passion has a long history in Western civilization, upheld by religious and cultural institutions. Women tend to be uncomfortable with their frightening passions and quick to negate their guilt-ridden incestuous impulses. Men tend to fear the power of female sexuality (Horney 1932). A passionate woman is perceived as flamboyant, phallic, "loose," and dangerous. These prohibitions can become translated into well-known resistances in clinical work (Holtzman and Kulish 2003).

It is less obvious that passion is nearly as scarce in our discussions of the male triangular situation as it is in the female.[2] In the case of men, too, do we lack a vocabulary for including in the triangular situation something more than renunciation, something positive and vital? Or is it that we simply disregard oedipal passions and turn our attention elsewhere? Some would take out the sexual component altogether. Friedman and Downey (1995), for example, in their discussion of the possible biological bases for the male (positive) oedipal complex, argue that there is evidence for a universal, inborn aggressiveness and competition between male animals, but not for the other sexual component of the triangular situation—an incestuous wish toward the female.

Individually and as a group, psychoanalysts have had difficulty articulating *passions* and, perhaps most particularly, *oedipal passions*. (As a group, we are careful and thoughtful, taught to put experiences into words and to titrate our emotions. While we are passionate about our work, we are often reluctant to admit it.) Our lexicon, handed down to us by Freud and subsequent generations—*preoedipal, oedipal, superego, instinct, erotic transference,* etc.—may connote *passions,* but to my mind, somehow distances us from them.

One exception to this generalization is Loewald (1985), who argued that Freud had in view the human passions when he spoke of instincts and their vicissitudes, and thus the psychoanalytic account of the oedipal complex

---

2 I am thankful to Marvin Margolis for this observation.

is best described in these terms. For Loewald, libido is a force emerging from the ego by which the ego strives to keep itself connected with the world from which it is overall differentiating itself. Because instincts are essentially communicative, the individual invests meaning onto significant people in the very act of libidinally engaging with them. Loewald's theory is at once a theory of instinct and object relations, and their interplay. Motivational, instinctual forces represent intrapsychic and bodily demands, the form of which take shapes initially through communication with the mother. Throughout a highly complex course of psychic development, both subject and objects are constituted through interactions within an erotic field.

In an essay on the place of Eros in the work of Loewald, Lear (1996) elucidates how Loewald thinks of passion as central to psychoanalysis. First, in the analytic situation, passion is generated as crucial emotional experiences, such as the oedipal crisis, are relived and re-created. According to Loewald, "the transference neurosis is the patient's love life as it is relived in relation to a potentially new love-object, the analyst" (1971, p. 311). Because the analyst's interpretations tend to facilitate psychological growth in the analysand, these communications can be considered erotic, in terms of the Socratic idea of Eros as a developmental force. Second, for Loewald, the love of truth in our field is in itself a passion. Certainly, coming to grips with the truth lies at the heart of the oedipal conflict—for Oedipus's struggle was to fix his eyes on the truth, as it is every child's or every analysand's struggle around the unpleasant truths of one's own urges and the truths of the primal scene (see Michels 1986).

Passion is the name Bion (1963) gave to the process of integrating and utilizing one's most basic and important emotions to make meaning. This seems to me to dovetail with Loewald's thinking about how the individual, being impelled from within, endows his relationships with passionate meanings. The psychoanalytic endeavor, therefore, is in this way of thinking a passionate one, by definition. This would also put oedipal passion squarely within the therapeutic situation in another way, correlating with the Kleinian linking of the ability to make meaning with mastering the oedipal situation. So, both the analytic investigation and the ensuing transferences and countertransferences are inevitably endowed with (oedipal) passion.

Several psychoanalysts have attempted to elucidate and define passionate romantic love, and have implicitly or explicitly linked it with oedipal dynamics. For example, Kernberg (1974, 1977) asserts that mature romantic love involves simultaneously a transgression into the forbidden domain of sensuality and the arena of the primal scene, and a transcendence of the limits of gender and generation. Bergmann (1997) also discusses passions in the therapeutic relationship in the context of forbidden desires.

In his comprehensive essay on romantic erotic love, Ross (1991) asks why, in their theorizing, analysts have so persistently avoided confronting the sensual passions of adult sex and love. He notes that Freud primarily viewed adult passions in terms of their infantile prototypes, transfigured by later moral and realistic constraints. Moreover, analysts have focused on the *content* of love relationships, rather than on the form and quality of the affects—that is, the passions—involved. In a brief discussion of countertransferences and resistances to oedipal passions in the clinical situation, Ross suggests that analysts may begrudge their patients, especially the younger ones, their passions. I think that, in general, adults may wish to forget and distance themselves from adolescent turmoil and thus begrudge the younger generation their passions (Kulish 1998).

For Ross, the essence of passionate sexual love is the feeling of danger and of putting oneself into an altered state of mind. It is a complex and sustained affective disposition, object-directed and impelled. More than a repetition and reworking of earlier infantile predispositions, it is neither synonymous with "genital primacy" nor regressive. Falling into romantic language, Ross emphasizes that sexual love involves a psychic and illusory reaching for the unattainable, the "soul" of the lover. He then elaborates the oedipal danger that he feels gives romantic love its passion: "Perhaps most important in terms of psychic structure, passionate love demands a moral or ethical accommodation—a reorganization of the superego so that it can countenance hitherto forbidden wishes" (1991, p. 471). In an earlier study of Western and Hindu love tales, Ross and Kakar (1986) included another ingredient of passion: early longings for the maternal object. Similarly, Person (1988) defines romantic love as a compound passion.

Other analysts have speculated that it is the scarcity and unattainability of the love object that heightens passionate enticement. Freud (1912) wrote that "some obstacle is necessary to swell the tide of the libido to its height" (p. 187). In her clarifying discussion of different dynamics of love, desire, and *jouissance* in the writings of Lacan and Mitchell, Bernstein (2006) speaks to this sense of unattainability. Lacan's *objet a* is defined as the illusory fragment, a kind of leftover psychic whiff from the primal lost object that is projected onto the desired love object. Thus, love is an uncanny game of narcissistic illusions in which one is wanted for what one does not have, and one desires what one cannot have. Echoing Lacan, Mitchell (2002) alludes to the narcissistic riskiness of romance over time.

Even more adamantly than Ross, Stein (2006) links oedipal conflicts to the experience of passion. She characterizes passion as a partial overcoming of prohibition; excitement is an "oedipal triumph over internalized parents, incorporated in a prohibiting superego" (p. 763). In the course of development, early bodily pleasures become revitalized and resuscitated by breaking the repressive barriers erected around them.

According to Stein, the most poignant, frenzied, and obsessive passions come from states of absence, sin, and abuse. The element of passion in romance can be explained by a repeatedly and fantastically enacted transgression of oedipal prohibitions. Passion is experienced through an "unforgetting" (p. 767). The oedipal roots of romance make love stories into narratives of pervasive longing, the overcoming of obstacles, and unending quests. Thus, romance is "a story that privileges the passion of the ongoing narrative itself" (p. 769).

Passion throughout life resonates with oedipal undertones, Stein continues. She writes:

The excitement and curiosity of the oedipal situation—a situation that is not limited to a certain age or a particular developmental stage—fuel and erotize passion. Passion always implies a hurdle and its overcoming, a desire not met, a suffering and being tantalized.

Passion therefore always carries connotations of a conflicted or forbidden desire, ranging from unconsummated love to the spikes of lust and longing within a long-standing relationship. [2006, p. 771, italics in original]

Like Green and Grunberger, Stein bemoans the apparent fact that we have almost ceased talking about oedipal situations in psychoanalysis. Have we collectively "forgotten," she asks, "the intensely exciting, conflicting, and forbidden feelings about the parents who exclude the child and the excitement we had as children about this forbidden knowledge?" (p. 772). I believe, as Stein suggests, that the intense and painful nexus of feelings associated with the Oedipus complex make it easier to turn our attentions elsewhere. Her use of the word *unforgetting* conveys an important experiential process, implying an active defensive force, and is a useful way to think of the therapeutic work of overcoming obstacles to oedipal passions.

Thus, Stein's and Ross's conceptualizations of passion conflate all passion with oedipal conflicts. This link is present in Bion's and Loewald's writings as well. I am impressed with the idea that human passion imbues the world with individually experienced meaning, and the complementary idea that this searching for truth and meaning is interlaced with oedipal strivings.

Contemporary writers speak to the necessities and risks of analysts' allowing themselves to feel passions in the therapeutic encounter. While passions within the analyst can lead to dangerous trespasses of ethical boundaries, Gabbard (1996) nevertheless advocates the analyst's full emotional participation in the analytic relationship. Influenced by Bion, he urges the analyst to make use of himself as a container for projection identifications and toxic affects. Others (Dimen 1996; Knoblauch 1996) contend that we cannot turn the body aside, either in our theories or in ourselves, as we sit and listen to our patients. Bonasia (2001) notes the disappearance of concrete sexuality from psychoanalytic scenarios in the literature, as well as a dearth of theories about sexual countertransference. He delineates "oedipal" countertransferences (p. 254) that may be manifested by a phobic avoidance of a patient's sexuality or conscious sexual fantasies, on the one hand, and amorous fantasies whose excitement results primarily from the patient's status as a prohibited object, on the other.

Some suggest that the passions connected to the oedipal situation must inevitably be renounced. From his historical review of Freud's views of the role of the father, Perelberg (2009) arrives at a fuller comprehension of the oedipal fantasy incorporating contemporary ideas of the unconscious transmission of fantasies across generations. The Oedipus *story* depicts the universal infantile fantasy of patricide, while the Oedipus *complex* reflects the psychosocial institution of a symbolic "dead father" as representation of the law and regulation of desire. Perelberg argues compellingly that the sacrifice of sexuality is the "central tragic element of the oedipal structure" (p. 713).

From this review of the psychoanalytic literature on oedipal passion, several key ideas emerge oedipal passion reflects the attribution of meaning to emotions; it rests on the ever-present libidinal engagement with objects; it is accompanied by the sense of danger and transgression; and it results from the overcoming of superego prohibitions. The experience of oedipal passion has been broken down into its elements and positioned as a key aspect of the analytic endeavor itself. Oedipal passion is an amalgam, a changing mix of strong affects, including transgression, danger, and sexual excitement, as well as jealousy, narcissistic disappointment, and rage. I would argue that the resulting combination, experientially, is more than the sum of its parts.

Thus, oedipal passion is difficult to verbalize or to break down. The stirring and dramatic music of grand opera, which so often tells a classical oedipal tale, can express this complex chorus of emotions perhaps better than words can.

These understandings also help explain why oedipal passion must continually be, as Stein (2006) puts it, "unforgotten." To the extent that we cannot acknowledge these resistances, we are likely to run into trouble clinically. I will focus on how some of these oedipal "countertransferences"—for want of a better word—look in action. Individual oedipal countertransferences are often supported by or embedded in our theoretical constructions, making them even harder to recognize.

CLINICAL EXAMPLES

I will illustrate some of the obstacles to understanding oedipal passion, which I have outlined above, with two clinical vignettes. The first case demonstrates how the fear of sexual passion, fostered by religious and familial beliefs, infiltrated the psyche of an individual female patient. This woman helped me understand that feelings of inhibition, inferiority, and lack in relation to men can cover over and in fact defend against sexual passions, especially oedipal passion. This clinical picture replicates psychoanalytic theories of women that are couched in the language of inferiority and render sexual passions invisible. Contemporary concepts that make more room for female passion would have helped me clarify this picture.

"Oedipal" countertransferences or blind spots were undoubtedly present, but resulted in a manifest enactment on my part in the second vignette. Resistance to the recognition of my own oedipal conflicts and passions reinforced my male patient's resistance against his own loving and oedipal passion. The second case illustrates a more general resistance to the awareness of cross- generational passion, and to the power of the generational barrier that is central to the triangular situation and the incest taboo.

Agnes

Some years ago, I treated Agnes, a depressed, phobic, sexually inhibited woman who had spent years in a joyless and sexless marriage. She came from a strictly religious home. Her father, an army officer, was stern and rigid. The patient had three elder brothers who were allowed more privileges, while she was kept under closer control. All were constantly reminded of their family's responsibility to keep up appearances in the community. Immediately after college, in keeping with family tradition, Agnes married an army man—an apparent "oedipal" choice, like her father both in his choice of career and his overbearing personality.

An important screen memory from age three was of dressing up with delight in her mother's clothes and painting herself with her make-up. When Agnes had paraded in front of her stern and religious father, his response was devastating. Demanding that she take off her finery, he intoned: "No daughter of mine will be a slut!"

The patient's mother was more permissive than her father, but long-suffering and subservient to him. She was very proud of, but apparently envious of and competitive with, her pretty daughter. In adolescence, as Agnes struggled to separate from her mother, she alternated between somewhat rebellious behavior, such as seeing older boys, and an anxious reliance on her mother for guidance. She was confused by the double messages she received from her mother. The mother encouraged her to be popular and to dress so as to attract boys, by sewing her outfits and encouraging her to enter beauty contests, but at other times would turn on her critically for such behavior. Agnes had many boyfriends who pursued her, but she chose her husband over a more exciting

261

sports star whom she dated intermittently during her adolescence and college years. The mother often talked about how she wanted her daughter to catch a rich husband, someone not in the service.

Once, after Agnes was married, her mother accompanied her to the gynecologist's office. On the way there, Agnes confided some of her sexual hang-ups to her mother. The mother's response was to announce that *she* could count on the fingers of one hand the number of times she had had intercourse without an orgasm.

In spite of some gynecological complications, Agnes was able to have two children, who were the joy of her life. Just before she entered treatment, she had a hysterectomy because of painful endometriosis.

Two factors in the patient's history contributed to her anxieties about sexuality: the mother's confusing competitiveness, and the father's severity and condemning attitude. For Agnes, entering the mother's domain of sexuality had become associated with danger. This frequent, inhibiting fantasy in women—that sexuality belongs to the mother—can be traced to the female triangular period (Holtzman and Kulish 2000).

Shortly after she began treatment, Agnes began to talk about her sexual inhibitions. Emboldened, she decided to face these more directly and to try to resume sexual relations with her husband. After a session in which she talked of her resolve, she called her husband at work to tell him of her thinking. He dropped everything to rush home to have sex, as she had been the one, presumably, to be avoiding sex. The next day they had sex again. On the following day, her husband, with no further explanation, announced that he wanted a divorce. Her husband was a difficult, narcissistic man, so the idea of divorce in itself was not so troubling. But in subsequent months, we came to understand that this sequence of events was a devastating repetition of her childhood rejection by her father.

This series of events appeared to be a serious setback to Agnes's progress. The patient had been overtly encouraged to assert her desire by being able to speak about sex in the treatment, and covertly must have felt encouraged by my accepting attitude. I worried about the possible dampening of her trust in the treatment and unforeseen effects of these events in the transference.

Indeed, difficult years followed in which she hid out at home and avoided social contact outside of family and work. The divorce had left her a single, working parent, financially strapped. She felt dependent on the analyst, and at separations complained miserably of her loneliness and of feeling abandoned. Not directly but by implication, she blamed me for her plight. She often talked bitterly of her resentment toward the men in her life—her father, brothers, and husband—and of her jealousy of their power and freedom. She wallowed in her sense of inferiority to men and was quite willing, indeed eager, to talk literally about "penis envy." Her feelings of being deficient, castrated and castrating, were genuine, and evident in early dreams filled with rockets or amputated limbs, etc.

In one dream, set in a room overlooking a football rally, a coach was being congratulated. He said to the patient, "Football players go on and on and get the praise; cheerleaders, nobody remembers." Her associations led to her identification with her subservient mother—the cheerleader—and her anger at the analyst as football player, the one who got the praise and credit for any gains she might make.

In the first two years of the analysis, Agnes was a very "good" patient, like the very "good" little girl she had always tried to be. In the transference, she endeavored to please m e by dutifully paying her bills, coming on time, and keeping her associations tidy and neat, as she felt she needed to be with her mother.

Often she experienced me as critical and demanding, like one or the other of her parents, although alongside this, an idealized maternal transference began to develop: the analyst was a woman who seemed, unlike herself, to "have it all."

As she began to understand and overcome her symptoms, in the third year of analysis, Agnes showed some interest in changing her lonely but safe existence. She came into one session bemoaning her fear of entering the dating scene. She declared that she felt as though a scarlet letter "U" for "Uptight" was written on her body. I remarked that Hawthorne's scarlet letter was not "U," but "A" for "Adultery." This infuriated her. With a raised voice, she exclaimed, "Why should I get into delving like this?"

I pointed out that it was more comfortable to feel uptight and inadequate than to feel what might be underneath—that is, the scarlet letter for adultery, for sex.

After a pause, Agnes mused, "So I'm not uptight, but interested?" Then her thoughts went to times when sex had been good with old boyfriends, one in particular who was a "great kisser." "I wasn't attracted to my husband, probably ever, in the first place. I probably chose him to run away from somebody who was really attractive to me."

With great difficulty, she recounted for the first time the details of an adulterous affair she had had early in her marriage, over which she had long suffered in secret. Next, she began to talk about her daughter, who had been born some time after the affair. This child had a minor birth defect. In reality she knew the child was her husband's, but she recalled that at the time of the child's birth, she had harbored painful fantasies that the baby was the fruit of the affair.

In retrospect, I think that the patient's fury expressed her experience of me as behaving like her mother. Agnes must have perceived me at that point as a judgmental parent. In correcting her about the scarlet letter, I was upping her, showing her my literary superiority—just as her mother had upped her about how many orgasms she had. Probably some competitiveness was stirring within me below the level of awareness, and had been for some time, hidden beneath the tacit working paradigm I had in my conscious mind. At the time, however, I was thinking about the analytic process in terms of a primarily dyadic maternal transference with its manifest themes of compliance, dependency, and depression.

In the next session, Agnes reported a long dream that took up much of the session. It occurred on Mother's Day while she was taking a very long nap from which it was hard to arouse herself. In the dream itself, she was taking a nap in two different settings, and each time was not able to get up from it. In each setting, she found herself sliding off a cot or bed, and was kissed—once by an older man and once by a younger one. Her parents were present, watching her or perhaps leaving. One of her few explicit associations was to the rolling-off movement as "like at the end of the sex act." She mused, "Maybe I am trying literally to wake up in terms of this analysis, in terms of knowing myself. Once during this week, I had a comfortable feeling about being a sexual female, but then it disappeared .... I'm making *some* moves forward."

Although there were intriguing hints here of a sleeping beauty being awakened by a kiss, or primal scene connotations (parents watching), or a shift in internal object relations (parents leaving), I interpreted the defensive aspects: "Whatever this dream is about, it seems clearly to show mixed feelings. You say the dream is about trying to wake up, and yet there was tremendous difficulty in reality and in the dream in waking up." (Note also the connection between knowing oneself and oedipal or primal scene material.)

Agnes replied, "I think this anxiety is about what I suspect I might be. I might be a *very sexual woman.*"

Soon after this came a series of guilt-filled sessions with worries about her children and observations about how she burdened herself. She came into a session berating herself for having very uncharacteristically forgotten an important parent-teacher conference about her daughter. I interpreted that she seemed to be punishing herself, and that she experienced her daughter's birth defects as a punishment and a proof of her guilt.

At this point, Agnes broke down and began to sob, "How could I do this? This is my punishment. I created a child who is eternally a reminder of what I did. It hurts .... I can't even breathe." Thus, the daughter was the embodiment of her sin, her scarlet letter.

In subsequent sessions, Agnes came to see that she felt her longstanding painful and humiliating gynecological difficulties were also punishments for this sexual misdeed, as well as for earlier ones—such as masturbation and the dressing-up episode—in childhood. It took some months of analytic work to understand that she was living out an unconscious imperative to punish herself for the affair by cutting off her sexual passions forever. This self-castration, castration in the broadest sense of the term, brings to mind Jones's (1927) idea of *aphanisis,* the complete extinction of the capacity for sexual enjoyment.

Agnes summarized her insights: "I have spent a lifetime denying myself …. My life has been a series of repentances and sacrifices …. That sweet child is my ultimate punishment." The next day, she reported, "I kept thinking over and over as I was driving home last night, *'The point is I enjoyed it; the point is I enjoyed it. It would not have been so bad if I had not enjoyed it!'*"

And I think this *was* the point. It was not only the *facts* of the sexual misdeeds that engendered such torment and guilt. Agnes felt guilty not only for the adultery, with its forbidden sex—the affair was yet another in her history of oedipal entanglements with forbidden, exciting men or older father figures—but primarily *for its intensity, its oedipal passion.*

In the following sessions, she voiced her resistance: "I'm scared, scared to come. My sexuality made this happen." She went on to talk of her fears of "going hog wild" if she were to let her inhibitions go. Perhaps she would become promiscuous, a prostitute, would turn to kinky sex, etc. Then—externalizing the source of the sexuality—she envisioned me as a sorceress who lured her into such evils.

As she reentered the social scene and finally found a new boyfriend/lover, Agnes began to enjoy passionate sex. Significantly, when she talked about her sexual experiences, she often specified—with pleasure and pride—how many multiple orgasms she had had. Here, clearly, was her oedipal rivalry, as she unconsciously took her turn at winning the orgasm game with her mother/ analyst.

This period marked the beginning of a major shift in the patient's life and her analysis. Gone was the good little girl; she had been replaced by a feisty, angry, rebellious, and openly competitive woman. While triadic material was discernible in this woman's psyche from the first, it now moved more into the open. Later, a Cinderella fantasy emerged—that I would become a fairy god-mother who would help her get her prince (a variant both of the earlier fantasy of the analyst as the seducing sorceress, and of her mother sewing clothes for her so that she could catch men).

Agnes dreamed, for example, that she had to clean a large mansion while a big party from which she was excluded went on next-door. At one point, she openly railed at me for going off on vacations with my husband and not finding a Prince Charming for her. Looking back now, I can see that even in this fanta-sy—the classical fairy tale of Cinderella with clear triangular content—oedipal passions were held at bay, for both analyst and patient. A fairy godmother, after all, has only Cinderella's best interests at heart; there is no intense jealousy or rivalry. I probably felt more comfortable in the role of fairy godmother than as the depriving and jealous stepmother or wicked witch.

For Agnes, inhibition and a feeling of inferiority had served as a lifelong defense against her sexuality, which frightened her in its intensity, its anal-like, out-of-control associations, and its oedipal, incestuous meanings. Experiences such as the one of her father calling her a slut provided the groundwork for this little-girl feeling that her sexual impulses were unacceptable and bad. While she felt inferior as a female and envious of her brothers, the "penis envy" covered over her presumably more basic fears about the wildness and intensity of her female sexual desires. It also hid from awareness her sexual passion.

In the course of her analysis, Agnes remembered having felt very pretty when she was younger, and that she had enjoyed the feeling of power her sexual attractiveness and sexuality gave her over men. Her memories of these long lost pleasures could be conceptualized within the framework of a primary and positive *sense of femaleness,* to borrow Elise's (1997) term. Here is a clinical example of the potential helpfulness of such concepts of primary femininity and ways of conceptualizing female passion. Otherwise, Agnes and I would have been left with only the idea of her penis envy or castration, which in this case were used defensively to cover conflict-ridden sexual passion.

Several obstacles lay in the way of my being able to glimpse this woman's oedipal passion and to articulate it. The patient herself tried to hide her sexuality behind concepts of inferiority and penis envy, concepts that at the time were the mainstay of theoretical understandings of female sexuality. This woman's oedipal passion was long kept at bay by her characterologically masochistic stance, probably in identification with her mother and as a result of unconscious guilt and need for punishment. While I was aware of the triangular oedipal meanings of her behaviors and fantasies, their passionate intensity became more accessible and real to me when they resonated and activated feelings in me, and I could become the interpreter of my own "countertransference and counter-resistance," as Loewald (1979, p. 159) put it.

Tom

The second patient I will present, Tom, came into analysis circuitously. First there was a marriage counselor whom he saw at the end of a very short-lived marriage. For a year, he went to a male therapist whom he fled after being told, reportedly, that his "core conflict was homosexuality." After that, the counselor gave him the names of two female analysts, one of whom was me. He chose me because he felt uncomfortable that the other analyst's office was in her home. Some years later, he revealed that he also felt that she—unlike me—was the kind of woman to whom he might feel sexually attracted.

When Tom began working with me, he was in his thirties. He roared up to his sessions on a huge Harley motorcycle (purchased right after he began seeing me), dressed in full regalia—black leather vest, chaps, and boots, long hair pulled back into a ponytail. He told me that he was intensely depressed over his inability to play his guitar and write music. From his late adolescence through his twenties, he had been in a rock band. He wrote his own music and had gotten an offer from a major record producer; for reasons that were not clear, however, he had not been able to take up this offer. He felt desperate about his stifled creativity and his "nowhere" life.

Derisive of monogamy, Tom asserted loudly that he could never see himself settling down with one woman. He spent most of his spare time going to bars to pick up women, but felt inhibited and awkward unless he loaded up with alcohol. He smoked marijuana daily and masturbated a great deal.

Nevertheless, he was financially successful; he owned a construction company. Tom's intelligence, desperation, and seeming interest in psychoanalysis overrode my initial qualms about the seriousness of his problems, so I agreed to see him for psychotherapy, which was converted to analysis after four years.

Not surprisingly, Tom proved to be difficult. He came to sessions high, often late. His associations consisted almost exclusively of detailed and mutedly despairing accounts of his adventures in picking up women. He spoke in slang-ridden, crude style, as if he were talking to another male musician—"Hey, dude!" He spoke often of his hopelessness about ever getting his creativity back and conquering his depression; he thought that eventually he would kill himself. I felt this was a real possibility, as he often drove while drunk and had wrapped himself around a tree several times. Throughout the years of treatment, I often worried about Tom, and I felt that he was keeping me at bay. But for some reason, I never shared his hopelessness.

It soon became clear that Tom suffered from a Madonna/whore complex.[3] The women to whom he was sexually attracted were trashy and brassy, one-night stands. He preferred women with big breasts. He *liked* the woman to whom

---

3 Freud's first published use of the term oedipus complex (1910, p. 171) was in connection with this kind of object choice.

he had been married and thought she was sweet, but he had lost sexual interest in her almost immediately after the wedding, and began to have trouble sustaining an erection with her.

Tom had two long-standing girlfriends: Roz, a sexy blonde with whom he enjoyed very good sex but whom he labeled as intellectually inferior; and Mary, whom he respected and could talk to, but in whom his sexual interest diminished the closer they became. (He had become friends with Mary after entering treatment.) The *L* word slipped through once or twice, however, as he inadvertently spoke of loving her.

On the surface, Tom's background did not seem to match this picture of perverse tendencies, addictive personality, and depression. His parents were solid citizens and apparently caring. He adored his father, a very quiet man who had been a fighter pilot, built the family home, and was a retired high school principal. He pictured his mother, in contrast, as an overly controlling housewife, doting and infantilizing. It disgusted him, the way she still fussed over him and treated him like a child. He recounted a telling screen memory suggestive of early sexual overstimulation: Sitting at his mother's feet at about three years of age, he reached up to touch her thigh. She pushed his hand away and said he was too old to do that—*anymore.* He had two older sisters who had teased him and belittled him mercilessly.

Tom said that he respected me as a professional, but absolutely refused to acknowledge any other positive feelings toward me at all—"None of that transference shit!" He became absolutely enraged if I suggested that he had any feeling about my vacations or any feelings of vulnerability whatsoever. He was afraid to recount dreams and especially to associate to any of them, for fear of what I might make of them; the previous therapist seemed to have based his ideas about Tom's supposed homosexuality on his dreams.

Tom was very touchy, and in the years before we began analysis I proceeded very slowly. I tried to deal with his narcissistic vulnerability by carefully interpreting his defenses against feelings of vulnerability and helplessness and his fears of closeness. I interpreted his need to blot out inner feelings of emptiness, loneliness, and depression by drinking, engaging in compulsive sex, and smoking pot. I attempted to interpret his perverse defenses (Coen 1998), and when eventually I told him that it seemed he had to keep his sexual feelings separate from his caring feelings, he reluctantly agreed. We came to a mutual understanding that Tom himself articulated: "Don't you know, Dr. K, this *is* the transference! Yes, I need to keep you at a distance, like I do everyone else."

It was this increased insight into his problems, this softening of his narcissistic macho stance, that led me to propose analysis, but the analysis got off to a scary start. Tom increased his drinking and his reckless, dangerous driving. He extended his sexual acting out to older and fatter women, with a few redheads [my hair coloring] thrown in, all of whom he described with derision. At the same time, he batted away any hint of a suggestion on my part of the transference implications in their similarities to me.

A year and a half into the analysis, he was arrested for drunk driving. His arrest and overnight in jail terrified him. He was able to acknowledge that he felt helped by my steadying presence and attempts at understanding his anxieties during this time. He decided it was time to try giving up marijuana, and he swore never to drink and drive again.

In this context, Tom experienced a dissociated Isakower-like experience on the couch. He reported a

...strange sensation, like a feverish dream, my body swimming. The left side is sinking, like I should be falling way to the floor, like airplanes in formation, and one of them just sort of falls off the edge .... The object is so huge it fills your whole vision like the point of a pen that just gets bigger and bigger, and you feel very small. The weight of the pen is like a battleship above you ... right here, right now.

Isakower (1938) described a group of bodily phenomena like this (which usually occur upon falling asleep)—sometimes with the sensation of a large object coming toward one—as regressive reexperiences of the state of being at the mother's breast (that is, preoedipal). This incident with Tom opened up a meaningful line of interpretation in the following months about "too much mother," which resonated with him. For the first time, Tom dropped his idealization of his father enough to admit that his father had not supported him against his intrusive and possibly seductive mother. Within the treatment, he increasingly let me interpret his vulnerable feelings toward me within the transference, and could sometimes admit to them.

Then we had an important mutual enactment. One week, with a short break coming up, I had to cancel a session unexpectedly. Tom himself cancelled on the following Monday in a characteristic tit-for-tat pattern that he had until then angrily and flatly denied. He began his Tuesday session by describing how he had not felt well the day before; he was tired and had cancelled a date to take Mary for a special dinner. He complained of feeling "cranky" during the day. "My non-existent love life. Getting nowhere." He mumbled something that sounded like "I can fall in love" (unclear if he said *can* or *cannot* fall in love). "But I keep things on the surface."

I said, "You can't let yourself get close and won't let yourself love." I told him that I thought he had to blow off Mary and me in order not to be too close. He nodded. Encouraged, I added that he cancelled after I cancelled, and that he did not like to be the one on the receiving end of a cancellation.

Tom replied, "It means *you* are in control. When you called to cancel, I thought, 'Hell, *she* cancels whenever she wants, so I can!' Thinking like that helps toexplain away the feeling. I put everybody on hold, too. Normally I don't ask Mary for a formal date, and it wasn't good I blew her off."

He continued:

Oh, I had an interesting dream Friday night. That night, I wanted to go the Blue Martini [a sleek bar near my office, not his usual kind of haunt]. Roz and I went there and I got drunk [the first time he had gotten drunk in a while], so she drove home and I passed out when I got home.

You were in the dream—that's the first time I've dreamt about you. We were going to meet at your home. Your husband was there working in the garage, and some kids—maybe yours. He showed me the way into your office. I sat on a hearth next to a fireplace. After a bit you showed up. You took a seat at the end of the couch, so I sat down on the floor at your feet and leaned up against the couch with my back to you, between your legs. Then at some point I had to change my clothes. I was embarrassed to ask where I should get dressed. You were there, busy, your back to me—the last appointment of the day [as that session was]. Your husband was still working in the garage.

Tom's associations led to "the time I went to that other doctor's house. I wasn't comfortable in her home, no waiting room. I knocked and she hadn't finished with the previous patient. I was embarrassed."

I remarked, "As in the dream."

"Yes." He paused. "I think on Thursday you were wearing a suit with a jacket, like you usually do. But then you took your jacket off and were wearing a sleeveless top during most of the session. When I got up to leave I saw … more of your skin showed."

I had completely forgotten this incident. It had been overly warm in the office that day. I had been dimly aware of discomfort at revealing my aging arms.

Actually, I almost always wear long sleeves. Defensively and without thinking, I said, "It was hot that day."

"Not to me," he said.

I said, "So it seemed seductive."

"Yes." Then he added, "In the dream, the way I was sitting at your feet, it would be like someone—you were rubbing my neck."

I interpreted that he was having sexual feelings toward me that made him very anxious (as did his feelings toward his mother, as I was able to bring in later), and that he tried to push himself away from me—so much so that he got drunk and cancelled the session. Both the feelings and the dream had been stimulated by his experience of my taking off my jacket. I observed that he had been trying not to have any personal feelings or curiosity about me, and in the dream, here he was in my home, in the middle of my life.

Tom began the next session by saying that he was very anxious to have me understand something. He had read that the analyst is supposed to be "a blank screen." Yet he admitted that he *had* been curious about me, and was now concerned that I might think he was so self-centered that he did not care about me or was not interested in me.

In the next few weeks came a multitude of dreams, to which he was able to associate a bit—some had seemingly triangular themes of punishment and castration, or sadomasochistic primal scenes. One, for example, involved Tom sneaking into the childhood house of his ex-wife to have sex with her, but being caught by the patriarchal father; in another, after trying to kill a snake, he was chased and snapped up by a huge lizard, a Komodo dragon. He recalled episodes of guilt-ridden teenage masturbation and the nightmares associated with them, and admitted to worries about possible diminished sexual interest and potency as he got older.

In the midst of this, Tom suddenly said he was thinking that he would try to break off with Roz, but:

I feel guilty. It isn't fair to her. Besides, although it's good sex, it's too easy to call her up. I have to quit looking for instant gratification. The time I spend with her keeps me from moving on, meeting someone else, or at least doing constructive work. I think I do have something to offer some-

one; I'm not a bad catch. I am intelligent, make a good living …. Yes, I'm shy, but I'd be a good man. Can't say I'm not capable of loving. I could treat a woman well. I want to be able to meet a high-quality woman … with a brain, someone I could respect, talk to, have interests in common with, and someone young enough to have children. If I could put the love and sex together, I could love someone …

It had taken us a long time to get to this, a long time before Tom could allow himself a glimpse of this early triangular material. His obvious concerns about his masculinity and disavowed feminine identifications were becoming more accessible. I was well aware that until this point there had been no triangular space (Britton 1989), no place for what some analysts call the analytic third (Ogden 1994). But in retrospect, I wonder, too, if my own oedipal conflicts were holding us back, even while I dealt with Tom's narcissistic vulnerabilities and the need to foster trust. What about my failure to imagine that a good-looking and macho, younger man might be attracted to my old arms—was this a defense against my own incestuous desires and fantasies?

My stifled imagination and Tom's formidable phallic-narcissistic defenses together created a mutual resistance (Boesky 1969). We were both content to believe that Tom could feel no attraction to me, but only to the "other kind" of woman. The enactment occurred as my removal of my usual, "proper" garb— probably re-creating early seductive behavior of his mother's—allowed both of our incestuous fantasies to break through. My act of exposure stimulated the incest taboo, evoking anxiety in both analyst and patient. Here is an instance in which an accessible vocabulary for passionate desire in the cross-generational situation might have helped me recognize my own conflicts earlier.

FURTHER DISCUSSION

Some years ago, in the face of the myth that you could not analyze elderly patients, I began an analysis with a depressed 77-year-old man. To my surprise, he immediately fell into what felt like a full-blown oedipal transference. He was in love in the lovely way a five-year-old boy is with his mother. He brought in his prized stuff for me to admire, standing right up against the door as he waited anxiously for the session to begin. Like an adolescent wooing his first love, he strove to entertain and impress me (and to counteract his sense of his own diminishing abilities and strength) with tales of his macho adventures during his youth.

What I want to stress here is my surprise. Why did this surprise me? Smith (1995) writes about the analyst's experience of surprise. Smith describes the shifts in the analyst's defensive organization that allow for this experience. Surprise marks mutually created resistances and enactments. So *why* was I surprised in this instance? Because the patient was old enough to be my father?

Yes, surprise was the affect that accompanied a break in the oedipal barrier, a crossing of the generational ground—the same ground so gingerly crossed by my father and me in relation to the Fenichel book. The crossing of generational ground is never done dispassionately. Here my surprise came with a breach in my complacent and well-established stance against *the actual experience* of cross-generational passions. Remember Freud's angry and inexplicable exhortation to his patient, H. D., the poet (which she took as an injunction against her affections): "I am an old man. You do not think it worthwhile to love me" (Doolittle 1956, pp. 21, 93).

In order to help this patient and my patient Tom—both very unhappy men—to be able to love, I had to let them love me passionately. And as my instructor had warned, I had to let myself love them in return. In the case of Agnes, I had to let myself become pulled into the passionate competition that is part of the loving/hating force field of the triangular drama. With both Agnes and Tom, it was Stein's (2006) "unforgetting" that opened up the oedipal material—an unforgetting of uncomfortable oedipal emotions of childhood and adolescence, by both analyst and patient—that made for a mutual loosening of resistances.

CONCLUSION

The many new theoretical and technical developments that have extended our understanding of triangular conflicts in the therapeutic encounter have helped me greatly in my clinical work, as I have tried to demonstrate. Among these tools are in the case of Agnes, the concept of primary femininity and broader understandings of the role of penis envy, and the role of the analyst's libidinal engagement in analytic process; and with Tom, the idea of the analytic third, and the need to pay attention to narcissistic sensibilities and vulnerabilities both of the patient and myself. And in both these cases, the importance of co- created resistance and the inevitability of mutual enactments were key elements.

But barriers still arise, technically and theoretically, in our resistance to the idea of *passion,* so fundamental to love and the oedipal situation. We are still lacking, or not availing ourselves of robust concepts and language for passion in the triangular situation, and without these we may lack important perspectives for understating our patients' and our own "oedipal" issues. The scientific language of ego psychology—*libido, object, erotize,* in which many of us were acculturated—can distance us from the subject matter of oedipal passions. Such language sanitizes, neutralizes, "-izes" passions.

The solution goes beyond language, however. Why is it that, periodically, an alarm is raised that our psychoanalytic theories have abandoned sexuality and "forgotten" the oedipal complex? As so many analysts beginning with Freud have suggested, the answer lies within ourselves. Our individual resistances to our oedipal wishes, and especially to their accompanying *passions,* reinforce theoretical rigidities and misunderstandings and keep them alive. And the very nature of oedipal passion—its complexity, its connection to a sense of transgression and danger—makes us shy away, even as it remains unnamed but basic to psychoanalytic inquiry and the search for meaning. We overlook oedipal passion or, as Stein (2006) suggests, we forget it, both within ourselves and—as a group—within our theories. Freud warned of the horror of incest, and we continue to collectively turn our eyes away from it.

REFERENCES

Benjamin, J. (1998). *Shadow of the Other.* New York: Routledge.

——— (2004). Beyond doer and done to: an intersubjective view of thirdness. *Psychoanal. Q.,* 73:5–46.

Bergmann, M. S. (1997). Passions in the therapeutic relationship. *Canadian J. Psychoanal.,* 5:73–94.

Bernstein, J. W. (2006). Love, desire, jouissance: two out of three ain't bad. *Psychoanal. Dialogues,* 16:711–724.

Bion, W. R. (1963). *Elements of Psycho-Analysis.* London: Heinemann.

Boesky, D. (1969). The reversal of *déjà raconte. J. Amer. Psychoanal. Assn.,* 17: 114–141.

Bollas, C. (1 996). Figures and their functions: on the oedipal structure of psychoanalysis. *Psychoanal. Q.,* 65:1–20.

Bonasia, E. (2001). The countertransference: erotic, erotised and perverse. *Int. J. Psychoanal.,* 82:249–262

Britton, R. (1989). The missing link: parental sexuality in the Oedipus complex. In The Oedipus Complex Today, ed. J. Steiner. London: Karnac.

Chodorow, N. (1976). The Reproduction of Mothering. Berkeley, CA: Univ. of Calif. Press.

Coen, S. J. (1998). Perverse defenses in neurotic patients. *J. Amer. Psychoanal. Assn.*, 46:1169–1194.

Davies, J. M. (1994). Love in the afternoon: a relational reconsideration of desire and dread in the countertransference. *Psychoanal. Dialogues*, 4: 153–170.

Dimen, M. (1996). Bodytalk. *Gender & Psychoanal.*, 1:385–401.

Doolittle, H. (1956). A Tribute to Freud. New York: Pantheon.

Elise, D. (1997). Primary femininity, bisexuality, and the female ego ideal: a reexamination of female developmental theory. *Psychoanal. Q.*, 46:489–517.

——— (2000). Woman and desire: why some women may not want to want. *Studies in Gender & Sexuality*, 1:125–145.

Feldman, M. (1990). Common ground: the centrality of the Oedipus complex. *Int. J. Psychoanal.*, 71:37–48.

Fonagy, P. (2008). A genuinely developmental theory of sexual enjoyment and its implications for psychoanalytic technique. *J. Amer. Psychoanal. Assn.*, 56: 11–36.

Freud, S. (1910). A special type of choice of object made by men. S. E., 11.

——— (1912). On the universal tendency to debasement in the sphere of love. *S.E.*, 11.

——— (1912–1913). Totem and Taboo: Some Points of Agreement between the Mental Lives of Savages and Neurotics. *S.E.*, 13.

Friedman, R. C. & Downey, J. I. (1995). Biology and the Oedipus complex. *Psychoanal. Q.*, 64:234–264.

Gabbard, G. O. (1996). *Passion's Risks: A Review of Love and Hate in the Analytic Setting.* Northvale, NJ/London: Jason Aronson.

Green, A. (1995). Has sexuality anything to do with psychoanalysis? *Int. J. Psychoanal.*, 76:871–873.

Grunberger, B. (1980). The oedipal conflicts of the analyst. *Psychoanal. Q.*, 49: 606–630.

Gu, M. D. (2006). The filial piety complex: variations on the Oedipus theme in Chinese literature and culture. *Psychoanal. Q.*, 75:163–195.

Harris, A. (2005). *Gender as Soft Assembly.* Hillsdale, NJ: Analytic Press.

Hirsch, I. 1994). Countertransference love and theoretical model. *Psychoanal. Dialogues,* 4:*171–192.*

Hoffman, L. (1999). Freud and feminine subjectivity. *J. Amer. Psychoanal. Assn.,* 44(suppl.):*23–44.*

Holtzman, D. & Kulish, N. (2000). The femininization of the female oedipal complex, part I. *J. Amer. Psychoanal. Assn.,* 48:*1413–1437.*

——— & ——— (2003). The femininization of the female oedipal complex, part II. *J. Amer. Psychoanal. Assn.,* 51:*1127–1151.*

Horney, K. (1932). The dread of women. *Int. J. Psychoanal.,* 13:*348–360.*

Isakower, O. (1938). A contribution to the patho-psychology of phenomena associated with falling asleep. *Int. J. Psychoanal.,* 19:*334–345.*

Jones, E. (1927). The early development of female sexuality. *Int. J. Psychoanal.,* 8:*459–472.*

Kernberg, O. (1974). Mature love: prerequisites and characteristics. J. *Amer. Psychoanal. Assn.,* 22:*743–768.*

——— (1977). Boundaries and structure in love relations. *J. Amer. Psychoanal. Assn.,* 25:*81–114.*

Knoblauch, S. H. (1996). The play and interplay of passionate experience: multiple organizations of desire. *Gender & Psychoanal.,* 1:*323–344.*

Kulish, N. M. (1991). Mental representation of the clitoris: the fear of female sexuality. *Psychoanal. Inquiry,* 11:*511–536.*

——— (1998). First loves and prime adventures: adolescent expressions in adult analyses. *Psychoanal. Q.,* 67:*539–565.*

——— (2000). Primary femininity: clinical advances and theoretical ambiguities. *J. Amer. Psychoanal. Assn.,* 48:*1355–1379.*

Kumin, I. (1985–1986). Erotic horror: desire and resistance in the psychoanalytic situation *Int. J. Psychoanal. Psychother.,* 11:*3–20.*

Lear, J. (1996). The introduction of Eros: reflections on the work of Hans Loewald. *J. Amer. Psychoanal. Assn.,* 44:*673–698.*

Loewald, H. W. (1971). The transference neurosis: comments on the concept and the phenomenon. In *Papers on Psychoanalysis*. New Haven, CT: Yale Univ. Press, 1980, pp. *301–314.30*

——— (1979). Reflections on the psychoanalytic process and its therapeutic potential. *Psychoanal. Study Child*, 34:*155–167*.

——— (1985). Oedipus complex and development of self. *Psychoanal. Q.*, 54:*435–443*.

Marcus, B. F. (2004). Female passion and the matrix of mother, daughter, and body: vicissitudes of the maternal transference in the working through of sexual inhibitions. *Psychoanal. Inquiry*, 24:*680–712*.

Martinez, D. L. (2001). Clinical uses of the concept of primary femininity. *J. Amer. Psychoanal. Assn.*, 49:*1379–1390*.

Mayer, E. L. (1995). The phallic castration complex and primary femininity: paired developmental lines toward female gender identity. *J. Amer. Psychoanal. Assn.*, 43:*17–36*.

Michels, R. (1986). Oedipus and insight. *Psychoanal. Q.*, 55:*599–617*.

Mitchell, S. (2002). *Can Love Last? The Fate of Romance Over Time.* New York: W. W. Norton.

Ogden, T. H. (1994). The analytic third: working with intersubjective clinical facts. *Int. J. Psychoanal.*, 75:*3–19*.

Pelaccio, J. (1996). Masturbation fantasies in a pre-latency girl: early female body fantasy conflicts as a major determinant in the experience of primary femininity. *J. Amer. Psychoanal. Assn.*, 44:*333–350*.

Perelberg, R. J. (2009). Murdered father, dead father: revisiting the Oedipus complex. *Int. J. Psychoanal.*, 90:*713–732*.

Person, E. S. (1988). *Dreams of Love and Fateful Encounters.* New York: Norton.

Pollock, G. H. (1986). Oedipus examined and reconsidered: the myth, the developmental stage, the universal theme, the conflict, and the complex. *Ann. Psychoanal.*, 14:*77–106*.

Richards, A. K. (1996). Primary femininity and female genital anxiety. *J. Amer. Psychoanal. Assn.*, 44(suppl.):*261–281.*

Ross, J. M. (1991). A psychoanalytic essay on romantic, erotic love. *J. Amer. Psychoanal. Assn.*, 39(suppl.):*439–475.*

——— & Kakar, S. (1986). *Tales of Love, Sex, and Danger.* New York: Basil Blackwell.

Rothstein, A. (1979). Oedipal conflicts in narcissistic personality disorders. *Int. J. Psychoanal.*, 60:*189–199.*

Searles, H. F. (1959). Oedipal Love in the counter-transference. *Int. J. Psychoanal.*, 40:*180–190.*

Smith, H. F. (1995). Analytic listening and the experience of surprise. *Int. J. Psychoanal.*, 76:*67–78.*

Stein, R. A. (2006). Unforgetting and excess, the re-creation and re-finding of suppressed sexuality. *Psychoanal. Dialogues*, 16:*763–778.*

Steiner, J. (1989). *The Oedipus Complex Today.* London: Karnac.

Tyson, P. (1994). Bedrock and beyond: an examination of the clinical utility of contemporary theories of female psychology. *J. Amer. Psychoanal. Assn.*, 42: *447–467.*

Webster's Third International Dictionary (1976). Springfield, MA: G. & C. Merriam Co.

Wrye, H. K. (1993). Erotic terror: male patients' horror of the early maternal erotic transference. *Psychoanal. Inquiry*, 13:*240–257.*

——— & Wells, J. (1989). The maternal erotic transference. *Int. J. Psychoanal.*, 70:*673–684.*

CHAPTER 10:

The Patient's Objects in the Analyst's Mind

(2014). Psychoanal. Q., (83)(4):843-869

In every analysis, the analyst develops an internal relationship with the patient's objects—that is, the people in the patient's life and mind. Sometimes these figures can inhabit the analyst's mind as a source of data, but at other times, the analyst may feel preoccupied with or even invaded by them. The author presents two clinical cases: one in which the seeming absence of a good object in the patient's mind made the analyst hesitate to proceed with an analysis, and another in which the patient's preoccupation with a "bad" object was shared and mirrored by the analyst's own inner preoccupation with the object. The use and experience of these two objects by the analyst are discussed with particular attention to the countertransference.

It is the nature of the psychoanalytic enterprise that the inner lives of analysts and patients become enmeshed. In the transference, the countertransference, and the therapeutic interaction, we come to represent objects to each other. This phenomenon is the core of the psychoanalytic process, and as such it takes center stage in our clinical reports. Yet in every analysis, the analyst develops an internal relationship not only with the patient, but also with the patient's objects, that is, the people—parents, spouses, children—who occupy the patient's life, feelings, and thoughts. Here I use the word *object* to refer to the internal mental representations of these people and to internal object relations.

We look constantly to the ways in which we and our patients become each other's objects, but not so much to this related phenomenon: that our patients' objects also become part of our inner experience (Jacobs 1983). Sometimes these figures present themselves comfortably to us as a welcome source of data about the patient's mind and life; at other times, they seem strangely absent or formless. Sometimes the analyst may become preoccupied with them, finding him- or herself thinking about them often, or in extreme cases may feel totally invaded and overtaken by sadistic, controlling gangsters (Rosenfeld 1971). Such experiences always reveal something about the patient's internal world, but if the analyst's view of these figures, and his or her relationship to them, becomes too fixed, it can become a challenge to listen flexibly and openly to the patient's psychic reality.

In my view, several interrelated factors contribute to why and how our patients' objects seem to migrate from their minds into our own: the nature of the patient's inner objects and object relations; the state of the transference and countertransference; the analyst's technique and theories that guide his or her thinking; and the analyst's personality and state of mind. It seems to me that in the present here and now of any analytic relationship, not all inner objects or object relations of the patient are available, visible, or active. Transferences that impart these objects shift; for complex reasons that relate to patient *and* analyst, one constellation may be more salient in one analysis and to one analyst than in another analysis and to another analyst. A failure of the analyst's experience of the patient's objects to shift, due to countertransference, may lead to stalemates in the process.

Ferro (1992) is one of the few psychoanalysts to write about these phenomena. He describes three different analytic models for interpreting "characters"—the patient's objects—in the analytic narrative: the structural, after Arlow (1985), in which the characters are understood as living people around which conflicts revolve; the Kleinian, in which characters are "de-codified" and can be understood as projections of bodily phantasies onto or into the analyst (I am using *phantasy* here in the specifically Kleinian sense); and Ferro's own relational-unsaturated analytic field theory.

284

I find Ferro's model particularly helpful in thinking about the clinical situation. Ferro (1992) likens the patient's objects to characters that appear in a narrative: "The character in a narration is both a construction of the text and a reconstruction of the reader" (p. 70). The analytic narrative, then, is the text written by the patient as author and the analyst as reader. As they appear in the text, the patient's objects are both a construction by the patient and a reconstruction by the reader/analyst. This metaphor appeals to me because it captures the complexity of the transference-countertransference situation from which the characters—the patient's objects—come to life in the analyst's mind. These characters, even though they emerge from the patient's narratives, are co-created by the analyst.

Emphasizing these complex mutual interactions between analyst and patient, Jacobs (1983) writes explicitly about the analyst's experience of the patient's objects. He explicates how the patient's objects can have a variety of meanings for the analyst, which can become potent forces in influencing his or her reactions to the patient. For example, the process of reconstruction of the patient's history may be significantly influenced by the analyst's perceptions of the patient's objects. The analyst's inner representations of the people in the patient's life may reactivate oedipal conflicts and material concerning the analyst's own family. As Jacobs summarizes:

> Not only are they [the patient's objects] related to self- and object representations past and present, but they may, in his [the analyst's] imagination, be part of a network of interactions involving the patient, his family, and other of his objects as the result of the reawakening in the analyst of fantasies, memories, and expectations derived from his sibling and family relations. [1983, p. 641]

Jacobs makes another important observation: he suggests that the analyst's unconscious identifications with the patient's objects may contribute to countertransference responses that are *especially hard to detect.* Parallel to a splitting of the transference, there may be a splitting of the countertransference, as an object in the patient's life becomes the target of one side or the other of the analyst's personal ambivalences.

In this paper, I will illustrate these ideas with an exploration of two vivid experiences that I had with objects in the minds of two of my patients. I focus on my countertransferences that shaped my experiences of these objects and created difficulties in the analytic process. I will track my inner responses and fantasies about a key object of each patient, link these responses with what was going on in the analytic field—in the changing transference- countertransference interplay—and speculate about what the changes in my experience might have meant and what psychic functions they played.

Shifts in my internal experience of the patients' objects seemed both to reflect and even to bring about developments in the analytic process. While I was not consciously aware of it at the time, in both cases, I sought out and even created my own version of my patient's object as a way to cope with puzzling and highly distressing elements in the relationship between the two of us.

Case 1: Tom

My patient Anna was in her late fifties, divorced for twenty years, with two grown sons. She conveyed a deep emptiness and depression. In her presenting complaint, however, the only concerns she mentioned had to do with her relationships with her sons and her new daughter-in-law. Her older son and his wife spent many weekends enjoying Anna's backyard pool, and she was so terrified of alienating her son that she felt unable to tell him that it was too much. She was also afraid that Tom, her current boyfriend, was getting fed up with the young couple's constant presence. I soon discovered that such fears that people in her life would become angry with her and leave her dominated

Anna's mind; within a few weeks, she was having these fears about me as well. I also learned that Anna had made a serious suicide attempt while her marriage was breaking up, and that she had a sexual encounter with her marriage counselor (a male) at the time. On her way home from that incident, she had said to herself, "Now it is truly hopeless," and made the attempt on her own life.

These specific anxieties aside, however, the patient appeared totally flat. All affects were absent, and it appeared that she had no words for feelings. The patient herself did not use the word *depression* at all, yet depression was there as a palpable presence.

After several months of psychotherapy, I began to think that Anna should be in analysis. But I hesitated, asking myself whether she would be able to tolerate the opening up an analysis would bring, and worrying about her suicidal potential. In a move unusual for me, I sought a colleague's advice about the wisdom of starting an analysis with this patient. Without conscious intent, I picked as my consultant a man whom I knew to be optimistically convinced that analysis was for everyone, so naturally he advised me not to hesitate to begin. In retrospect, I am sure that what I was really asking was whether *I* could tolerate the intense affects and deep depression that I anticipated I would have to live through with this patient. I did not understand this at the time.

From the very beginning, the analysis was marked by Anna's profound terror of abandonment. Our first break, around Christmastime, brought the conviction that I would never return. As she felt in relation to everyone in her life, she feared I would leave her if she displeased me in any way. Her constant preoccupation was that she would drive me away. "Whatever I say, you won't like me," she whispered.

As Anna's history unfolded in bits and pieces and over many months, I began to understand her depression, her seeming emptiness, and her fear of abandonment. She related her history at first with a bare-bones outline of the major facts, and then with snippets of data and memories, loaded down with unspecified affects. I will summarize here the history that we constructed over time of the patient and her objects; this history's coherence emerged only slowly. The emerging narrative helped me make sense of my patient's pained presentation and my inner experience of her.

Anna's mother had abandoned her at birth because she did not want a baby, especially a girl. This history was openly acknowledged in the family. Only after ten or twelve days did the paternal grandmother collect her from the hospital. Anna's mother did not have anything to do with her care; Anna's father, who worked long hours, hired a nurse who left when Anna was probably about eighteen months old. Some time later, a full-time housekeeper was hired; she stayed with the family throughout Anna's childhood, and Anna continued to maintain a close relationship with her. Anna could retrieve no early memories of her mother, only memories stemming from later childhood.

Her father was the only parent whom Anna felt she had, and she appeared to be attached to him. A traumatic incident had occurred early in their relationship. She reported what I labelled as a screen memory from the age of three: she was sitting on her father's lap, and he was tickling her. As she recounted this, she wondered if she had become sexually excited (and I wondered if the father had gotten excited). Her father pulled away, declared an end to the tickling and cuddling, and her sense was that he had totally shied away from any such physical or affectionate behavior from then on.

Anna said that her father often referred to her as "oversexed." Yet she felt that he "liked" her and was pleased by her accomplishments. Much later in the analysis, we came to understand that the sexual encounter with her marriage counselor was a reenactment of this early trauma. Her thought that "Now it is truly hopeless" reflected her feeling that she had lost her father, in a way, as well as her mother.

Throughout her childhood and adolescence, the patient reported, she was left almost totally to her own devices. She remembered wandering the streets alone as a child with the money her father had given her for food in her pocket. Her mother was an alcoholic and her father a heavy drinker; the parents "partied" all the time. Anna described her mother as an angry, bitter person who clung possessively to her father and was jealous of any attention he gave to Anna. He provided her with whatever money she needed during her growing-up years. He died a few years before Anna and I met, and her inheritance funded her analysis.

In the first months of the analysis, what I experienced was primarily the patient's profound sense of insatiable emptiness and unarticulated badness. The objects in her current life—her sons and her boyfriend, Tom—were described in terms of her terror of their disapproval and potential abandonment of her, but they remained fuzzy in my mind. These fears of abandonment and her unhappy demeanor conveyed a sense of depression that seemed to infuse the consulting room. As mentioned, her affect was generally flat; at times she would weep, seemingly inconsolably, without any clear connection to what she was saying. My concern was to make sense of her flat emptiness.

In the first year of the analysis and for several years to follow, on many occasions, the patient exhibited unusual behavior during her sessions, which was painful to watch. She would writhe and rock wordlessly on the couch. As I explored this behavior with her, I realized that it was a re-creation of her frequent masturbation, bodily based and without visual content. She experienced a painful something, an almost tangible substance, inside herself—like a kind of abdominal cramp. The most basic sensation was of an insatiable "sexual" feeling—an emptiness that could not be filled, but that impelled her to masturbate to relieve the tension. She had the fantasy that menstruation might help: blood flowing out would help, being rid of something inside would help.

Her masturbation gave her only temporary relief and left her feeling frustration and pain in the belief that she could never be satiated.

It was not possible to be in the room with this person, trying to come into contact with her unbearable sense of emptiness, without feeling a sense of desolation myself. I needed history, theory, insight—something quantifiable to help us both. So I began to interpret this bodily feeling, especially as it came up in the transference, as an early longing to be fed, cared for, and contained by me as a longed-for mother. Also, I began to focus on Anna's nameless sense of intrinsic badness that would drive people away—a badness that stemmed basically from her being female (the basis for her mother not wanting her), her intense sexual feelings (called "oversexed"), and her anger (as yet unacknowledged).

I understood Anna's feeling of an insatiable emptiness that could never be filled as a fantasy, yet at this point I was worried about it. I wondered whether it might be an expression of a developmental lack of psychic structure (Tyson 1996), and whether her inability to verbalize her affects was a consequence of unrepresented, unsymbolized, or inchoate mental states (Bion 1962; Green 1998). More than being worried about the meaning and implications of her emptiness, I felt uncomfortable—alone at sea and in need of something to hold on to.

Even the patient's descriptions of the people in her life at present seemed amorphous, vague, and flat. She talked a lot about her two sons, so I was form-ing some picture of what and who they were. But of Tom, her boyfriend, I had very little sense. He seemed a dim figure to me—just *there*. Anna complained vaguely about him: he was reliable but boring and uncommunicative. She hinted that sex with him was only so-so. However, he was moving in with her, and there was a likelihood that they would get married.

Then came a session in which I experienced a sudden insight about Tom. Anna was planning to make some renovations to her home, for which she had to obtain approval from the community zoning board. The morning after a public hearing in this regard, she reported what had happened. Tom had gone with her to the hearing. She had been very nervous and stuttered when she got up to explain her rationale for the changes to her property. Several men on the board had given her a hard time; they fired questions at her and it appeared they would vote against her. She had become flustered.

Tom, usually a quiet man, had then asked permission to stand up to speak. When the board had asked what his interest in the matter was, he had said,

"Well, I am the man who intends to be with this lovely woman for a long time. I intend to move in and marry her." The members of the board had laughed and subsequently approved her request.

Anna told me that she thought Tom had turned the tide not so much by his words as by the impression of respectability and solidity that he conveyed. Then she began to talk about her old housekeeper.

As I was listening, words suddenly came into my head like a bolt of lightning that lit up in my mind: "*He loves her!*" I do not remember what I actually said at that moment, but I think I murmured something to this effect aloud: "*He loves you.*"[1]

From that moment on, I felt Tom's presence in Anna's life more clearly—as a solid, supporting, and loving man. And I experienced his presence within myself as well—as a comforting anchor in a sea of emptiness, a psychic ally in the psychoanalytic enterprise.

In retrospect, I realize that I was searching for a sense of some sort of good internalized object in the patient's mind, which *I* needed her to have. It was painful to bear witness to her absolute terror of abandonment and to her internal emptiness in an area where any positive, caring object might dwell. Certainly, she could not find a positive image of her mother anywhere in her mind; I saw only a void where such an imago might be.

I think my words, "He loves you"—and, more important, my accepting attitude toward her—conveyed a complex message. First, it gave her my permission to be loved by a man, a permission she certainly did not get from her mother's jealous possessiveness of her father. It was probably received as a communication of my love for and protection of her as well. I wanted her to have a loving internal object, and I conveyed this to her in whatever words I

---

1 Birksted-Breen (2012) described sudden visual or dreamlike images that appear in the analyst's mind during reverie—images that offer a meeting ground between the concrete and symbolic in patients who demonstrate an absence of symbolic thinking within the analytic situation.

said. This was the root of both the sudden utterance and the hopeful attitude I conveyed. But above all, it conveyed my relief—at least she had someone now who loved her, and I had an ally whom I could hold on to in my mind. That ally, whom I manufactured, made it easier for me to tolerate her pain.

In the session that followed, Anna seemed a shade brighter and talked about her determination to be more sexually responsive to Tom. My sudden words marked another set of links that were hovering at the edge of my unconscious.

The patient's associations went from house renovations and Tom to the loved housekeeper—that is, from the possibility of renovations in her analysis to a good object: Tom/housekeeper/analyst.

But allowing herself to move closer toward a new object in her life and in her mind brought anxiety. A few months later, she reported a dream of being flooded by water, "water out of control." Her immediate association was: "Tom and I set a date to be married …. Maybe I feel like my feelings will be out of control." Later, she reported having told him that she was used to being alone. "If I weren't coming here, I fear I wouldn't be getting married," she told me. "I feel like the feeling maybe comes out here."

In a subsequent session, Anna reported feeling anxious: "I'm not good about having somebody around. I always said I didn't want to marry anybody I cared about enough so that if that person died, it would be painful. I've been masturbating a lot …. I feel dead, still, in the water."

I speculated that Anna's mother had never been with her when she was an infant, so that Anna was never able to take her in as an internalized presence. Perhaps this explained her reference to "dead, still in the water"—that is, *stillborn*, never able to see herself reflected in her mother's face. (This evokes Green's [1998] ideas about the imago of the dead mother in a child's mind.)

In the initial part of the analysis, I needed Tom as an external ally because I felt that Anna had not yet taken me in as a good object, but only as a potentially hurtful and rejecting one, so that her depression seemed dangerous to me.

This need for an inner ally was an unconscious one; I was aware only of an uneasiness and puzzlement that centered on trying to make sense of her deep and formless depression.

As the analysis went on, through the differing transferences that took shape, many representations emerged: that of a lost and fleeting mothering object (probably Anna's first nurse); an uncaring and neglectful mother who preferred males; a warm, caring housekeeper; a harsh and unaccepting maternal grandmother who did not like her; and a father. But there was no early sustaining and holding mother from infancy.

In retrospect, I can see my seeking the counsel of a certain male colleague as an expression of my need to find an object situated outside my patient's mind, and even outside the dyad—an object I could take in, lean on, and hold for support. In a totally unconscious identification with Anna, I was looking for a father who could take the place of the absent mother. And it is now clear to me that I was searching for a good object, one that could be counted on and that could provide structure, for both the patient and for me.

Case 2: Dimitri

In this case, again, it was the patient's romantic partner who played a dominant role, in both her mind and in mine. I experienced this object differently at different times throughout the treatment, and I would like to explore here what this might mean about the analytic process.

My patient, Helene, a woman in her mid-forties, was in severe crisis when she began seeing me. A few months before, she had discovered that Dimitri, her husband of twelve years, had been having an affair. He blamed her for this, saying that she was too self-assured and not supportive enough of him, and that he wanted a divorce.

She turned for help to her former analyst, Dr. P, and was shocked and dismayed to learn that he had retired. Dr. P called me, explained the situation, and gave me a brief history of his work with Helene and an impression of Dimitri. This particular attention to Dimitri did not strike me as odd at the time, given the situation, but retrospectively, I think it is meaningful. That is, the figure of Dimitri was significant to Dr. P, as it turned out to be for me.

My first impression of Helene was of a tall, stunningly beautiful woman whose presence—even her perfume—filled up the waiting room. But it was clear that she felt totally devastated, abandoned, and betrayed by both Dimitri and Dr. P. Focusing on the present circumstances, she told me that Dimitri, ten years younger than she, had left her for a younger woman, a Russian like himself.

Helene had met Dimitri when he was studying engineering on a student visa, while she was a young business executive. With her business expertise, she had helped him form and run a highly successful company in which they both continued to work—a company based on a sophisticated computer system that he had created. The Pygmalion-like story that she told over the following months portrayed how she had made Dimitri over—from a poor, rough immigrant into a jet-setting executive with expensive tastes. I heard about her own earlier history only later and in isolated fragments.

It was clear that Helene had benefited from her previous treatment and was very attached to Dr. P. She told me that he had helped her learn to trust and to understand the origins of her problems. At first, there were few other people—besides Dimitri, Dr. P, and her animals—whom I heard much about. She had rescued two dogs who had been abused, sheltering them and nursing them back to health and helping them trust human beings again.

Early on, we focused on the patient's angry and disappointed feelings about Dr. P, which clouded her ability to engage with me. In the meantime, Dimitri began having panic attacks and came back to her. They reconciled, but she remained obsessed with his betrayal, suspicious and frightened that he would betray her and leave her again, especially as he continued to blame her for his actions.

Dimitri filled the sessions. Helene recounted his mistreatment of her in many ways. She was jealous of and resentful about the money he had spent with the girlfriend. She talked of his constantly demeaning her by putting her down in front of the employees at work, giving her no credit and claiming her ideas as his own. She described his impulsivity, temper tantrums, demandingness, childishness, and narcissistic rants. She was trying to be submissive to his demands in order to keep the marriage together, and it was striking to note that she could not let herself be angry at him, but instead spoke of how much she was in love with him and how exciting he was to her. The two continued to spend money lavishly, going off on spur-of-the-moment weekend trips to exciting places. She continually asked me to help her understand him: How could he act this way? Was he right? Was she wrong?

A picture of Dimitri formed in my mind: I saw him in a controlling, sadistic position in their sadomasochistic relationship, and Helene in masochistic enthrallment with him. Like Helene, I began to feel that I could not be rid of him. Even though I knew better, in my mind, he took on the enduring role of "the villain of the piece."

A similar metaphor emerged in Helene's first reported dream, from the first month of treatment: "I was in another city and carrying a snake around. I realized it was bent—uncomfortable—I put it in a garage. Tina [a girlfriend] put it in the dishwasher, and it came out like a statue. I was angry, picturing how it had died. Then I was in an airport with Dimitri, with my arm around him. I realized he had lost all his muscles."

Her association went to snakes in the Caribbean, where she frequently traveled with Dimitri. "I often dream of being somewhere else, somewhere foreign. Dimitri has been a snake recently .... Boris [a Russian associate of Dimitri's] said something about somebody being a snake in the grass in the business ...."

Helene then began to associate to her girlfriend Tina, along with several other women—various friends and a friend's mother—who were "non-nurturing" and not to be trusted. Then she mused, "Dimitri was losing his muscles [in the dream]! I don't know—he's always talking about his muscles. He wants to be admired."

She talked about how Dimitri had told her to dress more conservatively at work because it was hard to concentrate. "I feel he is trying to dismantle me," she continued, "so that he can stand on his own, shine on his own." She went on for some while in this vein and then said, "I felt drugged yesterday—from sleeping pills and Xanax, perhaps. Like I was going to faint. Why do I feel drugged or poisoned? I don't understand."

I said, "You feel like you're in an altered state of mind." "Yes, like in a foreign state."

"The dream seems to be saying you are afraid that, with our work here, you will lose the relationship with Dimitri—it has weakened muscles and is losing its strength."

"Yes—plus I don't trust him."

I added, "Like a snake in the grass."

She responded, "Hmm. That's interesting. It's true that Dimitri and I are so intertwined. He's had a breakdown, and then I feel like I have one."

Then came a stream of questions about how to handle Dimitri to keep him from leaving again. I replied that she perceived me as being like the women in the dream—not nurturing, not to be trusted. On the way out, she commented: "I like your dream interpretation."

I would like to be able to say that this comment validated a good interpretation that addressed Helene's initial anxiety about the analysis. In truth, however, I think she was actually thanking me for having positioned Dimitri—and not herself or me—as the snake in the grass. Thus, both she and I could put aside for the time being the anger that I did not think she was ready to manage, letting it be contained in and represented by Dimitri; we could therefore overlook her castrating and erotic impulses evident in the dream imagery: a snake that was put into a dishwasher and became a statue, a snake that died. I focused on what I understood of the dream—her mistrust of me and what the analysis might bring, perhaps the dissolution of her needed sadomasochistic relationship with Dimitri—but I found the rest of the dream confusing.

At this time in the treatment, I felt it necessary to underscore his cruelty and un-dependability (and not mine), and to agree with her that he seemed unstable. In fact, Helene's barrages about Dimitri totally dominated the content of the sessions. I think that in this way, just as Helene felt dominated or let herself be dominated by Dimitri, I felt dominated by him, too. She could not get him out of her head, and neither could. I speculate that focusing on him as victimizer helped me get out from under this sense of domination.

Moreover, there was an Alice-in-Wonderland quality to the patient's world with Dimitri, and my principal focus was to try to engage her and help both of us *think* in the face of its seductions and confusions. Thus, at this point, I was dealing with Dimitri as an object and with an object relationship (a sadomasochistic one) that I felt Helene needed to "see" and understand more clearly. At the same time, he became for me a "real" object outside the analytic relationship, rationalized from the viewpoint (and my background) of ego psychology in terms of adaptations to the outer world and ego strengths, such as reality testing. I thought she needed to see that she was being controlled by him. Here my unconscious identification in the countertransference lay with her as a victim controlled by a sadistic object.

As Helene told me stories of particularly abusive (I thought) interchanges between her and Dimitri, it was clear that she would become confused, not trust her perceptions or judgment, and then take in the blame he seemed to be putting on her. For example, when something would go wrong at the business, Helene would try to get answers from Dimitri, who she felt would try to shut her out from important meetings. Giving her incomplete figures that did not make sense to her, he would then call her stupid for not understanding and blame her for the current work troubles. She would then become confused and begin to doubt herself.

At one point in the first year of the analysis, I used the term *gaslighting* to describe such interchanges with Dimitri. Calef and Weinshel (1981) described the phenomenon of gaslighting in terms of the back-and-forth processes of introjection and projection that occur in sadomasochistic interactions. The victims in these interchanges "struggle with the feeling that their minds are being 'worked over,' their thoughts influenced, and the validity of their perceptions undermined. Meanwhile the victimizers perpetrate these distortions, disavowing them and even claiming that they themselves are the victims" (p. 46).

That struck Helene; shortly afterward, she bought a book about gaslighting and watched the classic movie of that name. I told her that she wanted me to help her figure out Dimitri and the world around her, a confusing world that I thought she must have experienced as a child. For the first time, she began to fill me in about her background, through a series of memories of painful, crazy-making incidents with both parents, which certainly amounted to gaslighting. They labeled their self-serving, sadistic, or neglectful behavior as having been done for the patient's own good, and any distress about it was her fault.

For example, Helene told me that, as a teenager, she was unexpectedly invited by her mother to take a special trip to a Caribbean island. On the first night after their arrival, Helene found herself locked out of their rented condo for hours; it turned out that her mother was entertaining a lover whom she had apparently planned to meet up with on the island. When Helene complained the next morning, her mother blamed her for being ungrateful and selfish.

Helene told me that her mother had been very young, just eighteen, when Helene was born, and she resented her daughter for ruining a hoped-for modeling career. The patient described her mother as competitive and completely self-absorbed, never thinking of or caring for her, and said that her mother often abandoned her to the care of her harsh, Old-World paternal grandmother. Her father was more engaged, but also narcissistic, erratic, and explosive, attacking her verbally when things went wrong with the mother. Her parents divorced when Helene was in her teens. Finally, Helene refused to see her mother again, after repeated incidents in which the patient felt totally and painfully let down by the mother's gaslighting of her.

In these early months, I felt that Helene kept a certain distance from me. As she reiterated her feelings of distrust of Dimitri, I began to point out the parallels between her feelings toward him and her feelings toward me in the transference. She admitted to not wanting to trust me or anyone, ever again. In the first months, I struggled with the feeling that the patient would leave the treatment, would abandon *me*. And indeed, after every major separation, she would announce she was quitting. She frequently went away on weekends and was cavalier about informing me that she would miss appointments.

As we explored this behavior, the patient revealed her conviction that I did not think about or remember her at all, that she simply did not exist in my mind when we were apart. The acting out diminished after I interpreted that she wanted me to be the one who worried about being forgotten. Later, we got to her terror that she, being left alone, would disappear or cease to exist. Helene's responses to separations and my corresponding countertransference of feeling abandoned suggested a deeply troubled and shaky attachment to the early maternal object, mirrored in her clinging relationship to Dimitri. Gabbard (2012) articulated how sadomasochistic configurations can function to bind and cover early trauma and narcissistic problems of loss and attachment; Helene's conflicted attachment to Dimitri clearly served such functions.

Gradually, Helene began to separate herself from Dimitri's grip, both internally and externally. They lived separately during the work week and got together on weekends. She decided to disengage from their company—even though she feared Dimitri was driving it into the ground—in order to help the marriage, and because she felt her attempts to co-run it were becoming increasingly futile and damaging. As a result of these changes, Helene became less anxious but more visibly sad. As she made these moves, I felt relieved. At that point, I felt that progress in the treatment depended on both of us getting a perspective on Dimitri, as well as on her psychic use of him (note that I am saying *her* psychic use of him, not mine).

But the preoccupation with Dimitri continued. I felt somewhat freed from him, however, and a little more able to be heard by the patient, especially in relation to the transference. She announced that she *did* trust me, but not the process — "look what a mess I still am!" The transference, split in this way, reflected split-off aggressive fantasies, still embodied—in both our minds, to varying degrees—in Dimitri.

Two years into the treatment, catastrophe struck again. First, one of Helene's beloved dogs died suddenly. During this period of grieving, she brought the other dog directly into the session so I could meet him—a concrete manifestation of the patient's objects entering the analyst's space. The way I understand this is that Helene's inner world of objects was so shaken and shaky that she had to bring her remaining dog to me so that *I* could experience and verify the reality of its existence. Castelnuovo-Tedesco (1978) suggested that this need to find external validation for internal objects may be especially pressing during times of loss and mourning.

Second, Dimitri took a long trip home to Russia without her, ostensibly to explore his roots. When he returned, he subjected her to self-absorbed rants about his discoveries for hours, according to her account; she finally became fed up and angry. Then one Monday morning, I received a terse voicemail message from Helene who, to my surprise, was in California. In a cold, caustic voice, she said, "Thanks for all your help," and told me that she was not returning to treatment—or even to the state—ever. She meant never to return.

I felt blindsided, but the next day another call came. Dimitri had again asked for a divorce. Helene was in a panic, and she wanted to talk to me. We set up frequent sessions by phone until she could return home and until I got back from a trip away—a period of about three weeks.

The next two months were very difficult. When Helene returned in person, she seemed to be unraveling. Always carefully dressed before, she now appeared unkempt, distraught, lost. She pasted on a desperate smile at the beginning and end of the sessions. I was concerned about her psychic cohesiveness and the depth of her depression as she described her terror of emptiness and total abandonment.

I had long suspected that Helene abused alcohol; now she admitted to drinking to anesthetize herself to emotional pain. Session after session of Dimitri ensued: a constant, pain-filled barrage delivered tearfully and apologetically—did I think he was really leaving this time; how could he not be thinking of her and suffering as she was; how could this be, etc., etc. It was very hard to keep from answering these queries; the impulse was to soothe a suffering and crying infant.

At this point, Dimitri was no longer in my mind as he had been before. That image—the bad object—seemed to have dissolved, replaced by my clinical concerns and my need to understand this obsessive and desperate lament centered around him.

At first, I told Helene that she wished me to be all-knowing and was enraged at me that I had not been able to prevent this from happening—hence the call from California. I said that she used this obsessive and repetitive litany to keep Dimitri within her and to avoid the terror of her inner world (and herself) dissolving. That is, I thought that Helene's ongoing complaints about Dimitri were serving as a transitional object—they were soothing, if painful. I was no longer thinking about Dimitri as I had before. *Did Dimitri disappear from my consciousness because of my growing and fuller understanding of the uses to which the patient's object was being put?*

Helene said, "I know what this is about: my mother and my early experiences with her. But how come nothing you say or that anyone says goes in? [She was also barraging friends with the same questions.] How come I don't change?" I felt, actually, that she *was* letting in some of my words—as evidenced, for example, by the very fact that she could step back from her constant lament to ask this question.

Eventually, the patient began to come out of this stage and her perspective widened. In one session, she described feeling disoriented and afraid: "I need to hurry up and get happy. Without these business problems, my life would be emptier. It isn't good to be clinging to a bomb. The business is a monkey on my back, yet as much as it is a pain, it is a connection to Dimitri. I wonder why he couldn't put his otherness [that is, all the failings he disowned in himself] into someone else and not me—I get it all." She revealed that, three days before Dimitri told her he wanted a divorce, she herself had said, "I can't do it any more."

In another session, Helene tearfully complained about having been to an ear doctor, saying that he had hurt her and made her cry; she did not want him to drain her ear and hurt her even more. I interpreted the obvious parallel to me and to the painful analytic process.

She then began to obsess about Dimitri again and invited me to speculate on how Dimitri might be feeling. I said, "You need concrete evidence that you are in his mind and my mind, too. You want me to reassure you and make the pain go away." I felt that the patient had difficulty tolerating strong affects.

A week later, she came to a session a few minutes late. "I was frozen out of my car. Had a bad night. Nightmares. Woke up anxious. Took three-fourths of a Xanax and it knocked me out. It all stemmed from an e-mail to Dimitri about needing a conference call about several important business issues. It was businesslike but not stroking his ego. The automatic reply kicked in that he was out of the office—I imagine he is on vacation with a woman. And I see there were several unusual withdrawals of $500 on the wrong slips and scribbled, as if he is losing it. It all made me feel so bad."

I asked about the nightmares. "Okay, but first I want to tell you one more thing that happened." She then recounted that she had met a man whom she liked. She felt that he was coming on too strong, however, and she told him she was not feeling well and not ready for a close, one-to-one relationship yet. He texted her saying that she should just be straight and tell him she was not interested. She felt bad about this. (Here is an example of Helene's being in the position of doing the rejecting, of being the one in control.)

"So my dream—I lost my wallet, like what happened last summer on vacation [when she had had a miserable time with Dimitri, gotten drunk and sick and lost her wallet]. And lost my cell phone. The person who was supposed to call wasn't calling. I guess that is Dimitri, or my father [or, as I think now, she was the person who did not call the man who was interested in her, and who often did not call me when she missed an appointment]. Then I was losing my animals—couldn't keep track of them. I was in my house, and a friend, a realtor, was there. All my stuff was there. People who had bought the house had abandoned it. A new realtor said the sale didn't go thorough …. Animal food was there. Long abandoned." There was a pause as she silently cried.

"I was trying to pick up some of my things and then went somewhere with Sally, my cousin," Helene said, continuing her narrative of the dream. "We were sitting watching TV in a place like the one we rented when we went to California last month. In reality, it was like being in a tomb because the windows were all taped up—horrible. Then, sitting on a couch waiting for a car. It was not coming, not coming. Then we were driving a car, going around a cul-de-sac, and I was saying to myself, 'Put on the brakes.'" She paused. "Then Sally was moving away. I'm thinking, 'Don't go.'"

Then the patient said, "I woke up thinking I miss Dimitri so. I don't want the relationship to be over. Is this all real? Lots of times in the past, I would wake up and think, 'Did this really happen?' Like with my dog. And then I'd realize, 'Oh, my God—he's dead.' Readjusting to reality. In the time after Dimitri's betrayal, I'd wake up a lot. Had this kind of dreams and then I'd assess the reality. Lots of times it was, 'Oh, yes, thank God, he's here,' but then sometimes I'd think there's a problem and I'd say, 'I have to fix it.' Like with this guy yesterday—I felt I had to contact him and tell him I was sorry."

"I always have this recurring dream," Helene went on. "Like the kind of dream in which you've missed a class, you know? I've forgotten my animals are still alive. Horrified I've been neglectful. Like the house in the dream, which I dream about a lot ..."

I said, "The dogs in your dreams represent you. You've been afraid that you would be forgotten and go unattended by me, as you feel Dimitri and your mother have forgotten you."

The patient cried, and there was a long silence. Then she said: "Yes .... Lots of times I don't respond, but I heard everything you said and I think it's true. You are right that the animals are me. I don't want to abandon my children, like my mother did. Therefore I'm overly involved [referring to her animals]."

"And I do feel like I'm living in an abandoned, ghostlike place that used to be my life," she continued. "I'm sitting there saying he's gone. I want him to be frozen [that is, frozen in place]. I can't bear the fact that he's with someone else. So if I get little pieces of info—like he's taken money he shouldn't have from our account—it's like unrequited love. I feel like I have no right to feel sorry for myself. I have the world in front of me. What's wrong with me?"

I answered, "You have been in a place like purgatory—clinging to Dimitri in order not to feel empty and dead inside, but afraid to move on. Like this morning, when you were frozen out of moving—forward—to be with me."

At this point, I was dimly aware of feeling more positive and sympathetic toward Dimitri. Then, after this session, I had a dream in which an unknown but attractive man asked me to take care of and feed his baby by a previous wife.

He paid off some money to the Russian mafia. In the dream, which was pleasant, there seemed to be a sense of openness.

When I awoke, I thought that the man seemed to be a combination of three people: the actor George Clooney, whom I find rakish and good-looking; a family friend who had shown himself to be untrustworthy; and Dimitri. As I reflected on the dream, I asked myself whether my patient's object had found particularly fertile ground on which to form a negative image in my mind because of my experiences with my family friend—and, second, whether the sense of openness in the dream had to do with my sense of there being some new breathing and thinking room in the analytic situation as the patient's attachment to Dimitri changed.

My dream seemed to anticipate the emergence of the paternal aspects of Helene's attraction to Dimitri and, optimistically, a more triadic picture or space (Britton 1989). Indeed, in the months that followed, the patient began to talk about her father and her current relationship with him, and about her relationships with other family members and friends about whom I had heard almost nothing before.

Helene also announced that now she wanted to get to her anger at her mother. The dream began to undo our mutually created defense: Dimitri, no longer all bad guy and now an oedipal object whose allure I could understand, cheerfully moved out of the way and asked me to take care of his baby, the patient. As for the pay-off of money in my dream, I wonder if a silent countertransference had been building up throughout the treatment—a sense of being drained by Helene's constant preoccupation with Dimitri, and thus my being *owed* something. I could now put myself in Dimitri's shoes as the object of Helene's attempts at control.

I have tried to demonstrate how the object of Dimitri entered my mind and assumed different visages through a changing set of identifications and counter-identifications (Racker 1957). I think I needed to construct an image of Dimitri to help me handle shared uncomfortable affects in the dyad of Helene and me: anger, confusion, and helplessness.

Finally, a word about the name *Dimitri,* which of course I chose to disguise the real person. I realized as I wrote this paper why I had picked that name. A few months before, I had reread (probably not by accident) a classic suspense novel, a tale of espionage and assignation. The narrative traces the trail of a murdered man through Eastern Europe—a mysterious man, notorious and sinister, yet intriguing. The name of the novel, by Eric Ambler, is *A Coffin for Dimitrios.*

DISCUSSION

In both these cases, in different ways, I became caught up with a person in my patient's life—or, more accurately, with the patient's internal object representations of that person, present or absent, in her mind. In both cases, the patient's sense of attachment to her inner objects was shaky.

In the case of Anna, the seeming absence of an internal good maternal object was very troubling to me. This lack of internal structure is always a matter for serious consideration in terms of evaluating the patient's psyche and understanding his or her problems, and may or may not figure in a decision to offer an analysis to that individual. In this case, however, it was much more than an intellectual matter for me. As I have attempted to demonstrate, this absence resonated internally and unconsciously within me to produce a wordless apprehension. Had I been totally overtaken by this fear, I could easily have pulled away from a deeper involvement with the patient by keeping her in psychotherapy at once or twice a week, or by drawing away from her in other ways.

L. Ehrlich (2004, 2010) discussed the importance of unconscious fears and inhibitions within the psychoanalyst that keep him or her from recommending and/or deepening an analysis. She suggests three major considerations in the analyst's reluctance to begin a new analysis: a defense against powerful affects, a co-created resistance, and a manifestation of the analyst's own conflicts. Undoubtedly, Anna was a case in point and an example of all these factors.

With Anna, it was only with my sudden awareness that her boyfriend loved her and my voicing this thought aloud that I became aware of my unconscious fears of deepening the analysis and my identification with the patient's terrified sense of aloneness. Her telling the details of what her boyfriend had said and how he had conducted himself supplied me with some data about him. I used these details to create an inner representation of an object that I thought she needed, and certainly that *I* needed, in order for me to proceed more comfortably in the initial stages of this analysis. At the time, I was not able to become aware of or to make use of other important meanings of this internal event—the maternal role that I had stepped into of reversing the mother's possessiveness in relation to the father, a role that allowed for a more developed and triangular dynamic, and one that included giving Anna permission to be loved.

In the second case, Helene's incessant preoccupation with her bad object drummed him into my mind. My experience of Dimitri as a bad and obstructing object became fixed and interfered with my ability to understand what was going on in her mind and between us in the transference. At first, like her, I was confused and unable to think about the role that he played in her mind. My efforts to help Helene understand that Dimitri was like her parents, consistently gaslighting her, and that she was therefore putting herself in a position to be abused, were helpful, but only up to a point. I was working with the general idea that the people in the patient's life are transference figures, just as the analyst is. I agree with Castelnuovo-Tedesco (1978), who writes: "Characteristic of transference is the *intensity* of the universal need to rediscover in the therapist (and in other current objects) the objects of early childhood" (p. 23, italics in original). It was only when I came to see the defensive use to which both Helene and I were putting Dimitri that a deeper understanding of the transference and the countertransference was achieved.

My experience of Dimitri as a bad object, *my* bad object, made me unable to understand any hostility that might be arising in the therapeutic dyad and the control the patient exerted over me. Thus, I was a key participant in an ongoing resistance (Boesky 1990). This enabled the patient to split off her aggression defensively and to disown it, both of us keeping it out of the analytic dyad. As my bad object, then, Dimitri functioned to help me deal with my discomfort in the dyad. It was the object's fixity in my mind that was the problem, or, to put it differently, it was its quality of being "a dense object"—one with a thickness made up of multiple meanings that collapse into a singular, fixating meaning (Emery 1992)—that made for a sustained blindness.

Ferro's (1992, 1993) metaphor of the analytic enterprise as a narration written by the patient and read by the analyst is useful in thinking about these experiences, up to a point. The metaphor captures the idea that my internal images of Tom and Dimitri were co-creations. Anna and Helene were the original authors who portrayed their inner objects to me, and I, as the reader, elaborated them in my mind. But unlike those of a finished novel, the analytic plot and its characters change as they go along, edited and rewritten by both patient and analyst, who exert mutual influences on each other.[2]

With Anna, my sense of Tom as a loving person and my communicating this to her allowed her to see him differently and to open herself up more to him.

Similarly, as my understanding of my defensive use of Dimitri changed, so did my initial sense of him as villain; thus, I was better able to help Helene break free from the role of victim that she had assumed in her mind and in her life.

I am emphasizing here how much the characters of Tom and Dimitri were fashioned within my imagination. I needed these images to help me manage my countertransference—the discomfort within the dyadic situation that was becoming unbearable. In Anna's case, I needed a new object in my mind that seemingly did not exist in hers; in Helene's, I needed to share a bad object with her and then to create my own version of that object, which helped me find a more hopeful and optimistic sense of future change.

I suggest that this experience of the analyst's temporarily borrowing or reshaping the patient's objects to create a new version for the analyst may not be unique, but to my knowledge it has not been described elsewhere in the analytic literature. With these two patients, I created or partially created an object to help me cope with troubling feelings that arose in the analytic dyad.[3]

---

2 Fundamentally, of course, Ferro (1993) conceptualizes psychoanalytic treatment as a bi-personal field that comprises ever-changing dynamic processes.

3 This idea may have some overlap with the various concepts of the analytic third. As a concept, the third, while used widely by most contemporary psychoanalytic theoretical traditions,

I would like to emphasize that the uses of the patient's objects in the countertransference may be particularly hard to detect, as first suggested by Jacobs (1983). This is perhaps because the objects in a patient's story can become real to us as analysts. They take on a distinct gestalt, which forecloses their being scrutinized.

No one's object representations can be understood as directly synonymous with outer reality or with the real people whom we are told about. We know this from Freud (1917), who described the creation of an inner world, an ego and superego, from internalizations of lost objects. We also know it from Klein (1940), who gave us a view of the complex introjections/projections and reintrojections that make up the internal world of object relations.

Strictly and ideally speaking, therefore, we know that the pictures our patients give us about the people in their lives are distorted. We are trained to treat these objects as our patients' creations, which emerge from a long and complex developmental process.[4] We are encouraged to understand these figures as pieces of the patient, just as we perceive the figures in their dreams.

We listen to them as derivatives that carry the patient's feelings about us and give us pictures of the transference; that is, they open a deeper understanding of the patient's mind for us. But we are not so familiar with the notion that they are *our* creations as well.

While there is a legitimate place for discussion about adaptation to reality (and thus about external object relations and interpersonal conflicts), we would all agree that there are dangers for the analyst in becoming caught up in the patient's life in these ways—that is, in ways that involve accepting the patient's accounts as veridical. Jacobs (1983) and F. Ehrlich (1999), for exam-

---

remains ill-defined and is used inconsistently, often even within a particular school. There are many usages of the term, and several attempts have been made to classify these (Aron 2006; Muller 1999).

4 Increasingly, analysts have come to understand that the infant's early internal world is structured by the mother and other caretakers, and that internal representations of others emerge from interactive, affective-laden experiences (Stern 1995).

ple, describe the analyst's countertransference distortions about the people in the patient's life. F. Ehrlich became more acutely aware of such distortions in himself through his work with families and couples, in which he saw patients' children, spouses, or parents in person.

The contemporary emphasis on the here and now in the transference steels the analyst against the sorts of enactments and dilemmas I have described here.

Yet there are other inevitable pulls in the opposite direction—to become enmeshed in the patient's life, in the stories and memories the patient shares in analysis. As we listen empathically, we are pulled by our identifications with the patient and the characters he or she introduces to us—that is, by countertransferences, whether concordant or complementary, as Racker (1957) delineated.

These two types of countertransferences—identification with an aspect or feeling of one's self with a concordant feeling in the patient, or the unconscious taking on of a role complementary to a transferential figure in the patient's mind—were interwoven throughout both the analytic processes described in this article's clinical vignettes. But what I am specifically talking about here are countertransferences that become personified and organized in the analyst's mind around a figure borrowed from the patient's narratives. As I have attempted to demonstrate, we can too easily overlook or become oblivious to our role in shaping our own inner versions of these objects and what they might mean.

While both these cases are dramatic in different ways, such intrusions of, or preoccupations with, a patient's objects are common occurrences for analysts. If unchecked and unacknowledged, they can, as in these cases, hinder and interfere with the analytic process. On the other hand, an awareness of the possible meanings and functions of such preoccupations can help the analyst elucidate important unconscious fantasies and recurrent defensive strategies in the patient, as well as to identify unchecked countertransference reactions in herself.

REFERENCES

Ambler, E. (1939). *A Coffin for Dimitrios.* New York: Vintage, 1990.

Arlow, J. (1985). The structural hypothesis. In *Models of the Mind: Their Relationships to Clinical Work,* ed. A. Rothstein. Madison, CT: Int. Univ. Press.

Aron, L. (2006). Analytic impasse and the third. *Int. J. Psychoanal.,* 87: *349–368.*

Bion, W. R. (1962). *Learning From Experience.* London: Heinemann.

Birksted-Breen, D. (2012). Taking time: the tempo of psychoanalysis. *Int. J. Psychoanal.,* 93:*819–835.*

Boesky, D. (1990). The psychoanalytic process and its components. *Psychoanal. Q.,* 59:*550–584.*

Britton, R. (1989). The missing link: parental sexuality in the Oedipus complex. In *The Oedipus Complex Today,* ed. J. Steiner. London: Karnac.

Calef, V. & Weinshel, E. (1981). Some clinical consequences of introjection: gaslighting. *Psychoanal. Q.,* 50:*44–66.*

Castelnuovo-Tedesco, P. (1978). "The mind as a stage": some comments on reminiscence and internal objects. *Int. J. Psychoanal.,* 59:*19–25.*

Ehrlich, F. M. (1999). Countertransference to internal objects. *Contemp. Psychoanal.,* 35:*603–615.*

Ehrlich, L. T. (2004). The analyst's reluctance to begin a new analysis. *J. Amer. Psychoanal. Assn.,* 52:*1075–1093.*

——— (2010). The analyst's ambivalence about continuing and deepening an analysis. *J. Amer. Psychoanal. Assn.,* 58:*515–532.*

Emery, E. (1992). On dreaming of one's patient: dense objects and intrapsychic isomorphism. *Psychoanal. Rev.,* 79:*509–535.*

Ferro, A. (1992). Two authors in search of characters: the relationship, the field, the story. *Rivista di Psicoanalisi,* 38:*44–90.*

——— (1993). The impasse within a theory of the analytic field: possible vertices of observation. *Int. J. Psychoanal.*, 74:*917–929*.

Freud, S. (1917). Mourning and melancholia. S. E., 14.

Gabbard, G. (2012). Masochism as a multiply-determined phenomenon. In *The Clinical Problem of Masochism*, ed. D. Holtzman & N. Kulish. Northvale, NJ: Jason Aronson.

Green, A. (1998). The primordial mind and the work of the negative. *Int. J. Psychoanal.*, 79:*649–665*.

Jacobs, T. J. (1983). The analyst and the patient's object world: notes on an aspect of countertransference. *J. Amer. Psychoanal. Assn.*, 31:*619–642*.

Klein, M. (1940). Mourning and its relation to manic-depressive states. In *Love, Guilt, and Reparation and Other Works, 1921–1945*. New York: Delta, 1975, pp. *344–369*.

Muller, J. P. (1999). Consultation from the position of the third. *Amer. J. Psychoanal.*, 59:*113–118*.

Racker, H. (1957). The meanings and uses of countertransference. *Psychoanal. Q.*, 26:*303–357*.

Rosenfeld, H. (1971). A clinical approach to psychoanalytic theory of the life and death instincts: an investigation into the aggressive aspects of narcissism. *Int. J. Psychoanal.*, 52:*169–178*.

Stern, D. (1995). *The Motherhood Constellation*. New York: Basic Books.

Tyson, P. (1996). Object relations, affect management, and psychic structure formation: the concept of object constancy. *Psychoanal. Study Child*, 51:*172–189*.

CHAPTER 11:

Twos and Threes: Musical Chairs in Female Psychic and Social Life

(2018). J. Amer. Psychoanal. Assn., (66)(3):443–472

With Deanna Holtzman

I wish to acknowledge my co-author, colleague, and dear friend, Deanna Holtzman, with whom this paper was created and written. She died in 2016, just after the first draft of the paper was completed. It is fitting that this paper about friendships among women and girls marks the end of a long and fruitful collaboration.

Jockeying for position in the context of a threesome is a major preoccupation in female social behavior, and in female inner experience, throughout the life cycle. This oscillating phenomenon can be thought of as "twos and threes." While such configurations are often understood in terms of sibling rivalry or social influences, the focus here is on underlying female triangular dynamics. "Twos and threes" are differentiated from the more familiar rivalries among siblings and from the concept of sibling oedipal triangles. Clinical examples and a contemporary novel by Tana French are presented to demonstrate that concealed and overlooked female oedipal or persephonal conflicts may underlie these experiences and appear in the transference and countertransference.

Women of all ages have memories of rivalry and exclusion in relationships with other girls. Such experiences may occur in early childhood, but they come to the fore with greater intensity in adolescence. Three girls may try to maintain a three-

WHAT DO SEX AND GENDER HAVE TO DO WITH IT?

way relationship but find that their threesome is always under threat of dissolving into a twosome from which one of the three is excluded. If a new configuration emerges, the excluded party seeks to restore her access to the twosome and may then become herself the excluder of a third. This typical scenario is like musical chairs—two chairs and three people.

We call this the phenomenon "twos and threes." We believe that jockeying for position in the context of a threesome is a major preoccupation in female social behavior, and in female inner experience, throughout the life cycle. Our aim here is to understand the unconscious dynamics of such behavior, which so often dominates and complicates the lives of women and girls. While psychoanalytic writing about these relational patterns typically attributes them to the dynamics of sibling rivalry (see, e.g., Davidson 1975), we think that another powerful dynamic, a triangular one, arises from the so-called oedipal/ persephonal phase.[1] We will also differentiate these patterns from the more familiar rivalries among siblings by expanding Sharpe and Rosenblatt's concept of sibling oedipal triangles (1994) and referring to Juliet Mitchell's ideas about lateral relationships among siblings (2013). We will offer clinical examples to demonstrate how the triangular dynamics are embedded or overlooked in material that appears to refer to siblings or peers. We will speculate as to why this configuration seems more prevalent in female relationships than in male relationships.

Alliances among girlfriends fluctuate. Oscillations arise in a threesome as the parties take on shifting unconscious identifications and differing roles. Early problems with her mother may remain alive in a daughter, emerging in two-against-three patterns in childhood and adolescence. A girl may, for example, identify with one or the other member of a secure mother/daughter dyad or, by contrast, with the mother who chooses the rival daughter, or with the daughter left out by the parental couple. The excluded one often unconsciously represents the

---

1 We would rather refer to the female triangular situation as simply "persephonal" but will use the terminology persephonal/oedipal. We will use "oedipal" to refer to the male triangular situation and when paraphrasing and discussing the psychoanalytic literature.

mother, on whom the girl has guiltily turned the tables. This oscillation of two into three and three into two characterizes entry into, and struggles within, the persephonal/oedipal phase. Such dynamics may also infiltrate social relations among adult women.

Here is an example from an eighty-year-old woman in analysis:

When my husband and I go out, I am no good if there are three couples. It is much more pleasant with just two couples. I think it reminds me of childhood in middle school. There were two girls, Georgia and Karen, and I liked Georgia better. They were mean and did not include me. I felt so excluded. I remember other times that this happened. In second grade I was best friends with Marilyn next door and we spent a lot of time together.

Then there was a kid by the name of Sue living a few doors down the street. I was friendly with her and then Marilyn and Sue became friends and I was jealous of their relationship. I felt like the "odd man out." Now that's how I feel when there are other couples. If there are three couples, I can't hear or enter the conversation—it ends up with the other two talking socially. I start out chatting and then fizzle down. I get tired out. I don't have the stamina—to butt in and join in.

Otherwise, I feel just like out of the pair and the other two women are talking. I end up being primarily a listener. I am not good with a "threesy." That's how I felt with my mother and father and with my father and my brother—not preferred.

Here the painful feelings of exclusion are as poignant as they were when this woman was a child. Note that she reverts to the language of childhood as she talks—the girls were "mean." She reexperiences the exclusion by her girlfriends, the memory of which evokes feelings of exclusion from the parental pair (especially by her father, from whom she always wanted more attention and love)

315

and then of sibling rivalry with the brother her father preferred to her. The surface scenario recalls sibling and peer rivalries in which three females vie for a favored position. But other rivalries and jealousies also seem to be at play, indicative perhaps of both facets of the persephonal/oedipal triangular situation. On the one hand is a sexual wish to be preferred by a man (her father), in which the interloper is a rival woman (her mother); on the other, the patient, identifying as a male (the "odd man out"), wishes to exclude a rival male (her father) from a couple made up of herself and the other woman (her mother). The internal set of identifications is similarly complex.

The scenario of twos and threes seems to evoke painful feelings of humiliation and exclusion characteristic of the triadic experiences of childhood and the primal scene, when children become aware of their exclusion by the parental couple. Our clinical experience has shown that unresolved triangular conflicts can bequeath to girls and women a lifelong dilemma with threesomes, which must perpetually be managed and reworked. The cast of characters may vary but the unconscious task remains the same: to orchestrate a twosome into a threesome or a threesome into a twosome. Threesomes composed of whatever combination of sexes can take on these unconscious oedipal or persephonal meanings and dynamics.

THE PERSEPHONE COMPLEX AND ITS OSCILLATIONS

In previous works (Holtzman and Kulish 2000, 2003; Kulish and Holtzman 2008), we explored the typical triangular dynamics in little girls and women and suggested that the Demeter/Persephone myth captures them better than the story of Oedipus. We proposed that the female oedipal complex be renamed the Persephone Complex. As described by Freud (1923, 1933), the "positive" oedipal complex for a boy is marked by sexual longings for his mother and hatred and competitiveness toward his father, who has become his rival. Fears of castration and punishment motivate the boy to repress his desires and identify with his father. In applying the Oedipus myth to female psychosexual development, Freud described a more complicated pathway: Like the boy, the girl is initially attached to her mother, but then as she turns her sexual interest to her father, the mother becomes her rival. Unlike the boy, she has difficulty resolving oedipal conflicts, as she lacks the strong impetus of fear of castration (being already "castrated").

Lampl-de Groot (1928) expanded on Freud's ideas about the "negative" oedipal stage, which precedes the positive stage, in which the girl, like the boy, wants to conquer the mother for herself and sees the father as a rival. But because of the girl's feelings about her lack of a penis and castration, she relinquishes these phallic concerns and enters the positive oedipal stage. Thus, because she has difficulty giving up the first love object, the mother, "the female Oedipus complex vanishes only gradually, is largely incorporated into the normal development of the woman, and explains many of the differences [such as narcissism, lack of libidinal interest] between the mental life of women and of men" (p. 337).

This account has been subject to much revision on many counts from its inception and over the years. To begin with, it rests on a heteronormative assumption that a normal, linear course of development results in a girl's "achievement" of an attachment to her father as her love object. Many, if not most, contemporary psychoanalysts endorse a nonlinear, dynamic approach to development (Yanoff 2000; Knight 2011; Elise 2002). Second, as we and many others see it (Ritvo 1989; Burch 1997; Fischer 2002; Kulish 2006), at the entry into the triangular oedipal period the girl does not replace her first sexual object but *adds another;* she wishes to retain the love of mother and her nurturing even as she competes with her for the father's love and attention. We argue that the so-called negative and positive aspects of the triangular period do not follow the lockstep sequence described by Freud and his early followers but rather occur but rather occur simultaneously.[2] At the same time, her intensified sexual longings toward her mother also provoke fears of losing her love and care. Third, the meanings and role of penis envy in girls have been reexamined and are no longer seen as major motivators for the unfolding of female triangular relationships (see, e.g., Jones 1933; Grossman 1994). Rather, what is stressed instead of a sense of lack and renunciation of inborn masculinity are a girl's close ties to her mother and identifications with her and the importance of feelings about her female body and its life-giving potentialities (Balsam 2001, 2015; Elise 2002; Kulish 2000). Fourth, we argue that *separation issues are therefore typically part of the female triangular situation,* as is the need to conceal rivalries and aggression toward the mother. The story of Persephone portrays these understandings about female development. It is a tale about women and fertility. It centers on the girl's need to balance her love for (and her time with) her mother Demeter, goddess of grain and fertility, with love for her husband (and uncle) Hades (the father figure). A compromise brokered by Zeus allows Persephone to spend part of the year with her mother and part with her husband/father. That is, Persephone does not lose or renounce her mother in taking Hades as her partner. Direct aggression is not aimed at the mother, but appears in Demeter's rage at losing her daughter and the retaliatory famine she visits upon the earth. It is a story of a mother's intense, passionate love for her daughter.

The twos and threes phenomenon reflects Persephone's dilemma and the central motif of trying—sometimes more successfully and sometimes less—to balance a three-party system. It is harder to negotiate issues of loyalty and equality of affection among three parties than between two. The social life of girls is characterized by similar needs and dilemmas. When two draw closer to each other, the third feels deeply, painfully wounded. At the same time, as

---

2 The traditional terms—"negative oedipal," referring to the love object of the same sex, and "positive oedipal," referring to the object of the opposite sex—are unfortunate and should be replaced to rid the concepts of value-laden connotations.

seems typical of girls, the two don't want "to hurt anyone's feelings," just as they don't want to jeopardize the relationships with their mothers. The consequent feelings of betrayal, exclusion, and humiliation revive the dramas of the persephonal/oedipal period and the primal scene. These oscillations between twos and threes are attempts to repair these painful feelings and anxieties. The Persephone/Demeter myth depicts its dramatic resolution to such conflicts through the oscillations of the seasons.

Much has been written in the psychoanalytic literature about the developmental transition from dyadic relationships into triadic relationships— that is to say, "twos into threes." Modern Kleinians like Britton (1989, 2004) and O'Shaughnessy (1989) link the concept of being able to tolerate a "third" position and the capacity for self-observation and accepting reality. For Britton (1989), "triangular space" is bounded by the three persons in the oedipal situation and all their potential relationships. He speaks of the ability to tolerate the link between the parents in the oedipal situation: "If the link between the parents perceived in love and hate can be tolerated in the child's mind, it provides him with a prototype for an object relationship of a third kind in which he is a witness and not a participant. A third position then comes into existence from which object relationships can be observed. Given this, we can also envisage being observed. This provides us with a capacity for seeing ourselves in interaction with others and for entertaining another point of view whilst retaining our own ..." (p. 87). This achievement of being able to accept a threesome is not easily attainable or stable.

O'Shaughnessy (1989) describes some lasting psychic reactions to the early oedipus complex (or primal scene): the child, feeling excluded, is "driven to fracture and obliterate out of sight the oedipal parents ... not only impossibly stimulated but also outside and alone" (p. 143). For the Kleinians, early oedipal anxieties are thought to arise at the onset of the depressive position, that is, earlier than posited by Freud (see Brown 2002).

Ogden (1987) depicts the extensive psychological reorganization required at the threshold of the female oedipus complex: "The child becomes aware of her parents as people who have an intimate relationship with one another that does not include her. At the same time, an intense, triangulated set of whole-object relationships is established in which the father is taken as love object, while the mother is established as an ambivalently loved rival.... . The question of whether the little girl is in love with her mother or her father (in love with an internal object or an external object) never arises. It is both.... . The little girl does not have to reject the mother in order to love the father" (p. 489). We would emphasize both; the girl does not have to reject the father in order to love the mother, either.

RELATED PSYCHOANALYTIC LITERATURE ON SIBLINGS

Neubauer (1982, 1983) offers a useful context by defining rivalry in general and carefully distinguishing among rivalry, envy, and jealousy (1982). *Rivalry* is striving for exclusive access to another; *envy* refers to the mental attitudes of discontent with oneself, together with an urge to possess and to identify with the imagined superior achievement and potency of others; *jealousy* is resentment of the love a third person receives or expects from another. With jealousy comes a turning against the "new third person" (p. 124). He argues that both rivalry and jealousy are defined in the context of triadic relationships, while envy is an expression of the dyadic relationship and does not directly focus on a third person (1983, p. 326). Neubauer suggests that rivalry may be resolved by competition and coexistence; jealousy, by the repossession of the object's care. Envy, however, reflecting as it does deep dissatisfactions with the self, is a malignant factor and cannot easily lead to solutions (pp. 122-123). For jealousy to come into play, additional developmental factors must be added to the rivalry; it is "rivalry on the oedipal level" (p. 124). That is, the individual has reached the oedipal level and is dealing with feelings and rivalries he experiences in the interplay among three people.

Sharpe and Rosenblatt (1994) introduce the concept of the sibling oedipal triangle (SOT) and differentiate it from parental oedipal triangles. Basically, the two types of triangles are composed of different figures: in parental oedipal triangles, two parents and a child; in SOTs, two siblings and a parent or two siblings and a much older sibling who is in a parental position. They call SOTs "oedipal-like" (p. 491), however, and link them to traditional triadic oedipal dynamics on the basis of similarities in dynamics and structural elements. In SOTs there is a sexual component to the fantasy of exclusive love from the parent. For example, two younger female siblings may compete for the love and attention of an older brother. Such a three-way drama can be infused with sexual desire and jealousy, just as in traditional oedipal triangles, with which SOTs can coexist. These kinds of affects and sexual loadings differentiate SOTs from strictly sibling dynamics that revolve around earlier desires for care and nurturance.

Thus, Sharpe and Rosenblatt extend triadic dynamics and structures to different configurations within the family, arguing that these sibling dynamics are not to be considered, as often they are, simply defensive displacements from the parental oedipal triangle. Sharpe and Rosenblatt maintain that these SOT conflicts are "often more difficult and complex to resolve than normal parental oedipal conflicts but they may have more intense and lasting effects" (p. 520). They suggest that unresolved SOTs can lead to the same tendency to repeat conflicts in the choice of love objects as do unresolved oedipal issues. In an interdisciplinary study, Hanly (2016), applying Sharpe and Rosenblatt's concept of sibling oedipal rivalry to Jane Austen's *Sense and Sensibility,* convincingly demonstrates that the "novel brings to life, with the vividness and coherence of great literature, forces and fantasies in oedipal sibling rivalries" (p. 1057). Hanly argues that the novel demonstrates how sibling struggles reenacted in adolescence and family life can further growth in separation.

Sharpe and Rosenblatt distinguish between preoedipal sibling rivalry (which they see as dyadic) and developmentally more advanced oedipal sibling triangles (in which the internal world encompasses triangulated object representations). The prototype of preoedipal sibling rivalry is the birth of a sibling intruding upon a very young child's dyadic relationship with a parent. Sibling oedipal triangles involve developmentally whole objects, guilt feelings over the wish to eliminate the rival sibling, and fear of loss of the rival sibling's love and fear of retaliation. By contrast, in dyadic or preoedipal sibling rivalry there is a less advanced level of object relationships, superego development, and cognitive capacity; thus, the young child is not worried about losing the love of the rival sibling or capable of holding an internal three-way object relationship. In other words, the child has not reached the depressive position, and hence is not conflicted or guilt-ridden about his or her feelings toward the sibling rival.

We find Sharpe and Rosenblatt's arguments to be in accord with our own clinical experience and theoretical ideas, though they do not speak in terms of the oscillating twos and threes we focus on here. We propose a further extension to the social world: that is, to the triadic relationships of females beyond the family. We suggest, in addition, that the surface genders of the configurations may conceal underlying triadic (oedipal or persephonal) meanings.

While psychoanalysts have written extensively, especially in clinical reports, about conflicts and dynamics in sibling relationships, there is a noticeable gap in psychoanalytic theory relating to siblings. An exception is Mitchell (2003, 2013), who feels that too frequently sibling dynamics have been explained away in terms of oedipal dynamics (which is not our intention). She contrasts oedipal familial intergenerational relationships that can be described in terms of a vertical developmental axis with sibling processes that fall on a horizontal axis.[3] She stresses the importance for psychic development of "sibling trauma"

---

3 Mitchell distinguishes between Freud's concept of sexual differences, which fall on the vertical axis, and gender diversity, which falls on the horizontal axis.

that typically occurs at the age of two to three between the stage of narcissism and the oedipal stage. It is marked by a desire to kill the sibling and by incestuous urges and distinctive unconscious defenses against that wish: neither the projective identification of the preoedipal nor the repression of the oedipal, but rather splitting and dissociation. These reactions occur in response to the feared loss of the mother and the actual loss of the identity of being the baby.

In reaction to the trauma, the toddler identifies with the baby who replaces it. It is at this point in development, Mitchell argues, that gender acquires its subjective meaning: "The toddler gains access to its own gendered self through the 'other' of the sibling" (2013, p. 26).

From this scaffolding are built important aspects of the social world: brotherhoods and sisterhoods are established and the basis of lateral social exchanges and rights in kinship and labor are laid down. Significantly for our argument here, Mitchell points out that as the sibling trauma is resolved through the process of socialization (especially through the efforts of the mother), the child's ability to disidentify with the baby paves the way for later adjustment in the oedipal phase. In sum, Mitchell's formulations about the horizontal structuring of attitudes and conflicts about siblings may provide ways to understand differences in how triadic relationships are played out later in development.

Similarly, Steele (2010) offers compelling data on capacities that develop in infancy that may help the child later in coping with triangular issues. She indicates that conclusions from infant research and clinical experience make it clear that triadic relationships do not begin with the child's entrance into the oedipal phase, but have earlier roots in infancy. She summarizes an extensive body of research indicating that the infant-mother and infant-father relationships are separate and independent but that security in both of them promotes development and contributes to skills related to oedipal resolution. Specifically, security in the early mother relationship forecasts empathic skills, concentration, and theorizing in the domains of emotion and mind, while security in the early father relationship is associated with conflict resolution in peer relations, doll play, and mental health outcomes in middle childhood and puberty. Steele builds on Abelin's observations (1975) that the child's first efforts to engage in the triadic relationship of father/mother/child help to build a capacity for a third perspective.

Recent findings from infant research (Fivaz-Depeursinge, Lavanchy-Scaiola, and Favez 2010) demonstrate some evidence that young infants can relate to more than one parent at a time. Such capacities could be thought of as possible precursors of "triadic" interaction, shaped by patterns of communication within the family.

In sum, there are broader issues at play here, as well as unresolved triadic ones to which we attribute the pervasiveness of the phenomenon of twos and threes. Psychoanalytic theories and sociological research support the notion that for girls, interpersonal relationships matter intensely and that the aggression that may arise therein poses significant difficulties.

UNDERSTANDINGS OF THE PHENOMENON OF TWOS AND THREES

Object Relations

Chodorow (1978, 1994a,b) advances a theory of early object relationships suggesting that girls value relationships more than boys do, while boys value autonomy more than little girls do. Like Stoller (1968), she argues that the typical parenting arrangement in which the primary caretaker is the mother means that little girls negotiate separation developmentally from the same sexed object (mother). Thus, in female development the need for closeness with mothers and related conflicts become important. Persephonal/oedipal phase issues are also typically colored by relational issues. In contrast, the little boy typically separates from the opposite sexed parent (the mother); therefore, in establishing his masculine identity as separate from the mother, he is frequently more preoccupied with issues of autonomy and independence than girls are. In later writings Chodorow (1994b) cautions against overgeneralizations about gender and stresses individual differences.

Inhibited Aggression

Many psychoanalysts have written about the general cultural prohibitions against the expression of anger and aggression in girls and women (see, e.g., Nadelson et al. 1982; Gabbard and Wilkinson 1996; Person 2000). Lerner (1980) suggests that this inhibition reflects girls' fears of their own omnipotent destructiveness and preoedipal separation/individuation difficulties in the mother-daughter relationship. Tyson (1989) and Fenichel (1931) have explicated the preoedipal antecedents of girls' problems with anger in their relationship with the mother. Offering data about middle school children very much concordant with our observations, Knight (2011) noted that that girls turned their aggression on themselves and were worried about their "meanness," while boys were anxious about their overt and violent aggressiveness getting out of control. We argue that girls' inhibition of aggression also reflects the dynamics and conflicts of the female triangular persephonal situation (Holtzman and Kulish 2003). Fears of loss of the mother and her love come to the fore for girls in the context of triangular erotic conflicts. It is highly dangerous for a little girl to express murderous aggression and jealousy toward her mother, which must be denied or repressed. Thus, inhibition of a subjective sense of themselves as aggressive agents becomes a pervasive defense for women and girls (Hoffman 1999).[4]

---

4 Note that in the Hamstead Clinic's diagnostic profile manifest aggressive behavior of oedipal boys is typical. Anna Freud suggested these manifestations could be understood as a defense against castration anxiety (Koch 2012, p. 16).

Popular and Sociological Writings about Girls' Social Life

Recent writings on patterns of aggression in preadolescent and adolescent girls have aroused considerable interest in the popular press and academic literature. Hadley (2003, 2004) reviews these writings and the more formal research that has come to characterize girls' aggression as "indirect" or "relational," as compared to boys'. These writers follow the ideas of Chodorow (1978) and Gilligan and her colleagues (Gilligan 1982; Brown and Gilligan 1992) about the importance of relationships for girls. Our concept of twos and threes is illustrated in these detailed observations, as the ways in which we have observed clinically that girls behave and express aggression in threesomes corresponds with the vignettes appearing in popular texts.

For example, in a bestselling book for popular audiences, the parental educator Rosalind Wiseman (2002) describes the group dynamics of girls in terms of "queen bees" and "wannabes"—the girls who are popular and lead the group and the girls who want to be them. There are some that are neither. Like many of these writers, Wiseman gathered her data from journalistic interviews she conducted with groups of adolescents across the country. Wiseman describes dynamics among school-age girls that closely resemble the phenomena of twos and threes, and calls them "typical" (pp. 239-247). Sometimes a girl will be the excluded one in the group, the "third wheel," and sometimes the excluder. This kind of behavior leads to the "mean girls" term that has become so well known in the popular culture of movies and books, referring to girls on the inside of a group who are mean to girls on the outside. Wiseman offers advice to mothers: "If you have more than one girl over, you're just paving the way for girl drama" (p. 64).

In contrast, Wiseman's book on group dynamics among boys (2013) makes no mention of such dramas and triangularities. Rather, boys' competition is played out more widely, and being on top is based not on being "nice" or popular but on athletic ability. Most boys have a best friend and socialize within a three-to-five boy inner circle, with a few more guys on the periphery (p. 45), not in groups of twos and threes. In these two books, Wiseman offers no explanations for these patterns or why the behaviors differ between the genders. We include her work, however, to document the widespread awareness of the phenomenon of twos and threes in girls.

Research studies by social scientists on gender differences in aggressive behaviors in children and adolescents across many countries confirm and extend reports like Wiseman's. As summarized by Hadley (2004), they provide reliable evidence that girls in general express aggression differently from boys. Boys are more direct and often more physical, while girls tend to express aggression covertly and indirectly, and through relational maneuvers, including manipulative behavior like flattery or gossip. These relational behaviors increase markedly in the middle school years. The studies also show gender differences in patterns of social grouping, with girls typically forming tighter, smaller peer groups. Hadley (2004) discusses possible explanations for these general research findings in terms of societal expectations and values and evolutionary theories offered by Campbell (1995) and Brown (2003). In summary, there are many reasons for these differing expressions of aggression between boys and girls—social, psychological and biological.[5]

Adolescence

Since triadic persephonal issues arise with a vengeance at adolescence, the phenomenon of twos and threes emerges with greater salience and clarity at this time. Competition with other girls and the mother is heightened, as is the need to manage accompanying fears of rejection. Such underlying feel-

---

5 There is much evidence that male mammals demonstrate more rough-and-tumble play than do girls (see, e.g., Friedman and Downey 1995).

ings become particularly clear and poignant when one girl begins to date and spend time with a boyfriend, at the expense of her relationship with a female "best friend." The girl left behind feels painfully alone and excluded, and the triadic situation and primal scene may be evoked. In such instances, it is the "negative" oedipal complex that may be activated—the girl's erotic longings for the mother who prefers the father.

Alliances among teenage girlfriends reflect shifting unconscious identifications and positions the way a kaleidoscope reflects shifting images. Homoerotic and heterosexual desires oscillate between the "negative oedipal" and "positive oedipal" desires, reflecting old persephonal conflicts between desire for one parent and loyalty toward, and love of, the other. The painful alienation of the excluded party is characteristic of the primal scene. One patient as a young adolescent once saw her parents having sex. At that moment she thought, "I don't recognize what they have turned into. They pay no attention to me. I don't matter." But it is equally a conflict for the girl if her father manifests a preference for her, which she fears might evoke her mother's hostility, or vice versa.

Triadic conflicts like these may be played out in interpersonal relationships with peers. For example, a patient remembers the searing, painful feelings when two of her girlfriends went to a carnival without her. In telling the story, she equated those feelings with the time her boyfriend broke up with her and took up with another girl. These two memories—one of the twos and threes among peers, the other of a persephonal/oedipal triangle—were linked by the same painful affects of jealousy and exclusion and suggest similar underlying dynamics and sources.

The popular mystery novel *A Secret Place,* by Tana French (2015), vividly portrays the dynamics and emotions of twos and threes in adolescence. It is set in an exclusive girls' boarding school in Ireland where one of the teenage students is murdered. The solution lies in the unraveling of complicated feelings among a set of girls, including feelings of loyalty, exclusion, and, in this case, literally murderous rage. Two girls share a secret place on the grounds where they sneak out to meet. These two tell a third about the place and take her there: "'You never showed us this place before,' Holly says. Selena and Becca glance at each other and shrug. For a second, Holly feels almost *betrayed*—Selena and Becca have been boarding for two years, but it never occurred to her that they would have separate stuff together—until she realizes that now she's part of it too" (p. 22).

Moreover, the girls have vowed to do without boyfriends to keep their friendship circle unbroken, but when one of them breaks this vow, things get nasty and a series of events ensue that lead to murder: "sometimes she wants to punch Selena right in the soft pale daze of her face and keep punching. Not because she got off with Chris Harper and lied to them and broke the vow that was her idea to begin with; those aren't even the problem. But because the whole point of the vow was for none of them to have to feel like this. The point was for one place in their lives to be impregnable. For just one kind of love to be stronger than any outside thing; to be safe" (p. 374). These are the painful feelings many girls try so hard to avoid.

In this book murderous rage, and the narcissistic wound of being excluded and betrayed, are enacted in behavior: As in real life, when an adolescent girl starts to date boys, her close girlfriends can feel betrayed and abandoned. The core dynamics are twos versus threes. Holly's realization that "it never occurred to her that they would have separate stuff together" serves equally as an iconic reaction of the third, intruding upon the primal scene.[6] A girl's realization that parents (or classmates) have separate lives and experiences together that do not include her set off feelings of shock and betrayal. Perhaps these students are right to insist on their official rock-solid camaraderie to avoid dangerous competition. In this novel poisonous jealousy about being left out leads to murder.

---

6 We are aware that these feeling may also echo feelings connected with intrusions into the original fantasied blissful dyad of mother and child.

TWOS AND THREES IN BOYS VERSUS GIRLS

Clinically, although we have treated many men in analysis and psychotherapy, we have rarely encountered the twos and threes phenomenon, as described here, in their accounts and memories of their social life. On the surface, men do not seem to fret about being excluded from a lunch with two of their friends.

Boys have rivalrous interactions, but typically they do not develop into endlessly revolving threesomes. We did, however, observe one clinical incident of a boy reporting a twos versus threes experience. Like many girls, he seemed especially interested in maintaining close relationships with others. It may be relevant, though, that this boy grew up with twin sisters who were close to his age. Surely other clinicians who work frequently with adolescent and preadolescent boys have observed more of these experiences in boys.

Of course, we are not saying that men and boys are not very much concerned with or do not have difficulties with triangular relationships. For example, men often come into treatment not able to resolve a triangular drama they have created with a wife and mistress. This may be a man's way of dealing with the oedipal conflict by making sure that two women are fighting over him, thus ensuring that the person left out of the threesome is never oneself.

It may also be that the gendered differences suggested by Chodorow's work may offer another vantage point on this issue: the suggestion that girls and women value close relationships, while boys and men value autonomy and independence, may mean that men need to take a "strong," "who cares" attitude about hurt feelings in their social relationships. Describing the fate of a boy's oedipal strivings in middle childhood, Ross (1977) writes that "a child of this age will err in the other direction from the self-reference of his earlier years, now removing himself from the problems with which he grapples, as if they had nothing personal to do with him. The primal scene, his own sexual feelings, for that matter his wishes to be nurturant or generative—these no longer interest him. He is concerned instead with 'mates' …" (p. 341). In a discussion of the social (and psychological) construction of femininity, Benjamin (2004) argues that an oedipal boy's attitudes toward femininity may express his "need to locate an object that can contain excitement and can hold the place of passivity," culturally the "daughter" position (p. 48). She goes on to suggest that in an oedipal boy's mind, a sister may also play this role. Thus she offers a theoretical suggestion of how male oedipal conflicts are played out in the sphere of siblings or peers.

Just as the paradigms for the female and male oedipal complexes have differences, we are suggesting that triadic dynamics and conflicts seem to be played out differently in the social life of girls and boys. We second Chodorow's caution about making generalizations regarding gender differences. As social institutions such as family structure and cultural proscriptions for gender change, the underlying triadic/persephonal dynamics and patterns that we have been addressing may change as well.

CLINICAL EXAMPLES OF TWOS AND THREES

Case I

Mrs. E. is a married woman in her late twenties in analysis for a couple of years for mild feelings of depression and insecurity. She reports a relatively good relationship with her mother, but complains that her mother has always been very devoted to her father, which has always left her without enough energy for Mrs. E. and her brother and sister. She has always suspected that her mother prefers her sister to her. Mrs. E. comes in five minutes late for a session, the time and day of which the analyst had changed. Confused, she had texted to ask about the time. She explains she was late because she was helping a woman with directions.

The patient, who constantly feels she may not be liked or wanted, begins talking about a birthday party given her by several girlfriends. At first she didn't want to invite her sister, who is several years older and not really part of the group, but she insists that she doesn't want to hurt anyone's feelings.

Eventually she did invite the sister but, after some pondering, not her mother—because she is "of a different generation." Her difficulty with the decision reflects her obsessive concern about who is excluded and who isn't and about hurting feelings. Then she says, "I don't know if I am crazy. Some things really bother me too much. I *did* handle that situation well. No one's feelings were hurt. Why can't I get over it?"

Then she switches to another incident that bothers her concerning her girlfriend W., whom she has known since childhood. She explains how W. has always been "mean," and describes her as "competitive" (as if competitiveness were a bad thing). Recently, she recounts, she and W. had a lunch date and at the last minute W. canceled. Mrs. E., deciding to go out anyway, saw her friend lunching with another woman. Here is betrayal and yet another rejection. She said to herself, "That's it—this is a mean girl." She thinks she will remain friends with W., however (because of her need to be friends with everyone). But then another rejecting incident occurred, and Mrs. E. announced to her husband, "I won't take it anymore!"

Here the patient's anger is evident to the analyst, probably brought on by the analyst's changing the time but expressed through her displaced descriptions of and preoccupation with her social interactions. Mrs. E. continues the session by telling the analyst that two days earlier she had seen W. walking down the street with another "mean" woman. She asks herself, "Why should I care? I have my friends, yet it bothered me to see them together." She imagines that the two women "hate" her and are talking about her. Then her thoughts switch to her father: "I can't talk easily with my father. The relationship has been distant because he has difficulties relating and I've distanced myself from that pain.

But he always has seemed to be close to my mother." She adds, "My mother— when she talked to me about the party, she was critical in insisting I invite my sister." When she told her husband about all of these feelings, he was very supportive but puzzled. He asked her, "Why can't you get over it? It wouldn't bother me at all."

The analyst suggests that she can't "get over it" because she is so angry and feels that she cannot express her anger to her mother, her father, and today to her analyst, who switched her session around. Mrs. E. agrees, uncomfortably. She finishes the session by talking about her husband and how supportive he is. We can see that she needs a man who will soothe her inner fears of not being wanted, not desired, not chosen. Perhaps she is also contrasting the husband's support with that of the analyst and other women who let her down. We also can speculate that earlier "horizontal" conflicts with her sister, about which we know nothing at this time, may have set the tone for her subsequent triangular conflicts; but after an inner struggle she includes her sister, not their mother, in her birthday party.

This core of this session revolves around more typical sibling rivalry or, perhaps more accurately, sibling oedipal rivalry, two siblings vying for the love of the mother, on a developmentally higher, object-related level, as described by Sharpe and Rosenblatt. The patient is competing with her sister for their mother's favor and seems to feel that the mother/analyst prefers a third party (the sister) to her. She is unconsciously angry and hurt, perhaps that the analyst changed the time for someone else's benefit, and acts that out by coming late. But there are also brief glimpses of the traditional persephonal/oedipal triangle—mother, father, and daughter who is jealous of the father's closeness to mother. In the middle we see jealousy playing out in the twos and threes phenomenon of being snubbed by a peer. Who the peer might unconsciously represent—mother, father, sibling—is not clear here. Throughout this session we can see variations of twos versus threes. The shadow of the persephonal/oedipal triangle that comes up associatively suggests that this is more than simple dyadic sibling rivalry, but the theme of two versus threes predominates from the very beginning, as the patient begins by creating a third—the person she stops to help, leaving the analyst waiting.

This acting out presages the theme of the session, which emerges in the material to follow: feelings of being excluded and recurring expressions of various rivalries. The dynamics are set for the two-versus-three phenomena, and her confusion about the time change is symptomatic. In helping someone who makes her late, she may also be identifying with the analyst, who she imagines was helping someone else. Thus, she excludes the analyst and makes her wait.

Note that Mrs. E.'s husband seems bewildered by all this drama; as we have said, boys seem to have an easier time than girls do in managing "two versus three" in relationships, and are less obsessed with that kind of social problem than girls are. We have speculated that this difference is another reflection of girls' need to hold on to their mothers as they move away into the world of adult sexuality.

Case 2

This session in the analysis of Ms. T., a single woman in her early thirties, begins with a dream: "I'm kissing a guy in a weird way in a corner. I look and where spectators are standing is his wife. And she was talking about how her relationships with people are always a problem." Ms. T.'s thoughts turn to experiences in early adolescence, and she says, "Girls are excluders. They are able to go in twos and not threes. I'm always feeling in the middle. It's just not fair." Here again is the theme of painful exclusion, explicitly stated in terms of twos and threes. She complains about what happens when she introduces her friends to each other. She feels that the two become friends, displaying no loyalty to her, and that she becomes marginalized.

She goes on to say that a friend, who holds a superior position at the PR firm where they both work, is giving a party to which she has not been invited. The reason, she was told, is that one of the intended guests, Ms. P., is her immediate boss and would be uncomfortable if Ms. T., an underling, were there. Ms. T. complains bitterly that Ms. P is more important than she is to her friend, and therefore her needs must be catered to. "Like I am dangerous and going to hurt her!" This outburst is a denial of the murderous rage unconsciously evoked by her jealousy and exclusion.

That association sparks the memory of another part of the dream: "I'm stuck outside a house. I walk around with just a towel on and I try to find the entrance to get back in." The image of a towel had come up many times in Ms. T.'s analysis. It alluded to an important primal scene experience in which her parents had hurriedly covered themselves with a towel when she walked in on them. In the first part of the dream, there are other possible allusions to the primal scene—for instance, spectators watching the patient in a "weird" kiss. (The analyst thinks that perhaps "weird" refers unconsciously to homoerotic desires of the patient toward her, but feels she must leave this aside at this point.) "P. [the boss] is just like my mother, insecure," Ms. T. goes on. "I felt that my mother would feel left by me and jealous maybe if I was prettier, younger, and more successful in school than she was. I was supposed to be loyal to her, just like P. expects me to be loyal to her. [The patient is saying that P., who is included in the party over her, represents her mother.] I felt this loyalty thing when I was talking to her about how this other guy in the firm is so experienced and I wanted to work with him. P. yelled, 'I'm fed up with hearing about him!' I guess she didn't want to hear me praising a man and feeling that he was so great, better than her maybe. I felt that both my mother and P. wanted to thwart my development."

"I felt that I couldn't love both my mother and my father: that it could only be one or the other or they would be jealous."

At this point relatively early in the analysis the patient idealized the analyst and contrasted her seeming equanimity with her jealous mother and the equally jealous Ms. P. Only later did this image crumble to allow negative and competitive feelings to emerge in the transference.

This example shows the loyalty conflict of the Persephone story clearly. The patient explicitly begins with the idea of twos and threes during adolescence, but quickly gets into persephonal/oedipal triangles as she attempts to deal with the feelings characteristic of such unresolved conflicts by means of an unconscious re-creation. In her evoking her supervisor's (mother's) jealousy by praising the man and evoking her jealousy, the patient tells us that what has been evoked for her is the difficulty of negotiating a threesome and balancing loyalties and desire toward father and mother. Also evoked are old feelings of being excluded from a threesome—in the present a peer, a female boss, and herself, overtly a SOT, but a persephonal/oedipal triangle just beneath—at first she, a rival girlfriend, and the supervisor— which quickly morphs into another configuration: she, a male coworker, and the supervisor, and then finally settling on the triangle of mother, father, and herself. Reversing the roles to become the one doing the excluding, she undoes this narcissistic wound. Here in this session, as in real life, triangular and preoedipal themes are interwoven, united by feelings of jealousy and exclusion around both female and male figures. Where there has been trauma (parental ineptitude, preference, or overstimulation, as in this case), there may be a greater vulnerability to jealousy and feeling left out, and more conflicts and eventual difficulties.

Case 3

Mrs. Z., in her mid-forties and a lawyer in a large firm, was in her third year of analysis. She had become friendly and involved with two other women, K. and J., who worked with her, and they often had lunch together. All three were ambitious and wanted to become partners. An underlying competition was in motion.

The following session occurred after the analyst had taken a short break, and the patient had canceled the session after her return to go to the beach (an action-oriented response to exclusion), obviously connected to the transference and feelings of rejection. However, when the analyst had tried to explore these connections, the patient denied that her cancellation had any meaning. She was usually more insightful, so this defensiveness suggested strong underlying emotion.

She says, "I guess I am a jealous person." The analyst asked her to elaborate. "Yesterday I was feeling that K. and J. are better lawyers than I. They feel I am not as good as they are. It makes me feel really bad. And to make it worse they left early and went to lunch without me. I can't get past this sibling stuff!" (We had discussed her feelings about K. and J. in terms of her rivalries with her siblings.) The two of them seem to be more in with T. [one of the older male partners], kidding around and talking about cases. And they seem closer together than they are with me." On other occasionsMrs. Z. has reported being praised and getting good feedback from this man. "I have to work harder; it seems to me, than K. and J."

After a few moments' silence she says," I am thinking about my father and how he and I would kid around and play with the dog. My mother was so tough all the time. She would take away pleasantness, spoil the fun, and be critical of our kidding around." Then, after a pause, she continues, angrily: "The only reason you would ask me about my being away was to take away fun [this seems to express an unconsciously co-created transference—a critical maternal superego]. I was not jealous about your going away [note the disavowal and negation returning to the opening affect here and the patient's denying of any meaning to her going away]—just sad at your going away, probably to be with your family or husband."

The analyst remarks: "So you did have other painful feelings that were expressed by your staying away on Friday." The patient nods and becomes thoughtful.

This session starts with what seems like jealousy around easily recognizable rivalrous sibling issues. (The patient had an older sister, close in age, and a younger brother.) The twos versus threes dynamic is obvious. But as the session progresses, we see that the exclusion by the two women seems to have re-evoked persephonal/oedipal/triadic conflicts: fun with her father in an erotized tone (playing with the dog), followed by the memory of her mother's perceived critical attitude about the fun, and perhaps having fun with her father.

Then the patient herself brings in the affect of jealousy, which the analyst has not mentioned, and the feeling of being left out by the analyst; she alludes to the analyst's trip with her family and her husband—the latter suggestive of a primal scene. In an attempt to manage the painful feelings of rejection and not being included, she unconsciously retaliates by rejecting the analyst in turn and going off with her own husband and family.

The analyst was surprised by the patient's intense resistance at first, and felt herself pulled internally into being somewhat critical, like the mother who takes away the fun. Competition with her peers, K. and J., for T.'s attention seems on the surface like sibling oedipal rivalry (two siblings vying for a parent's or older sibling's favor and attention), but the patient's associations are entwined around her father, her mother, and herself, along with triadic persephonal/oedipal exclusion and painful narcissistic wounds.

Two years later, preoccupations with this triangle composed of Mrs. Z. and her friends K. and J. receded, as erotic feelings and fantasies toward the analyst took center stage in the analytic relationship and began to be understood.

Triadic themes also emerged, as the patient jealously imagined the analyst having sex with her husband, or as she tried to make the analyst feel left out by hinting that she was finding a captivating male replacement for her.

Occasionally K. and J., as well as T., appeared secondarily as characters in dreams linked with the figure of the analyst. Following is a session that signaled the beginning of this turbulent period in the analysis.

The patient begins: "I had a dream last night. Ted [her thirteen-year-old son] had a friend over. They were playing Pokemon. I was enjoying the two of them. Then when I was going to , I was thinking about how we had talked about how you write about sex and I had said, 'You write about sex and that's why I picked you.' What does it mean I picked you and what does it mean about you?" So, the dream:

> I'm looking for you to give you something and wanted to tell you I found a rare Pokemon. I was in your house and all the walls were white. It was all open space. I looked down the hall into the kitchen. You had on a little skirt that skaters wear and a bed jacket on and blue slippers which were roller blades and you were skating around the kitchen... . There was a white, curly-haired dog. You put the roller skates on the dog on the front paw and back paw. I asked what has this to do with sex. You answered, "We'll have to research it." ... there were a lot of books in a loft. Then I became uncomfortable. Your skirt went up. Saw your hip and leg. "Ugh," I said, "I don't want to see this!

"I think of my mom's leg," she says. "When you called Monday to say you were sick, I panicked. K. wears her skirts short, shorter than I do. More attractive to men than I am. This dream doesn't feel so important."

The analyst remarks on the anxiety:" I think you are getting to some uncomfortable feelings that *are* important."

The patient replies, "I don't know what to make of this dream. For a long time I have had dreams where I am searching. Or there were feelings of being trapped and looking for a way out. This one was all open. [The analyst was aware of a sense of lightness and playfulness in the room. She wonders if that signals progress—a shared open analytic space like Britton's triangular space (2004)—to observe what was going on.] In recent dreams, I was looking for Dr.B. [her former male therapist] for a tryst.... . I have been working with K. on a case. Working intensively. It is like intercourse—we get lost in it."

"I saw too much of my mother when she was getting dressed and undressed when I was a kid. It was irritating, overstimulating.... . I had gone into the bedroom earlier in the day, putting on my sweatpants. I turned and saw Ted watching me. I had left the door open. I set the thing up, not consciously. I felt bad. The look on his face was sexual. How could it not have been sexual for me?" She pauses.

The analyst suggests that in the dream Mrs. Z. was looking at the analyst.

The patient nods: "Yes.... . It was traumatic to see my mother in the hospital [a few years before]. I think she was wearing a bed jacket then." The patient associates to the roller blades: "You were being a kid. I didn't know whether to take you seriously. It was exciting and wrong and crazy. K. has this white dog. It thinks I'm the greatest. It is attached to me."

(The analyst is thinking that the curly-haired dog may represent herself, suggesting an acknowledgment, if unconscious, of a positive bond between them. But it is the curly-haired dog that is crazy about the patient, not the patient who is crazy about the curly-haired analyst. And it was a dog that had brought the patient shared pleasure with her father. She is also aware of a sense of pleasure and a stirring excitement within herself.) Going back to the how the patient introduced the dream, the analyst asked," Is my writing about sex exciting to you?"

The patient laughs. "Absolutely! Voyeuristic, I guess." Analyst: "What's that about for you?"

The patient hesitates, then says, "Have you had similar sexual experiences to mine? Do you enjoy sex with your husband?" She goes on to talk enviously about how the analyst seems to have her sexuality well-channeled in writing. She then reports that she imagined bringing the analyst soup when she was sick, and how she would like to bring in her recent positive evaluations from work because it was hard for her to integrate the good in herself and feel accomplished. She finishes the session by saying, "I had the dream after you told me that what I said was insightful. It was like a hug. I do think you like me…

. I don't' think K. likes me lately. This is mixed in with the analysis somehow…. . I'm getting along better with J. lately though. My mother didn't like me. It was hurtful. I know Dad liked me and was proud of me." (The feeling her mother did not like her is undoubtedly partly her projection, although the mother was critical and severe, not fun-loving like the father.)

This session does not contain clearly triadic material, except that there are three figures— the patient, K., and a dog—and the reference to a tryst with a male therapist. The sexual feelings, replays of an earlier excitement with her mother, seem like those of a little girl on the cusp of the triangular stage looking at her sexual mother with curiosity and awe. She experiences the analyst as seductive, exciting, and excited by her. Yet the sexuality belongs to the mother and not yet to the daughter. There are indications of unconscious anger at her analyst/mother for leaving her, covered by solicitousness (the chicken soup), but she loves and needs her and her positive regard as well. The idea that working with K. is like intercourse suggests working with the analyst has become erotized for her.

Here the friends from the twos and threes situation, K. and J., and the analyst are brought together—who likes her and who doesn't—and then equated with parents, one of whom likes her while the other does not. The triangle of friends becomes the parental triangle. The curly dog, a packed image, connects to K., perhaps to the analyst, and to her father, and may also represent a younger child or baby. If we look at the characters in the dream as all representing parts of the self, then we have the skating analyst, who is the disavowed but wished-for sexual self (and the cold researcher who excites but does not gratify); the curly-haired dog who represents the side of the self, the child, who is very attached to the analyst and mother and to the patient herself, the onlooker.

341

A few months later came another dream, in which she is beginning to acknowledge her erotic feelings toward the analyst: "A blending of your office and Joe's [a gay colleague]. I hugged him. Is that my homosexual thing toward you?" She laughs anxiously.

With termination is sight almost two years later, and triadic issues being worked through (we concur with contemporary thought that the persephonal/oedipal complex is never really "resolved"), Mrs. Z. describes a dream after having good sex with her husband: "I dreamed of being part of a family. You were there, too. There was a picture of you when you were a little girl. Curly hair but gray." (This is reminiscent of the dog in the dream above.) "Cute. In the dream, you write songs in addition to the book and that's why your husband married you. [She laughs.] He fell in love because of the music you made."

Thus, the overly exciting sexual book has become beautiful music that the marital couple make together, perhaps picturing the analytic creation or baby made by the analytic couple. It would seem that the patient had reached a point where she could tolerate, even joke about, the parental couple, as in Britton's concept of triangular space (2004).

By the time Mrs. Z. terminated and had worked through her triadic conflicts, as well as significant early trauma, she was more comfortable with her positive loving feelings toward the analyst/mother, as well as in her relationships with female friends and colleagues. There was no more preoccupation about who liked whom better. In a session a few weeks before terminating, she speaks of what good friends she and K. have become and how now she is enriched by being part of a small group of friends that includes K. "K. went to lunch with J. the other day. She had asked me first, but I couldn't go and it didn't bother me like it would have before. I am glad those childish feelings are gone, or almost gone," she adds laughingly.

DISCUSSION AND SUMMARY

The adolescent girl in *A Secret Place,* the lawyer Mrs. Z., the eighty-year-old woman with the "mean" friends—all get caught in the tangles of twos and threes. That is, the unconscious wish to turn a threesome into a twosome, and the attendant unconscious conflicts, occupies much of a female's social life, if not worked through earlier. We have observed that the phenomenon can become intergenerational, as some of the clinical material suggests. Mothers of daughters may be motivated by their own underlying problems that reflect unresolved triadic conflicts of the persephonal phase. These mothers then become caught up in their daughters' dramas of who is mean to whom or who is being left out and try to intervene, often making matters worse.

As we suggested, this phenomenon appears more prevalent in females than in males. Is this really the case? Are our clinical impressions skewed, given our practices and interests? Is it because, as we have mentioned above, boys handle their aggression and competition differently—that is, more directly, even physically? Is it because boys play out their oedipal conflicts differently, with more overt competition and less worry about losing their mothers? Is it because boys have these same feelings of exclusion and rivalry, but do not let themselves become aware of them? Is it because girls are more invested in and more anxious about relationships than boys? What are the internal psychological explanations of these phenomena and the apparent gender-related differences? And finally, an interesting question: why is it that twos and threes are played out over and over in the configuration of *three females,* even though, as we have tried to show, unconsciously they may represent other figures of both genders? The three female figures can refer to females; we have observed twos and threes phenomena in a few lesbians we have treated in which jealousy centers on a female rival of the lover. Does this pattern occur because it is so common that postoedipal school-age children are thrown together and play separated by gender? Could it be that in the group dynamics of school-age boys, if we are alerted to them, we might find underlying triadic themes and patterns? For example, one such triad is bully, victim, and observer(s), as delineated by Kerzner (2013). Because gender is fluid and constructed on complex unconscious identifications, it takes on changing and varied configurations (Harris 2005).

In our experience, as illustrated in the examples, the clinical material around twos and threes often seems on the surface to present editions of typical sibling rivalry, but these explanations do not always suffice. As patients tell us of their experiences, their associations soon shift to persephonal/oedipal memories, themes, and conflicts. Just as in dreams, what becomes confusing is that the characters in the stories they recount to us may unconsciously represent other figures—for example, one of the three figures in the primal scene, or a sister vying for an elder brother or parent (in a sibling oedipal triangle). Because of the accompanying affects of exclusion and jealousy, events that are experienced as sibling or sibling oedipal rivalries may then trigger underlying oedipal conflicts, or vice versa. In other words, the intenseexperiences in preadolescence and adolescence that evoke the twos and threes material may pull up a clump of memories of painful rivalries and feelings— both sibling and oedipal. (It should be noted, however, that we have observed the twos versus threes phenomenon in girls and women who have no siblings.) And as research suggests, all these may rest on early patterns stemming from infancy.

Attention to several key factors can guide us clinically in trying to identify and understand such experiences: (1) underlying fantasies, if they can be discerned;

(2) accompanying affects (anger, jealousy, sexual desire and excitement); (3) level of object relationships; (4) how aggression is handled; (5) the actual family situation and configuration in the history; (6) the state of the transference and countertransference at the time.

The emotional quality of twos and threes phenomena—the constant oscillations between intense efforts to balance a three-party system and the accompanying impulses to exclude someone—convince us that we are seeing triadic dynamics associated with the primal scene. These oscillations are particularly characteristic of the female developmental paradigm that we call the Persephone complex. We offer these observations as preliminary speculations and hope they stimulate further investigation and discussion.

REFERENCES

Abelin, E. (1975). Some further observations and comments on the earliest role of the Abelin, E. (1975). Some further observations and comments on the earliest role of the father. *International Journal of Psychoanalysis* 56:293–302.

Balsam, R.H. (2001). Integrating male and female elements in a woman's gender identity. *Journal of the American Psychoanalytic Association* 49:1335–1360.

——— (2015). Oedipus Rex: Where are we going, especially with females? *Psychoanalytic Quarterly* 84:555–588.

Benjamin, J. (2004). Deconstructing femininity: Understanding "passivity" and the daughter position. *Annual of Psychoanalysis* 32:45–57.

Britton, R. (1989). The missing link: Parental sexuality in the Oedipus complex. In *The Oedipus Complex Today: Clinical Implications*, ed. J. Steiner. London: Karnac Books, pp. 83–101.

——— (2004). Subjectivity, objectivity, and triangular space. *Psychoanalytic Quarterly7* 3:47–61.

Brown, L.J. (2002). The early oedipal situation: Developmental, theoretical, and clinical implications. *Psychoanalytic Quarterly* 71:273–300.

Brown, L.M. (2003). *Girlfighting*. New York: NYU Press.

——— & Gilligan, C. (1992). *Meeting at the Crossroads: Women's Psychology and Girls' Development*. New York: Ballantine Books.

Burch, B. (1997). *Other Women*. New York: Crown Publishers.

Campbell, A. (1995). A few good men: Evolutionary psychology and female adolescent aggression. *Ethology & Sociobiology* 16:*99–123*.

Chodorow, N.J. (1978). *The Reproduction of Mothering: Psychoanalysis and the Sociology of Gender.* Berkeley: University of California Press.

——— (1994a). Family structure and feminine personality. In The Homeric Hymn to Demeter, ed. H.P. Foley. Princeton: Princeton University Press, pp. *243–265.*

——— (1994b). Femininities, Masculinities, Sexualities. Lexington: University Press of Kentucky.

Davidson, L. (1975). Comments and criticisms. *Contemporary Psychoanalysis* 11:*255–258.*

Elise, D. (2002). The primary maternal oedipal situation and female homoerotic desire. *Psychoanalytic Inquiry* 22:*209–228.*

Fenichel, O. (1931). Specific forms of the oedipal complex. *International Journal of Psychoanalysis* 12:*412–430.*

Fischer, R.S. (2002). Lesbianism: Some developmental and psychodynamic considerations. *Psychoanalytic Inquiry* 22:*278–295.*

Fivaz-Depeursinge, E., Lawanchy-Scaiola, C., & Favez, N. (2010). The young infant's triangular communication in the family: Access to threesome intersubjectivity? Conceptual considerations and case illustrations. *Psychoanalytic Dialogues* 20:*25–140.*

French, T. (2015). *The Secret Place.* New York: Penguin Books.

Freud, S. (1923). The ego and the id. *Standard Edition* 19:*12–66.*

——— (1933). New introductory lectures on psychoanalysis: Lecture XXXIII. Femininity. *Standard Edition* 22:*112–135.*

Friedman, R.C., & Downey, J.l. (1995). Biology and the oedipus complex. *Psychoanalytic Quarterly* 64:*234–264.*

Gabbard, G.O., & Wilkinson, S.M. (1996). Nominal gender and gender fluidity in the psychoanalytic situation. *Gender & Psychoanalysis* 1:*463–481.*

Gilligan, C. (1982). *In a Different Voice: Psychological Theory and Women's Development. Cambridge*: Harvard University Press.

Grossman, L. (1994). Contemporary theories of female sexuality: Clinical applications. *Journal of the American Psychoanalytic Association* 42:*233–241*.

Hadley, M. (2003). Relational, indirect, adaptive, or just mean: Recent work on aggression in adolescent girls—Part I. *Studies in Gender & Sexuality* 4:*367–394*.

——— (2004). Relational, indirect, adaptive, or just mean: Recent work on aggression in adolescent girls—Part II. *Studies in Gender & Sexuality* 5:*331–350*.

Hanly, M.F. (2016). Sibling rivalry, separation, and change in Austen's *Sense and Sensibility. International Journal of Psychoanalysis* 97:*1057–1075*.

Harris, A. (2005). Gender as Soft Assembly. Hillsdale, NJ: Analytic Press.

Hoffman, L. (1999). Passions in girls and women. *Journal of the American Psychoanalytic Association*47:*1145–1168*.

Holtzman, D., & Kulish, N. (2000). The feminization of the female oedipal complex: Part 1. A reconsideration of the significance of separation issues. *Journal of the American Psychoanalytic Association* 48:*1413–1437*.

——— & ——— (2003). The feminization of the female oedipal complex: Part 2. A reconsideration of the significance of aggression. *Journal of the American Psychoanalytic Association* 51:*1127–1151*.

Jones, E. (1933). The phallic phase. *International Journal of Psychoanalysis* 14:*1–13*.

Kerzner, S. (2013). The crucial role of the "third" in bully/victim dynamics. *Psychoanalytic Inquiry* 33:*116–123*.

Knight, R. (2011). Fragmentation, fluidity, and transformation: Nonlinear development in middle childhood. *Psychoanalytic Study of the Child* 65:*19–47*.

Koch, E. (2012). Discussions in the diagnostic profile research group. *Psychoanalytic Study of the Child*66:*281–315*.

Kulish, N. (2000). Primary femininity: Clinical advances and theoretical ambiguities. *Journal of the American Psychoanalytic Association* 48:*1355–1379*.

——— (2006). Frida Kahlo and object choice: A daughter the rest of her life.
Psychoanalytic Inquiry26:7–31.

——— & Holtzman, D. (2008). *A Story of Her Own: The Female Oedipus Complex: Reexamined and Renamed.* Lanham, MD: Aronson.

Lampl-de Groot, A. (1928). The evolution of the Oedipus complex in women.
International Journal of Psychoanalysis 9:332–346.

Lerner, H.E. (1980). Internal prohibitions against female anger. *American Journal of Psychoanalysis40:137–148.*

Mitchell, J. (2003). *Siblings and Violence. Cambridge,* UK: Polity Press.

——— (2013). Siblings: Thinking theory. *Psychoanalytic Study of the Child*
67: *14–34.*

Nadelson, C.C., Notman, M.T., Miller, J.B., & Zilbach, J. (1982). Aggression in
women: conceptual issues and clinical implications. In *The Woman Patient,*
ed. M.T. Notman & C.C. Nadelson. New York: Plenum Press, pp. *17–28.*

Neubauer, P.B. (1982). Rivalry, envy, and jealousy. *Psychoanalytic Study of the
Child* 37:*121–142.*

——— (1983). The importance of the sibling experience. *Psychoanalytic Study
of the Child* 38:*325–336.*

Ogden, T.H. (1987). The transitional oedipal relationship in female development. *International Journal of Psychoanalysis* 68:*485–496.*

O'Shaughnessy, E. (1989). The invisible Oedipus complex. In *The Oedipus Complex Today: Clinical Implications,* ed. J. Steiner. London: Karnac Books, pp.
129–150.

Person, E.S. (2000). Issues of power and aggression in women. Paper presented
to the American Psychoanalytic Association, New York, December.

Ritvo, S. (1989). Mothers, daughters, and eating disorders. *In Fantasy, Myth,
and Reality: Essays in Honor of Jacob A. Arlow, M.D.,* ed. H. Blum, Y. Kram-

er, A.K. Richards, & A.D. Richards. Madison, CT: International Universities Press, pp. *371–380*.

Ross, J.M. (1977). Towards fatherhood: The epigenesis of paternal identity during a boy's first decade. *International Review of Psychoanalysis 4:327–347.*

Sharpe, S.A., & Rosenblatt, A.D. (1994). Oedipal sibling triangles. *Journal of the American Psychoanalytic Association 42:91–523.*

Steele, M. (2010). The quality of attachment and Oedipal development. *Psychoanalytic Inquiry 3:485–495.*

Stoller, R.J. (1968). The sense of femaleness. *Psychoanalytic Quarterly 37:42–55.*

Tyson, P. (1989). Infantile sexuality, gender identity, and obstacles to oedipal progression. *Journal of the American Psychoanalytic Association 37:1051–1069.*

Wiseman, R. (2002). *Queen Bees and Wannabes.* New York: Harmony Books.

——— (2013). *Masterminds and Wingmen.* New York: Harmony Books.

Yanoff, J.A. (2000). Barbie and the tree of life: The multiple functions of gender in development. *Journal of the American Psychoanalytic Association 48:1439–1465.*

CHAPTER 12:

Reckoning with Sexuality

(1019). Int. J. Psychoanal., (100)(6):1216-1236.

A review of Freud's ideas about the sexual drive and sexuality reveals reoccurring questions: What is the relation between the sexual drive and its somatic underpinnings? Can we integrate formulations couched in terms of meaning with those couched in terms of energy? What is the relation of the sexual drive to other drives, psychic structures and affects? The author focuses on two further questions: what can we understand about the experience of sexual passion, and why is there so much anxiety, regulation, and opposition in regard to sexuality, both individually and generally, even within psychoanalysis itself? The author argues that the discomfort with and repudiation of sexuality are related to the nature of the sexual drive itself and to its origins in early childhood and are tied to many of the issues that have marked its history in psychoanalysis. The author discusses a clinical case of a man who tried to isolate and eradicate his sexual drive. His felt absence of sexual drive is an individual instance of the larger discomfort and unease with the truths about human sexuality around which Freud built his theories of development and mind.

INTRODUCTION

Freud's assertion that we are compelled by unconscious mental forces was and continues to be profoundly unsettling. All the more so since he suggested that these forces are largely sexual in nature. Sexuality was at the centre of his theories of the mind and its psychopathology. Early on he discovered that "damned up" sexual impulses lay behind the strange hysterical symptoms of his first patients; then he postulated that sexual trauma accounted for the symptoms of obsessional neurosis. Delving deeper, he changed course: it was not sexual traumas but unconscious sexual fantasies originating in early childhood that were the nexus of neurosis. This *infantile* sexuality was comprised of seemingly perverse elements which were folded into normal adult sexuality later. Thus, all mental phenomena were characterized by unconscious sexual conflict, enervated by sexual energy and imbued with sexual meanings. As theoretical gaps and clinical observation demanded, Freud changed his conceptualizations about the sexual drive many times over the course of his life. His followers added to and modified his theories; defectors and detractors focused their objections on the centrality of sexuality in the theory. In the decades that have followed Freud's death, generations of psychoanalysts have continued to grapple with his theories of the sexual drive and infantile sexuality.

I will outline the central issues in these arguments and developments. This selected look at Freud's concept of the sexual drive and its place in the mind suggests that for psychoanalysis there remain many unanswered questions and areas to explore about the sexual drive and sexuality: what is the relation between the sexual drive and its somatic underpinnings? Can we integrate formulations couched in terms of meaning with those couched in terms of energy? What is the relation of the sexual drive to other drives, psychic structures, and affects? I raise these general questions to see how they may clarify and influence my own thinking and technical approaches to sexuality in the clinical situation. I will focus on two further questions. First, what can we understand about the experience of sexual *passion*, a subject that, until recently, is conspicuously absent in the literature? The second and related question is why is there so much anxiety, regulation, opposition, and moralizing in regard to sexuality, both individually and generally, even within psychoanalysis itself?

I, for one, strongly believe in the centrality of sexuality both theoretically and clinically. Along with many others (Green 1995; Fonagy 2008; Kulish 2011) I have bemoaned the minimization of sexuality, particularly the Oedipus complex, in contemporary psychoanalytic thinking. Many have argued that newer theoretical developments in psychoanalysis have diluted or taken us away from the importance of sexuality. But I think that many of the theoretical developments in other areas, such as narcissism, aggression, or attachment, help us better understand sexuality and the sexual problems of our patients. I believe that the sexual drive cannot be divorced from other aspects of the personality, especially from the objects to which it is directed—one of the major points of contention from the beginning.

Our theoretical inclinations, whatever they may be, lead us to highlight some aspects of the clinical picture and ignore or be blinded to others. They can buttress particular countertransferences or biases. Moss (2010) warns against the complacency that comes from leaning on our theories and not thinking.

Theories can be used to distance oneself from the emotionality and intensity of the clinical material. Even drive theory itself couched in its scientific language can be used to distance a clinician from the intensity of the sexual drives present in the consulting room.

In this paper I will argue that the discomfort with and repudiation of sexuality both within and outside of psychoanalysis are related to the *nature of the sexual drive itself* and to its origins in early childhood and are wrapped up in many of the issues that have marked its history in psychoanalysis. I will present a clinical case of a man who has tried to isolate and eradicate his sexual drive. His felt absence of sexual drive is one individual instance of the larger discomfort and unease with the truths about human sexuality that Freud discovered within himself and around which he built his theories of development and mind. I will utilize selected contemporary ideas about sexuality and sexual passion that complement an ego psychological and developmental model to understand and work with this man's seeming lack of sexuality. These ideas address some of the theoretical dilemmas in early theory and have helped me to understand the seeming lack of sexuality found in the case. I try to explain this man's fear of sexuality in terms of an early experience of sex as "excess," heightened by early difficulties in regulating affects and mirroring. These issues interdigitated with early narcissistic and separation issues and later sexual development.

CONTROVERSIES AND QUESTIONS ABOUT THE SEXUAL DRIVE

There have been several excellent critical reviews of the history of Freud's drive theory and its subsequent theoretical developments: Brunswick (1954), Dahl (1968), Compton (1981a, 1981b, 1981c, 1981d, 1983, 1985), Greenberg (1991), Stein (1998a), Kernberg (2001), Ghent (2002), and Scarfone (2015). I will pull from these writings four central issues that pervade current thinking about sexual drives and the larger area of sexuality.

Mind/Body

In the 1980s Compton wrote a series of lucid and comprehensive articles on Freud's drive theory. He pointed to the recurring problem of mind/body with which Freud struggled. Describing the concept of drive as "a frontier between the mental and somatic," Freud distinguished between inborn biological instincts and drives, their psychic representations, the definition I will be using in this paper. Freud never ceased in his efforts to explicate the links between drives and the underlying biology and to make his growing discipline a respectable, empirical science. Compton pointed out the many difficulties in this effort: psychoanalytic/clinical and neurophysiological statements reflect two different languages and frames of references, a problem that remains today. Even so, I believe that as new ideas and contradictions to psychoanalytic theory arise from the neurosciences, psychoanalysts must consider the implications seriously, and I have included some of these suggestive findings in this paper. For me, however, the more pressing and interesting clinical issues concern the body and embodiment, especially when we are considering sexuality. Starting with Freud and the "body ego" (1923), the course of ego and sexual development begins in the earliest bodily contacts between mother and infant. I will return to these connections later with the ideas of maternal eroticism.

Energic Considerations

A second controversial and difficult question concerns the energy or sources of excitation of the sexual drive. The term "libido" was used variously by Freud as an adjective or noun meaning sexual or a sexual appetite, but also and importantly as an abstract concept of sexual energy. According to Compton (1981a), Freud shaped his ideas of mental energy by filling in theoretical gaps in drive theory with neurophysiological hypotheses and language known to him at the time. This may have been particularly true of his concepts of mental energy such as the continuity hypothesis, the necessity of the system to maintain excitation at a constant level; the reflux arc; specific kinds of drive energies; or the relaxation/oscillation model. Some of these concepts have relevance to the phenomenology of sexual passion and desire, which I will discuss later. In the 1950s and 1960s, ego psychologists, such as Loewenstein, Rapaport, Klein and Holt (panel report, Dahl 1968) questioned basic aspects of the theory of instinctual energy. Many (Compton 1981b; Greenberg 1991; Zepf 2010) concluded that the doctrine of psychic energy would best be considered as a set of descriptive *metaphors*, not as explanations. For Kernberg (2001), for example, *affects* are the primary motivators of behaviour[1]

I have never been comfortable with the energic metaphors, which may help us to understand, or think we understand, how drives work in the mind, but serve as stopgap explanations. I am convinced by my readings about drive that there is no need to hold to the idea that all mental energy is sexual, although the idea reinforces the sense of the centrality of sexuality in mental life.

The Place of The Sexual Drive in Regard to Other Drives

For Freud the sexual drive was one of the two basic motivating forces in the mind. In his earliest theories, it was the sexual drive and the ego, self- preservative drive;[2] later it became the sexual drive, Eros and the aggressive drive, Thanatos. Early supporters such as Adler, Rank, and Jung began to split off from Freud on the centrality of the sexual drive, postulating other primary drives.[3] However, most major theorists, such as Klein, Winnicott, Loewald, and even Kohut, hold to a concept of sexual drive.[4] Solms (2012) tells us that neuroscience supports the concept of sexual drive, but he argues that Freud made the mistake of assuming there was only one kind of pleasure. It is noteworthy that in this profusion of different theories about basic drives, sexuality almost without exception has a place.

---

1 For neuroscientists, affects, originating in anatomically identifiable neural circuits and not a hypothesized psychic energy, are the prime movers of human motivation (Schwartz 1987; Solms 2012). Neuroscientists also caution us that there is no evidence for a special kind of mental energy (Hadley 1992).

2 Some would hold on to Freud's original self-preservative or ego drive (Novey,1957; Schmidt-Hellerau, 2005).

3 Many also psychoanalysis, as for example, Lampl-de Groot (1956), have never accepted the concept of the death drive.

4 Currently neuroscientists prefer the term "motivational system" to "drive" (Pansepp, 2012; Migone and Liotti, 1998).

For me, the more compelling and clinically relevant question is not how many primary drives there are in addition to the sexual drive, but rather how the sexual drive interacts with other motivational systems or aspects of the mind. I am willing to consider that there are other motivational systems, such as attachment or the epistemophilic instinct (Katz 2001) active in the human psyche and that have a place in understanding the mind and sexuality. There is much evidence from developmental research and the clinical situation that attachment and sexuality appear to interact and support one another (Modell 1990; Silverman 2001). A good example of an attempt to integrate the sexual drive with attachment/recognition theory (Benjamin and Atlas 2015) will be discussed later in conjunction with my clinical case.

The Relationship of Drive to Object

The beauty of Freud's conceptualization of sexual drive is in its explanatory power to describe what is observed clinically. Freud's concept of the sexual drive (1915), while based on endogenous and continuous excitations and pressures, was characterized by plasticity in source (bodily zones), aim, and object. Thus, the countless possible permutations and outcomes in an individual's sexual life could be accounted for, including the complexity of the sexual object with its interchangeability or its fixity. Ingeniously, Freud suggested that sexual, libidinal energy "leaned" at first on the inborn life— preservative drives that orientated the infant to the mother. Sucking on the breast then became a source of libidinal pleasure, imbuing the mouth as an erogenous zone. (Note the theoretical difficulty here: the idea of "leaning on" makes logical sense, it is but a metaphor, and furthermore Freud eventually abandoned his early concept of a life preservative drive.).[5]

---

5 Solms (2012) adds to the argument by stating that the erogenous zones are objects not sources for the sexual drive.

We separate drive and internal object for the sake of classification and exposition, but in fact they are intertwined. Even as he attempted to outline a scientific, bodily based system of drive, Freud always connected object with drive. After 1915, Freud occupied himself increasingly with the importance of the objects of the sexual drive and related fantasies. The prototype of sexual fantasy for Freud was the infant soothing itself by hallucinating the need- satisfying lost object. The object or its loss was part of the formation of sexual fantasy.

Of course, in Kleinian thinking, unconscious aggressive and sexual fantasies are mental representations of the instincts and are inherently relational. The aim of the instinct is characterized by a specific type of object relatedness. Such pre- existing, pre-verbal bodily potentialities allow the infant to select from and organize the world around him. The infant's inner reality is slowly comprised through a series of introjections, projections, and projective identifications in the form of bodily symbolic fantasies (Ogden 1984; Blass 2017).

In the intervening years since Freud, the inner world of objects and the external interpersonal environment were given increasingly more importance in the shaping of drives, seen as less dependent on their inborn, programmed sources. The evolution of psychoanalysis from a one-person to a two-person theory is correlated with this change in focus and understanding of the drives. In 1983 Greenberg and Mitchell suggested that object relation theories and drive theories were incompatible. Yet in 1991 Greenberg reaffirmed the importance of the sexual and aggressive drives, while stressing their dependence on environmental influences. Many (if not most) psychoanalytic writers (Dunn 1993) agree on this point, as do the neurobiologists (Schwartz 1987; Hadley 1992; Sheperd 2005; Solms 2012). Over the years, I have become convinced that drive and object, drive and environment cannot be separated.

In sum, a review of the concept of the sexual drive has convinced me that it is time for its reformulation. Psychoanalysis needs to free itself from views built upon nineteenth-century neurology and biology and to take account of contemporary neuroscience, to relinquish the concept of libido as an energy source and related definitions of sexual discharge which comprise our lexicon and influence our theoretical and clinical thinking, to give up our adherence to binaries and to consider how various motivation systems and affects might relate to sexuality, and to incorporate new ideas about passion and desire.

CONTEMPORARY THINKING ABOUT SEXUALITY: A PHENOMENOLOGICAL FOCUS ON PASSION

With these questions in mind, I will turn to some contemporary psychoanalytic thinkers whose works and ideas about sexuality I find promising and innovative: Laplanche, R. Stein, and Fonagy, and some American women, notably Balsam, Elise, Dimen, and Wyre. In general, these writers focus more on phenomenological, clinical-near aspects of sexual experience, a focus which I have found a useful starting point in my own thinking about sexual issues.[6] Most of these writers stress the importance of the early maternal (or parental) dyad and maternal eroticism in the development of sexuality. I focus on these theories because they help to explain the paradoxical felt absence of sexuality in my clinical case. They outline variable pathways from early experiences

---

6 Kohut (1959) muses about a more experiential approach to sexuality and sexual drive: "the concept of sexuality has led to much confusion and argument. The sexual quality of an experience is neither adequately defined by the content of the experience not by the body zone... analysts have not emphasized enough that the sexual quality of an experience is one that cannot be further defined. True, it is understood by analysts that we mean by sexual something much wider than genital sexuality and the pregenital sexual experience includes sexual processes, sexual locomotion and the like. Yet, it is instructive to pregenital sexual experience of childhood and adult sexual experience (whether in foreplay, in perversions, or in intercourse) have thus a not further definable quality in common that we know to be sexual, either by direct experience or after prolonged and persistent introspection and removal of internal obstacles to introspection (resistance analysis). And we may, therefore, say that for the infant and child a large number of experiences have that quality that adults are most familiar with in their sex life; our sex life thus provides us with a remnant of an experience that was, early in our psychological development, much more widespread" (pp. 476-477). He then goes on to talk about "drive" which gets at the inner experience of a sexual impulse—the experience of wanting, wishing: "a drive, then is an abstraction from innumerable inner experiences" (p. 477).

theorized in terms of attachment, aggression, or narcissism to later experiences in the sexual arena.

Laplanche (Laplanche and Pontalis 1968; Laplanche 1997, 2004, 2007) draws on the work of Ferenczi (1933) to posit a primal seduction or awakening into sexuality by the parent. Laplanche explores the construction of the sexual drive within the infant as a result of its earliest experiences with the caretaker, usually the mother. The caretaking adult cannot help but respond to the child *unconsciously* with sexual feelings and unwittingly communicates these fantasies and affects in all of his or her close encounters with the child.

Laplanche furthers Freud's theory of "leaning on" in which the sexual drives "lean on" the original self-preservative instincts satisfied during caretaking. For example, while the mother feeds and cuddles her child, she responds sensually and sexually, her breasts being endowed with sexual meanings and sensations to her, her body responsive to touch, and wishful fantasies in her mind. These communications are unconscious, un-verbalized, and continuous. Thus, the child encounters confusing, mysterious sensations, minute silent signals that it cannot understand or begin to integrate but nonetheless awaken and begin to shape its own sexual feelings and desires, stimulating a sensual/sexual set of inborn responsiveness, in addition to the bodily zones postulated by Freud.

What is first taken in as sexuality by the human infant, therefore, is something mysterious, overwhelming, and unspoken, and perhaps remains so, something to be passed down to ensuing generations. In this asymmetrical process, Laplanche postulates that instinct is transformed into human sexuality and the subject is constituted.

In his illuminating explanation of Laplanche, Scarfone (2015) explains the seduction theory: "primal seduction does not replace early seduction or infantile seduction; it does not invalidate their importance but instead provides them a foundation" (55–56). I disagree with Laplanche, who feels the sexual instinct springs up only at puberty, and maintain that there are inborn, endogenous, and continuous sexual sources in infancy and early childhood. I would say that sexual drive is *shaped, but not constructed, by the other*.

Ruth Stein extends Laplanche's ideas in a wonderful series of papers (1998b, 2007, 2008) on the lived experience of sexuality. In 1998 she articulated the strange, uncanny otherness of sexuality. In the initial silent seduction of the human infant into the world of adult sexuality, the mother's message is enigmatic, non-transparent, and not symbolizable. Thus, the experience of sexual desire carries the inherent quality of the enigma of the object. The lingering effects of the enigmatic desire and message from the other may appear clinically in patients' intense curiosity or sensitivity to what their analysts desire from them. This is all in the usual course of things. Trouble comes if mothers *fail* to eroticize their child's body. This failure can lead to hysteria as sexual and bodily experience becomes split off.

There is also a quality of uncontrollability about sexuality that may be traced to such early experiences. Stein (2008) thus formulates a second quality of the experience of sexuality as "excess." This sense of excess reflects the asymmetrical nature of the early child/mother interactions so ripe with sensations and unconscious bodily/sexual fantasy. In these early moments, what impinges on the child and what it experiences becomes "too much."

Green (1997) further elaborates the sense of otherness of sexuality that Laplanche and Stein describe. There is a double "otherness" in the experience of sexual desire. This otherness reflects the otherness of the sexual partner as well as the otherness of the subject *to himself* when he experiences erotic excitement, a surprising intensity which makes him a stranger to himself. He suggests that this intensity might explain how sexual experience can so easily cover other feelings and drives, as in what we term "sexualization."

Similarly, Fonagy (2008) traces the sense of strangeness and alienation of sexual experience to the early parent–infant relationship. Based on attachment theory and research, he and his colleagues (Fonagy et al. 2002) show that inaccurate and non-responsive mirroring of infants' affect states by caregivers lead to later problems in symbolization, sense of self, and dis-regulation.

Further, research shows that mothers find it particularly difficult to mirror accurately signs of sexual excitement (erections, masturbatory behaviours), routinely present in infants. Without such mirroring there can be no full experience of containment or indeed even of owning early feelings of arousal. Fonagy speculates that the internalization of an incongruent response to frustration gives the psychosexual core its unique combination of urgency and incongruence (2008, 23). Such theories of Laplanche, Stein, and Fonagy, which explore the subjective experience of sexual desire, also throw light upon the needs for its repudiation and suppression.

Many other contemporary psychoanalysts place the beginnings of infantile sexuality and human sexual experience in the early close, bodily relationship between mother and infant. Among these are Wyre (2006), who so beautifully explicates maternal erotic transference and countertransference, and Kernberg (2001), who reiterates the central role of erotization in the mother–infant relationship for later libidinal development. Lemma (2015) stresses the importance of a mother's love of her infant's body for the development of a solid positive sense of self, body, and sexuality: "Through her gaze and her touch the mother invests her baby's body with her libido. I want to suggest that, for both genders, the too-desiring, or the not-desiring-enough mother of early childhood can compromise the development of the body self. Desire lies at the heart of the earliest relationship …" (31). It follows that compromise of the development of body self then can compromise the blossoming of sexual desire.

Dimen (1999) takes up the subject of how psychoanalysis may be eluding the subject of sexual passion. Herself from the relational school, she bemoans the fact that sexuality is being re-interpreted simply as a relation not a *force* and has lost its passion. She suggests that where libido was, now there are objects and attachment. (That is, she reiterates the theoretical need for some concept of drive.) At the same time, she argues that the contemporary psychoanalysis has not really shifted away from sex: "The new thinking takes off from Melanie Klein's relocation of genitality in the preoedipal period, which places sexuality squarely in the middle of the emergence and structuralization of the self in its relation to others" (p. 416).

Taking a footnote from Freud (1905, 135n2), in which he states why he chose the term "libido" over the word "lust" to represent a sexual instinct, Dimen retrieves the subject of lust to examine its meaning. For Dimen, "If libido describes why you want to have sex, lust says what it's like while you are having it" (430). Sex is driven by a force demanding discharge, according to Freud. But Dimen points out that much of the pleasure in sexual experience is not simply a seeking of discharge and a reduction of tension, but rather comes from a suspended state of unconsummated desire, a state that may be shared intimately with another person. I would suggest that such a state may not be easily tolerated by some people, perhaps individuals who have difficulties with affect tolerance, as in my clinical case. This brings us back to thinkers such as Solms (2012) or George Klein (as cited in Dahl 1968), who suggest that other kinds of discharge and conceptualizations of pleasure/unpleasure might be needed to explain sexual experience fully.

Dimen suggests that desire without promise of satisfaction is a legacy of the Oedipus complex. Many others speak to this sense of desire for what we do not possess as a recipe for the experience of passion or excitement. Something or somebody that leaves us dissatisfied is all the more desired.[7] Examining drive and desire from the point of view of Freud and Lacan, Gammelgaard (2011) writes: "fundamental to the path of drive toward satisfaction is a circular movement around the object. We usually overlook this because ... this object— from the point of view of drive—exists only as an absence, a void which can be cathected to any object. ... Thereby it functions to designate the location of the Other's presence" (971). Here, she makes an important point.

---

7 This comes close to Lacan's object of desire (1986).

I have suggested that the passions of the Oedipal complex have been underappreciated by psychoanalysis and that discomfort with passion *in itself* is one of the reasons for the continued need for the repression of Oedipal conflicts (Kulish 2011). Furthermore, from early on there was no place for female passion in psychoanalytic theories (Irigaray 1985; Hoffman 1999; Kulish 2011; Balsam 2012). Females' sexual and bodily experience was conceptualized in terms of a sense of lack and inadequacy; female libidinal development was outlined in its relationship to a male body and male experience; libido itself was viewed as basically masculine; questions about female agency and desire were left out of the dialogue.

In contrast, the idea of passion was central for Loewald (1985). He argued that Freud had in view the human passions when he spoke of instincts and their vicissitudes, and thus the psychoanalytic account of the Oedipal complex is best described in terms of human *passions*. For Loewald, libido is a force, emerging from the ego, by which the ego strives to keep itself connected with the world from which it is differentiating itself. According to Loewald, "the transference neurosis is the patient's love life as it is relived in relation to a potentially new love-object, the analyst" (1971, 311). Because instincts are essentially communicative, the individual will thrust meaning onto significant people in the very act of libidinally engaging with them. Thus, the analytic situation becomes an erotic field. Here we find sexuality linked intimately with connections to objects, and with meanings of objects and not their cathexes.

On this erotic field, analyst and patient join in an erotic dance. Elise (2017) uses Kristeva's (2014) concepts of maternal eroticism to compare the erotic transference/countertransference to a dance: an embodied choreography within the analytic dyad that parallels the early maternal dyad. For Kristeva, the mother's active holding and rhythmic attunement is a needed backdrop for the release of another being into the world. The mother relies on her eroticism to nurture the child lovingly and the child relies on the mother's eroticism to develop a vibrant sense of self. Kristeva weaves together body and mind and weds eroticism and the maternal. For her, maternal love is the prototype of human passion. Kristeva asserts that maternal eroticism, perhaps even more than childhood sexuality, must be repudiated by society. Again, we return to the idea of repudiation of sexuality and its link to early development, which we will see in my individual clinical case.

Kristeva (2014) and Balsam (2012) complain that the body (especially the female body) has been forgotten in modern psychoanalytic theories. Balsam (2014) applauds Kristeva, "who does not get caught up in the mind/body dichotomy and moves effortlessly straight from Freud's sense of biological instinct as representable in the mind to dwell in the live moment of the psyche's occupation of the body" (94). I would add that while the subject for psychoanalysis is the mind and we identify the sexual drives as the representations of sexual instincts in the mind and observe the representations of body, via the ego, in the mind, we cannot forget that there are two minds and two bodies in the consulting room, speaking in different languages, verbalized and non-verbalized.

Finally, it is because passions are unsettling in their own right and because sexual drives are tied to lost objects and to forbidden Oedipal objects that sexuality can become so conflicted. Adult sexuality is entwined with infantile sexuality, which we all would forget or deny. The sexual drives in childhood are tied to parents and siblings and thus inherently incestuous. We would like the picture of the past to be empty of forbidden sex and unsettling sexual passion, brushed in neat pastels, not awash in turbulent, fierce colours.

THE CLINICAL SITUATION

We do not have to adhere to the idea that libido is the source of all mental energy or that the sexual drive is one of two basic drives to affirm that sexual impulses and issues permeate the analytic situation. The sexual drive is so compelling and intrinsically unsettling that it emerges sooner or later in all patients, whether or not their presenting complaints are sexual. Certainly, if a patient does not mention sexuality sooner or later, I begin to wonder. Sexuality enters the session in many ways: overtly in a presenting problem of impotency or frigidity, in accounts of problematic marriages devoid of sex, in disguise in dreams, in the patient's body language, in a seductive action or exhibitionistic display by patient or analyst, in strange, unexplainable symptoms, in anxieties that have no source, and most basically in the transference/ countertransference and unconscious interchanges between patient and analyst. It is both invasive and elusive. Often it is in its absence that it conceals its presence, or in its presence that it conceals its absence.

A Case of a Man with "No Libido"

Mr. B, a 38-year-old accountant, was referred to me by his former psychotherapist who recommended psychoanalysis. Mr. B's problem was that he had never really had sex and was very ashamed about this. He had sought help in the past with a sex therapist who had arranged for him to be with a sex surrogate. With this woman he was able to have an erection and to penetrate her on one occasion, but he had not carried this experience over into trying to have sex with anyone else. He had dated women over the years, but always fled before the relationship might become more intimate. Mr. B admitted that he did masturbate frequently with a required fantasy: he watches as two men cut his hair short. (Later in the course of the analysis he revealed that it sometimes might be a woman who cut his hair.) I found Mr. B to be motivated and intelligent and agreed that psychoanalysis was in order.

Mr. B appeared extraordinarily anxious. He had just moved from another city to a new position working under a demanding boss. This move meant he had to leave his therapist, a woman he liked and had grown to trust, so starting with me was very difficult. He also found his new job and the company very difficult; the situation seemed "unsustainable." In the first year of his analysis, Mr. B talked of literally nothing else but his anxiety, his job, and the difficulties there. The only people he talked about were his boss and another young man, D, who worked in the company. He was angry at D because D had pushed him away when he got a new and controlling girlfriend. Mr. B felt this was doubly painful since it represented what he feared would happen if he got into a relationship with a woman: he would be controlled.

Mr. B perceived his mother as controlling, infantilizing, and extremely critical; his father as passive and stubborn. His mother was so anxious that the family always gave into her requests in order to quell her anxiety. The father tried to ignore the mother's criticalness, but the two bickered incessantly. Yet Mr. B felt his parents loved him and each other. When the patient was in grade school, he had frequent temper tantrums. Looking back, he thought he was trying to get attention and express his feeling of not being understood. He was teased in school but his parents more or less told him to just ignore the teasing and his feelings.

He was especially tortured by the girls. For example, he was told by one that another little girl "liked" him. But it all turned out to be a huge hoax, and he was deeply hurt and crushed. He always performed very well at school and had a few close male friends. Throughout his adolescence and college, he never dated or had any sexual urges towards anyone, female or male. "No libido" he insisted, except for his hair-cutting fantasy, which he called a "fetish" after some exploration about sexual problems on the internet. He announced that he did not want to give up his fetish—"It is *mine*."

The patient recalled that the fetish began at summer camp, which he attended when he was 12 years old. On the bus ride to the camp, some veteran boys who had been there before told him that he "would never make it at camp." He recalled that one night his cabin mates began talking and kidding around about shaving. It was around then that he began having the fantasy. He remembered having the fantasy before he began to masturbate in late adolescence.

The patient and I both considered that his long-standing worry about something being "wrong" with him might come down to being gay. Certainly, the scenario with him, his friend D, and D's girlfriend had, to me, undertones of a "negative Oedipal" triangular situation. In our analysis of the situation the material revolved around the patient's longings for and disappointments with his father, who, he felt, did not stand up for him with the mother. In thinking about his sexuality, the patient said he had never been aware of sexual desires for a man. He felt what was wrong and shameful was that he had no sex drive and that people would discern this. In fact, his parents took him to a doctor to get hormone shots when he was about 13, "to push me into puberty." He recalled that, "Nobody explained anything to me and I didn't really feel behind."

The patient reported many dreams and quickly was able to associate and try to figure them out. His first reported dream in the second week of analysis was: "I am in a house, looking out a big glass window. [There is a large window next to my couch.] Two tigers are trying to crash through the window and I am terribly afraid." His association to the tigers was that they were women. This became a shared language of the analysis—"tigers" as shorthand for women and his fears about them. It was striking that in the first two or three years of the analysis, Mr. B's dreams were populated almost exclusively by males, except his mother.

Often in his dreams he was with his parents or alone travelling, trying and not being able to get somewhere.

Mr. B had erections on several occasions during the first years of analysis: once when watching a movie about a developing close and loving relationship between a man and a woman; once when vacationing and spending time with a likeable young woman beside a swimming pool; once fleetingly on the couch when he was talking about wanting to find the perfect woman—someone who listened and was understanding and non-critical. The patient could acknowledge, but quickly jumped away from, the awareness that these feelings corresponded to his feelings for the analyst, but certainly, he averred, no sexual ones.

The first two years of the analysis were marked by the patient's anxiety. In fact, for months Mr. B struck me as a ball of anxiety that needed to be soothed and contained. This became a prevailing countertransference pull—to soothe and reassure him, as one would with a small child. He revealed he misused sleeping medications and alcohol to soothe himself and control his anxiety. The sessions were filled with anxious accounts of his worries, tortured ambitions, and conflicts at work and his interactions with his colleagues and especially his boss, whom he admired and tried hard to please. He would reassure himself constantly that he was doing a good job. He worked long hours and had little or no social life, no thoughts about anything outside of work. Occasionally he would visit his parents. With me, he also tried to do a good job. It was clear that he needed to be the one to come up with the interpretations and insights (indeed he was insightful and intelligent), and at first, I felt I had to let these narcissistic defences alone. Retrospectively I see that while he described a controlling mother, in this way I felt controlled by his behaviour to try to comfort and soothe him.

At the months passed, silences began to develop. At first, he found my silences intolerable and assumed, like his parents, I was not listening or understanding him. If in the face of silence I questioned him or interrupted his silences, he then became agitated and felt I was like his controlling mother; if I remained silent, I was like his parents who could not help him. He picked up the slightest anxiety or hint of criticism on my part, which made me, in his mind, like his mother. He was often angry at me and despairing about the analysis. After some cycles of these interactions and my interpretations of them, he could see his part in making me into a controlling or non-empathic mother. Later he could tolerate my not talking and appreciate that I was listening in my silences.

In the third year of analysis, he began to talk about his interests in the cities he visited on his business travels. He developed some interests in art and movies and for the first time began to read something other than self-help books and business tracts—some novels and history. He developed new friendships, most notably a very close friendship with a woman co-worker with whom he could confide his feelings. A few women began to appear in his dreams. He became more outgoing, joining some social groups and making several new male friends, and especially a married couple whose children he loved. He began to talk sadly about wishing he might have a family of his own, and was increasingly aware of loneliness. He could crack jokes and talk about politics during his sessions. An interesting mind and fuller and more connected person was emerging.

Sexuality was not overtly in the picture. He avoided talking about his fetish, which I tried at times to tie to his narcissistic self-reliance, to be "worked on" and fixed up and especially his need to keep everyone, including me, out. He came to understand that it represented a way of keeping his mother out.

Getting a haircut as a child was a rare occasion when she was on the periphery; he was in someone else's hands. He felt his fear of women and of being married was tied to his view of his parents: his mother controlling his father and not wanting to be in the father's position. I could see that the fantasy disguised and defended against castration fears and that the aggression which he was set to see in women and feared in me also represented his own projections—two angry breasts transformed into two threatening tigers, the two cutting barbers. That is, he needed to see women, and not himself, as controlling and aggressive.[8]

---

8 This recalls a well-known case (Blum (1978; Freedman, 1978) in which a man's fetish about being shaved by a barber represented fears of castration and death. And was reminded of Blum's famous case of the man who had a similar sounding fetish about being shaved (Blum,

Yet he appeared disembodied, sexless. I felt totally disembodied myself. He would look at me fleetingly at the beginning of each session, mutter a hello, then, eyes averted, head straight to the couch. I felt like a talking head, my body invisible; he seemed oblivious if I coughed, moved, or was out of sorts. The two roles he attributed to me as a woman were tiger or comforter, but not much else. In his competitiveness in wanting to be the first to come up with an insight, I thought I was his father who it seemed always had to be right. In his wanting to please me, I was his mother.

He rebelled against outside pressure, saying he hated "having a gun to his head." In the course of our work, he came to realize that the gun was his own voice or that of his mother—"My mother in my head." That voice was a constant source of anxiety and criticism (and unconscious connection with her).

Mr. B despaired of being able to have sex with a woman and being able to please her. He was afraid of rejection, humiliation, and failure. At one point, he demanded that I, like the sex therapist, find him a sex surrogate. I suggested that he wanted me to be the one to initiate him into sex (an interpretation which he did not seem to hear until a year later). Only when I said that getting a surrogate did not make sense at that point and that we needed to work through his fears did he agree in relief. This interchange was a piece of a larger ongoing unconscious enactment on my part. Later in the analysis I was surprised to learn that the surrogate was a younger attractive woman. I realized then that I had unconsciously assumed she was an older woman, really rather unlikely. I had been carrying the unconscious fantasy of being the older woman who would initiate the young man into sex—my matching counterpart to an Oedipal fantasy of a young adolescent, which appears in themes of many famous films, such as *The Graduate* or *The Reader*. I had also slipped into the

---

1978; Freedman, 1978). Blum suggested that the patient's fears of castration and sadomasochistic preoccupations reflected a history of childhood traumata during World War II.

fantasied position of the possessive mother who did not want her son to be with another woman.

Then in the third year of analysis I noticed that the patient's fly was unzipped. This seemed to happen frequently, but it was not always clear because he often wore loose shirts not tucked in. I found myself checking his fly and feeling uncomfortable about it—both about my looking and what to do— should I say something? When? What? What did this mean? After some hesitation, I drew his attention to the fact his fly was frequently open and suggested that he wanted me to pay attention to his body, to his penis, to the sexuality he tried to keep out of our sessions and his life. He listened to this, granted its plausibility, but continued to appear in the office with his fly unzipped. He attributed this to the fact that our sessions were early in the morning and he often was very hurried and half asleep.

The open fly was a sexual tease, both beckoning and rejecting me. A sadomasochistic scenario of seducer and seduced was created between us by my letting myself be the paralysed onlooker to his continuing exhibitionistic action. It was some while before I could recognize this enactment. Other kinds of behaviours in the sessions paralleled this teasing. Mr. B would constantly declare he was going to make this change or that change in his life to move out of a stand-still—then nothing would come of it. In one sense this back and forth—saying "I can do this" and then "No, I can't"—reflected his constant need to reassure himself that he was ok and nothing was wrong with him, but I realized gradually that its effect on me in the countertransference was subtly to raise hopes that we were getting somewhere and then dash them, in this way playing with my sense of effectiveness and making me feel, as he did, ineffective and hopeless. When I addressed the teasing behaviours with the patient, he spoke of how he wanted me to have *no desires for him in any way*— that is, neither of us should have any desires for the other. He insisted he wanted to be free from the constant pressure of his mother's needs. And yet, he was unconsciously sexually teasing me, giving proof to the presence of sexual urges and anger that were hidden, but there all along.

In the fourth year of the analysis, after continued work on his defences against feelings of vulnerability and connectedness with me, the patient said he realized how much he wanted to break out of his walled-in loneliness and find a woman who would understand his lack of sexual experience. He was afraid of being rejected and found to be wanting. The patient speculated that his mother did not want him to marry—she who nagged at him about every-thing he should do, never said a word about his being single. He knew for a fact that she disapproved of homosexuality, but he thought that she did not want him to be with a woman either. In this context in which I had been in-terpreting his conflicts about separation from his mother and his family and becoming a grown man (as evidenced in his dreams in which he was always with his family), the patient said, "Maybe my leaving my fly open is a rebellion against her." At this point in the analysis, he often overslept and was late and the sessions were marked by frequent tortured silences. I talked to him about how he tried to keep himself in limbo in his life and in the analysis, and that he was feeling rebellious towards me.

He dreamt about a big cat, not a scary tiger, "but it just looked big and wouldn't hurt me … How big a deal I make it. Over-sexed in my head." Note the lack of clarity here—was it the cat or himself who was over-sexed? This image is a first sign of his sense of excess about sexuality. In a second dream on the same night, his mother is in the hospital and they don't know if the situation is fatal. A baby is stuck inside her. His associations led to his speculation that maybe the baby was his mother inside him and that his mother's influence was dying. I suggested that maybe he was the baby stuck inside of her.

Following is material from a session around this time that illustrates his emerging sexual feelings in the transference:

The talk of becoming sexual is making me so anxious! It's like my fe-tish—it prevents me from doing what I want in life. [I felt helpless at that moment and was aware I wanted somehow to push or help him to get going.] One thing that stops me is sex. My mother-in-my-head stops me. My flaws stop me from exposing myself. I want to go on a date, open up … The sex surrogate was understanding. If only the sex therapist had not pushed me … I think we are breaking through to something.

I murmured my agreement. Sharply, he asked, "Why do you say that?" I think he was picking up my need to push him and sensing a hint of sexual desire in my tone. I think my countertransference of wanting to push him to get going and to help him out sexually also reflected my identification with his pain and loneliness. I was finding it hard to bear my helplessness and frustration at standing by and outside his aloneness and isolation, month after month. I said, "You wish I would be your analyst, mother, sex therapist and sex surro-gate all at once."

"Yes."

After a pause, he said in a longing tone, "The sex surrogate was young. If you were younger, you could be my sex surrogate."

I was stung by the hostility embedded in this mixed message—I might want you, but you are too old. In contrast, as the time was up, he said with a bit of a smile, "See you tomorrow." This was the first time in the analysis he had said anything like that—an acknowledgement of his continuing link to me. Perhaps unconsciously his comment was also a way of undoing his earlier rejection of me.

A few weeks later he reported a dream: "I am on a train watching somebody masturbating. Like me watching myself but trying to hide it. It is clear I am worried somebody will catch me … sexual … out in the open and thinking something's wrong with me. This fits with that dream last week of my mother taking a CEO position in the business. She says mean things. And the way she relates to me, it's like you can't tell where one person ends and the other begins."

I pointed out that he felt sexual feelings were bad, to be hidden, like masturbating and being caught.

He continued, "This morning I checked my fly to see if it was open ... Last night I watched a TV show—'Law and Order'. Women were molested by a teacher and they killed and castrated him." At that moment I understood why I had hesitated in pointing out his open fly—not wishing to be seen as humiliating and castrating and to be pulled into the ensuing dangers of sexual excitement and sadism.[9] I said, "It is dangerous to have sexual desires for both the man and the woman and for you in here with me." He nodded and then reported, with some hesitation, that the previous night he went to a social function and was hoping to meet a woman there. This was typical: to acknowledge a fear and then immediately to try to reassure himself, or placate the listener, by negating it.

The patient and I had come to understand that one meaning of his open fly was to have me recognize, accept, and appreciate his masculinity, his body, and his penis. In this period of the analysis, he remembered for the first time that his grandmother, a woman he perceived as more accepting than his mother, had commented on his open fly when he was little—perhaps three or four years old. This was the first time in the analysis he had talked about the significant role she had played in his life. When his mother had worked part-time, this grandmother had looked after him. He wondered if his grandmother "noticed something" about him his mother did not. Listening, I thought about Laplanche and speculated about silent, confusing messages he may have picked up from his mother about masculinity and sexuality. These silent, confused messages were projected onto me in his teasing, yes and no behaviours.

---

9 Here is the darker side of sexuality, equated with the death drive by Laplanche (2015) and pictured as excessive, perverse and "demonic."

Here is an excerpt from a long dream following this sequence. In it is the theme of strangeness and strangers, which had been appearing in dreams and his thoughts for several months:

I was in X [the city in which he grew up] trying to get to my house [from childhood]. I kept asking people where Michigan was, as if it were in there and here at the same time. There were a lot of people there of Arab descent. Strangers. I saw people get out of a car and I felt afraid because everybody was Arabic. Then white guys got out of a car. Drunk. Naked. Doing something sexual. [I asked, "What?"] Maybe women in the car. I thought the one guy would kill me ... Everywhere there were strangers. It seemed strange, alien. I couldn't find where we were going. Then there were religious Jews and religious Arabs outside praying. I felt alone, confused ... Maybe I want to move home. I thought to myself before I got here—if you try to talk me out of moving there I will be angry.

I said, "You want to put outside yourself your wishes about changing and moving away from what feels safe, to put one side of the conflict into me and to get me to fight with you to stay with me." I talked to him about how hard it was for him to connect to someone outside his family—how hard it was for him to make the unknown known and the unknown person known.

"Yes," he said, "As with sex."

In the following weeks, for the first time, he had a primal scene dream in which he came upon his parents having sex. He speculated that if that had happened in his childhood, he would have been jealous of their relationship, and of both of them. I considered these signs of triangularity in the material and the emerging sexual feelings in the transference/countertransference as significant progress and deepening in the relationship.

DISCUSSION

Examining the interactions between the sexual drive and other aspects of mental functioning expands our understanding of the issues in this case. Silverman (2001) describes the complex relationship between libidinal desire and the attachment system, especially the affect-regulation function. In a recent article by Benjamin and Atlas (2015) the authors explore the difficulty in tolerating sexual excitement and intimacy in terms of the ideas of Laplanche, Stein, and Fonagy et al. on sexuality as excess and contemporary ideas about infant attachment and affect regulation. Benjamin and Atlas contend that processing and tolerating sexual excitement depends on the earlier development of being able to regulate affects. Both the early unconscious parental messages about sexuality, on the one hand, and a mother's failure to help the infant contain affects and excitement, on the other, create a situation of excess, or "too muchness" for the infant (although to my mind the two conceptions of excess seem different, from different frames of reference). If recognition and regulation by the mother fail, there is a premature process of self-soothing which prefigures auto-erotic fantasy. Put in other terms, the internal maternal object is perceived as not being able to serve as a container for projections of sexuality. The child's experience of aloneness with psychic pain is a sequela of failures of recognition and/or overstimulation caused by inadequate or overwhelming responses from the caretaker.

Fonagy argues that for such individuals sexual intimacy in adulthood becomes problematic and dangerous. Thus, sexual feelings and enjoyment are experienced as alien, an imposed burden. Needing another can become dangerous and allowing another with whom one can share one's sexual excitement safely turns into a difficult obstacle to overcome. For patients with these difficulties, perhaps such as Mr. B, the ability to experience an adult erotic transference in the room is a therapeutic achievement.

Such formulations can explain the dilemmas of my patient in allowing himself to have sex with another person, a "stranger." Benjamin and Atlas illustrate their ideas with a case of a man who, with his unmanageable tensions and difficulties around being a "real man," sounds very much like Mr. B. Corresponding with their description, Mr. B too felt alone with his psychic pain. Certainly, I thought that his severe and chronic anxiety, his efforts and need to reassure himself, and especially my countertransference of wanting to soothe him suggested early problems in affect regulation. Through the lens of my own feelings, I imagined an anxious mother who could not contain or soothe him as an infant and a child, or recognize him as a separate male being.

While this explanation of early problems in affect regulation makes sense, there is more to the story. My patient developed narcissistic defences in order to feel in control and handle the disappointments and anger of his neediness and aloneness. His internal experience of sexual excitement could be described as one of excess (the over-sexed cat) but also its opposite, deficiency ("no libido"). For this man, sex was alien, dangerous, and uncontrollable and had to be isolated. Sex with and by oneself was safe; intercourse with a person outside the family circle was equated with sex with a stranger practising strange religious rituals, like the religious Jews and Arabs in his dream. A central unconscious fantasy was that the outside world is a dangerous place. While the early unassimilated messages from the adults around him may form the foundation for this sense of strangeness and alienation, the patient deciphered messages from his mother that could be symbolized and recognized: anxious messages, mixed up with his own unconscious fantasies, to remain close. Not only did he feel he did not get enough help from either parent in containing affects, he also identified with his anxious mother and her anxiety as a way to stay close to her.

Through the first years of the analysis, the work by necessity focused on the patient's anxieties about his worth and stability, his narcissistic conflicts and defences, his need to isolate himself, and his conflicted dependence on and identification with his mother. It took years for the patient's unconscious and hidden sexual drives and fantasies to emerge overtly in the transference.

Sexuality announced itself in the sessions via the patient's symptomatic behaviour, by which he was trying to communicate a need to be seen as a male, to exhibit his sexual desire, and to entice and humiliate me. In my countertransference, I was tempted to look, to seduce, or be seduced. I was afraid of hurting Mr. B, becoming a tiger myself. In this interaction, the meaning of the fantasy "fetish" became clearer—as narcissistic withdrawal into safety and autoeroticism and an escape from castration fears and fears of aggression towards and from women. While he yearned for closeness with his father, the central fear appears one of surrender to the image of a castrating, controlling, and overwhelming woman. He wished for his father to intervene, to teach him, by strength and example, how to deal with such a woman.

Central to this case was the presence of the internalized object—the mother (and analyst) in his head who whispers to him to stay close and not to leave and to stay away from strangers. Constantly critical, this voice suggests that he is incapable, an infant in need of the mother's constant guidance and presence. It makes growing up, becoming a man, having one's own family beyond reach. Did his mother unconsciously communicate her uneasiness about his maleness—the something "wrong with him" along with her un- verbalized and disavowed sexual desires? Certainly, such confused and conflicted sexual fantasies occupied his mind. In any case, these were the unconscious feelings of which I became aware in the role of "other" in my countertransference reactions—at first disembodied, then disconcerted, and finally sexually alive.

Mr. B tried consciously to keep his sexual body out of the picture, but it sneaked in through an unconscious symptom of forgetting to zip up his fly. Bodily issues are prominent in this man. He felt like something was the matter with his body—something vague, having no sex drive, not enough hormones, or the opposite, being "oversexed" and dangerous. Mr. B had to draw attention to a part of his body in an unconscious gesture to get me to recognize his body and ultimately to find my way back into mine.

CONCLUSION

From its beginnings, the concept of the sexual drive has occupied a central position in psychoanalysis. Through the years, it has been challenged, modified, or expanded. We continue to struggle with the mind/body question. Too often we solve this conundrum by concentrating on the mind, yet renewed attention is being given to the body. Contemporary psychoanalysts do not have to adhere to the idea that libido is the source of all mental energy, that sexual pleasure is to be understood narrowly in terms of the relief of a built-up tension, or that we must swear allegiance to only two major drives. Psychosexual development is no longer considered by most as following a linear, predictable course, an unfolding of endogenous instincts. While we may hold to Freud's ideas that sexual drives derive from a biological base, we have come to appreciate how they are shaped by the outside environment. I believe that the human infant is not a blank, asexual being; its inborn sensuality and sexual readiness develop in conjunction with cognitive and other functions. Its readiness for eroticism is nourished by maternal eroticism. From the beginnings of its life the infant is sheathed in sensual bodily contacts and surrounded by erotic murmurings of the mother and other adults in the family.

More recent psychoanalytic writing on the nature of the sexual experience and passion has given us a fresh look at all these issues. Contemporary ideas have extended the scope of our psychoanalytic interests from Freud's explications of the sexual drive to the larger realm of sexuality that encompasses drives, objects, aims, sexual object choice, gender, desire, and passion. This expanding universe has brought changes in theory and technique and bids us to open our minds about the subject itself. I have highlighted the work of

Laplanche, Stein, and others who elucidate the experience of sexual passion and used their ideas to help me better understand the case of a man who was not able to have a sexual relationship. In both Freud's theory of sexual drives and infantile sexuality and Laplanche's theory of the unconscious inter- generational transmission of enigmatic sexual messages, sexuality remains inevitably and irrevocably unsettling. The ubiquitous presence, infantile origins, and enigmatic power of sex have led and will continue to lead to its suppression and repression, individually and socially. This is the continuing challenge for psychoanalysis.

REFERENCES

Balsam, R. H. (2012). *Women's Bodies in Psychoanalysis.* New York: Routledge.

——— (2014). "The Embodied Mother: Commentary on Kristeva." *J Amer Psychoanal Assn* 62: *87–100.* doi: 10.1177/0003065114523781

Benjamin, J., and G. Atlas. (2015). "The too Muchness of Excitement: Sexuality in Light of Excess, Attachment and Affect Regulation." *The International Journal of Psycho-Analysis* 96: *39–63.* doi: 10.1111/1745-8315.12285

Blass, R. B. (2017). "Reflections on Klein's Radical Notion of Phantasy and its Implications for Analytic Practice." *The International Journal of Psycho-Analysis* 98: *841–859.* doi: 10.1111/1745-8315.12674

Blum, H. P. (1978). "Psychoanalytic Study of an Unusual Perversion—Discussion." *J Amer Psychoanal Ass* 26: *785–792.* doi: 10.1177/000306517802600404

Brunswick, D. (1954). "A Revision of the Classification of Instincts or Drives." *The International Journal of Psycho-Analysis* 35: *224–228.*

Compton, A. (1981a). "On the Psychoanalytic Theory of Instinctual Drives—I: the Beginnings of Freud's Drive Theory." *The Psychoanalytic Quarterly* 50: *190–218.* doi: 10.1080/21674086.1981.11926950

——— (1981b). "On the Psychoanalytic Theory of Instinctual Drives—II: the Sexual Drives and the ego Drives." *The Psychoanalytic Quarterly* 50: *219–237*. doi: 10.1080/21674086.1981.11926951

——— (1981c). "On the Psychoanalytic Theory of Instinctual Drives—III: the Complications of Libido and Narcissism." *The Psychoanalytic Quarterly* 50:*345–362*. doi: 10.1080/21674086.1981.11926958

——— (1981d). "On the Psychoanalytic Theory of Instinctual Drives—-IV: Instinctual Drives and the ego-id-Superego Model." *The Psychoanalytic Quarterly* 50: *363–392*. doi: 10.1080/21674086.1981.11926959

——— (1983). "The Current Status of the Psychoanalytic Theory of Instinctual Drives—I: Drive Concept, Classification, and Development." *The Psychoanalytic Quarterly* 52: *364–401*. doi: 10.1080/21674086.1983.11927037

——— (1985). "The Development of the Drive Object Concept in Freud's Work: 1905-1915." *J Amer Psychoanal Assn* 33 (93): *98–115*.

Dahl, H. (1968). "Panel Reports—Psychoanalytic Theory of the Instinctual Drives in Relation to Recent Developments." *J Amer Psychoanal Assn* 16: *613–637*. doi: 10.1177/000306516801600314

Dimen, M. (1999). "Between Lust and Libido: Sex, Psychoanalysis, and the Moment Before." *Psychoanal Dial* 9: *415–440*. doi: 10.1080/10481889909539334

Dunn, J. (1993). "Psychic Conflict and the External World in Freud's Theory of the Instinctual Drives in Light of his Adherence to Darwin." *The International Journal of Psycho-Analysis* 74: *231–240*.

Elise, D. (2017). "Moving From Within the Maternal: The Choreography of Analytic Eroticism." *J Amer Psychoanal Assn* 65: *33–60*. doi: 10.1177/0003065116688460

Ferenczi, S. (1933). "Confusion of Tongues Between Adults and the Child." In Final Contributions to the Problems and Methods of Psycho-Analysis, 156 167. London: Karnac Books. 1994.

Fonagy, P. (2008). "A Genuinely Developmental Theory of Sexual Excitement and its Implications for Psychoanalytic Technique." *J Amer Psychoanal Assn* 56: *11–36*. doi: 10.1177/0003065107313025

——— Gergely, E. Jursit, and M. Target. (2002). Affect Regulation, Mentalization and the Development of the Self. New York: Other Press.

Freedman, D. A. (1978). "Of Instincts and Instinctual Drives: Some Developmental Considerations." *Psychoanalytic inquiry* 2: *153–167*. doi: 10.1080/07351698209533441

Freud, S. (1905). "Three Essays on the Theory of Sexuality." *SE* 7: *125–245*.

——— (1915). "Instincts and Their Vicissitudes." *SE* 14: *117–140*.

——— (1923). "The ego and the id." *SE* 19: *1–66*.

Gammelgaard, J. (2011). "Love, Drive and Desire in the Works of Freud, Lacan and Proust." *The International Journal of Psycho-Analysis* 92: *963–983*. doi: 10.1111/j.1745-8315.2011.00355.x

Ghent, E. (2002). "Wish, Need, Drive: Motive in the Light of Dynamic Systems Theory and Edelman's Selectionist Theory." *Psychoanal Dial* 12: *763–808*. doi:10.1080/10481881209348705

Green, A. (1995). "Has Sexuality Anything to do with Psychoanalysis?" *The International Journal of Psycho-Analysis* 76: *871–873*.

——— (1997). "Opening Remarks to a Discussion of Sexuality in Contemporary Psychoanalysis." *Int. J. Psycho-Anal* 78: *345–350*.

Greenberg, J. (1991). Oedipus and Beyond: A Clinical Theory. Cambridge MA: Harvard University Press.

——— & S. Mitchell. (1983). Object Relations in Psychoanalytic Theory. Cambridge: Harvard University Press.

Hadley, J. (1992). "The Instincts Revisited." *Psychoanalytic inquiry* 12: *396–418*. doi: 10.1080/07351699209533903

Hoffman, L. (1999). "Freud and Feminine Subjectivity." *J Amer Psychoanal Assn* 44 (supplement): *23–44*.

Irigaray, L. (1985). "The Blind Spot of an old Dream of Symmetry." In Speculum of the Other Woman, edited by G. Gill, *13–129*. Ithaca, NY: Cornell University Press.

Katz, M. (2001). "The Implications of Revising Freud's Empiricism for Drive Theory." *Psychoanal Comtemp Thought* 24: *253–272*.

Kernberg, O. F. (2001). "Object Relations, Affects, and Drives: Toward a new Synthesis." *Psychoanalytic inquiry* 21: *602–619*. doi: 10.1080/07351692109348963

Kohut, H. (1959). "Introspection, Empathy, and Psychoanalysis –an Examination of the Relationship Between Mode of Observation and Theory." *J Amer Psychoanal Assn* 7: *439–483*. doi: 10.1177/000306515900700304

Kristeva, J. (2014). "Reliance, or Maternal Eroticism." *J Amer Psychoanal Assn* 62: *69–85*. doi: 10.1177/0003065114522129

Kulish, N. (2011). "Obstacles to Oedipal Passion." *The Psychoanalytic Quarterly* 80: *3–32*. doi: 10.1002/j.2167-4086.2011.tb00075.x

Lacan, J. (1986). *The Seminar of Jacques Lacan: Vol II. Four Fundamental Concepts of Psychoanalysis* J-A Miller, edited by A. Sheridan. translator. London: Penguin. (Original work published 1973).

Lemma, A. (2015). Minding the Body: The Body in Psychoanalysis and Beyond. London: New Library of Psychoanalysis.

Lampl-De Groot, J. (1956). "The Theory of Instinctual Drives." *The International Journal of Psycho-Analysis* 37: *354–359*.

Laplanche, J. (1997). "The Theory of Seduction and the Problem of the Other." *Int J Psycho-Anal* 78: *653–666*.

——— (2004). "The So-Called 'Death Drive': a Sexual Drive." *Brit J Psychother* 20: *455–471*. doi: 10.1111/j.1752-0118.2004.tb00164.x

——— (2007). "Gender, sex, and the Sexual." *Studies in Gender and Sexuality* 8: *201–219*. doi: 10.1080/15240650701225567

——— (2015). Between Seduction and Inspiration: Man. New York: The unconscious in Translation. forthcoming. (Quoted by Scarfone).

—— & J. B. Pontalis. (1968). "Fantasy and the Origins of Sexuality." *Int J Psycho-Anal* 49: *1–18*.

Loewald, H. W. (1971). "The Transference Neurosis: Comments on the Concept and the Phenomenon." In *Papers on Psychoanalysis, 301–314.*, 1980. New Haven, CT: Yale Univ. Press.

Loewald, H. W. (1985). "Oedipus Complex and Development of Self." *The Psychoanalytic Quarterly* 54: *435–443*. doi: 10.1080/21674086.1985.11927112

Migone, P., & G. Liotti. (1998). "Psychoanalysis and Cognitive-Evolutionary Psychology: An Attempt at Integration." *The International Journal of PsychoAnalysis* 79: *1071–1095*.

Modell, A. H. (1990). "Some Notes on Object Relations, "Classical" Theory, and the Problem of Instincts (Drives)." *Psychoanalytic inquiry* 10: *1821–1196*. doi: 10.1080/07351699009533806

Moss, D. B. (2010). "Like Drives, Cultural Products Exert a "Demand on the Mind for Work"; an Introduction to two Exemplary Essays." *The Psychoanalytic Quarterly* 79: *159–170*. doi: 10.1002/j.2167-4086.2010.tb00443.x

Novey, S. (1957). "Are-Evaluation of Certain Aspects of the Theory of Instinctual Drives in the Light of Modern ego Psychology." *The International Journal of Psycho-Analysis* 38: *137–145*.

Ogden, T. H. (1984). "Instinct, Phantasy, and Psychological Deep Structure –a Reinterpretation of Aspects of the Work of Melanie Klein." *Contemporary Psychoanal* 20: *500–525*. doi: 10.1080/00107530.1984.10745750

Pansepp, J., and L. Biven. (2012). *The Archaeology of Mind: Neuroevolutionary Origins of Human Emotions.* New York: WW Norton & Co.

Scarfone, D. (2015). *Laplanche: An Introduction.* New York: The Unconscious in Translation.

Schmidt-Hellerau, C. (2005). "We are Driven." *The Psychoanalytic Quarterly* 74: *989–1028*. doi: 10.1002/j.2167-4086.2005.tb00234.x

Schwartz, A. (1987). "Drives, Affects, Behavior—and Learning: Approaches to a Psychobiology of Emotion and to an Integration of Psychoanalytic and Neurobiologic Thought." *J Amer Psychoanal Assn* 35: *467–506*. doi: 10.1177/000306518703500208

Sheperd, M. (2005). "Toward a Psychobiology of Desire: Drive Theory in the Time of Neuroscience." *Modern Psychoanal* 30A: *43–59*.

Silverman, D. K. (2001). "Sexuality and Attachment: A Passionate Relationship or a Marriage of Convenience?" *The Psychoanalytic Quarterly* 70: *325–358*. doi: 10.1002/j.2167-4086.2001.tb00603.x

Solms, M. (2012). "Are Freud's "Erogenous Zones" Sources or Objects of Libidinal Drive?" *Neuropsychoanalysis* 14: *53–56*. doi: 10. 1080/15294145.2012.10773688

Stein, R. (1998a). "The Enigmatic Dimension of Sexual Experience: The "Otherness" of Sexuality and Primal Seduction." *The Psychoanalytic Quarterly* 6: *594–625*. doi: 10.1080/00332828.1998.12006067

——— (1998b). "Panel: Review of the Psychoanalytic Theory of Sexuality." *The International Journal of Psycho-Analysis* 79: *995–998*.

——— (2007). "Moments in Laplanche's Theory of Sexuality." *Studies in Gender and Sexuality* 8: *177–200*. doi: 10.1080/15240650701225534

——— (2008). "The Otherness of Sexuality: Excess." *J Amer Psychoanal Assn* 56: *43–71*. doi: 10.1177/0003065108315540

Wyre, H. K. (2006). "Sitting with Eros and Psyche on a Buddhist Psychoanalyst's Cushion." *Psychoanal Dial* 16: *725–746*.

Zepf, S. (2010). "Libido and Psychic Energy–Freud's Concepts Reconsidered." *Int Forum Psychoanal* 19: *3–14*. doi: 10.1080/08037060802450753

Persephone, the Loss of Virginity and the Female Oedipal Complex

(1998). Int. J. Psychoanal., (79):57–71

With Deanna Holtzman

The ancient myth of Persephone and her mother, Demeter, has been characterized as the most important myth about women and the mother-daughter relationship. Previous psychoanalytic interpretations of the myth have neglected its depiction of the girl's defence against a sense of agency over her sexuality. The authors present two examples of the use of this myth by an analytic patient and the writer, Edith Wharton. Both women consciously identified in childhood with the figure of Persephone. Aspects of the myth contributed to a central unconscious fantasy that illuminated their dynamics and sexual conflicts. The authors argue that the Persephone myth is essentially a portrayal of the oedipal dilemma that emphasizes a conflict of loyalty towards father and mother, fear of loss of virginity and adult sexuality and its peaceful resolution. The female oedipal conflict is seen as different from that of the male, because the girl competes with the mother on whom she must depend as primary care-giver. Separation issues are encompassed within the female oedipal phase proper. It is proposed that the Persephone complex is better suited to representing women's issues than is the myth of Oedipus.

INTRODUCTION

The ancient myth of Persephone and her mother, Demeter, has been characterized as the most important myth about women and the mother- daughter relationship (Rich, 1976; May, 1980; Lincoln, 1991). It tells the story of the abduction of Persephone, Demeter's mournful search for her, their separation and reunion for part of the year, and the establishment of the seasons. Traced to at least 2000 BC, the myth represented the central motif around which the Eleusinian Mysteries were celebrated in the ancient world.

Women, as well as men, participated and had central roles in these and other fertility rites that honored the goddess Demeter (or Ceres, Roman Goddess of Grain). We will present two examples of the importance of this myth to two women, an analytic patient and a famous writer, Edith Wharton. Both women strongly identified with Persephone and the myth became the basis for a central unconscious fantasy that illuminated their dynamics and sexual conflicts. Through the use of this myth, we hope to elucidate certain aspects of the female oedipal complex and women's initiation into adult sexuality, topics that have been neglected in psychoanalytic thinking.

There are myriad versions of this myth. We will draw upon the oldest and most complete, *The Homeric Hymn to Demeter* (Foley, 1994). The story is as follows: Kore/Persephone, the young daughter of Demeter and Zeus, is gathering flowers in a meadow with other young girls. As Kore plucks a particularly beautiful narcissus that has attracted her, the earth opens suddenly and she is abducted by Hades, God of the Underworld and Death. Nobody hears her screams and cries. (Some versions of the story make a rape more explicit). When Kore next appears in the Homeric Hymn, she is with Hades in the underground. The scene pictures Hades 'reclining on a bed with his shy spouse, strongly reluctant …' It is important to note that prior to her stay with Hades and presumably to the loss of her virginity, the girl is known only as

'Kore' which in Greek literally means the 'maiden'. Thereafter, she takes on the new name of Persephone.

In the meantime, Demeter descends from Olympus to search the earth frantically for her daughter. In her fury and pain, Demeter causes famine and drought to spread over the earth. Zeus is induced by this catastrophe to persuade Hades to release Persephone. However, Persephone is tricked by Hades to eat a seed of the pomegranate (in some versions seven seeds). Thus, she has broken an injunction not to eat in the underworld and is now bound to Hades. In classical mythology, eating the seed symbolically implies sexual union (Foley, 1994, pp. 56-7).[1] In other versions this act of eating the pomegranate is variously and ambiguously interpreted as voluntary or involuntary, with or without the girl's conscious awareness.[2] A compromise between the gods is worked out by which Persephone spends one third of the year with Hades, and two thirds with her mother. This compromise is the ancient explanation of the origin of the seasons. Winter rules while Persephone is away from her mother and she lives with Hades, and the earth flowers in spring and summer while she is with her mother. The poem ends with Demeter founding the Eleusinian rites.

The myth has been studied by many scholars and writers, including classicists, feminists, sociologists and psychoanalysts. It has been reworked by poets and novelists in many forms and variations. Fairfield (1994) has explained the universal appeal of this myth in terms of pre-oedipal separation-individuation issues. She presents Kore as representative of the child of either sex who experiences itself as feminine in a primary maternal identification,

---

1 As psychoanalysts we recognize that the idea of eating seeds is a common children's fantasy of oral impregnation.

2 The ambiguity and variability in telling and retelling the story of the seeds in the different versions of the myth first suggested to us the idea of conflict and defensiveness around the question of the volition of woman's sexual impulses. Freud (1916) wrote that modifications, repetition, vagaries and circumlocutions in dreams are evidence of censorship and conflict. Acknowledging the cultural, historical and other reasons in variability in myth, however, we know that there is a danger in leaping to interpretation of myth as dream.

and the abduction by Hades as the paternal presence in early triangulation. Foley (1994) emphasizes the cultural-historical meaning of the myth, which describes the effect on women of arranged marriages and the ensuing separation from family. McClelland (1975) states that the myth exemplifies the feminine attitude towards power. In an important sociological contribution, Gilligan (1982) relates the myth of Persephone to her research on contemporary female adolescence. She compares the mysterious disappearance of the sense of self in female adolescents to an underground map 'kept secret because it is branded by others as selfish and wrong' (p. 51). In a similar vein, Krausz (1994) interprets Persephone as portraying the voicelessness and invisibility of womanhood.

Lincoln (1991) interprets the myth as a scenario or rite of women's initiation. Other underlying meanings of the myth that have been proposed include: archetypal mother-daughter imagoes (Jung, 1967), divided femininity because of patriarchy (Irigaray, 1991), bisexuality (Hirsch, 1989), or a girl's renunciation of phallic strivings and acceptance of femininity (Arthur, 1994).

Special attention has been given to the meaning of the pomegranate in the story. Lubell (1994) summarizes: 'The pomegranate with its astonishing number of seeds and brilliant red juice has long been seen as a complex symbol combining womb or fertility with images of bloody death' (pp. 37-8). Lincoln (1991) adds, 'Furthermore, the red colour evokes associations not only of mortal wounds but also of menstrual blood, the blood of defloration, and the blood of parturition' (p. 85). It was the one food that women were allowed to eat during the second day of fasting in the Eleusinian mysteries.

Several writers read the Persephone myth as a depiction of a form of the female oedipal complex. Chodorow 1994 notes Freud's emphasis on the girl's pre-oedipal attachment to her mother and its carry-over into the oedipal period. She notes that Persephone represents such a case: 'torn from and always maintaining her attachment to her mother, Demeter' (p. 10). Tyson (1996) also speaks of the myth of Persephone as an example of a partial resolution of the oedipal conflict, in which the girl feels she must take care of her mother. None of these various interpretations z, as we will, the aspects of the story that provide a defensive covering to girls' sexuality.

We will argue that the Persephone myth captures a female 'oedipal' conflict and its more typical resolution better than the original oedipal drama, which is modelled on a male's story. In our examples, we will emphasize three aspects of the Persephone/Demeter myth: firstly, its strong representation of the girl's loss of virginity and entry into adult heterosexuality, secondly, as a compromise formation resolving conflicts over love and loyalty towards mother and father, and thirdly, its clear paradigmatic value as the hallmark of the female Oedipus complex.

CASE STUDIES

The following clinical vignette demonstrates the powerful meaning of a central unconscious fantasy connected to the childhood reading of the Persephone story. Mrs. P began psychoanalytic treatment, four times weekly on the couch, when she was in her late thirties. She complained of depression, recounted a history of prior alcohol and drug abuse, and voiced her conviction that she was fated to kill herself. Childless, she blamed herself because of an abortion in her early twenties. She consoled herself with her gardening, which represented one of her few pleasures and had been a passionate interest since childhood. She was the youngest of five children, three boys and two girls. Her father, a doctor, was alcoholic yet admired and idealized by the entire family. Her mother, described as prudish and critical, became increasingly depressed and dependent upon alcohol by the time the patient entered puberty. The patient felt herself to be the one chosen in the family to be her mother's companion and caretaker. Unlike her sister, she had not been encouraged to date. Neither of the girls was pushed to achieve academically as the boys were.

In her treatment it became clear that Mrs. P was sexually inhibited and conflicted, unable to talk about sex. She viewed sex as dirty and frightening. She did reveal that beginning at the age of 7 or 8, she was abused sexually by her older brother who would lie on top of her while both were naked and simulate intercourse. Whether penetration occurred was unclear. She resisted the increasing evidence that her alcoholic father had also been involved in some sexual abuse (fondling) of her nieces and nephews.

Several years into the treatment, Mrs. P reported having repeated dreams after the previous session, in which she had insisted that the comedian Woody Allen could not be guilty of charges made against him of misconduct with his stepdaughter. With a great deal of shame, hesitation and reluctance, she recounted one of the dreams. 'I don't know why it's so hard':

'You and I were in this place and I went to the bathroom, a shared bathroom. I had left in the sink—Why can't I say it—It's so horrible—a douche bag. I left the bathroom and realized you would go in and see it and I was so embarrassed ...'

The dream made her think of an incident she had not thought of for years and about which she had never spoken to anyone. At the age of 12, she had got what she now thought was a vaginal discharge. Her father took her to a doctor's office where, for some reason she did not comprehend, she was catheterized. The nurse in a harsh tone asked, 'Are you active?' 'Sexually active?' the analyst asked. (The analyst's naming of 'sexual' rather than a more neutral question may represent a mini-enactment of the role of the intrusive mother/nurse.) 'No, I think physically. I wonder if my hymen was broken.' The patient recalled that she was found to have had a yeast infection, for which there was medicine to be applied vaginally with a plunger. The mother was the one who applied the plunger, in a ritualistic manner. As she continued, the patient began to obsess about whether her older sister was always present at these ministrations. She complained to the analyst how, 'This was all humiliating'. Then the patient recalled how she had first used pads, 'not tampons', when she began to menstruate.

When later in the session the analyst asked if the patient had any discomfort or bleeding with her first intercourse, the patient replied, '*No. Never. Not at all. Never. It was nothing.* I don't even remember when I had intercourse for the first time'. Allowing herself to be used at men's whims, she had made herself dead drunk every time she had sex in college. Obsessing, she recounted how the first time might have been with this boy, or perhaps it was somebody else. We have found that such occurrence of doubting, denial and use of negations is characteristic of material associated with the breaking of the hymen and the loss of virginity (Holtzman & Kulish, 1997). In addition, the doubting and negation surrounding the memory of the breaking of the hymen in this instance is clearly associated with protection against guilt-laden oedipal memories of traumatic familial experiences and fantasies, all with strong sado-masochistic meanings. There are hints about childhood sexual abuse by her father and/ or certainly confused fantasies about him. The gloss on the dream—'I don't know why it is so hard'—gives more credence to the memories and hints of childhood sexual experience and trauma. The remark seems to reflect a girl's confused reaction to an erect penis. Her unconsciously arranging not to know which man definitely first penetrated her has dynamic significance. By its ambiguity it allows for the expression of an unconscious incestuous wish to be deflowered by the father and defends against it by blotting out knowledge of this guilt-ridden possibility and meaning. In our experience such a dynamic is not rare. The harsh nurse is the embodiment of the forbidding mother who punishes the girl for her desires. In the transference she re-created the scene with the analyst as the passive onlooker to her humiliation, and also cast her again as the forbidding and intrusive mother.

It was not until a year later that the Persephone fantasy emerged. In the context of her father's death (her mother had died some years earlier), Mrs. P began sorting through household items and old letters. In going through her mother's letters, she was struck by memories from early childhood of happier times with her mother. Both the letters and her memories captured a loving closeness that had eluded the patient up until that time. In this context she remembered how as a child she had been fascinated by and loved the story of Persephone. She recounted the story and how she identified with Persephone's love of flowers. She connected the story with a childhood compulsion to dig in the earth, to find secret and nameless buried treasures. Her story omitted one important detail. There was no reference to the role of Hades, an omission which the analyst pointed out to her. The patient was astounded and she associated to a long-standing obsessive fear of being sold into 'white slavery'. She feared that she would be drugged, abducted, and forced into unspecified, horrifying sexual activities with men. One form of symptomatic anxiety was a phobic avoidance of doctors and medical procedures that would entail an anaesthetic. It had not occurred to her that this phobia was related to her father's being a doctor.

In a session shortly after Mrs. P talked about her fascination with Persephone, she reported two detailed and terrifying dreams from the same night. The dreams further clarify some of her sexual fantasies and resonate with references to the myth of Persephone and its unconscious meanings to her. In the first, occurring in an underground setting, she is captured and unable to escape from a cult in which three girls are forced into sexual acts. She was forced to have sex with a little boy. The punishment for the girls' refusing is dismemberment of one or another body part, or something thrust into an eye. In one part of the dream she is ordered to put her foot in a bucket. She is terrified because it is clear to her that her captors are going to cut off her foot. The sense in the dream was that if she tried to escape, 'the whole thing would happen over and over again'. (Perhaps there was an unconscious pun here: the 'hole' thing happening over and over again may also refer to the mother's use of the vaginal plunger and the abuse by her brother and possible penetration of her bodily 'hole'.) The long, complicated second dream is set in a morgue 'where there are just dead bodies.' Later the dream becomes pleasant, in different surroundings. A woman leads her to a steamy, clear and beautiful prehistoric lake, in which they swim together. A huge giant is on the shore.

Her associations to the dreams went to her sexual experiences with her brother L and her sense that she could not refuse him. The three girls brought to mind the number of brothers in her family. Something thrust into an eye brought back a memory from childhood in which she poked her eye by accident. L, who could be kind to her comforted her and reassured her that 'she had not damaged herself forever'. (Many of her associations to these dreams, for example, the references to seeing and being a passive onlooker, point to primal scene meanings, which we will not elaborate here.) The bucket of water was an old-fashioned bucket with a wringer, which reminded her of her mother's old-fashioned washer. She wondered if her brother L had once caught his hand in its wringer. She mused about her father: 'The giant seems phallic-like and that brings me somehow to my father. I don't want to implicate my father in all of this'. Her thoughts brought up again the idea of white slavery, and led to the insight that she perceived her barrenness as punishment for the childhood sexual activity with her brother. The analyst at this point interpreted Mrs. P's feeling of being stuck in the past with her family, a prisoner destined to keep repeating the past and the scary experiences and feelings from the past.

While she did not consciously remember the sexuality and the rape as integral to the Persephone myth, these dreams and her associations communicate her unconscious apprehensions of these aspects of it. Both dreams, set in the underground world, with the dead, are associative links to Persephone's journey to the underworld, where she encounters sexuality. Mrs. P's anxiety about penetration and virginity is revealed in her fears about being damaged forever. She perceives the female role as one of being a victim of abuse and rape, from which she tries to defend herself. There is ambiguity about who is castrated, sterilized or mutilated—her brother or herself? One aspect of the fear of loss of virginity is the unconscious link of the loss of the hymen with mutilation and castration. Her own mutilation and castration become the retribution she expects for her own castrating impulses towards her brothers and father. She is afraid of being penetrated and hurt, but unconsciously also wishes to be the penetrator or to castrate.

She is drawn, in her mind, submissively to her father and her brother, yet at the same time she yearns for the beauty of closeness with the mother/ analyst, perhaps depicted by the swim in the primordial lake. Her submissiveness and passivity with men allow her to be 'involuntarily' sexual while remaining close and loyal to her mother. Her associations link the conscious identification with Persephone to unconscious childhood fantasies of bodily damage due to incest. The fears about harm to bodily parts—a hand caught in the wringer or feet being cut off—were clearly sexualized in this dream. She associated her bodily fears with her chronic phobic avoidance of medical examinations. At this time she did not understand that her fears served as a defensive cover for her unacceptable desires for sexualized genital procedures performed on her by her physician/father as well as intrusive, sexualized anal/ urethral/vaginal procedures by her mother with the plunger or douche. Thus we see positive and negative oedipal themes, and heterosexual and homosexual themes, in these sadomasochistic fantasies. The sadomasochistic coloration has been intensified because of her childhood trauma.

In the ensuing months she saw the way in which she ran from or denied her own sexuality both in and out of the treatment. For the first time she broached the subject of sex with her husband, although very negatively: 'I hate sex! Men always want sex, to intrude, push'. The analyst pointed out that Mrs. P perceived sex as outside herself originating from the man, and that she never pictured it as pleasurable. 'That's right. That's how it is', she replied. Gradually, however, the patient began to understand the defensive need in her attitude as the analyst repeatedly showed the patient how guilty she must have felt about her sexual fantasies and experiences as a child and adolescent and her fears of her sexual impulses as a grown woman. The most dramatic example of this process was stimulated by a current experience that had clear echoes of her experience as an adolescent at the doctor's office. Bothered by a recurrent discharge, she went to a specialist in yeast infections. She was told she had no medical condition, just 'normal secretions'. As she tried to tell the analyst of this, her horror and disgust were so profound that she could barely get the word 'secretion' out, and only in a whisper (secretion = secrets?). The analyst asked what was so horrifying, but the patient could only shake her head in distress.

Gently the analyst suggested, 'It is so disturbing for you to think that you might have normal secretions, evidence that you have sexual sensations, which are to you so dirty and not normal that you cannot even let yourself know you have them'. Miserably, the patient nodded her agreement. Yet in the following sessions the patient's tone was more hopeful and for the first time she could voice the desire to work on solving her current sexual difficulties.

Some months later the conflict became externalized on to the analyst. Mrs. P reported that when she thought about sex she heard 'an interference' in her head. 'But you want me to talk about sex'. The analyst interpreted this as a projection of Mrs. P's own sexual interests and pointed out her conflicted needs to please the analyst, perceived as the demanding mother. Additionally, we speculate that 'an interference' may have represented the hymen that the analyst was invited to penetrate, thus recreating traumatic scenes from Mrs. P's childhood and adolescence.

Ultimately, Mrs. P was herself able to link this defensiveness with the manner in which she unconsciously engineered the loss of her virginity as a passive, non-volitional act. She gained insight into the meanings of her fears of 'white slavery' as guilt-ridden, unwanted oedipal wishes that repeated the fears and excitements of her childhood sexual trauma. Her own willing participation with the brother was acknowledged.

One year later, Mrs. P found herself with many positive improvements in her life. She had taken on much more responsibility at work through the encouragement of her female boss. In so doing she became aware of ambitiousness and competitive feeling towards female colleagues. She remembered that when she was a child, she was supposed to pass a swimming test, but after she got almost all the way across the pool, she could not let herself finish. It was 'something to do with' her mother, although she thought the feeling came from within herself. Then her mind went to sex. 'Sex would also take me away from my mother. It's OK if you have sex to have a baby but not for other reasons, and you absolutely can never enjoy it!'

It appears that the event of the father's death evoked many memories, and led to the re-discovery of her earlier loving relationship with her mother. The simultaneous pairing and highlighting in her mind of both of these relationships with father and mother re-evoked earlier conflicts in loyalty between father and mother, and brought into clear focus in the treatment her oedipal dilemma and the meaning of the contents and the intrapsychic use of the Persephone material. This myth represented her triangular oedipal resolution—her fantasy of preserving a relationship with her mother who pursues, searches for and loves her, while at the same time allowing for her own close involvement with the father/brother in the secret underworld of sexuality and death. Her unconscious conviction was that she could not keep her mother and be sexual at the same time. Her utilization of the Persephone myth demonstrates an unconscious resolution of this problem.

Disregarding a prohibition by eating a single or several seeds of the forbidden fruit, and thus gaining sexual knowledge is, in our view, the cornerstone of the tale of Persephone. In our study of virginity (1997) we found that the disobeying of a prohibition, clearly sexual in nature, is a frequent motif representing the guilt-ridden conflictual entry into the world of sexuality for girls. Forbidden sexual knowledge, alluded to in the story of Persephone, is a central theme in the life and work of the American writer, Edith Wharton.

Aspects of the Persephone/Demeter myth occur overtly and repeatedly in her thoughts, in autobiographical diaries, and in her literary works. Referring to the pomegranate seeds, a principal biographer (Erlich, 1992) says, 'The garnet-colored seeds, sewn throughout Wharton's work from early to late ... mark the trail we have been trying to follow towards the center of this imagery complex' (p. 43). Wharton, like Mrs. P, suffered from major sexual difficulties and phobias.

Born into a wealthy New York socialite family in 1862, Edith had a relatively lonely childhood. Her two brothers were thirteen and fifteen years older. Her father inherited his wealth and she identified with his intellectual and artistic interests. Like Mrs. P, she was an ardent and passionate gardener.[3]

Her mother was experienced as forbidding and cold, deeply involved in social life and beautiful clothes. The era in which she lived has been characterized by prudery around sexual matters. Wharton portrayed her family, especially her mother, as excessively prudish, even for the times. The prohibition around sexual knowledge was particularly inhibiting to this brilliant and sensitively precocious child. In her diary she writes,

> *I was always told ... It's not nice to ask about such things ... Once when I was seven or eight, an older cousin had told me that babies were not found in flowers, but in people. This information had been given unsought, but since I had been told by mama that it was 'not nice' to inquire into such matters, I had a vague sense of contamination, & went immediately to confess my involuntary offense. I received a severe scolding, and was left with a penetrating sense of 'notniceness' which effectually kept me from pursuing my investigations farther; & this was literally all I knew of the processes of generation till I had been married for several weeks ... A few*

---

3 Lewis (1985) writes of Wharton's 'remarkable achievement' of her book Italian villas and their gardens and adds that the focus is on the second of the two title phrases. He described her 'profound addiction, amounting to an obsession with enclosed as against unbounded spaces: with houses themselves, the arrangement of rooms within houses, the make-up of properly designed gardens.

days before my marriage, I was seized with such a dread of the whole dark
mystery, that I summoned up courage to appeal to my mother, and begged
her, with a heart beating to suffocation, to tell me 'what being married
was like.' Her handsome face at once took on the look of icy disapproval
which I most dreaded (1922, pp. 33-5). ... these elements were habitual
sources of metaphor in her fiction ... those metaphors were invariably
used to describe the inner nature of women' (pp. 120-1).

Her childless marriage to Edward Wharton, according to most biographers, was virtually sexless and certainly unhappy. It was not until the age of 45 that a passionate love affair with Morton Fullerton awakened her sexuality. He was a purportedly bisexual, promiscuous journalist who was involved sexually with his cousin, who had become his adopted sister. Wharton documented her sexual awakening with Fullerton in passionate poetry and moving passages in her diaries and letters: 'whatever those months were to you, to me they were a great gift, a wonderful enrichment; and still I rejoice and give thanks for them! You woke me from a great lethargy ...' (Erlich, 1992, p. 105).

One of Edith Wharton's childhood symptoms was a phobia of crossing thresholds, which can be linked to her fears of loss of virginity and of penetration. The terror hit her precisely at the point of crossing the threshold, from the outside into the interior of her house. The idea of thresholds is frequently associated with the loss of virginity, which can be represented as the crossing of a threshold from childhood into adult sexuality. On another level, we interpret her fear of crossing the threshold as representative of a conflicted fear/wish of being penetrated or penetrating, sexually. She described it as a 'dark undefinable menace, forever dogging my steps, lurking, and threatening' (Wharton, 1933, pp. 16-18).[4] Her childhood fear of ghosts, which accompa-

---

4 Wharton's phobia of thresholds may be related to a fascination with thresholds which abounds in her literary works and in her architectural interests. For example, her first published

nied the threshold phobia, seemed to lift after the love affair with Fullerton and she wrote a series of ghost stories for the first time. We feel that her fear of losing her virginity and entering adult sexuality, as evidenced by the threshold phobia, is related, and can be traced to an intense oedipal tie to her father. We deduce this through an analysis of context, contiguity, repetitive themes and experiences in her life, diaries and literary works.

Indeed, incestuous themes provide some of the most dramatic and poignant moments in her work. These themes often encompass two women in competition for a man, as in for example *Ethan Frome* (1911), or *The Bunner Sisters* (1916). Frequently an uncle or a guardian lusts after a young woman, as in the novella *Summer* (1917). The unpublished fragment, 'Beatrice Palmato' (Wolff, 1977), describes in explicit terms consummated sex between a father and a daughter. Many literary critics have noted the predominance of these incestuous themes. White (1991) postulates that Wharton had been a victim of childhood incest, although there is no direct evidence for this.

Wharton recounted her youthful disdain of fairy tales and adoration of the tales of the Olympian gods and goddesses. When she was about 5, a friend of her father's would put her on his knee and entertain her with the myths. In her autobiographical account, she clearly identifies the characters in the myths with the adults in her life. Her father's library became the centre of her passion for reading and knowledge. Her mother carefully attempted to censor and control that knowledge. In the following quote from her autobiography we see how reading and knowledge became sexualized and linked to Persephone:

> *But this increase of knowledge was as nought compared to the sensuous rapture produced by the sound & sight of the words ... they sang to me so bewitchingly that they almost lured me from the wholesome noonday air*

---

work, *The Decoration of Houses,* has two chapters devoted to doors and thresholds (Wharton & Codman, 1902).

401

of childhood into the strange supernatural region where the normal plea-
sures of my age seemed as insipid as the fruits of the earth to Persephone
after she had eaten of the Pomegranate seed (Wharton, 1922, p. 10).

This magnetic attraction to Persephone and the pomegranate seed can be documented in a variety of Wharton's works.

In her early short story, 'The House of the Dead Hand' (Wharton, 1904), a daughter and father are linked by artistic and intellectual interests that exclude an uninterested mother. The father's purchase of a painting with the daughter's dowry money prevents her from being able to marry the man she loves. This sensuous painting, the daughter's property, is kept hidden in the depths of the house, shrouded from light by velvet curtains. The father allows chosen visitors to view it on condition that they never reproduce it. But even after her father's death, the girl remains unable to free herself from her incestuous bond to him. A strikingly gratuitous detail in the story is that visitors may view the painting only from the vantage point of standing on the pomegranate bud on the carpet, with a red curtain that is pulled away. Wharton interjects the pomegranate into a tale rife with oedipal conflict and forbidden sexuality. In the Beatrice Palmato fragment mentioned previously, Wharton uses a bud explicitly to represent the clitoris, as for example: 'she felt the secret bud of her body swelling ...' (Wolff, 1977, p. 304).

In a poem in the form of a dialogue entitled 'Pomegranate Seed' published in 1912, Wharton retells the Demeter/Persephone myth. Here, she emphasizes childlessness and gives multiple symbolic meanings to the pomegranate seed—from a baby, ovary, semen, sexuality, to death. The poem also movingly portrays the love, sadness and anger between mother and daughter. In addition to such works characterized by themes of Persephone, Wharton even created fictitious characters such as Margaret Aubyn in *The Touchstone* (1900), who wrote literary pieces related to Persephone and the pomegranate.

Finally, the ghost story, called one of her best, 'The Pomegranate Seed' gives an explicit reference to the Persephone myth in an explanatory footnote.

Wharton's explanation of the myth includes Persephone's abduction and 'broken vow of sexual abstinence.' (Neither Wharton nor the *Homeric Hymn* specify to whom this vow is made.) This story is Wharton's reworking of the Persephone myth with generations and genders reversed. An off-repeated configuration in Wharton's writings appears here in which two women and a man are the main protagonists. In the plot, a young woman has married an older man, whose first wife has died and left him with children. He becomes increasingly withdrawn and distant after each of the mysterious deliveries of grey letters in an unknown hand. The new wife is jealous and concerned about his increasingly diverted interest: 'she felt her husband was being dragged away from her into some mysterious bondage' (Wharton, 1936, p. 777). As the story unfolds, the letters are ghostly demands and summonses for him to join his dead wife. Finally, he disappears. Possessiveness by the older woman, the first wife, has asserted itself. As in a typical Wharton outcome, what looks like an oedipal victory for the younger woman is short-lived and disaster ensues. In Wharton's reversal, which mimics the little girl's situation, it is the younger woman, rather than the older Demeter, who is left alone and grieving.

In summary, in a long series of autobiographical and fictional writings by Edith Wharton, there can be found a repetitive, rich and intriguing inter-weaving of content about Persephone, the prohibited pomegranate, forbidden sexuality, and oedipal and incestuous themes. We think that there is convincing evidence that these fantasies dominated her personal mental and sexual life as well.

DISCUSSION

The conscious identifications with Persephone for Mrs. P and Wharton, both literate and precocious little girls, are evident in the clinical and biographical material. Through the work of the analysis with Mrs. P and the inferences from literary and biographical analyses of Wharton's life and writings, the unconscious meanings of the Persephone story to these women emerged with clarity. For both Mrs. P and Wharton, the Persephone myth embodied unconscious fears of intercourse and the loss of virginity, their views of sexuality for a woman as a concrete or implied form of enforced rape or bondage from which it is difficult to escape, and an oedipal conflict with all its incestuous implications. Both of these women experienced their mothers as forbidding, sexually prudish, and excessively involved in social proprieties, difficult objects with whom to identify. A shared legacy from these childhood experiences was a harsh superego. Both girls, one being born at the end of a large sibship and one after an interval of thirteen years, must have felt pangs of being unwanted and yearned ambivalently for closeness with their mothers. Because the Demeter/Persephone myth embodies this intense but ambivalent relationship with the mother, it appealed to these girls. For both it provided an unconscious defensive structure in which their own sexuality and responsibility for it was disavowed. Because of the more conflicted relationships with their mothers, there was a greater inhibition in the ability to take responsibility for their sexuality, which in their minds belonged to their mothers.

Many contemporary psychoanalytic writers have suggested that conflicted pre- oedipal relationships with the mother predispose girls to later difficulties in owning and enjoying their sexuality. Chasseguet-Smirgel (1970) posits that the little girl's need, in the course of early development, to free herself from the image of an omnipotent, castrating mother commonly leads to idealization of the father or the phallus and to a denial of her female sexuality. Benjamin (1990) describes the sexual difficulties that arise for girls because they must identify with the mother who, in normal development, is seen as an object of, not subject over, sexual desire. Torok (1992) writes of anal conflicts that interfere with the assumption of sexual desire: 'The superimposition in the same object of both mastery and rivalry blocks the way out of the anal stage and forces the girl to renounce her desires' (p. 168). Hoffman (1996) has argued persuasively that psychoanalytic theory has had difficulty in conceptualizing feminine subjectivity, that is, women's capacity to take agency over sexual pleasure, a capacity often conflicted for many women.

In these two examples we see both the conscious use of this myth for defensive purposes and in the presence of a more general dynamic constellation. Although aspects of Mrs. P's and Wharton's relationships and their families were troubled, we believe their dynamics are not unusual nor unique. While these are two perhaps exaggerated examples, we believe that they point to important aspects of more 'normal' or typical female development. Similarly, the pathological dramatic examples in men also help to illuminate the meanings of typical male oedipal development.

Thus, the explanatory power of this myth exceeds these immediate examples. Yearnings for the mother, pre-oedipal issues, especially around eating, and separation-individuation themes are certainly a part of the complex tapestry evoked by this popular myth. Fairfield (1994) emphasizes elements of early triangulation. We would argue further that Persephone is most centrally an incestuous oedipal and certainly a sexual drama. Its main characters, Demeter, Zeus and Hades, are siblings. Thus, Persephone is ravished by and becomes the queen of her uncle. Note that Persephone herself is the offspring of Zeus and Demeter—sister and brother. *What other psychoanalytic interpretations of this myth have overlooked is the girl's defensive abdication of her own agency and ownership over her sexual desires in order to preserve a closeness with the mother.*

What sets the entire tale into motion is Kore's abduction/rape. 'Kore' is the Greek word for virgin or unmarried girl. In *The Hymn to Demeter* it is only after she has been with the abductor Hades that Kore acquires the name Persephone.

405

Thus it is the tale of the transformation of a virgin into a sexually knowledge-able woman. According to a classical scholarship, 'Meadows in Greek myth are liminal sites, associated not only with the transition to sexuality and fertility but with the underworld … The motif of abduction from a meadow and a group of maidens suggests the girl's readiness for marriage' (Foley, 1994, pp. 33-4). We have found in our previous study (1997) that the loss of virginity is often fantasized in the minds of women and men as a rape and abduction from the world of childhood—a liminal or threshold phenomenon.

The forbidden nature of sexual knowledge in both its intellectual and Bib-lical sense is well-known through the story of Adam and Eve and the forbid-den fruit from the tree of knowledge. It characterizes the transitional element noted above, from innocence to sexuality/mortality. In the Persephone myth, the forbidden fruit is the pomegranate. Eating the pomegranate seed implies that the girl has been initiated into sexuality and has accepted it within her.

Classically, when a bride ate food in her husband's house, she accepted her transition to her new life in the husband's domain. Pomegranates in mythology are associated with blood, death, fertility and marriage. The eating of the seed also suggests impregnation. The flower symbolism in the tale and its connection to virginity, sexuality, and childbirth has been noted by us and others (Lupton, 1993) previously. Wharton's diary quoted above clearly illustrates her notion about babies being found in flowers. Mrs. P too, was obsessed with planting and flowers, and consciously and unconsciously linked them with her unfulfilled desires for babies. Thus, Persephone's picking of the flowers connotes loss of virginity and impregnation. The girl's ambivalence about sexuality is reflected in oscillations between desire and unwillingness. This brings to mind Mrs. P's use of doubting, denial and negation when recounting her loss of virginity and Wharton's symptoms of anxiety around her upcoming marriage.

Utilizing the resolution of Kore/Persephone, the girl can keep and remain loyal to her mother and be sexual at the same time. For Persephone, to each relationship there was a season, a division by time spent with each but clearly involving three characters, mother, father and daughter. The three participants, Demeter/Hades/Persephone share time together two by two: mother with the virgin Kore, and husband/lover with the sexual Persephone. (We observe that for Oedipus as well there certainly was not a resolution with the three parties living happily ever after.) While manifestly she is forced into sex and bondage, she becomes the powerful spouse and queen of a new domain. This paradoxical core of the story of Persephone, so often overlooked, represents a pleasing solution to a little girl's oedipal dilemma. It can be argued that competition between mother and daughter, so central to an oedipal drama, is not a part of the manifest narrative of Persephone and Demeter. In *The Hymn to Demeter* there is only a frantic, loving, searching mother who longs for her daughter.[5] Yet the entire story can be interpreted in terms of its defensive stance against competition between mother and daughter. For Persephone direct competition with the mother is overshadowed by the conflict between sexuality/father and innocence/mother. It is because of its many-layered psychological meanings, and particularly its solution to oedipal and sexual conflicts, that the myth of Persephone and Demeter appealed to Mrs. P, Wharton, and, we think, to many, many women. And what of its appeal to men? We wonder if in addition to bisexual identification or psychic bisexuality, the appeal of the Persephone/Demeter myth provides for males another chance to glory in the fantasy of a prescribed or enforced return to intimacy and closeness with a loving mother.

This myth may help us to understand further the female Oedipus complex and the ways in which it differs from that of the man. Contemporary object-relations theorists, such as Chodorow (1978), have suggested that separation is especially difficult and salient for the little girl as compared to the little boy.

Chodorow posits that in the course of development, the girl must separate from the primary object, the mother, while she has the task of identifying with

---

5 Competition is evidenced in another portion of the myth in which Demeter and a mortal woman struggle for possession and influence over a baby boy

her, the same-sexed object. Identifying with the opposite-sexed object, the father, on the other hand, helps the boy with separation from the mother, but leaves him more vulnerable to an exaggerated need for autonomy. Chodorow posits a more permeable, less defined boundary between mother and daughter that implies a greater tie to the mother. These suppositions about boundaries, however, are open to question, as they seem to us to be too generalized.

Certainly, we have observed that separation from the mother and the maternal relationship are highly prominent in females as they think about defloration and sexuality. In many versions of the myth Persephone cries poignantly for her mother as she is abducted. Social and cultural realities are some important determinants for this feeling of loss and separation. In many societies marriage brings separation, sometimes total separation, for the girl from her mother, family and home. Called upon to move into a new role and identity, she leaves past and childhood behind.

We do not feel that the observation about the prominence of the role of separation from mother around defloration for women *necessarily* demonstrates a permeable boundary between self and other, or regressive, pathological or pre-oedipal interpretations. Separation material is frequently erroneously or automatically construed as infantile or pre-oedipal. Rather we would say that separation themes occur at all stages of development. The female oedipal configuration includes earlier conflicts within it, just as the male configuration does. The female oedipal phase proper entails a strong involvement with the mother around sexuality. This is not representative of or identical with the pre-oedipal concerns about nurturance, control or individuation.

What is unique to the feminine positive oedipal organization derives from the fact that rivalry occurs with the same-sexed parent, the mother, who is generally the primary caretaker. The girl has to maintain a relationship with her mother/caretaker, while at the same time compete and identify with her.

Similarly, Person (1982) stresses that the little girl is more intimidated than the little boy during the oedipal period because her rival is also her source of dependent gratification. Tyson (1989), Lax (1995), Chasseguet-Smirgel (1970), have all made related points about the importance of the girl's tie to the mother in the shape, progression into or resolution of the girl's Oedipus situation. In contrast, in the positive oedipal configuration, the boy is not confronted with competition with the major caretaker/mother on whom he still must depend. We would stress that this need gives to the girl's oedipal phase a flavour of separation that should not always be read as infantile or pre-oedipal. It reflects the complexity of the highly sensitive psychological tasks facing the little girl as she traverses through the oedipal period.

Freud (1931) noted the increased length and strength of the pre-oedipal tie of the little girl to her mother, and posited a lack of motivation (i.e. castration) for a definitive oedipal resolution (1925) and the development of a strong superego. We argue that the particular circumstances of a girl's relationship to her mother produce an equally definite resolution, although it differs in its form. Other writers have addressed these issues. Chasseguet-Smirgel (1970), for example, speaks about a unique and powerful source of guilt in the oedipal situation of the girl, not found in that of the boy, that reflects anal conflicts with the mother. Others, such as Bernstein (1983a), Blum (1976) and Gilligan (1982) describe the specific forms and contents of the superego for the girl that derive from her relationship with her mother and the different configuration of her oedipal situation. Such writings invoke other factors than castration anxiety to explain moral development in girls. These include fears of feminine mutilation and other specifically feminine genital anxieties, fears of loss of love of both parents and fears of loss of the object. We believe that in addition to castration anxiety, fears of loss of love and of the object and conflicts about loyalty are central to moral development and superego formation in boys as well. A thorough discussion of the motivating forces for the girl's resolution of her oedipal dilemma and the formation of the superego, however, is beyond the scope of this paper.

Both the oedipal story and the Persephone myth concern sex and depict developmental incestuous origins of heterosexuality. Murder, castration, and conflicts over power and authority are essential and prominent in the male paradigm. In contrast, the maintenance of intimate relationships takes center stage for the female in the Persephone story. Violence and sexuality/death are present but not murder, castration and open competition; women's aggression is in the shadows. The punishment is dreadful and bloody for Oedipus; for Persephone it means 'unhappy exile' from her mother for part of the year and immersion in the other world of sexuality and death. Persephone also encompasses the so-called negative oedipal complex, the girl's love of her mother. McDougall (1970) suggests that female homosexual love of women must be integrated into the psyche in order to achieve a 'harmonious feminine nature'.

Thus, because the oedipal paradigm, manifestly a story with a male as a central protagonist, does not contain the loyalty conflict with the mother, it does not fit the girl's situation as well as Persephone. There are many other stories and myths about females that appeal to girls or capture aspects of the girl's triangular situation (see Bernstein, 1983b; Kestenbaum, 1983; Shainess, 1982), but in our minds they do not incorporate the organization of object relationships and the conflicts and defenses as well.

Elements of Persephone's dilemma are a part of every female's intrapsychic experience and oedipal complex. because the Persephone myth encompasses ideas of fertility and periodicity, virginity and its loss, the relationship with the mother and the importance of relationships in general, it better captures the female oedipal complex than does the Oedipus Rex story. We would suggest that the female Oedipus complex be replaced by 'Persephone Complex'. Further research and clinical data, however, will be needed in order to support our theses.

REFERENCES

Arthur, M. (1994). Politics and pomegranates: an interpretation of the Homeric Hymn to Demeter. In *The Homeric Hymn to Demeter*, ed. H. P. Foley. Princeton, NJ: Princeton Univ. Press, pp. *214–242*.

Benjamin, J. (1990). The alienation of desire: women's masochism and ideal love. In *Essential Papers on the Psychology of Women*, ed. C. Zanardi. New York: New York Univ. Press, pp. *455–479*.

Bernstein, D. (1983a). The female Oedipal complex. In *Female Identity::Conflict in Clinical Practice*, ed. N. Freedman & B. Distel. Northvale, NJ: Jason Aronson, 1993, pp. *101–142*.

Bernstein, D. (1983b). The female superego: a different perspective. *IJP*, 64: *187–200*.

Blum. H. (1976). Masochism, the ego ideal and the psychology of women. *APA*, (Suppl.), 24: *157–192*.

Chasseguet-Smirgel, J. (1970). Feminine guilt and the Oedipus complex. In *Female Sexuality*, ed. J. Chasseguet-Smirgel. London: Karnac, 1992, pp. *94–133*.

Chodorow, N. (1978). *The Reproduction of Mothering: Psychoanalysis and the Sociology of Gender.* Berkeley: Univ. California Press.

——— (1994). *Femininities, Masculinities, Sexualities.* Lexington, KY: Univ. Press Kentucky.

Erlich, G.C. (1992). *The Sexual Education of Edith Wharton.* Berkeley: Univ. California Press.

Fairfield, S. (1994). The Kore Complex: the myths and some unconscious fantasies. *IJP*, 75: *243–263*.

Foley, H.P. (ed.) (1994). *The Homeric Hymn to Demeter.* Princeton, NJ: Princeton Univ. Press.

Freud, S. (1916). Introductory Lectures on Psychoanalysis. *S.E.*15–16.

——— (1925). Some psychical consequences of the anatomical distinction between the sexes. *S.E.19.*

——— (1931). Female sexuality. *S.E.21.*

Gilligan, D. (1982). *In a Different Voice.* Cambridge, MA: Harvard Univ. Press.

Hirsch, M. (1989). *The Mother/Daughter Plot: Narrative, Psychoanalysis, Feminism.* Bloomington: Indiana Univ. Press.

Hoffman, L. (1996). Freud and feminine subjectivity. In 'The Psychology of Women: Psychoanalytic Perspectives'. *APA*, (Suppl.), 44: *23–44.*

Holtzman, D. & Kulish, N. (1997). *Nevermore: The Hymen and the Loss of Virginity.* Northvale, NJ: Jason Aronson.

Irigaray, L. (1991). *Marine Lover of Friedrich Nietzsche,* trans. J. C. Gill. New York: Columbia Univ. Press.

Jung, C.G. (1967). The psychological aspects of the Kore. In *Essays on a Science of Mythology; The Myth of the Divine Child*, C. G. Jung & K. Kerenyi. Princeton: Princeton Univ. Press, pp. *156–177.*

Kestenbaum, C.J. (1983). Fathers and daughters: the father's contribution to feminine identification in girls as depicted in fairy tales and myths. *Amer. J. Psychoanal.*, 43: *119–127.*

Krausz, R. (1994). The invisible woman. *IJP*, 75: *59–72.*

Lax, R.F. (1995). Motives and determinants of girls' penis envy in the negative oedipal phase. *J. Clin. Psychoanal.*, 4: *297–314.*

Lewis, R.W.B. (1985). *Edith Wharton.* New York: Fromm.

Lincoln, B. (1991). *Emerging From the Chrysalis.* New York: Oxford Univ. Press.

Lubell, W.M. (1994). *The Metamorphosis of Baubo.* Nashville, TN: Vanderbilt Univ. Press.

Lupton, M.J. (1993). *Menstruation and Psychoanalysis.* Chicago: Univ. Illinois Press.

May, R. (1980). *Sex and Fantasy.* New York: Norton.

McClelland, D.C. (1975). *Power: The Inner Experience.* New York: Irvington.

McDougall, J. (1970). Homosexuality in women. In *Female Sexuality*, ed. J. Chasseguet-Smirgel. London: Karnac, 1992, pp. *171–212*.

Person, E. S. (1982). Women working: fears of failure deviance and success. *J. Amer. Acad. Psychoanal.*, 10: *67–84*.

Rich, A. (1976). *Of Woman Born: Motherhood as Experience and Institution.* New York: Norton.

Shainess, N. (1982). Antigone, the neglected daughter of Oedipus: Freud's gender concepts in theory. *J. Amer. Acad. Psychoanal.*, 10: *443–455*.

Torok, M. (1970). The significance of penis envy in women. In *Female Sexuality*, ed. J. Chasseguet-Smirgel. London: Karnac, 1992, pp. *171–212*.

Tyson, P. (1989). Infantile sexuality, gender identity, and obstacles to oedipal progression. *APA*, 37: *1051–1069*.

——— (1996). Mother/Mate: a developmental dilemma and a crossroads in development. Paper presented to 'Transitions in Women', Symposium of the Michigan Psychoanalytic Society.

Wharton, E. (N. D.). *The Romantic Ballad of ye Portuguese Plums*. Bienecke Rare Book and Manuscript Library, Yale University.

——— (1900). *The Touchstone*. New York: Scribner's.

——— (1904). The house of the dead hand. In *The Collected Short Stories of Edith Wharton*, ed. R. W. B. Lewis. New York: Scribner's, 1968, pp. *507–529*.

——— (1911). *Ethan Frome*. New York: Scribner's.

——— (1912). *Pomegranate Seed. Scribner's* Magazine, 51: *284–91*.

——— (1916). *The Bunner Sisters*. In *Xingu and Other Stories*. New York: Scribner's.

——— (1917). *Summer*. New York: Appleton.

——— (1922). *Life and I*, manuscript version of A *Background Glance*. Beinecke Rare Book and Manuscript Library, Yale University.

——— (1933). *A Backward Glance*. New York: Charles Scribner's Sons, 1964.

——— (1936). Pomegranate seed. In *The Collected Short Stories of Edith Wharton*, ed. R. W. B. Lewis, New York: Scribner's, 1968, pp. *763–788*.

——— & Codman, O. (1902). *The Decoration of Houses*. New York: W. W. Norton & Co., 1978.

White, B.A. (1991). Neglected areas: Wharton's short stories and incest. *Edith Wharton Rev.*, 8: *3–11*.

Wolff, C.G. (1977). *A Feast of Words; The Triumph of Edith Wharton*. New York:

CHAPTER 14

The Femininization of the Female Oedipal Complex: Part I: A Reconsideration of the Significance of Separation Issues

(2000). J. Amer. Psychoanal. Assn., (48)(4):1413-1437

With Deanna Holtzman

Freud's insights about the oedipus complex have been universalized to include the psychology of the girl. The authors argue that this crucial developmental phase for girls has uniquely feminine characteristics that have not been fully recognized or cohesively incorporated into psychoanalytic theories. This paper addresses these differences, which are based on characteristic patterns of object relationships, typical defenses, and social considerations. The authors argue that "female oedipal" is an oxymoron, and propose that this constellation be named "the Persephone complex" after the Greek myth of Persephone, which seems to capture better the typical situation of the little girl. They focus on the issue of separation and its complicated and necessary role in the triangular situation of females. Using illustrations from clinical material, the authors argue that the frequent appearance of separation material linked to triangular heterosexual competitive fantasies can and should be differentiated from material in which ideas about separation stem from dyadic and earlier issues. Misunderstanding how these separation conflicts tie into triangular "oedipal" relationships can lead to a "preoedipalization" of the dynamics of girls and women.

Psychoanalytic thought has long considered the oedipus complex a cornerstone of psychic development. Based on the story of a male, and emerging from

Freud's understanding of his own unconscious conflicts, the paradigm posits a triangle in which a boy loves his mother and competes with and wants to get rid of his father. These insights have been universalized to include the psychology of girls, and an analogous triangular situation was postulated: that is, the girl loves her father, and competes with and wants to get rid of her mother.

However, triangulation for girls is not simply a mirror image of what happens in boys. It has unique feminine characteristics that have not been fully recognized or cohesively incorporated into our psychoanalytic thinking and lexicon. In this paper we will address these uniquely feminine characteristics, which are based on gendered differences in object relationships, defenses, and social considerations. Further, we argue that the term "female oedipal" is an oxymoron. We will focus on the issue of separation and its complicated and necessary role in the female triangular phase proper. We will use clinical material to demonstrate that the virtually ubiquitous appearance in girls of separation material linked to triangular heterosexual competitive fantasies can and should be differentiated from material in which ideas about separation do not include any so-called "oedipal elements" and express earlier dyadic issues. The concerns about separation so often attributed to females demonstrate triadic as well as dyadic object relations, and "oedipal" as well as preoedipal conflicts.

One idea about the difference between the triangular situations of little girls and little boys has run through psychoanalytic writing from Freud on down through his apologists to his critics and his revisionists: that is, the importance to the girl of her relationship to her mother, and its role in the development, shape, and resolution of her "oedipal" situation. It is this relationship on which we will focus, concentrating specifically on the importance of issues of separation from the mother in girls' triangular conflicts.

In a previous paper (1998) we argued that the Persephone myth is a better fit for the description of the little girl's situation than is the Oedipus myth, and we suggested that the term "oedipal complex" be replaced with "Persephone complex." For over a thousand years, the Eleusinian mysteries, celebrating fertility and the Demeter/Persephone myth, were the most important of the widespread Greek mystery cults and rituals (Foley 1994). The myth tells the story of Kore's (Persephone's) straying from her mother to pick flowers, her sexual abduction by the lord of the underworld, her mother Demeter's mournful search for her, and the establishment of the seasons by their separations and reunions over the cycle of the ensuing years.

Our source for this tale is the Homeric *Hymn to Demeter* (see Foley 1994), in which the story goes as follows: Kore/Persephone, the young daughter of Demeter and Zeus, is gathering flowers in a meadow with other young girls. As Kore plucks a particularly beautiful narcissus that has attracted her, the earth opens suddenly and she is abducted by Hades, God of the Underworld and Death. Nobody hears her screams and cries. (Some versions of the story make a rape more explicit.) When Kore next appears, she is with Hades in the underworld. Hades is pictured "reclining on a bed with his shy spouse, strongly reluctant." It is important to note that prior to her stay with Hades and (presumably) the loss of her virginity, the girl is known only as "Kore," which in Greek literally means "maiden." Afterwards she is known by the new name of Persephone.

Demeter, goddess of fertility and Persephone's mother, descends from Olympus and frantically searches the earth for her daughter. In her fury and pain, she causes famine and drought to spread over the earth. Zeus is impelled by this catastrophe to persuade Hades to release Persephone. However, Persephone has eaten some pomegranate seeds. (In some versions she is tricked or forced by Hades; in others, she takes the seeds willingly.) She has broken an injunction not to eat in the underworld, and is now bound to Hades. A compromise is worked out among the gods, by which Persephone spends one third of the year with Hades and two thirds with her mother.[1] This compro-

---

1 The proportion of time that Persephone spends with hades and with her mother varies from version to version of the story. In some it is half and half. The number of seeds ingested also varies.

mise is the ancient explanation of the origin of the seasons. Winter rules while Persephone is away from her mother and living with Hades, and the earth flowers in spring and summer while she is with her mother. The poem ends with Demeter's foundation of the Eleusinian rites.

Persephone's story is the story of a close mother-daughter relationship, of separation and reunion, and of a way of resolving conflicts about entering the sexual world. The positive feminine oedipal situation requires the girl to maintain a relationship with her mother while at the same competing with her. We emphasize that the Persephone story involves a sexual triangle in which the girl creates a compromise solution by separating in time and space her relationship with a woman/mother and a man/father. She oscillates between two worlds: as Persephone in the murky, sexual world of Hades where she rules as queen, and as Kore in the sunny, safe world of Demeter where she is an innocent virgin picking flowers. We see this as a clear paradigm of a heterosexual conflict of loyalty: the desire both to stay with mother and to run away with father. This is a little girl's dilemma.

Other writers have selected different stories, Cinderella or Electra, for example, as paradigmatic of the girl's oedipal situation.[2] Our objection to Cinderella, which Bernstein (1993) favored, is that aspects of the maternal object are split between the bad stepmother and the good fairy godmother. Splitting is generally an earlier, preoedipal phenomenon. In contrast, in the tale of Persephone, male and female (whole) objects are separated in time and place; this is a means of dealing with the conflicts of that later stage. Thus, we feel that the story of Persephone better captures a girl's typical solution to her "oedipal" dilemma. She is caught between her attachment to her mother and her attraction to her father. We selected this myth not because it necessarily represents the *ideal* of mature female development, or the *best* resolution of

---

2 Freud (1931) rejected the idea of Electra, proposed by Jung, as paradigmatic of the girl.

this situation, but because it represents a common defensive compromise by which the concerns of that stage of development may be managed.

In a previous work (1997) we demonstrated that themes of separation from the mother typically accompany women's memories and experiences of their loss of virginity and entry into adult heterosexuality. In addition, unconscious incestuous fantasies about the father are usually intertwined with this material. We found that the concerns about separation from a mother that accompany a daughter's stepping into her world as a heterosexual rival are not regressive, dyadic, or preoedipal, but are part of the triangular experience and development itself.

From the beginning, Freud (1925) noted differences in the oedipal situations of little girls and little boys. He stated that "the fateful combination of love for the one parent and simultaneous hatred for the other as rival is found only in boys" (Freud 1931, p. 229). According to his early theories, different reactions by girls and boy to the anatomical differences between the sexes—that is, penis envy versus castration anxiety—had major consequences for oedipal development, and ensured that entry into the oedipal situation, its length, its resolution, and its influences on the development of the superego are different for boys and girls, as are their eventual sexual aims and their choice of sexual object.

Dissatisfied with his early formulations about female psychosexual development, Freud welcomed contributions from female colleagues, who explained and elaborated aspects of female development through the exploration of the preoedipal phase. Lampl-de Groot (1927), Deutsch (1945) and Bonaparte (1953) emphasized preoedipal dyadic relationships between girls and their mothers to explain some of the observed differences between the female and male oedipal complexes. At the same time, they adhered closely to Freud's model for the oedipal situation itself.

These early ideas about the female oedipal complex, and the ways it resembles and differs from that of the male, have been addressed by subsequent analytic thinkers. Freud (1931) had cautioned that the duration of the girl's attachment to her mother should not be underemphasized. Lampl-de Groot (1927) supported Freud's formulations, and documented a negative oedipal complex that preceded the positive oedipal in the girl. Fenichel (1954) did not regularly find this constellation as a forerunner to the positive female oedipal in his case material. He stressed object relations, and presented clinical material to demonstrate that the woman's oedipal complex owed its special form almost entirely to a transfer of traits from the pregenital relationship with the mother onto the genital relationship with the father. The early Kleinians (Jones 1935; Klein 1928) proposed that an innate drive, rather than penis envy, impelled the girl into the heterosexual oedipal situation. Others also vigorously questioned the centrality of penis envy in female psychosexual development, in terms of its inevitability and its meaning (Chasseguet-Smirgel 1970; Grossman and Stewart 1976; Horney 1924; Schafer 1974). Researchers in early infant and child development (Moore 1976) pointed out that the observation of sexual differences did not come as late as Freud proposed, so that reaction to it could not explain the entry into the oedipal period. Others beside Fenichel questioned the inevitability of a negative oedipal preceding the positive (Edgecomb and Burgner 1975). There has been serious disagreement about the girl's supposed weaker motivation for resolving the oedipal conflict, and the implications of this for the formation of the superego (Bernstein 1990; Blum 1976; Gilligan 1982; Schafer 1974).

In this paper we will address the so-called "positive oedipal" triangular situation and the development of heterosexual interests in girls. Our focus will highlight the girl's conflicted entry into heterosexual triangular development. In the traditional "old-fashioned" family situation, a little girl, three to six years old, begins to feel that her mother, her primary object, is her rival for father's affection and interest. This rivalry threatens her basic security, because of frightening fantasies of loss of maternal nurture, and evokes conflicts about loyalties to the two parents. At this age, the little boy's primary caretaker and object of blossoming (positive) oedipal desires are one and the same: his moth-er. His rivalrous and angry feelings are directed primarily toward his father, on whom he does not depend in the same way as he does upon his mother.

Thus, separation issues are not as much in the foreground with the boy at this time as they are with the girl.

We are not saying that boys do not have separation issues. However, the typical situation for little girls at this stage of development (the entry into tri-angulation) brings up separation issues with particular intensity. Nor are we saying that girls' oedipal struggles are more difficult than those of boys—only that they are different. Ultimately, of course, both girls and boys have to deal with the developmental tasks of loosening infantile ties to internal parental objects and integrating disparate parental imagos.

In emphasizing one component of the triangular picture, separation issues, we acknowledge that we are extracting one aspect of a very complex process, and that we run the risk thereby of misconception and oversimplification. Indeed, different and intricate patterns of anxieties, urges, fantasies, defenses, and object relationships comprise the oedipal phase for each sex.

We deliberately speak of separation *issues*, not separation problems. Sep-aration and psychic development are interwoven, beginning in infancy with separation of self from object, and proceeding to the establishment of object constancy and a rudimentary sense of self, the achievement of a solid core gender identity, and a sense of bodily autonomy. Disruptions and conflicts in these areas can lead to major problems such as ego deficits and separation anxieties. And there are characteristic separation tasks that must be handled throughout *all* stages of development. Colarusso (1997) has outlined complex issues of separation-individuation as they occur throughout the life cycle. We will build on the observations of the many psychoanalysts who have written about the role of separation issues in the girl's oedipal complex.

Contemporary theorists such as Chodorow (1978) and Lerner (1980) have suggested that separation is especially difficult and salient for the little girl as compared to the little boy. Chodorow posited that in the course of development the girl must separate from the primary object, the mother, while she identifies with her as the same-sexed object. In contrast, his identification with the same- sexed object, the father, helps the boy with separation from the mother, but leaves him more vulnerable to an exaggerated need for autonomy. Chodorow suggested that the boundaries between mothers and daughters are more permeable and less defined than those between mothers and sons, and she argued that the girl's oedipal complex is affected by these configurations:

> *The turn to the father, however, is embedded in a girl's external relationship to her mother and in her relation to her mother as internal object.... Every step of the way, as the analysts describe it, a girl develops her relationship to her father, while looking back at her mother—to see if her mother is envious, to make sure she is in fact separate, to see if in this way she can win her mother, to see if she is really independent. Her turn to her father is both an attack on her mother and an expression of love for her.... The male and female oedipal complex are asymmetrical. A girl's love for her father and rivalry with her mother is always tempered by love for her mother, even against her will [pp. 126–127].*

Echoing these ideas, Burch (1997) linked them to the myth of Persephone. She cogently described the girl's attempt to hold on to the mother "while she embraces the father," and concluded that "the myth of Demeter and Persephone more aptly describes the daughter's developmental crisis" (p. 19).

Chodorow's arguments have been influential in laying forth the differences between girls' and boys' situations in family oedipal relationships. While we agree with many of her descriptions, we question her conclusions about the permeability of the girl's ego boundaries, which seem to us to be overly generalized and not necessarily true.[3] This kind of thinking has perhaps un-intentionally furthered the belief that girls are more prone to preoedipal pa-thology and fixation than are boys. Hoffman (2000) suggested that relational analysts tend to subordinate conflicts over oedipal passions to earlier relational issues, and that a lack of appreciation of girls' passion in psychoanalytic theory in general has resulted in a preoedipalization of their dynamics. "It thus makes sense to consider that it is much safer to talk about object relations than about powerful sexual and aggressive feelings" (p. 16).

Lax (1995) identified aspects of separation in the oedipal period, though in the context of penis envy. Person (1982) stressed that the little girl is more intimidated in the oedipal situation than the little boy (that is to say, less able to show overt hostility and competition) because her rival, the mother, is also her source of nurturing. Tyson (1989) and Chasseguet-Smirgel (1970) have made related points about the importance of the girl's tie to the mother in the shape, progression into, and resolution of the girl's oedipal situation. Benjamin (1990) and Torok (1992) suggested that conflicted preoedipal relationships with their mothers predispose girls to difficulties in owning and enjoying their sexuality.

CLINICAL MATERIAL

We have selected the following examples from many possible cases to elucidate separation issues experienced by female patients in relationship to their moth-ers within the context of heterosexual triangular situations. These patients were relatively well functioning, neurotic individuals with no serious impairments of

---

3 Research (Olesker 1990) has documented gender-linked differences in infants' and toddlers' achievement of the awareness of psychological separateness from their mothers. Girls seem to become aware of their separateness earlier than boys. We interpret this finding as support for the argument that girls tend to be more sensitized to and interested in issues of relatedness and separateness where their mothers are concerned, and not as an indication that they have more difficulty establishing the boundaries between self and internal primary object.

ego functions or object relations. In each of these examples there is a theme of conflict between two separate worlds. One world, the mother-daughter dyad, is contrasted with the other world, that of secret and dangerously exciting sexuality with a man. While the material appears initially to be organized around dyadic separation issues, eventually triangular competitive and sexual themes emerge as the central conflict.

Case I

The following session is from the second year of the analysis of a young woman about to be married, Miss R. In the session we will themes of attraction to a father figure, of missing her mother and competing with her, and of fears of bodily injury and separation as punishment for winning the rivalry are all present. The image of cutting off a finger in response to a pleasurable, but conflicted, experience occurs as well. Miss R's husband-to-be is a man she considers a good, comfortable choice, but not someone towards whom she feels strong passion. At this point in the analysis the patient was talking about her plans for her wedding and the analyst's upcoming vacation. The approaching wedding has re-evoked anxious feelings and fantasies that her father was always more interested in her than he was in her mother. In the sessions preceding this one, Miss R had spoken about her dog, imagining what it would be like to be the dog, and how miserable it would be to be pushed outside into the wintry cold away from desired warmth and closeness. She also reported a vignette about her hairdresser, who was "a bitch, beneath a nice exterior … so busy talking about a party she was giving while I had to sit there. There she was behind me showing off and I had to wait." The analyst interpreted Miss R's anger about being pushed away into the cold while the analyst was off enjoying her private life. In response, the patient became tearful and vented some of her hurt and anger at the analyst. This material appeared to be garden-variety dyadic reaction to separation from the analyst.

In the next session the patient began, "This is very close to my wedding, but I'm having these images that are just terrible—images about cutting tomatoes and cutting off the end of a finger. I think it was an image, but not a dream. I don't know. A terrible thing that gives me anxiety to think of, so I tried to think of a field of flowers. [Note the similarity of this imagery of a field of flowers to the setting of the Persephone myth.] But every time I thought of that particular image I felt the pain of it. In my chest. It's like my whole self. A whole bodily feeling. How easy it is to lose the extremities. It seems like all is going so well now that it scares me. Work is going good. Bob [her fiancé] and I have a lot of new friends. Last night we went to dinner with this guy and his date. I felt out of my league. I enjoyed the whole ambiance of the expensive dinner, but it all scares me. And then I come home and have images of cutting off my finger! It's like I can see the fruits of my efforts. I'd be the one chopping. It would be my finger. No one else would be responsible for it. It would bring me back to reality, the real world, and I would know this is the world I live in. This is a situation I could manage. As awful as it would be, it would be *my* hand and *my* problem."

The analyst asked her to tell her more about that. "I don't know. It's like everything keeps getting better and better, and it seems very scary. At the dinner we were at it's almost as if people are taking me away from things that are familiar to me. It's like I really missed my mom. My parents were out of town this weekend. I wanted to talk to her. I feel pulled away then."

The analyst asked, "Pulled away?"

"Pulled away from my mom. I now spend evenings with people she doesn't *know*. There's kind of a loneliness in me. Maybe like the same thing when I went to college. When I went away, I was there with all people my mom didn't know, and when we went to this dinner it's similar. I feel like I don't really belong, and I feel pulled away from what I feel is so comfortable. I'm becoming someone I'm not—in relationship to me. I don't know why I'm comparing all the time, but the whole thing makes me feel more alienated from my mother."

Miss R went on to say that the other guy, who is in the computer business, turns out to have the same first name as her father: Jim. She commented, "It is really strange that it's the same name. I'm afraid with this guy because he is so sophisticated…. He's a real good catch, but that bothers me because I don't want to feel that way—I'm engaged to Bob." Then she described how Jim R, the guy with her father's name, had said forcefully to his date at the dinner, "Taste this."

"I was attracted to him but I don't like domineering men. Whoa—that reminds me of my dad a little because he can be that way. 'Take a bite,' he'd say. I'd say no.[4] He wouldn't force it of course, but the date, she'd do whatever the guy said. And it was like Chuck, my former boyfriend, who was also in computers. And this guy… Wait a minute, I gave you the wrong name, the name I gave you, Jim R, is really a cousin of my dad. The guy's name is really Tim R. I don't know why I called him Jim R—I used to have a crush on Jim."

Her thoughts turned again to competition; this time she compared herself with Tim's date (her rival, the woman belonging to the father substitute). The patient said, "We both can't be good, we both can't be successful. It's like a see-saw. We both can't be up at the same time."

The analyst said, "This worry about alienation from your mother stems from your concern that you both can't be successful at the same time." The patient responded, "Well, I think that's true because we can never be together at the same level. Cutting off the finger is the same thing. It's like separating from a part of yourself. Like I could destruct and kill off a part of myself. Like if a little part of my finger was like my relationship with my mother and I cut it off.

Maybe going to dinner with that guy last night, the four of us, is like a separation. Maybe it's also a separation from my fiancé, because I was really

---

4 Note the similarity to the eating aspects of the Persephne myth, in which Persephone is enticed, fooled, or on her own eats pomegranate seeds—the forbidden fruit. It is this prohibited act that seals her fate, and forces her return each year to the underworld to reign as Hades' queen.

interested in the other guy. To be safely married to someone not so sophis-ticated as the other guy [and not as sexually exciting, we believe] is like my mother's world. If I step out of the world of my mom, I become disconnected. It's interesting and yet funny. With the same name as my dad, this guy seems more dangerous, like dangerous new territory. I don't trust this guy. Or my cousin. They'd be condescending with me just like my dad. It was exciting to enter into his territory but always humiliating."

This session had been preceded by separation material that appeared to be preoedipal, related to the mother-daughter dyad. It concerned two people, the analyst/mother and the patient/daughter, and the parent/dog, hairdresser/client themes of early loss—being pushed out, ignored, and rejected. It became apparent that this material had evolved into triadic sexual concerns. The patient was preoccupied with an attempt to balance two different worlds. She contrast-ed the world of the close-knit comfort of mother and family with the world of excitement and forbidden sexuality. She clearly linked her father with the male relative of the same name. The slip she made in the matter of the name demarcated the emergence of a conflict about an incestuous attraction with its accompanying anxieties and guilt. Her anxieties about competitive rivalry with her mother led to fears of being alienated from and losing her mother, and being punished by having a part of herself cut off. The cut-off finger can be understood and interpreted in terms of castration, but this patient's associations alerted us to the important awareness that it referred toss of her relationship with her mother as well.[5]

---

5   A cut-off member or part of a finger is an element that appears in many fairy tales such as "the enchanted pig" and "the little mermaid," both of which are discussed by Bettleheim (1975). He attributed to these images the notion of a girl giving up a piece of herself (the hymen) in order to achieve a sexual or marital partnership. In addition, he suggested that it symbolized fantasies of castration: loss of a phallus. Our material suggests a new interpretation. The cut-off part represents not only castration or defloration, but also being cut off from the mother. In her mind, the girl fears that in order to marry she must lose her mother.

The two worlds Miss R described concretely parallel the story of Persephone, who is queen of the underworld—"the world below"—and mate to her uncle Hades for part of the year, but who returns to be with her mother, Demeter, in the fertile "world above" for the rest of it. A balancing act is required to keep her mother's love and nurture while at the same time she becomes sexual with a man. Competitive rivalry, incestuous heterosexual attraction and anxiety, and conflicts around loyalty to one parent versus the other are all present.

In the transference a similar situation was developing. The patient talked about her competitiveness with the analyst, and her desire to be just like her and to possess everything the analyst had. She anxiously described a movie in which a young woman moves in with and wants to be like her new roommate. The patient recognized herself in this character. Eventually the character takes over the roommate's possessions, her lover—her entire life. The patient's competitive and aggressive feelings were emerging in fuller form.

Case 2

Mrs. L, a married woman in her forties, was in the fifth year of her analysis. In the clinical material to be presented the main theme is that winning the competition with her mother is dangerous and means loss. As in the previous case and the one to follow, the patient had associations involving losing a part of herself. This can be understood as fear of losing the mother, as well as of bodily injury as punishment for unacceptable wishes.

Prior to this session, Mrs. L had been talking about her mother, who, according to the patient, did not approve of her growing up. "Maybe she wanted me to stay a little girl." Mrs. L reported anxiety when she realized she had things in common with the analyst, such as the interest in books and art that she deduced from observing the analyst's office. She went on to describe how she and her mother would do lots of things together—cooking, for example—and how homesick she would become when she was not with her mother. She described her mother as sometimes depressed, thus available only erratically. "She would turn on and off in terms of her interest in me." These feelings about an unavailable mother sounded at this point like dyadic preoedipal material. The analyst interpreted the patient's parallel experience in the transference: that is, that the analyst, being not always available, seemed like her erratic mother. The patient responded, "I got so screwed up in my relationship with my mother. The more successful I got, the less she was there for me." Competition is visible here as a precipitant for the emergence of anxieties about separation.

The next session began with Mrs. L talking about her going away to college. "I remember when I went off to college in the big city. There would be drinking parties, smoking, smoking dope, drugs, marijuana. My mother would have had a hard time with that. I think that she had a vested interest in me staying a child. She was not aware of it, but it was there. The attachment that we had was so great. My mother often says, 'I love how you used to be.' My mother never saw that part of me. The cut-up part of me." The analyst asked, "Cut-up part?" The patient responded, "The silly part, the sexual part of me. That world was not known to her—the party me. It gave me a sense of myself. I was separated from my mother, which was good for me. I became a person unto myself; I wasn't that when I was with her. I figured out who I was. The first year was a very big adjustment. At first I was very lonely and very unhappy and then I found I preferred it; I liked it and I wanted to stay at school. When I was there, I felt separate. College was a very different world than the world at home. The world at home was so different I was shocked when I returned. The tempo of life differed—my mother around… I missed that world at college. I knew all about the seasons."

The patient replied to the analyst's question about what she meant: "When I got away from school and I felt I lost that part of myself. I would look at the sky and get a sense of time—spring, the smell of plants. I was never at college for the summer. Fall was gorgeous. At first the days lasted long like they do when you're younger. They go too fast when you are older. The rhythm of life was different. I felt when I was there, finally after a period of adjustment, I had grown up. I remember missing my mother a lot but then I got used to it and then I didn't want to come home after a while. The summers, they were hot—no air conditioning, sticky, unbearable, hot, and bugs. But at school you had no sense of the world outside.... In the dorm we lived next door to poverty, the ghetto.

Incest was the thing; it was all over. Lots of mentally retarded, with a lot of incest between fathers and daughters. These were poor, poor people.... There were a lot of flat-head faces [i.e., developmentally disabled]. Everybody talked about it, everybody knew about it. For my community service, I went into a house once with a dirt floor. There were pockets of communities like that, poverty like you would never believe. Some experience! There was one preacher who owned the whole neighborhood and I met his daughter. She couldn't wait to get out of that place.

"I remember so much missing my mother. She was upset that I was gone and yet I think she still had a life of her own. She missed me; she didn't fall apart, but she did miss me. However, she was never distraught. I was more missing her, more attached, at the beginning. I would come back and spend two months at home and everything was okay, and then I would be trying to get back to myself. I missed that part of myself. I would wake up there unburdened.... It's like there are two different worlds—my mother's world and my school world. I think that they don't have to be antagonistic.

"When I got married, again I felt like I lost half of myself. I had been very dependent on my mother, who I think felt that she was losing me. I was so attached to her. I felt unseparated from her. Just being with her made me feel better. I had a good marriage and I produced a life of my own. I was in my own world. Before that everything was close and good, and after that, when I would go back to the city where she was living, I would feel suffocated by her.

430

Something about the intensity. I would feel that I was a child, and I couldn't stand it. Something changed. I grew up. I started to feel separate. I had felt before that she could take my suffering away just by my being with her, and I felt that I could do the same for her. When I got married, some-thing switched. My husband and I had a life of our own, a house of our own, we were happy. My mother really didn't know me. She didn't know what I was like. Before, I would tell her all my worries. It was something about me being young. I would get annoyed later on, the way she would talk, but I felt like I was stuck in the category of 'little girl,' which drove me crazy. She would lecture to me. She would have a critical edge toward me or others."

When the analyst asked why the criticism, she was surprised by the patient's reply: "Well, there may have been something about competition, but I don't know what about. That I wasn't good enough. That was the feeling that I always had." The analyst interpreted the defense: "If you feel you are not good enough then you don't have to fear competition." The patient responded, "It feels like I have this hidden part of me, this competitive part. Dangerous. I do go after what I want. I don't know if my mother approved or not. After I was married [she married a man in the same profession as her father] I wasn't there for my mother. I couldn't go shopping with her. Couldn't spend enough time. I felt guilty. [Silence.] I am thinking of competitive. Competition means loss. The better I did, the less I had in common with my mother…. I felt I lost my mother when I went to work. One more separation. I felt like it was to go off and do something by myself, on my own, in a different space. It has something to do with competition."

The analyst asked, "How?"

"There were parts of my mother that were very feminine and vivacious and would go to parties, dress very feminine, very flirtatious—but not seductive. Appropriate. And she, I think, was really disappointed with my father. I remember her being angry with me. I had dated a boy for two years and we went somewhere to make out. My hair was disheveled, and she told me I was grounded, and she was mad.... Dating was OK but she did not want anything sexual. She was very threatened by real sexual passionate attachment.... All I want to do now is relax and dig in my garden. I want to play and dig in the dirt. In spring I would go into the garden and weed it. I just loved putting my fingers in the dirt and the smell of the dirt and the flowers. There is something about it that is calming. I love to watch things grow.... It piques my curiosity." The session ended with the patient returning to the theme of separations, this time in her experiences at camp.

All these separations—at camp, in college, in marriage, at work—represent "straying from mother." When Persephone strayed from her mother, abduction, rape, and eventually marriage and separation from her mother resulted. This patient, like Miss R, stresses the experience of two different worlds. The world of the intimate closeness with mother again contrasts starkly with the world of exciting forbidden sexuality, parties, and incest. Like Miss R, Mrs. L suffered loss as she entered the world of sexuality. The loss is of a part of herself, and yet she also *finds* a part of herself—the sexual part—that the mother does not know. As the two worlds oscillate, there is throughout this session a merging of separation themes—earlier with later issues and dyadic with triangular ones, such as loss of mother's care, or divisive competition. The patient's guilt is associated with incestuous erotic fantasies of competing with her mother. (Persephone strayed from her mother to go after what she wanted, a special flower, and was abducted.) "It's dangerous to go after what I want" is followed by expressions of guilt. The appearance of associations about seasons and about gardening seem at first glance peculiarly out of place, but they contain underlying meanings of birth, fertility, and periodicity that do seem to fit. Again, the story of Persephone playing in the garden, with the fluctuation of the seasons, is evoked.

Case 3

Miss A had been in analysis for a short time, and was just about to become engaged. Here again, the anticipation of taking on the role and place of the mother as a married woman brings fears of maternal loss and conflicting loyalties to father and mother. An enactment between analyst, fiancé, and patient demonstrates these conflicts.

In the previous session Miss, A had talked about a dream in which she had left some red luggage behind at a train station. She was with a group of people, all of whom had left their luggage. After some hours she returned to the station and was told that it was too late, and she could not get her luggage. She associated to a weekend trip to a rock festival with her boyfriend and a group of his friends. It had been his idea, and it was the first time she had gone on a trip like that. Although she had been apprehensive, it had turned out to be fun. The train reminded her of recent travels. Leaving luggage had something to do with getting married and fears about losing a part of herself. The red was a red flag about something—danger. She was worried that she would not be able to hold her own with her boyfriend. He was considerate, but forceful and sure of himself. She often was afraid that her ideas and needs would be submerged by the strength of his personality. She felt she was "less together" than he was.

We suppose that this phrase contains at least three meanings. In the first sense, she was talking about her emotional state. She felt that he was "more together," less open emotionally, altogether less vulnerable than she was. In the second sense, it referred to her previously articulated notion of the female genitals as "being open," and the male genitals "closed over" (Mayer 1985). Third, and most salient for our discussion, she and her mother would be "less together." Here "less together" referred to separation from her mother, who gave her needed support and care that she feared her boyfriend might not provide. In association to "everybody's luggage," the patient guessed that this referred to something she shared with others who were "in the same boat—like other women." [Retrospectively, we speculate that the "red luggage and being late" may have reflected fears and anticipations about being pregnant: that is, her period being late.] She had previously expressed conflict about having children. Thus, anticipation of being married was evoking feelings of vulnerability (her view of the woman's role).

The analyst suggested to Miss A that this idea of "being in the same boat" was connected with often stated worries that she would become like her mother in ways that she did not like. Earlier in this session the patient had talked about how her mother always let her father have his own way when they traveled. In general she pictured the parental relationship as one in which the mother was dominated by the father. The analyst reflected the patient's worries that she would duplicate her parents' relationship in her own future marriage. The patient agreed. Miss A had in fact uncharacteristically allowed her fiancé to dominate and direct their recent travel plans. The analyst felt that in general Miss A was a very strong and not at all submissive young woman. In this instance, her submissiveness was a stance that actualized the dangerous unconscious desire to take the mother's place. The analyst did not explore this desire at this time.

In the following session Miss, A reported that she had told the dream to her boyfriend, who said it had to do with losing one's freedom (this was clearly *his* concern). She had unconsciously acted out her stated fear, and allowed her boyfriend to be dominant in determining the meaning of the dream. But *she* thought, and stated somewhat hesitantly, that the dream was not about losing freedom, but concerned *friends*. It felt to her that the "something" she was losing might be friends, specifically girlfriends [that is, feminine support]. The analyst supported the patient's tentative explorations by saying that it was the patient's dream, and that it was the *patient's* associations that were important. Thus, the analyst entered a mini-enactment of competition with the boyfriend about whose associations to the dream were important. Miss A had set up a possible rivalry between his interpretation and that of the analyst.

Miss A then began to talk about how she had lost or left behind friends in her moving around the country, to go to college and more recently to follow her boyfriend to his new place of employment. She speculated about her future bridesmaids, one a girlfriend from grade school, one from college. She would like to get in touch with another old girlfriend with whom she had lost contact. She told a story about how she had gotten a brush-off when she had tried to contact another friend. She lamented that she had not been able to make very many new close friends since moving to the area. "The two friends I have made here are both women who have recently lost their mothers. I don't know what that means—a sick fascination with that somehow."

Her thoughts went to her mother, and about times in the past in which she experienced a closeness with her. These associations substantiated the notion that the patient's feeling of loss here referred to the loss of her mother.

She mused, "Sometime in the summer I might want to travel with a girl-friend, but how could I do that, travel with a friend, if I'm engaged? And how would it work being married and maintaining friendships with women?" The analyst asked, "So you are worried about losing your connection with your women friends?"

"Yes." She became tearful. "How can I balance that? How can I find ways to balance my old friends and this new world? The world of women and the world of men. How can I balance these worlds?" She began to cry harder. Her thoughts returned to the coming summer. Maybe she could travel with her women friends then, during that season, separate from her boyfriend. "But that doesn't make sense…."

She was worried about how she would balance her relationships with her mother/analyst and her husband-to-be. This worry was becoming more of a reality as she anticipated stepping into a world where *she* will be wife and mother. Maternal loss is clearly the danger she is experiencing in this material. One important meaning of "losing part of herself" is the loss of female companionship, support, and familiarity. Here again is Persephone's dilemma, by now familiar to us: how to balance these perceived conflicts between the worlds of the mother and of the father. The delicate balance that preserves female attachment, originating with mother, while moving into the world as a sexual woman with a man, is represented poignantly by Miss A's anxiety about how to have both without losing in either sphere. The issue of loyalty faced by this patient, which we feel is a typical feminine dilemma, is an example of the divergent type of conflict described by Kris (1988), which requires that one object or aim be given up in the interest of another.

DISCUSSION

In this clinical material we see issues of separation and triangular conflicts occurring simultaneously. In all three cases, fears of bodily damage intertwine with fears of loss in reaction to the threats of oedipal gratification. These female patients had relatively close and untroubled relationships with their mothers. In our previous work on the Persephone myth (1997), in which we used bi-ographical as well as clinical material, we also found these kinds of conflicts around separation. These previous cases showed greater difficulties in separat-ing from their mothers, manifested in these women's inability to marry or to enjoy sex. Troubled preoedipal relationships with their mothers made this later separation phase more perilous, and contributed to their sexual symptoms. Their conscious identification with the Persephone of Greek myth alerted us to an important central unconscious conflict: the division of allegiance between mother/caretaker and father/lover. Our current cases demonstrate and elabo-rate our thesis that separation issues during the "oedipal" triangular phase do not *necessarily* indicate earlier or major separation issues. Nor do they neces-sarily represent signs of major preoedipal pathology, fixations, or regressions.

All of these female patients, like many others in our clinical experience, have the idea that passionate sexuality, especially with a "forbidden" male, is opposed by the mother. Sexuality is seen as belonging to the mother and not to the girl. This perception produces the striking need in the girl to compart-mentalize intrapsychic representations of a sexual and nonsexual self. We view this compartmentalization primarily as defensive, in the interest of sustaining the tie to the mother while entertaining an erotized relation with the father. Thus passions and sexuality are relegated to a secret part of the self, separate from mother. The feminine body, with its unseen inner cavities and passages lends itself to this psychic sequestering. This kind of inner separation does not necessarily mean, as has been suggested by others, that girls have greater difficulty than boys in separating self from object. We suggest that this kind of psychic compartmentalization is a typical developmental occurrence, with adaptive as well as neurotically conflicted meanings.

The typical dangers of childhood—loss of the object, loss of the love of the object, castration, and superego guilt and/or punishment—have been thought to mark and signal a developmental chronology. However, as Brenner (1982) and more recently Nersessian (1998) have suggested, these feared calamities are inextricably interwoven with each other. Brenner writes that they appear in sequence during development, but later become so interwoven that they cannot be artificially separated (p. 94). We feel that there has often been a spurious assignment of level of development to the differing calamities— separation from and loss of the object and loss of the love of the object are considered necessarily preoedipal, while castration anxiety is seen as more characteristic of the oedipal period. If traumata around separation characterize the femi-nine triangular situation, but they are automatically schematized as early-or preoedipal, then it would follow logically, but erroneously, that girls tend to be fixated at earlier developmental levels. We argue that this view is erroneous both theoretically and clinically. Person (1988) has pointed out that fears of loss of love, which are part of the oedipal constellation for women, are often expressed in oral, sometimes cannibalistic, terms. We concur that competitive fears can take these forms because "the object of competition is also the source

437

of nurturant and dependent gratification" (p. 170). We also argue that castration fears are not necessarily characteristic of "later" developmental phases. Galenson and Roiphe (1971), for example, observed that castration anxiety occurs very early, preoedipally. Others, such as Sachs (1962), have argued that castration anxiety often carries very early preoedipal terrors of annihilation and separation. In our patients, we see the inextricable intertwining of castration and/or female genital anxieties with separation anxieties and oedipal guilts. For example, in our current cases, the appearance of fantasies of a "cut-up" or "cut-off" or "lost" part of the self were linked to the idea of a severed maternal relationship. That is to say, they referred to separation and not only to lost or damaged genital body parts.

Brenner (1982) writes that "passionate sexual wishes characteristic of the oedipal phase are most intimately bound up in every child's mind with object loss, that is, with the disappearance of one or both parents" (p. 103). We feel, however, that maternal object loss or separation has especially important significance for a little girl during the oedipal period. Because the mother remains nurturer while she is, at the same time, a sexual object for the boy, his positive oedipal yearnings are not as fraught with fears of her loss. Out of fear, he may renounce his sexual longings for his mother, but he is not required to give her up as caretaking object. Earlier dyadic needs for nurturing are easily masked by his triadic oedipal desires. Castration anxieties, therefore, are more visible in this situation. For the little girl the fact that her rival is the primary caregiver gives a greater weight to object loss and separation issues in her triadic picture.

Chodorow, Person, and many others have stressed such gendered differences. We emphasize that these differences between males and females do not necessarily reflect fixations at or characteristics from different levels of development.

We feel that this idea has important clinical consequences. Women are infantilized and demeaned if their separation fears are routinely perceived as primitive or infantile. Furthermore, misdiagnosis or misinterpretation of the level of the separation issues can produce a stalemated or endlessly regressive treatment. It is true that preoedipal issues around separation always influence and are intermingled with later separation material. The triangular separation issues we have focused upon, however, do not necessarily signal or originate in earlier separation problems.

The separation themes and defenses characteristic of triadic conflicts for women, as shown above, can be differentiated clinically from earlier material. First, they frequently are precipitated by important developmental steps in the lives of women, such as starting college, a first sexual encounter, marriage, or a new career. Second, they intertwine with rivalrous competitions with other women, such as a new job or a successful love affair. Above all, to be so designated, they necessarily appear in the context of triangular relationships, be they rivalries with mother for father's love (or vice versa), or the working out of loyalties between two compelling loved ones.

Desires for agency with regard to erotic sexuality and passion are frequently and typically concealed by females. A sense of agency is hidden behind inhibition, clinging, and secrecy. Women often hid their eroticism with the defensive stance of helplessness or externalization; Persephone claimed that "Hades made me do it." For Oedipus, in contrast, the defensive stance was that "I didn't know I did it": that is, disavowal or denial. The girl's defensive need is particularly exaggerated when realistic problems with a mother make such developmental forays into sexuality as dangerous in reality as in fantasy.

In her exploration of the preoedipal origins of women's problems with superego development and expressing anger, Tyson (1998) focused on the mother/daughter relationship. In several of her clinical vignettes, we note that separation conflicts were precipitated either by a fantasy about marriage or the actuality of an upcoming marriage. In one case, for example, a young woman about to be married struggled in the transference with fears that the analyst/mother would disapprove of the engagement and marriage. The patient expressed fears that she would be ejected, and not be able to see the analyst again.

Is this not the very dilemma we have been describing: the need to balance the fear of separation from the mother with the wish to move into the adult sexual world? Here again is the fantasy that heterosexual victory might mean the loss of her mother/female analyst.

Tyson also described the case of a little girl whose favorite game was to pretend that she was Cinderella and that her idealized fairy godmother gave her everything she wanted. Thus, she got the prince. With the fairy godmother as her procurer, she avoided the danger of assertively or aggressively taking what she wanted for herself. Tyson reported that the girl had a history of provoking her mother's anger and then fearfully clinging to her. Tyson's focus was on the preoedipal origins of these narcissistic entitlements and sadomasochistic interactions. We would add that this little girl's conflict around anger at that moment in the treatment had triangular meanings as well: that is, she wanted to marry the prince. As Tyson clearly illustrated, the rage and fear of abandonment had preoedipal determinants, but they emerged in full bloom with the "oedipal" wish to get the prince. Thus, we think that the oedipal situation with its anxieties about maternal loss gave added intensity both to her anger and to her conflicts about its expression.

This paper is an attempt to examine the paradigm of triangular development as it applies to women: that is, to "feminize" the so-called female oedipal complex and to clarify its clinical implications. We have found that issues of mother- daughter separation are a fundamental part of the female oedipal paradigm.

For that reason we feel that the triangular phase for girls is not well characterized by the Oedipus myth, and propose renaming it the "Persephone complex." Persephone's compromise between innocence and sexuality, her conflicting loyalties to her mother and her father, and her means of traversing the boundary between childhood and adulthood typify for us central aspects of female development.

In future work we hope to examine homosexual interests, the so-called negative oedipal conflicts, and the role of aggression and superego development in women. Many additional questions can be raised, and we look forward to further discourse with our colleagues.

REFERENCES

Benjamin, J. (1990). The alienation of desire: Women's masochism and ideal love. In *Essential Papers on the Psychology of Women,* ed. C. Zanardi. New York: New York University Press, pp. *455–479.*

Bernstein, D. (1983). The female Oedipal complex. *In Female Identity Conflict in Clinical Practice*, ed. N. Freedman & B. Distel. Northvale, NJ: Aronson, 1993, pp. *101–142.*

Blum, H. P. (1976). Masochism, The Ego Ideal, and The Psychology of Women *J. Amer. Psychoanal. Assn.24:157–191*

Bonaparte, M. (1953). *Female Sexuality.* New York: International Universities Press.

Brenner, C. (1982). T*he Mind in Conflict.* New York: International Universities Press.

Burch, B. (1997). *Other Women.* New York: Columbia University Press.

Chasseguet-Smirgel, J. (1970). Feminine guilt and the Oedipus complex. In *Female Sexuality*, ed. J. Chasseguet-Smirgel. London: Karnac, 1992, pp. *94–133.*

Chodorow, N. (1978). *The Reproduction of Mothering: Psychoanalysis and the Sociology of Gender.* Berkeley: University of California Press.

Colarusso, C.A. (1997). Separation-individuation processes in middle adult-hood: The fourth individuation. In *The Seasons of Life: Separation Individuation Perspectives,* ed. S. Akhtar & S. Kramer. Northvale, NJ: Aronson, pp. *73–94.*

Deutsch, H. (1930). The Significance of Masochism in the Mental Life of Women *Int. J. Psycho-Anal.*11:*48–60*

Edgcumbe, R. and Burgner, M. (1975). The Phallic-Narcissistic Phase—A Differentiation Between Preoedipal and Oedipal Aspects of Phallic Development *Psychoanal. Study Child*30:*161–180*

Fenichel, O. (1934). Further light upon the pre-oedipal phase in girls. In *The Collected Papers of Otto Fenichel.* New York: Norton, 1953, pp. *241–288.*

Foley, H. P. (1994). Background: The Eleusinian mysteries and women's rites for Demeter. In *The Homeric Hymn to Demeter,* ed. H.P. Foley. Princeton: Princeton University Press, 1994, pp. *65–75.*

Freud, S. (1925). Some psychical consequences of the anatomical distinction between the sexes. *Standard Edition*19:*171–179.*

——— (1931). Female sexuality. Standard Edition21:*221–243.*

Galenson, E. and Roiphe, H. (1971). The Impact of Early Sexual Discovery on Mood, Defensive Organization, and Symbolization *Psychoanal. Study Child*26: *195–216*

Gilligan, C. (1982). *In a Different Voice.* Cambridge: Harvard University Press.

Grossman, W. I. and Stewart, W. A. (1976). Penis Envy: From Childhood Wish to Developmental Metaphor *J. Amer. Psychoanal. Assn.*24:*193–212*

Hoffman, L. (1999). Passions in Girls and Women *J. Amer. Psychoanal. Assn.*47: *1145–1168*

Holtzman, D., & Kulish, N. (1997). *The Hymen and the Loss of Virginity.* Northvale, NJ: Aronson.

Horney, K. (1924). On the Genesis of the Castration Complex in Women *Int. J. Psycho-Anal.*5:*50–65*

Jones, E. (1935). Early Female Sexuality *Int. J. Psycho-Anal.*16:*263–273*

Klein, M. (1928). Early stages of the oedipus conflict. In *Love, Guilt and Reparation and Other Works: The Writings of Melanie Klein. Vol 1.* London: Hogarth Press, 1975, pp. *186–198.*

Kris, A. O. (1988). Some Clinical Applications of the Distinction Between Divergent and Convergent Conflicts *Int. J. Psycho-Anal.69:431–441*

Kulish, N. and Holtzman, D. (1998). Persephone, the Loss of Virginity and the Female Oedipal Complex *Int. J. Psycho-Anal.79:57–71*

Lampl-De Groot, A. (1928). The Evolution of the Oedipus Complex in Women *Int. J. Psycho-Anal.9:332–345*

Lax, R.F. (1995). Motives and determinants of girls' penis envy in the negative oedipal phase. *Journal of Clinical Psychoanalysis4:297–314.*

Lerner, H.F. (1980). Internal prohibitions against female anger. *American Journal of Psychoanalysis40:137–147.*

Mayer, E. L. (1985). 'Everybody Must be Just Like Me': Observations on Female Castration Anxiety *Int. J. Psycho-Anal.66:331–347*

Moore, B. E. (1976). Freud and Female Sexuality—A Current View *Int. J. PsychoAnal.57:287–300*

Nersessian, E. (1998). A cat as fetish: A contribution to the theory of fetishism. *Int. J. Psycho-Anal.7:713–725.*

Olesker, W. (1990). Sex Differences During the Early Separation-Individuation Process: Implications for Gender Identity Formation *J. Amer. Psychoanal. Assn. 38:325–346*

Person, E.S. (1982). Women working: Fears of failure, deviance and success. *J. Am. Acad. Psychoanal. Dyn. Psychiatr.10:67–84.*

——— (1985). The erotic transference in women and in men: Differences and consequences. *J. Am. Acad. Psychoanal. Dyn. Psychiatr.13:159–180.*

Sachs, L. J. (1962). A Case of Castration Anxiety Beginning at Eighteen Months *J. Amer. Psychoanal. Assn.10:329–337*

Schafer, R. (1974). Problems in Freud's Psychology of Women *J. Amer. Psychoanal. Assn.22:459–485*

Torok, M. (1970). The significance of penis envy in women. In *Female Sexuality*, ed. J. Chasseguet-Smirgel. London: Karnac, 1992, pp. *171–212.*

Tyson, P. (1997). Love and hate and growing up female. Paper presented to the Miami Psychoanalytic Society, November 9.

CHAPTER 15

The Femininization of the Female Oedipal Complex, Part II: Aggression Reconsidered

(2003). J. Amer. Psychoanal. Assn., (51)(4):1127–1151

With Deanna Holtzman

This paper examines and explores the manifestations of aggressive impulses in the so-called female oedipal complex. The authors describe how competitive aggression on the part of young girls, seemingly missing in children's stories and myths, is unconsciously inhibited, disguised, or externalized. They report similar phenomena in women patients involved in triangular conflicts, and present a selected review of the literature on the inhibition of aggression within the female triangular situation. Stressing dynamic patterns in the object relationships in the female triangular situation, the authors offer a psychological explanation for this inhibition. They present clinical material to demonstrate how overt murderous and competitive aggression toward the mother appears after considerable analytic work. They conclude that girls and women frequently relinquish a sense of agency over both aggression and sexuality in dealing with triangular conflicts, to preserve a safe relationship with their mothers.

Mirror, mirror, on the wall, who's the fairest of them all? With these words, the evil queen, Snow White's stepmother, expresses her competitive feelings toward all other females, and especially Snow White. When the magic mirror shows that Snow White has surpassed her, the queen's envy and rivalrous hatred of her beautiful stepdaughter erupts. She plots to kill her younger rival with a poisoned apple.

As in most fairy tales, Snow White, the heroine, is a beautiful, sweet, and innocent young girl. Dangerous rivalrous impulses are portrayed as emanating not from within the young girl, who is cast in the role of victim, but from outside her. It is the older woman, in her multiple guises of witch, stepmother, enchantress, and evil fairy, who is the purveyor of powerful aggressive motives and actions. Thus, competitive aggression is present in tales about females, but typically does not originate with the young heroine; it is displaced or projected, or it occurs by accident (Bettelheim 1975; Palmer 1988; Dahl 1989; Person 1988).[1] Some familiar examples are Heidi in *Heidi*, Dorothy in *The Wizard of Oz*, Wendy in *Peter Pan*, and the princess in "Sleeping Beauty." We have observed similar phenomena in women patients involved in triangular so- called oedipal conflicts; their aggression is unconsciously inhibited, disguised, or externalized.

In contrast, boy protagonists in children's tales are active, courageous, and adventuresome, going out on their own to slay dragons and win princesses. In the Greek story of Oedipus, the male's aggression is out in the open. In his travels Oedipus comes upon a man, Laius, with whom he argues as to who has the right of way. Not knowing that Laius is actually his father, he kills him.

Oedipus, again unknowingly, marries his mother, rules the kingdom, and has four children. This tale of murder and incest contributed to the insights into infantile sexuality that became the basis for Freud's understanding of the dynamics of the oedipus complex. The classic story was universalized over time to apply to girls, as well as boys. The theme of sexual impulses toward the opposite-sexed parent, and murderous rivalry toward the parent of the same sex, was the paradigm. However, the story of Oedipus is based on a male model and on early and incomplete psychoanalytic concepts of female psychosexual

---

1 Sophocles' and Euripides' versions of the story, Electra is masochistic, helpless, and envious, and renounces sexuality.

development. These ideas have been subject to intense scrutiny and reformulation in more recent psychoanalytic discourse. It is our contention that one
central gender-related difference in the dynamics of the triangular situation
is the role and the expression of rivalrous aggression.

We and others (Holtzman and Kulish 2000; Bernstein 1993; Person
1985) have argued that the Oedipus story does not adequately or accurately
fit the typical triangular situation of females. One reason for this is the
pattern of object relationships at the time the girl approaches the "oedipal"
stage of development. Typically, the major caretaker in the family is the
mother, who now becomes the daughter's rival. The girl's blossoming sexual
interest in her father (and mother) means that she is faced with a conflict
that threatens her basic security with her caretaker. Thus, a conscious sense
of agency with regard to overt expression of murderous aggression and
rivalrous sexuality is exceedingly dangerous. Chodorow (1978) has suggested that separation is especially difficult and salient for the little girl as
compared to the little boy. The little girl must separate from her mother,
the primary object, while at the same time identifying with her as the
same-sexed object. Thus, according to Chodorow, the boundaries between
girls and their mothers are less defined and more permeable, and the ties
stronger, than those between boys and their mothers. The situation for the
little boy is fraught with its own dangers, but is significantly different. In
the boy's positive oedipal situation, the rival is the father, who is not typically the major source of nurturing caretaking in the family. Chodorow's
arguments have been influential in laying forth the differences between
girls' and boys' situations in family oedipal relationships.

Chasseguet-Smirgel (1970), Person (1985), Tyson (1989), and Lax (1995)
have also made relevant points about the importance of the girl's tie to the
mother in the shape, progression into, and resolution of the girl's triangular
or "oedipal" situation. From a viewpoint similar to ours, Reenkola (2002) says
that when the mother becomes the rival of the girl, "this is a fateful combina-

tion. The ambivalence of love and hate towards the mother arouses immense guilt in a girl, having a powerful impact on the vicissitudes of aggression in women" (p. xv).

We have proposed that this developmental conflict for females, in which we have found that anxieties about separation from the mother are prominent, be called the *persephone complex*, from the Greek myth of Persephone. The story is as follows: Kore, the young daughter of Demeter and Zeus, is gathering flowers in a meadow with other young girls. She strays from her mother's side to pluck a particularly beautiful narcissus that has attracted her. The earth opens suddenly and Hades, God of Death and the Underworld, abducts her. (Some versions of the story make a rape more explicit.) When Kore next appears in the Homeric Hymn, she is with Hades in the Underworld, and has taken on the new name of Persephone. In the meantime, Demeter has descended from Olympus to search the earth frantically for her daughter. In her fury and pain, she causes famine and drought to spread over the earth. In response to this catastrophe, Zeus persuades Hades to release Persephone. However, Hades tricks Persephone into eating a seed of a pomegranate. Having broken an injunction not to eat in the Underworld, she is now bound to Hades. A compromise among the gods is worked out by which Persephone spends a third of the year with Hades, and the rest with her mother. This compromise is the ancient explanation of the origin of the seasons. Winter rules while Persephone is away from her mother, and when she returns in spring and summer, the earth flowers.

We feel that this myth beautifully portrays the conflicts and solutions of the girl as she takes her first steps into the world of sexual feelings for her father. In particular, the story of Persephone depicts a frequently occurring defense—that is, the disavowal of agency over sexuality. This idea was a direct outgrowth of prior work in which we discovered that a female's first experience of sexual intercourse always included, in some form or other, thoughts related specifically to her mother. These thoughts included fears of retaliation, competitive and rivalrous feelings, or victorious fantasies of embarkation onto the path of adult sexuality. It is our thesis that at the phase of triangulation, the same dynamic holds for the expression of aggression in little girls as it does for sexuality

It has been argued, however, that the myth of Persephone is not analogous or parallel to the story of Oedipus. We have been asked, "Where is the rivalry and rage toward the mother in Persephone, compared to the rivalry and rage toward the father in Oedipus?" We agree that aggression on the part of a female is not visible, except in the revengeful retribution of the mother, Demeter, who unleashes famine upon the earth until her daughter is returned to her. Aggression certainly does not seem to mark the relationship between Demeter and Persephone. We argue that agency over aggression, like sexuality, is disguised and inhibited in this story, as in the female triangular situation itself.

The purpose of this paper is to examine and explore the manifestations of aggressive impulses—their absence, expression, or disguises—in the female triangular situation. We focus on the psychological influences on aggression, although we are mindful of the sociological, cultural, and biological influences that contribute to females' attitudes toward aggression.[2]

REVIEW OF THE LITERATURE

It is striking how little can be found in the psychoanalytic literature about aggression in women; even less is available about aggression in the female triangular or "oedipal" situation. In contrast, themes of competition, castration, and aggression in the male oedipal complex are discussed regularly. In this review of the literature, when we are discussing other writers' ideas, we will stick with the language the original writer used to refer to the female oedipal

---

2 We have not addressed the complex questions involved in psychoanalytic definitions of aggression. Parens (1980) has explicated different aspects of aggression—self-preservation, mastery, reactions of rage to unpleasure, and destructive sadism.

constellation. In discussing our own ideas, we will use *triangular situation* or our designation *persephone complex.*

Many have written about the general cultural prohibitions against the expression of anger and aggression by girls and women (Bernardez-Bonesatti 1978; Lerner 1980; Nadelson et al. 1982; Bernay 1986; Guzder and Krishna 1991; Gabbard and Wilkinson 1996; Person 2000). In a discussion of the analysis of aggression, Gray (2000) has speculated about general cultural influences on the inhibition of aggression in vulnerable groups, such as women: "It seems possible that an evolutionary process, cultural rather than biological ..., could contribute to the development of chronic, characterological defenses of the ego. This might restrain their conscious aggression, thus supporting survival in an otherwise dangerous environment" (p. 222). In most societies, both men and women have placed negative values on women's aggression. Lerner (1980) discussed the reasons for the general inhibition of female anger or aggression, and indicated that the cultural definition of the healthy woman is one who is devoid of anger and aggressiveness. She suggested that this inhibition reflects women's fears of their own omnipotent destructiveness and separation/ individuation difficulties in the mother-daughter relationship. Bernay (1986) has observed that women do not allow themselves to be aggressive. Most women have incorporated an unconscious ego ideal that has historically understood aggression as evil. Nadelson and her colleagues (1982) pointed out that women experience aggression as if it were only destructive. We have observed that many female analysts and candidates become anxious about the idea that women are "aggressive" and object to it, insisting instead on the word "assertive."

On the other hand, many have argued that women's seemingly lesser aggression than men's is biologically based (Maccoby and Jacklin 1974). Based on recent observations in the behavioral and neurosciences, Friedman and Downey (1995) have raised questions about the ubiquity of the oedipus complex. They suggested that there is an innate biologically determined tendency for *sons* to feel rivalrous, competitive, and aggressive toward their fathers, and vice versa. Thus, this one component of the oedipus complex, universal among males, is not necessarily connected with erotic desire. They then argued that males are biologically more aggressive than females. They cited evidence of rough-and-tumble play, one category in which sex differences have been consistently reported in most cultures and seem to be independent of child-rearing practices. By implication, therefore, the aggressive competitive components of the Oedipus story would hold truer for males than for females.

Others have argued that application of the oedipus complex to girls is not viable, especially with regard to the aggressive components. When aggression is discussed as part of the female oedipal situation, it is frequently in the context of female masochism (Novick and Novick 1972). Plaut and Hutchison (1986), for example, emphasized the masochistic, inhibited reaction of the girl to the triangular situation in contrast to the more aggressive reaction of the boy. In a feminist view, Stiver (1991) argued that oedipal dynamics can best be understood in terms of patriarchal relationships, and that the major sources of anger in mother-daughter relations reflect the mother's degraded and inferior position in the family constellation. These writings unfortunately foster misunderstandings that "normal" female development is linked with masochism and passivity.

Chasseguet-Smirgel (1970) defined and described in the oedipal situation specifically feminine positions not found in the male. She suggested that one such feminine position involved a specific moment in development: the change of the object from mother to father. Unconscious fantasies of castration by, and in identification with, a castrating mother provide sources of anxiety and guilt stemming from aggression. The girl's attempts at resolution of anal-sadistic conflicts with the mother give rise to idealization of the paternal object representation. Although Chasseguet-Smirgel focused on a specific set of dynamics arising out of one particular family constellation, which limits its applicability, we agree with her stress on the problem of loyalty seen so typically in little girls at that period of development. She wrote: "I have tried to show conflicts which oblige so many women to choose between mother and husband as the object of dependent attachment" (p. 134).

We stress another source of anxiety in the triangular phase—separation worries about the loss of the caretaker, who is the object of dependent attachment. Chasseguet-Smirgel focused attention on anal-sadistic conflicts and associated guilt that the girl carries forward into, and that influence, the triangular phase. We are arguing that there are sources of guilt about competition with the mother that characterize the triangular situation itself. Like Chasseguet-Smirget, Torok (1970) described the girl's struggles with aggressive fantasies as she progresses from the anal stage into the triangular period, because of the "super-imposition in the same object [that is, the mother] of both mastery and rivalry, a universal difficulty in girl's development" (p. 168). This difficulty at times results in a dependence toward the man, "the heir of the anal Mother imago" (p. 168). For us, the loyalty and separation issues arise intrinsically from this period, and are not necessarily either a defensive outcome or a residue of earlier issues.

Following Freud, the motivation for the girl's change of libidinal object from mother to father has been attributed to anger and disappointment in her mother, especially as a "castrated," degraded object. In her discussion of the female oedipal complex, Lester (1976) stated that the turning to the father "is not necessarily accompanied by an aggressive flight from mother, although often antagonism and competition can be observed" (p. 523). Based on her clinical observations, Lester concluded that there is no evidence of a "loosening of the tie with mother" (p. 522), but rather continuous identification with her throughout the oedipal period. She stated that the turn to the father as erotic object occurs later, at latency. For Ogden (1987), this moment of change of object is best understood in terms of the unfolding of internal object relationships. In the context of the dyadic relationship between mother and daughter, the girl develops a transitional relationship with her mother to mediate the entry into the oedipal phase. She and the mother engage in a "dress rehearsal" for the later oedipal drama, in which the mother allows herself to be loved as a man via her own unconscious identification with her own father. Subsequently, the girl's discovery of the oedipal mother's "externality," that is to say her real relationship with the father, is experienced as a betrayal.[3]

Both of these authors rightly emphasize the importance of the mother to the girl in her transition into the triangular period, but they both retain in some fform the idea of a change in object. We argue that this moment should be characterized not as a *change* of object, but as an *addition* of a libidinal object. In a view very close to ours, Ritvo (1989) has commented that girls do not relinquish the tie to the mother, but rather learn to deal with their aggression against her while retaining the ties.

Only a few writers address the question of inhibition of anger toward the mother in the triangular situation. Keiser (1953), discussing a manifest oedipus complex in an adolescent girl, noted the absence of overt aggressive feeling.

When the patient expressed the slightest disparagement of her mother, anxiety appeared. In this instance, however, defenses against aggressive impulses toward the mother were particularly intense because she was the only remaining parent.

In this selected review, we observe an emphasis on the preoedipal influences on female aggression in the triangular period. Many authors have discussed problems with separation/individuation (usually preoedipal) in the girl's expression of anger toward her mother. Galenson and Roiphe (1982) have said that girls' strivings toward separation are experienced as threats to the maternal bond. Along these lines, Elise (1991) has argued that there are developmental differences according to gender in the handling of affects during the separation/ individuation process. She suggests that the so-called depressive affect observed by Mahler in little girls during the separation/ individuation process may be

---

3 Following Ogden, Wilkinson (1993) described how the girl must renegotiate her loyalty to her internal, preoedipal mother, while she begins to identify with the sexuality the external, oedipal mother shares with her oedipal father.

an indication of their ability to feel and express emotions of hurt and disappointment concerning loss. Elise also makes another important observation: that aggression is regularly depicted in Mahler's writings as facilitating healthy development in boys, and neurosis in girls.

The focus on early preoedipal issues holds true for Lerner's explanation of the general cultural inhibition of aggression by women. It also characterizes the work of Chasseguet-Smirgel and Torok, who emphasize the influence of anal struggles with the mother on the girl's entry into, and mastery of, the triangular situation. Tyson (1989, 1997) and Fenichel (1931) also explicated the preoedipal antecedents of girls' problems with anger in their relationships with their mothers during the triangular phase of development. A common thread runs throughout all these writings, however, and one with which we are in accord:the importance to the little girl of preserving her tie to her mother, and the effect of this tie on her expression and handling of aggression.

CLINICAL MATERIAL

We will now present three clinical examples of aggression connected with the heterosexual triangular conflicts (two women competing for a man) of three adult female patients in analysis. In all our clinical material the triadic nature of the conflicts is evident and currently alive in the transference, and we have italicized particularly striking examples of core inhibitions. The first two cases most clearly demonstrate the inhibition of aggression and competition toward a female rival: "Who's the fairest of them all?" The inhibition of aggression associated with persephonal development is seen frequently in the treatment of female patients, especially in the earlier stages of analysis. In our clinical experience, more overt and consciously tolerated murderous aggression toward the mother appears only after considerable analytic work, as in the third example. We also observe such overt aggression in cases characterized by extremely troubled relationships with the mother. In our previous work (2000), inhibition of agency over sexuality in our cases was notable. Sexuality and aggression are inextricably interwoven; we separate them only for purposes of our discussion.

Case 1

The following patient's intense defensive idealization of the analyst/mother functions as a strong inhibitor of anger. This idealization is related to the fact that her mother died when she was five years old. In the following clinical material, fantasies about sexual pleasure with a former boyfriend lead directly and immediately to thoughts about her mother's death. This sequence can be understood as the patient's conflicted unconscious linking of rivalrous, competitive, sexual feelings with the traumatic loss of her mother at the height of the triangular phase.

Miss M, a manufacturer's representative, was poised to begin a five-times-a-week control analysis after a year and a half of thrice-weekly psychotherapy. Her presenting problems centered around depression, and difficulties in her relationships with men She also reported "wild behaviors," including drug and alcohol use, promiscuity, and impulsivity, starting early in adolescence and continuing up to her present age of 29. When Miss M was five, her mother died suddenly. Her father remarried two years later. She was the youngest in a family of five siblings. Because she, being very young, invested so much of her neediness in her stepmother, her older and less needy siblings chastised her for not being loyal to her biological mother. During the psychotherapy it became evident to the analyst, but not to the patient, that she felt unconsciously guilty for her mother's death, and maintained the fantasy that her anger was the cause. Miss M related how she felt as a child that her attractive father adored her beautiful mother. She also felt angry that her mother had died and left her. Miss M's promiscuity seemed to be a cover for her desperate search for a mother via precocious heterosexual contacts.

The early therapeutic work began a true mourning process for the mother. A very eager patient, Miss M expressed her desire to come often, and asserted how much she loved coming. She told the analyst over and over how much she loved her, and that she felt she would make a wonderful mother. This hyper-idealization allowed little room for Miss M even to consider the possibility of any negative feelings or anger toward the analyst. Any attempt by the analyst to approach such feelings would elicit vehement denials. This conscious denial would then be followed by material with themes of death and tragedy— an older woman's terminal illness, or a mother's death in a TV show. Such sequences suggested a causal, but unconscious, link in the patient's mind between expression of anger and death. The following is a session shortly before the patient was to begin her analysis.

The patient came in breathless, coffee cup in hand. "I have been running around all day. Tomorrow we have the presentation. I have been all over the place. Thank God for coffee. I want to continue talking about what we were talking about yesterday—the idea of pleasure—not being able to enjoy it or tolerate it. Ron [the patient's old high-school boyfriend] has asked me to go with him to a football game in a couple of weeks. I was talking to Mary [a much older sister] about it. A part of me wants to go with him. I think it will be fun.

But a part of me doesn't want to go. I don't want to lead him on. I know he wants more from me. Also some of our mutual friends will be there. I really enjoy them. But I think they will really be annoyed if I am with Ron. Like Mary, they'll say, "How can you be with him? Just leading him on, not really interested in him.'"

The analyst said: "Talk more about this idea of having pleasure and everyone commenting about it." The patient replied, "Yes, I feel the same way. I am worried that I will be leading him on, and also I don't want others to get upset… the whole idea of pleasure. Anyway, I will probably just get drunk, not to enjoy it."

To a series of queries from the analyst, the patient said, "Well, I think he will try to kiss me and I know I really enjoy it and then I also remember the time with Brian [another former boyfriend] in the back of the van. We were really kissing and making out … It just feels like I can't enjoy it and if I am out of it, drunk, *I don't have to take responsibility for it, for the pleasure.* This is the problem: I'm thinking for some reason about my mom dying." (Note that the thought about her mother dying comes up in the context of taking responsibility for guilt- ridden pleasure, a pleasure that females around her condemned). She started to cry. "Maybe … Mom used to make things pleasurable for me. When she died, I have to … It is like I don't want to give up the idea of someone doing it for me, making it happen for me… Well, thinking of this old friend, Donna, from the old church I used to attend, who sends gift boxes to me every year. Most of the time I don't even open them."

The analyst asked, "What about not opening the box?"

"Well, anything from Donna would have the same message as my old church. It's the school of thought that says that things are predetermined. It's Calvinist thinking, a belief in predeterminism, heaven or hell. My dad believes in it, believes he is going to heaven. You can do whatever you want. So it's OK that he was such a jerk. I don't agree with it, the idea of being the chosen one… *I have this idea now that we make things happen for ourselves. I felt I would go heaven but after my mother died I felt I would go to hell.*" We interpret this to mean that Miss M felt that once she took agency for her actions, which include death wishes toward her mother, she would be sentenced to hell. This is the second reference in this session to the patient's taking responsibility for actions or feelings—sexual and aggressive—that lead to hell or death. The defining triangular configuration is contained in a few phrases: a reference to her Dad, denial of positive feelings toward him, the death of her mother, and her guilt for her wishes.

Here the analyst intervened perhaps too quickly, and did not follow the train of associations about going to hell. Instead she took up the idea of beginning the analysis: "I wonder if the idea of being chosen, predetermined, and pleasure is being triggered by our talk of starting analysis here."

"Yes, I feel anxious, I know we have talked about it and I really want to do it but it makes me anxious. You know when I was walking in today, I saw myself in the window. Here I was in a skirt, my hair pulled back really looking like an adult and I thought, I am one, I *have to take responsibility but it makes me anxious*."

The analyst said, "Perhaps there is a worry that there will be all sorts of needs and longings stirred up and I won't be able to help you and that I will leave you on your own to figure it out. Also it seems the idea of being "chosen" is present. Perhaps you feel like the chosen one, but it doesn't seem to feel so good.

Perhaps you view my recommendation of analysis as you being the chosen one and it seems confusing. We can try to understand more of your confused and conflicted feelings."

Being chosen as a control case seems to have stirred up a host of feelings, fantasies, and anxieties for this young woman. She is gratified that she has been chosen by this wonderful new mother substitute, who is fulfilling her longings for her lost dead mother. At the same time, there is a hint that being chosen might mean that other wishes, frightening sexual fantasies—to "make out" or even do more with a guy of whom no one approves—might emerge and be condemned by the analyst/mother. It seems that the patient links such fantasies with punishment—the punishment of losing her mother. It is too early in the analysis to interpret that the patient may also feel that her competitive strivings caused the mother's death. It is poignant and striking that the patient so clearly documents how her sense of purity and goodness plummets with her mother's death, from heaven to hell.

To avoid guilt, the patient projects her anger and self-disapproval onto her family and friends, who will "be annoyed," she fears, if she takes up with this former love. She perceives the male, not herself, as "wanting something more." "Being drunk" is used as a defense against acknowledging agency in her sexual and aggressive wishes. There is an oral mode of protection and gratification; this is also how she arms herself against the sense of deprivation and anxiety, bringing a cup of coffee with her as she enters the session. Inhibition and repression are sustained through action, substance abuse, externalization, and projection. The propensity toward action reflects the reality of early trauma in this woman's life. The trauma of the early loss exacerbates the unconscious guilt about, and defense against, aggression toward her mother, and fixates her in the magical thinking of childhood. The frozen anger appeared in the transference as excessive idealization of the analyst as the perfect mother.

Case 2

The following is from the second year of analysis of a thirty-five-year-old married woman, Mrs. P, who made significant improvements in overcoming depression and self-deprecating behavior. In the analysis, much work concentrated on her strong, erotized attachment to her father and her problems in differentiating herself from a controlling but loved mother with whom she had identified. In the course of the analysis she struggled with the emergence of dim memories from childhood that highlight her sexual feelings about her father, and possibly some sort of incestuous experiences; these thoughts were terrifying and very unwelcome. Nevertheless, improvements in self-esteem meant that she could procure a new, very satisfying job and buy a new home, very different from the kind of place her mother would have chosen. Both new job and new house made her feel "more grown-up." Yet at the same time she felt pulled into feeling as she had as a child. She reported feeling very stressed.

Over the previous week, Mrs. P had complained of a sense of everything being in disarray. In the session immediately before the one we will present, she described an image from a dream: "I picture my dad on a ladder, kind of like a poster, with the title, 'Midnight Marauder.' He looks happy, good-looking. "Midnight Marauder" brings a thought of him coming into my room in the dark."

Mrs. P began the next day's session by reporting that she had been contacted about a new and very prestigious position, which paid double her current salary. She announced to the analyst that of course she would not even consider this proposal, as she was so content with her current job, which was still quite new.

"Why not?" the analyst asked. The patient was quite taken aback, but in response she began to speculate about what she might indeed do with more money, and with other things she wanted in her life. "I didn't even interview, but I did meet with my current supervisor to tell her about this offer. It went swell. She did speak about a raise, but one that could not match the proposed salary. Talking last time did sort of open my eyes to thinking about what I do want. Or being able to buy things without worrying. I would like another degree—a Ph.D." Her thoughts went back to a couple of years ago when she had inquired about some of the Ph.D. programs in the area. She had set out to talk to someone at a local university (one with which the analyst was affiliated). She had gotten lost on the way and never even got to her appointment. Significantly, she had not told the analyst about these events at the time.

It emerged that the patient felt intimidated by the community in which the university was situated. She said, "The people there are so much brighter, more competent. I feel like it's something about competition. And there are conferences and concerts there that I would like to attend, but I don't even think to get tickets because I assume I can't get them."

The analyst asked whom she knew from there who was so bright. The patient replied, "People who graduated from there seem better. It doesn't seem rational. I'm mad and disappointed how I blew off my college and my grades." The analyst interpreted, "You use a blanket of inferiority in your mind to keep yourself from competing, competing with me, getting a Ph.D. like me. You probably connect the university with me, and so feel inferior to anyone connected with it. You feel you cannot compete with me."

Mrs. P replied, "I'm definitely not as good as you, or at least I feel that way. I feel that way about people from the Psychoanalytic Institute especially."

Mrs. P was inhibited in procuring a more prestigious job, more money, and more education. The extent to which she needed to diminish herself, keep herself down, is clear. This material emerged with direct allusion in the transference to competition, becoming equal with, not even better than, the analyst/mother. It is clearly related to the immediate context of emerging sexual material about the father, the good-looking "midnight marauder." Thus, the triadic conflicts, the fires of forbidden, sexual impulses toward father, and the competitive desires to be better than mother, must be put out with a blanket of inhibition and inferiority. Becoming equal with the parent, or like her, seems to carry with it ominous rumblings of destructiveness.

Both these patients commented on the experience of feeling or being grown up. This phenomenon in and of itself speaks to the push/pull feeling of being on the cusp on the triangular situation. Being grown up puts the female squarely into a position of being able to compete and take responsibility for herself. It is what these two women intensely long for, and at the same time fear. It means to them the loss of the early nurturing mother. In both cases the material is triadic, with the cast of characters including a female, a desired male, and a disapproving or competing female or chorus of females. These female voices whisper, "Don't lead him on," or "Don't be too successful," or you will lose the mother's love or approval, or the mother herself. Aggressiveness leads to loss.

Case 3

In comparison to the two cases above, the following patient demonstrates a capacity and tolerance for the emergence of aggression with some acknowledgment of agency—a function of considerable analytic work.

Mrs. A, a twenty-nine-year-old advertising executive, was in her fourth year of analysis. She was perceptive and psychologically sophisticated, and she made good use of her analysis, which enabled her to advance in her career. When she began treatment, she had been unable to work in a creative or effective manner. Analytic work had uncovered her unconscious competition and rivalry with her mother, which had contributed to her work inhibition. In the session to be reported, she manifested a form of conflicted aggression and competition with her mother and the analyst. The analyst's upcoming vacation and Mrs. A's recent acclaimed successes at work were exacerbating her anxieties in the transference.

Mrs. A commented that it had been difficult getting to the session because of the icy sidewalks around the analyst's office. She reported that she hesitated before telling the analyst this. When asked why the hesitation, she said that she was uneasy being critical of something about the analyst—that her sidewalks had not been salted. The patient then began talking about how her mother put her down if she expressed any of her own aspirations, concerns, or criticisms.

Her mother would do it in a "mean" way, which meant to the patient that she (the patient) had no right to such thoughts or feelings. The analyst pointed out that Mrs. A was intensely anxious because of her anticipation that the analyst would do the same.

The patient replied, "I wanted to kill her." (The interpretation freed the patient to express direct murderous rage, but only in the past tense.) The analyst said, "Wanted to kill her?"

"Yes. I remember wanting to kill her. And I felt like a worthless, shitty, awful person for feeling that. I remember her venom, her strength, and her power.

462

I wanted to have the ability to wipe her out. I wanted to be the powerful one because I always felt so small. I felt there was no one to help me.

Yet, the thing is, she would always be there. That's something. But there were times I remember very briefly when I wanted to obliterate, destroy, get rid of her. I wanted to be one up on her. This morning in aerobics, I did stretches, which I love. My stomach was bloated, which I can't stand because my mother had a big stomach. [Her mother had had four childbirths after the birth of the patient.] I was one up on her because I was young and pretty. How could I be that? I felt guilty about getting attention ... something in our both being female. It's like maybe I could be more attractive to my father. The thought was scary that he would like me better. She would be angry at me. I would want his affection, of course, not his sexual advances. [Note the defensive negation of sexuality.] Mother was angry at me for being seductive and flirtatious. I wanted to get her obliterated, and I used to fantasize I was father's favorite. But it's scary; how could I get rid of her? But I could be the prize daughter for my father. My mother, she was always there. *If I got rid of her who would take care of us?* But I do remember when I was three or four specifically—how do I remember back so far?—sitting with Dad on the couch. I think what I remember is wanting to be touching him. I felt I was very, very special and thought, We don't need mother. It was scary thinking that I had the power. I guess that's why I can't assert myself here and couldn't achieve because it means that someone else gets destroyed and certainly would be angry at me. [!] Is this what females go through? It's hard for me to experience the relationship with you. It seems okay to be smart and have aspirations, but that's not part of me. I expect you to put me down. I went and tried things but they never worked out. But I think that must have been wrong, to want to get rid of mother, and I must have realized it. Maybe I wanted Dad to touch me. I was afraid to tell him how close I wanted to be to him. He was a jerk, but being pretty was a good way to get his attention. But he was strong. But mother was always there. *What would happen if she really was gone? I had that fleeting thought."*

The analyst said, "What would happen?"

"Well, I needed her. She was the mom. I counted on her. She took care of me and my brothers and sister. Who would take over? Me? My little sister? And I just felt horribly guilty, inescapably, immutably awful, if I did [think about getting] rid of her. I was bad, dirty, ugly to want to get rid of her, but I felt I hated her. Although I was stirred up … the way I was treated by her and her meanness back to me, I couldn't compete. She was bigger, stronger, and she was awful, and yet, because I couldn't … I wanted to get rid of her. Scary … sexual toward my father? I fantasized maybe I was more desirable than she was. My father as I talk all through this analysis is a non-figure in my life. [Negation again.] How come? He existed. I didn't talk to him. I walled him off. He's still walled off, and mother was unreachable. Maybe you can help me. It makes me want to cry. Then I don't know if others feel the same way. This is awful to feel this way. It's painful. [Patient was crying.] But I do, I feel sorry for myself but I don't like to admit it.

Why do I have all this today?"

The analyst responded, "I think you wonder if I understand that this is related to my upcoming absence. You are feeling hurt and angry, even wanting to murder me and afraid I will retaliate, but you want me back, too."

Mrs. A said, "This is awful, painful. I remember feeling this same way when I was little—just devastated." She went on to say that she was afraid that there was something she would do which would make the analyst stay away, and something that the analyst would see—her ugliness. Then she said that her mother seemed so powerful, and could make her feel so powerless. "I'll do something to alienate you."

The analyst said, "My leaving makes you feel just as powerless. Also you seem to have the fantasy that my leaving is related to something negative about you." Mrs. A ended the session by saying, "My anger and my hurt stain you and you'll take that and you will be gone more. I'm frightened that you'll use my feelings against me."

The session following dealt with ambivalent transference feelings toward the analyst—love, admiration, and a desire for closeness alternating with derogation of the analyst's femininity and envy of her relationship with her husband. For example, the patient said, "It should be me going on vacation going with your husband, not you. Why you? I'm younger and prettier."

In this session we see the emergence of material that had not been recalled previously: that is, the desire to kill the mother and replace her. This is directly analogous to the typical paradigm of the male: kill the rival off to replace him. Yet here this material appeared only after many years of analytic work and interpretation of defense. The patient now was very different from the inhibited woman who had come into analysis. Our point, however, even here, is that the competitive urge was intermingled with much anxiety about loss of the mother and the mother's love. The murderous rage was attached to fears of loss of nurturance and comfort from the mother. The patient almost undoes her anger as she expresses it (as illustrated by her feeling that she had no right to it). Clearly, the material is triadic and competitive. The patient's statement that she is younger and prettier than the mother/analyst is the answer to the wicked queen's question in "Snow White" about who is the fairest of them all. The desire to have the man/father, to be pregnant and have a big stomach like the mother had, and to be the favorite chosen one are evident. The patient remembers her fear that she might be able to get what she wanted: that is, get rid of her mother/analyst. The warning "Be careful or you might get what you wish for!" is a common message in fairy tales. The patient's expectation and fear of punishment if that wish to win the competition were gratified demonstrate the boomerang effect of such death wishes. The patient's feeling is that ugliness instead of prettiness will be the legacy of her murderous rage, and that ultimately she will lose her mother.

DISCUSSION

The above case material demonstrates that fears of loss of the mother and loss of her love come to the fore in the context of triangular erotic conflicts. We argue that this does not occur because the little girl has not yet resolved preoedipal conflicts, or, as older psychoanalytic theory would have had it, because she has no penis and therefore is not motivated by castration anxiety. It occurs because concerns about separation from and abandonment by the mother are central for the little girl in the triangular situation. Loss of the mother is a major persephonal punishment for the little girl. These dynamics are an important part of the period of triangulation per se, and not simply a carryover from earlier developmental phases.

It is highly dangerous for a little girl to acknowledge and express her sexual wishes toward her father. She wants to be her father's chosen love, and to outdo and replace her mother. Yet she needs to remain bonded to her caretaker, and identified with her as a source of self-esteem. The more tenuous the mother-daughter relationship, the more difficult it may be for the girl to tolerate her own aggressiveness (see Silverman 1987). For a little boy, the destruction and reanimation of his oedipal rival is repeatedly expressed in active aggressive play. For a little girl, a more careful route is traversed. Murderous aggression and rivalry must be denied. Inhibition of a subjective sense of agency over aggression becomes a pervasive defense for women and girls (Hoffman 1999).

Thus, for the little Persephone, disguise of impulse is safer. Ideas of being "forced" to engage in activities that are fantasized or perceived as dangerous to mother are more acceptable than overt active impulses. Little girls whisper constantly to their mothers, have and share secrets; needing to be liked, they are exceptionally sensitive to relationships. They maneuver into exclusionary duos, forming and reforming pairs. They eschew open competition with other females, and are uncomfortable with threesomes. Their difficulty is reminiscent of Persephone, who can be with father/Hades part of the time and with mother/Demeter part of the time, but not with both at the same time. Men (as exemplified by Oedipus) are not unconscious about their competitive aggressive feelings; in fact they are often encouraged by society to be aggressive, although they may delink their aggression from its underlying motivations and genetic origins. But little girls have to be careful and compromising in order to traverse the dangerous but exciting persephonal period safely. When they become grown women, like Electra and Lady Macbeth, they can use men as powerful instruments to carry out their ambitious, rivalrous, and murderous dreams. Sexuality and aggression are very much intertwined in the little girl's mind at the triangular stage of development. In a young child, aggressive and libidinal impulses can be so closely woven together that they seem to be one strand; it is not possible to separate the patterns of regulation of aggression and libido. For example, Herzog (2000) carefully delineates how libidinal tensions and interests impact father-daughter interactions in regard to the modulation of aggression. He suggests that there are gender-specific regulatory patterns laid down in the family that become powerful determinants of how the child organizes aggressive drives and fantasies. For example, in a libidinally charged relationship with their fathers, girls may be especially attuned to how their fathers expect them to behave.

Boys, in comparison, who may be more difficult and "ask for it" more, will push to engage their fathers in maternally sanctioned limit setting.

From another vantage point, the little girl's body, with its inner cavities and flowing sensations, also influences this interweaving of sexual and aggressive impulses. Aggression, like sexuality, is incorporated into the female body image and body ideal in keeping with bodily contours and inborn temperaments (Downey 2000). The little girl finds more inward, interior ways to handle her aggressive and sexual feelings. A long-ignored paper by Lou Andre as-Salome (1916) discusses the female anatomical configuration—with the vagina a close neighbor to the rectum, actually "renting space from it"—and its effect on the "transposition" of the instinctual drives. This configuration leads to three levels of confusion for the female: confusion of zones, of motor functions, and of the means of control (anal and genital "thrusts" are experienced as uncontrollable). Following Salome, Richards (1992) emphasizes the flexing of the perineal musculature in the development of female genital awareness and sensation. According to Richards, the contraction of these sphincter muscles in toilet training results in a spreading sexual excitement, which is experienced as genital. Since the anus is intimately connected with aggression, it is not much of a leap to suppose that this inner spreading of excitation can be experienced as aggressive as well. Just as the little girl is able to hide her sexual feelings and arousal within her body, she is prone to express her anger secretly, by holding back rather than punching, by tears rather than shouts, by retaining an inner secret that gives the bearer power. As a popular journalist put it, "Within the hidden culture of aggression, girls fight with body language and relationships instead of fists and knives.... Silence is deeply woven into the fabric of female experience" (Simmons 2002).

Recent sociological and popular writings have described the major differences in how girls and boys express aggression. In a series of studies of female adolescents, these authors (Gilligan 1982; Simmons 2002; Talbot 2002) concluded that schoolgirls are frightened to own and to show their anger because they are afraid they will be isolated and ostracized. We are proposing an intrapsychic dynamic that would help to explain these reliable observations and suggest that these fears stem from the persephonal period. For the girl, to be isolated and ostracized at this time is tantamount to loss of the object or loss of the love of the object.

Aggression, like sexuality, is an integral part of the triangular period. We do not see it as the main motivating factor for developmental progression either into or out of the triangular situation. Rather, it must be mastered. In coping with the conflicts of that stage, little girls frequently give up their subjective sense of agency over aggression and sexuality. If the analyst is not sensitive to the importance of analyzing women's defenses against aggression, particularly the lost sense of agency over aggression, analyses can be stymied or stalemated. We have tried to demonstrate that a focus on how and why our female patients inhibit their unconscious competitive and aggressive wishes clinically within the psychoanalytic situation can lead to improved understanding and mastery of their triangular conflicts. This crucial phase has been neglected in contemporary reexaminations of female development in psychoanalysis.

Freud's writings about the girl's triangular oedipal situation was marked by oscillations and theoretical dilemmas. At first he made the mistake of thinking that the female and male oedipus complexes were analogous. Changing his mind about this, he became ensnarled in the complexities of the developmental differences he was proposing. Using male oedipal dynamics as the norm, Freud had to go into theoretical contortions to make female dynamics conform to these notions. He relied on the concept of penis envy to describe the girl's convoluted and difficult change in libidinal object and "phallic" aim from love for her mother to sexual interest in her father. The boy's entry into the oedipal phase was seen as less complicated; the mother remained object of his impulses from earlier to later stages of infantile sexuality. Freud proposed castration anxiety as the motivation for resolution of the oedipal conflict and superego development for the boy. For the girl, since she had no penis, the motivation for resolution and superego formation was weaker, and these developments might never be achieved at all. Thus, with a male measure as a basis for comparison, girls could neither enter the oedipal situation easily, nor could they get out of it. The use of a male norm made women appear abnormal—forever tied to their mothers, for example, or weaker in superego development.

What then are the aspects of the girl's triangular or oedipus complex that call for reexamination in the light of contemporary psychoanalytic thinking? First, her *entry into the triangular situation*. The discovery of the difference between the sexes, emphasizing penis envy as the motivating force for entry into the triangular phase and the turning away from the mother in disappointment and rage, is no longer accepted as a satisfactory explanation. We have emphasized the importance of separation issues for the girl regarding her entry into the triangular situation. We have also strongly argued that this development should not be characterized as a change of libidinal object for the girl—from mother to father—but as an *addition* of object. And, as we stated above, we do not believe that aggression necessarily motivates the girl's entry into triangular situation.

The second aspect that must be reconsidered is *the resolution of the triangular situation and the formation of the superego*. Also strongly under question in contemporary thinking is the notion that the presence of castration anxiety (and a penis) is necessary for the resolution of triangulation and for mature superego development. By that reasoning, girls can never, or only much later and gradually, resolve the oedipus complex, and their superego development is compromised.[4]

Finally, there are *the dynamics of the triangular situation itself*. In this paper, we have focused on the differences in dynamics that stem from the different object relations during the triangular situation for boys and girls and their influence on expressions of aggression and competitive strivings. We hope that this paper can contribute to the further elaboration of a uniquely female line of development.

REFERENCES

Andreas-Salome, L. (1915). Anal et sexual. In L'amour du narcissisme. Paris: Gallimard, 1980, pp. *91–130*.

Bernadez-Bonesatti, T. (1978). Women and anger: Conflicts with aggression in contemporary women. *Journal of American Women Analysts*33: *215–219*.

---

4 The Kris study group reported their findings from a review of case material. They concluded that for both men and women, concerns about punishment included fantasies of loss of the object, and loss of love, as well as castration (Hoffman 1994).

Bernay, T. (1986). Reconciling nurturance and aggression: A new feminine identity. In *The Psychology of Today's Woman: New Psychoanalytic Visions,* ed. T. Bernay & D. Cantor. Hillsdale, NJ: Analytic Press, pp. *51–80.*

Bernstein, D. (1993). Female Identity Conflict in Clinical Practice. Northvale, NJ: Aronson.

Bettelheim, B. (1975). *The Uses of Enchantment.* New York: Random House.

Chasseguet-Smirgel, J. (1970). Feminine guilt and the Oedipus complex. *In Female Sexuality: New Psychoanalytic Views,* ed. J. Chasseguet-Smirgel. Ann Arbor: University of Michigan Press, pp. *94–134.*

Chodorow, N. (1978). *The Reproduction of Mothering: Psychoanalysis and the Sociology of Gender.* Berkeley: University of California Press.

Dahl, E.K. (1989). Daughters and mothers: Oedipal aspects of the witchmother. *Psychoanal. St. Child*44: *267–280.*

Downey, T.W. (2000). The unfolding anatomy of aggression in one girl. Presented at the winter meeting of the American Psychoanalytic Association, New York.

Elise, D. (1991). An analysis of gender differences in separationindividation. *Psychoanal. St. Child*46: *51–67.*

Fenichel, O. (1931). Specific forms of the Oedipus complex. *Int. J. Psycho-Anal.* 12: *141–166.*

Friedman, R.C., & Downey, J.I. (1995). Biology and the Oedipus complex. *Psychoanal. Q.*64: *234–264.*

Gabbard, G.O., & Wilkinson, S.M. (1996). Nominal gender and gender fluidity in the psychoanalytic situation. *Gender and Psychoanal.*1: *463–481.*

Galenson, E., & Roiphe, H. (1982). The preoedipal relationship of a father, mother, and daughter. In *Father and Child: Developmental and Clinical Perspectives,* ed. S. Cath, A. Gurwitt, & J. Ross. Boston: Little, Brown, pp. *151–162.*

Gilligan, C. (1982). *In a Different Voice.* Cambridge: Harvard University Press.

Gray, R. (2000). On the receiving end: Facilitating the analysis of conflicted drive derivatives of aggression. *J. Amer. Psychoanal. Assn.*48: *219–236.*

Guzder, J., & Krishna, M. (1991). Sita-Shakti: Cultural paradigms for Indian women. *Transcultural Psychiatric Research Review*28: *257–301.*

Herzog, J.M. (2000). Female aggression and its relationship to the family, the culture and the individual. Presented at the winter meeting of the American Psychoanalytic Association, New York.

Hoffman, L. (1994). Superego analysis: Report of the Kris Study Group. *Journal of Clinical Psychoanalysis*3: *161–177.*

Hoffman, L. (1999). Freud and feminine subjectivity. *J. Amer. Psychoanal. Assn.*44 (Suppl.): *23–44.*

Holtzman, D., & Kulish, N. (2000). The femininization of the female oedipal complex, part I: A reconsideration of the significance of separation issues. *J. Amer. Psychoanal. Assn.*48: *1413–1437.*

Keiser, S. (1953). A manifest oedipus complex in an adolescent girl. *Psychoanal. St. Child*8: *99–107.*

Lax, R. (1995). Motives and determinants of girls' penis envy in the negative oedipal phase. *Journal of Clinical Psychoanalysis*4: *297–314.*

Lerner, H.E. (1980). Internal prohibitions against female anger. *American Journal of Psychoanalysis*40:*137–148.*

Lester, E. (1976). On the psychosexual development of the female child. *J. Am. Acad. Psychoanal. Dyn. Psychiatr.*4: *515–527.*

Maccoby, E., & Jacklin, C. (1974). *The Psychology of Sex Differences.* Stanford: Stanford University Press.

Nadelson, C. C., Notman, M., Miller, J. B., & Zilbach, J. (1982). Aggression in women: Conceptual issues and clinical implications. In *The Woman Patient,* ed. M.T. Notman & C.C. Nadelson. New York: Plenum Press, pp. *17–28.*

Novick, J., & Novick, K. (1972). Beating fantasies in children. *Int. J. Psycho-Anal.*53: *237–242.*

Ogden, T.H. (1987). The transitional oedipal relationship in female development. *Int. J. Psycho-Anal.*68: *485–498.*

Palmer, A. (1988). Heidi's metaphoric appeal to latency. *Psychoanal. St. Child*43: *387–398.*

Parens, H. (1980). An exploration of the relations of instinctual drives and the symbiosis/separation-individuation process *J. Am. Acad. Psychoanal. Dyn. Psychiatr.*28: *89–114.*

Person, E.S. (1985). The erotic transference in women and men: Differences and consequences. *J. Am. Acad. Psychoanal. Dyn. Psychiatr.*13: *159–280.*

——— (1988). *Dreams of Love and Fateful Encounters: The Power of Romantic Passion.* New York: Norton.

——— (2000). Issues of power and aggression in women. Presented at the winter meeting of the American Psychoanalytic Association, New York.

Plaut, E.A., & Hutchinson, F.L. (1986). The role of puberty in female psychosexual development. *Int. Rev. Psycho-Anal.*13: *417–432.*

Reenkola, E.M. (2002). *The Veiled Female Core.* New York: Other Press.

Richards, A.K. (1992). The influence of sphincter control and genital sensation on body image and gender identity in women. *Psychoanal. Q.*61: *331–351.*

Ritvo, S. (1989). Mothers, daughters, and eating disorders. In *Fantasy, Myth, and Reality: Essays in Honor of Jacob A. Arlow,* ed. H. Blum, Y. Kramer, A.K. Richards, & A.D. Richards. Madison, CT: International Universities Press, pp. *371–380.*

Silverman, D. (1987). What are little girls made of? *Psychoanal. Psychol.*4: *315–334.*

Simmons, R. (2002). *Odd Girl Out: The Hidden Culture of Aggression in Girls.* New York: Harcourt.

Stiver, I.P. (1991). Beyond the Oedipus complex: Mothers and daughters. In *Women's Growth in Connection,* ed. J.V. Jordan, A.G. Kaplan, J.B. Miller, I.P. Stiver, & J.L. Surrey. New York: Guilford Press, pp. *97–121.*

Talbot, M. (2002). Girls just want to be mean. *New York Times Magazine,* February 24, p. *24.*

Torok, M. (1970). The significance of penis envy in women. In *Female Sexuality: New Psychoanalytic Views,* ed. J. Chasseguet-Smirgel. Ann Arbor: University of Michigan Press, pp. *94–134.*

Tyson, R. (1989). Infantile sexuality, gender identity, and obstacles to oedipal progression. *J. Amer. Psychoanal. Assn.*37: *1050–1069.*

——— (1997). Love and hate and growing up female. Presented to the Miami Psychoanalytic Society, November 9.

Wilkinson, S. (1993). The female genital dress-rehearsal: A prospective process at the oedipal threshold. *Int. J. Psycho-Anal.*74: *313–330.*

CHAPTER 16

Countertransference and the female triangular situation

(2003). Int. J. Psychoanal., (84)(3):563-577

with Deanna Holtzman

This paper represents an attempt toward reconciling contemporary changes in psychoanalytic understandings of female development, particularly in respect to separation issues, with their clinical applications to female patients.

Psychoanalytic thinking typically has categorized separation conflicts as pre- oedipal, but the authors suggest that these are an integral part of the triangular situation of the girl. The authors argue that an allegiance to erroneous theory and/or individual blind spots have led to the infantilization, pre-oedipalization or cultural stereotyping of females, which constrains the effectiveness of their analyses. The authors present a selected review of the literature on gender-based countertransference biases in both male and female analysts, with reference to female 'oedipal' material. Analytic case material of two women is presented which demonstrates how theoretical misperceptions and countertransferences to triangular separation conflicts can produce an impediment to progression in analysis.

INTRODUCTION

This paper represents an attempt toward reconciling contemporary changes in psychoanalytic understandings of female development, particularly in respect to separation issues, with their clinical applications to female patients. We will attempt to elucidate some ways in which changes in theories about women might affect technical considerations and interpretive attitudes in the analyses of females by both male and female analysts. We believe that an allegiance to erroneous theory and/or individual blind spots have led to the infantilization, preoedipalization or cultural stereotyping of females, which constrains the effectiveness of their analyses. In this paper, we will, first, briefly summarize outdated and erroneous conceptions about the female 'oedipal' situation. We will try to demonstrate how psychoanalytic theory about separation may lead analysts to misread separation material when they encounter it in a clinical situation and often treat it automatically as pre-oedipal. Utilizing clinical data, we will try to demonstrate how being mired in older conceptualizations of the female 'oedipal' complex can result in a treatment that is derailed, lengthy, stalemated or even aborted. Second, we discuss common stereotypes and countertransferences around 'oedipal' material with female patients. Such blind spots are frequent in both male and female analysts. Besides misperceptions stemming from outdated and erroneous theory, personal countertransferences and blind spots frequently interfere with psychoanalytic treatment and understanding of 'oedipal' or triangular material in women.

As many writers have demonstrated, early psychoanalytic theories about female development reflected 'a masculine mythology of femininity' (David, 1970, p. 47) and were based on the girl's sense of deficiency and on penis envy (Schafer, 1974; Birksted-Breen, 1996; and many others). Penis envy was postulated as the impetus for the change of object from mother to father and, hence, the motor into the 'oedipal' situation. Compensation for the missing penis became the sole source of the desire for a baby. Theoretically lacking the boy's motivation for resolution to oedipal desires, i.e., castration anxiety, the girl was left marooned in an unresolved 'oedipal' situation and saddled with a weak and defective superego. The view of the female as a *garcon manqué*, castrated and deficient, with a purported lack of knowledge of the vagina left little or no room for female sexual pleasure or even other anxieties about the feminine self. Without ideas of a primary femininity, earlier theories could not articulate an intrinsic feminine sexuality that might be part of the triangular situation and the girl's sexual desire for the father (or the mother).

Freud's stunningly creative and veridical postulations about the oedipal complex were based on the story about a male as central protagonist and, as such, had a phallocentric cast. Our focus here will be on the female 'oedipal complex', which we feel is an oxymoron.[1] (Therefore, we refer to the female triangular situation, or the female 'oedipal' in quotes.) Moreover, the applications from the male oedipal complex to the female situation were never developed fully. Derivations from the early psychoanalytic theories of 'oedipal' development imply that women, as compared with men, suffer permeable self-object boundaries, are not able to give up or resolve 'oedipal' attachments and have narcissistic difficulties or weak superegos. All female development, including the triangular situation, was colored by a sense of deficiency with narcissistic and masochistic proclivities.

We, along with others (Chodorow, 1978; Bernstein, 1993; Burch, 1997; Holtzman and Kulish, 1997, 2000), have suggested that the tale of a male, Oedipus, is not appropriate in describing the typical triangular phase in female development. We have proposed that this developmental conflict be called the 'persephone complex', from the Greek myth of Persephone. We argue that this crucial phase for girls has uniquely feminine characteristics that have not been fully recognized or cohesively incorporated into psychoanalytic theories and technique. These concern the girl's entry into the feminine triangular situation,

---

1 Marianne Goldberger, MD, first suggested that 'female oedipal' is an oxymoron.

typical anxieties and defensive handling of aggression and sexuality that may characterize the triangulation situation itself, and the girl's unique compromises at resolution of the conflicts.

PERSEPHONE AND THE FEMALE TRIANGULAR SITUATION

In our previous work (Holtzman and Kulish, 2000) we argued that a misunderstanding of separation issues in the triangular situation has led to a distorted notion of females as immature. Psychoanalytic theory predisposes thinking about separation issues as having early, pre-oedipal origins. We contend, however, that separation issues are a regular component of triangular conflicts for girls, *sui generis*, not solely based on or originating in dyadic, pre- oedipal conflict and development. We are aware that triangular conflicts are not necessarily 'oedipal'. Abelin (1971) has documented early triangulation in terms of the father's role in helping the very young child separate from the mother, a pre-oedipal separation. Separation has a different meaning and emphasis for females than for males, and nowhere is it clearer in its significance as a major dynamic than for girls in the 'oedipal' situation. In the typical course of psychological development, little girls separate themselves from the same-sexed object, their mothers (Chordorow, 1978; Person, 1983; Ogden, 1987). Contemporary theorists such as Chodorow or Gilligan (1982) have argued that, because of an early closeness or enmeshment with their mothers that ensues from this fact, girls typically place high value on interpersonal relationships. In comparison, little boys, who separate from the opposite-sexed object, place more value on power and autonomy. We would stress another factor: that is, because the mother is the primary care taker in the usual family situation, separation from her is especially tricky and conflicted for little girls. We believe that competitive feelings toward the mother and developing sexual urges must be inhibited, repressed or projected because little girls are afraid to ruin or destroy their relatively safe positions with their mothers. In a view similar to ours, Reenkola described the triangular situation when the mother becomes the rival of the girl: 'This is a fateful combination.

The ambivalence of love and hate towards the mother arouses immense guilt in a girl ...' (2002, preface, p. xv). Confronted with the triangular situation and their attractions to their fathers, girls must carefully negotiate dual attachments to both parents. This idea was a direct outgrowth of our prior work, which found that a female's first experience of sexual intercourse always included, in some form or other, thoughts related specifically to her mother. These thoughts included fears of retaliation, competitive and rivalrous feelings, or victorious fantasies about the embarking on the path of adult sexuality. Hence, we argue that the rich and complexly evocative myth of Persephone, which depicts a balancing of loyalties between the parents, revolves around the theme of Persephone's separation from her mother, Demeter, and celebrates fertility, cyclical rhythms and female power, better describes the girl's developmental crisis (see also Burch, 1997, p. 21).

The story is as follows: Kore/Persephone, the young daughter of Demeter and Zeus, is gathering flowers in a meadow with other young girls. Kore plucks a particularly beautiful narcissus that has attracted her. The earth opens suddenly and Hades, god and king of the Underworld and Death, abducts her. Nobody hears her screams and cries. (Some versions of the story make a rape more explicit.) When Kore next appears in the Homeric hymn, she is with Hades in the Underworld. The scene pictures Hades 'reclining on a bed with his shy spouse, strongly reluctant ...' (Foley, 1994). It is important to note that, prior to her stay with Hades and presumably to the loss of her virginity, the girl is known only as 'Kore', which in Greek literally means the 'maiden'. Thereafter, she takes on the new name of Persephone. In the meantime, Demeter descends from Olympus to search {delete}frantically for her daughter. In her fury and pain, Demeter causes famine and drought to spread over the earth. Zeus is induced by this catastrophe to persuade Hades to release Persephone.

479

However, Persephone is tricked by Hades to eat the seeds of a pomegranate. (In some versions she is tricked; in some, forced; and, in others, takes the seeds willingly.) Thus, she has broken an injunction not to eat in the Underworld and is now bound to Hades. A compromise between the gods is worked out by which Persephone spends one-third of the year with Hades, and two-thirds with her mother. This compromise is the ancient explanation of the origin of the seasons. Winter rules while Persephone lives with Hades, and the earth flowers in spring and summer while she is with her mother. The poem ends with Demeter founding the Eleusinian rites.

We feel that this myth beautifully portrays conflicts of the girl as she takes first steps into the world of sexual feelings for her father. In particular, the story of Persephone depicts the very commonly seen female defense—the disavowal of the sense of agency over sexuality. We argue that the whole structure of the story, in its various versions, reflects this defense. That is, Persephone is 'forced' into her union with Hades. Yet the ambiguity of her participation in the eating which seals her fate is reflected in the various versions of the myth. It is our thesis that the same dynamic holds for the expression of aggression in little girls at this phase of triangulation as for sexuality.

The incestuous motif is clearly represented in this tale, as Persephone becomes queen and mate to her uncle. Demeter, Zeus and Hades are siblings. It can be said, however, that the myth of Persephone is not analogous or parallel to the story of Oedipus. We have been asked, 'Where is the rivalry and rage toward the mother in Persephone, compared to the rivalry and rage toward the father in Oedipus?' We agree that aggression, on the part of a female, is not visible, except in the revengeful retribution of the mother, Demeter, unleashing famine on the earth until her daughter is returned to her. Aggression certainly does not seem to mark the mother-daughter relationship between Demeter and Persephone. It is our argument that the sense of agency over aggression and sexuality is disguised and inhibited in this story, as in the female triangular situation, as it appears clinically.

COUNTERTRANSFERENCE TO FEMALE TRIANGULAR MATERIAL

In an overlooked and perhaps prophetic article from twenty years ago, Grunberger (1980) spoke of the resistance, individually and institutionally, to the oedipal complex, that 'nodal complex'. He pointed to narcissistic elements central to the oedipal conflict, which often are not resolved by analysts in their own personal analyses. He warned that these lacunae have consequences not only for the effectiveness of their analytic work with their own patients but may become played out in theoretical controversies which aim to obliterate or minimize the oedipal complex theoretically or to alter psychoanalytic institutions broadly. We will leave this general admonition aside, however, to outline some typical countertransferences to triangular material with female patients.

TYPICAL COUNTERTRANSFERENCES WITH FEMALE PATIENTS

Female analysts and female patients

It is interesting that the beneficial effects of the countertransference in this dyad are frequently stressed in psychoanalytic literature. This emphasis may reflect the positive value women place on relationships, as suggested above. Ruderman (1986), for example, wrote of the 'creative and reparative uses of countertransference' in women treating women. She agreed with Mahler that in treatment daughters might need to revisit their relationships with their mothers in order to explore and develop their own identities. Thus, she advocated the idea that female analysts continually need to rework and re- examine their own relationships with their mothers with reference to themes of separation and individuation. A common idea is that this female-to-female interaction can foster positive feminine identifications for the female patients who may be lacking such models.

On the more negative side, however, celebration of the beneficial effects of reworking of separation themes between women may obscure other issues. Female analysts often miss, or misinterpret 'oedipal' (and/or paternal) trans-ferences. According to many writers (Bernstein and Warner, 1984; Ruderman, 1986) female analysts respond defensively to the competition and envy of their female patients and often resist being seen as the rival 'oedipal' mother. Instead, they tend to get involved in or lost in earlier pre-oedipal mother-daughter issues (Mendell, 1993) and often become too merged or over- identified with their patients (Bigras, 1990). They become 'too maternal' and overprotective (Moldawsky, 1986). Meyers (1986b) warned of another pitfall in this dyad, in which patients and analyst collude in idealized 'good' mother transference, often erotized. The bad mother image is split off and displaced on a person outside the therapeutic situation, male or female (often, in our experience, the husband or lover). Also, this picture may mask unrecognized erotic oedipal father transferences.

Dahl (1989) proposed that the common fantasy of the terrifying 'witch' mother associated with the daughter's hostile attachment to her mother is better understood as an 'oedipal' fantasy than as pre-oedipal. The fantasy of the witch mother is multifaceted. It includes a secret excited longing for the mother and her body, projections on to the mother of envious hostile and jealous aspects of the daughter's love, experience of the mother as malignantly destructive of the daughter's efforts to obtain genital pleasure from other sources, and oscillation between the wish to be mother's erotic partner and the fear that the mother would destroy her if she knew her daughter had an alternative erotic object tie to a man. Earlier fantasies are now reworked in the 'oedipal' context. We find these ideas congenial with our own thinking.

Several writers in differing contexts mention the problem of overidentification with the female patient by the female analyst (Notman, in Stein and Auchincloss, 1984-5). This situation is particularly apparent when a woman chooses a woman analyst consciously with the idea that she will receive support for her attitudes. Bernstein (1991), for example, warned that it might be too easy for a woman to identify with another woman's hostilities toward men rather than analyze them. We would suggest that this focusing of resentment on men outside the office might detour hostility away from the analyst-patient relationship. Indeed, there is a lot of sentiment expressed in the literature that women analysts need to mentor their female patients (Kestenbaum, in Stein and Auchincloss, 1984-5; Eisenbud, 1986). Such sentiments and enthusiasm have their dangers. Positive mentoring can foster the analyst's own agenda and values, and allow unexamined countertransferences to germinate.

In a comprehensive and perceptive article, Bernstein (1991) discussed the dangers in the woman/woman dyad. She highlighted the awakened competitiveness, both pre-oedipal and 'oedipal', in the female analyst toward the patient and the patient's mother. The fantasy is 'we are going to do it better'. The analyst may foster a powerful regression in the presumable service of growth, but this may also become a resistance. The stance of insisting how bad the original mother was may also hide far more threatening erotic, loving feelings toward their mothers that both analyst and patient fear. McDougall (1986) provided a now well-known example of this fear. She described her countertransference reaction to a female patient: 'deafness' to the homosexual, negative 'oedipal' dimensions of the patient's fantasies.

Male Analysts and Female Patients

If biased in their expectations of women, male analysts may foster traditional female sex roles and replicate patriarchal power structures (Broverman et al.,

1970; Lerman, 1982; Myers, 1982). Male analysts may unwittingly foster unhealthy compliance on the part of their female patients. Lerner (1980) wrote of how females learn to protect the male ego through the socialization process. The male analyst may unconsciously encourage this behavior as a boost to his ego (Person, 1983). While silently assuming the paternal role, male analysts may unwittingly keep female patients caught up in an 'oedipal' dynamic or paradoxically infantalize them. There is overwhelming evidence that male analysts are more vulnerable to acting upon strong erotic countertransferences seductively or overtly (Myers, 1982; Meyers, 1986a; Bigras, 1990; Gabbard and Lester, 1995; Kernberg, 1995). Sexual boundary violations occur most frequently between male analysts and female patients (Dahlberg, 1970; Seiden, 1976; Butler and Zelen, 1977).

Shared stereotypes and social roles about gender operate silently in generating unconscious attitudes and biases in analysts toward their patients. Such unconscious attitudes, while strictly speaking may not be classified as countertransferences, nevertheless exert powerful influences in the analytic process, which are important to examine. Bernardez (1987) has labeled these characteristic reactions 'cultural countertransferences'.

Cross-Gendered Countertransferences

Analysts have various degrees of comfort in experiencing the self in the guises of the opposite sex. These blind spots have been documented by a number of authors (Chasseguet-Smirgel, 1984; Gabbard and Wilkinson, 1996). Many have argued that the reported differences in cross-gender transferences that seem to adhere to the manifest gender of the analyst were the result of countertransferences, or intolerances for cross-gender transferences (Goldberger and Evans, 1985; Raphling and Chused, 1988; Goldberger and Holmes, 1993).

There may be particular difficulties, that is, countertransferences or blind spots, in dealing with cross-gender oedipal transferences (Kulish, 1984, 1986, 1989). It has been suggested in the literature that the oedipal transference usually materializes along the lines of the manifest gender of the analyst, with the feelings toward the opposite sex being played out in displacement (Kulish, 1989). While this may be, it may also be that the analyst's internal difficulties in bisexual empathy and identification become strained in these instances. For example, several writers (Meyers, 1986b; Lasky, 1989) suggested that the male analyst might be uncomfortable in experiencing himself as the oedipal mother. Under the sway of the common unconscious fantasy that equates being a woman with being castrated, male analysts may fear perceiving themselves as a 'castrated' being or as a sexual object that can be penetrated. Gabbard and Lester (1995) pointed to a similar construction in some cases of sexual boundary violations between male analysts and female patients. The male analyst disavowed his participation in a cross-gender analysis as a genital male and convinced himself that he was providing maternal nurturance in his sexual acting out.

On the other hand, the female analyst may have difficulty experiencing herself as the 'oedipal' father. Processing cross-gender transferences that also involve roles that are not 'in synch' with the analyst's predominant sense of sexual orientation, as, for example, in a female patient's sexual fantasies about her female analyst in the so-called 'negative oedipal' transference, would add another layer of difficulty.

Gabbard and Wilkinson (1996) summarized two main threads running through recent theoretical contributions on gender—multiplicity and disavowal—that appear in a clinical tension between nominal gender and gender-fluidity in the transference-countertransference dyad. They suggest that the formidable difficulties in differentiating longings for pre-oedipal paternal nurturance, pre- oedipal maternal nurturance and genital oedipal wishes may be further complicated by the analyst's own subjective constructions of gender.

In a research project, which set out to examine some of these suggestions, Kulish and Mayman (1993) found evidence that therapists encouraged the development of gender-consistent transferences. More specifically, female therapists described more transferences pertaining to earlier oral issues, especially with their female patients, and less often recognized oedipal material than did male therapists. Males were more sensitive to competitive oedipal issues, especially with male patients.

Kumin (1985-6) described analysts' 'erotic horror' in the face of erotic transferences and countertransferences. The dysphoric feelings associated with the defense against the awareness of erotic transference can be characterized as erotic horror. The task, according to Kumin, is to accept patient's sexual desire without seductiveness or avoidance. We might conclude that women may lean toward avoidance in the countertransference to patient's oedipal sexual fantasies but have less difficulty with maternal/infant transferences, which include anal and oral erotogenic components. (Wyre and Welles, 1989; Lester, 1990). Men are thought to be more in touch with strongly erotic feelings in the transferences, but may err in the direction of seductiveness in the countertransference.

CLINICAL MATERIAL

In the following clinical case, an example of a countertransference around triangular sexual issues by a female analyst to a female patient, demonstrates the derailment of the treatment for a period of time. Sally, a middle-aged teacher, was approaching the end of her analysis. She had sought treatment because of severe anxiety, social phobias and inhibitions in all areas of her life, especially the sexual. She was the youngest and overly protected child of strict, but loving parents. The children in the family were always expected to put on a good front and live up to the highest ideals of conduct. Her father was a staunch minister who kept tight and critical watch on his children, especially his daughters. She remembered how he was extremely vigilant against her straying sexually. Her mother, who was more permissive, gave the patient mixed messages, such as be popular with the boys but stay away from sex. At the same time the mother would brag to her daughter about her own past and present sexual experiences, even detailing how orgasmic she was.

The patient approached the treatment as she did the rest of her life—she tried to be an obedient, good girl, who submitted to the forceful demands of her parents. Her first dream epitomized this central anal conflict: She dreamed *she was about to suffer a huge 'Sigmoid'*, a pun on the word 'Sigmund'. (Patients often experience the beginning of the analysis as a virginal sexual experience with the wish/fear of penetration (Holtzman and Kulish, 1997)). The analyst was experienced as both the strict critical father and the competitive demanding mother. It took several years of analysis before this characterological defense shifted to allow her underlying rebelliousness and anger to emerge toward the analyst. In the course of the treatment, she ended her long, virtually sexless and unhappy marriage, obtained a more rewarding job and began to feel much freer and happier with herself.

The following sequence of material occurred as she was working through her anxieties about seeking new relationships with men and trying to escape her severe inhibitions about sex. She had just begun to see a man, named Jim, who was interested in her. Jim was separated, but his divorce was not yet final. In the immediate week before, the patient had talked about her conflicted feelings of competition with some of her female co-workers in their standing with their male boss.

In the session, Sally began by talking about how she had felt pleased that she had handled a problem with her teenage son more calmly and with less self- recrimination than she had in the past. She then said, 'So on to Jim'. She reported that Jim had told her about a big brouhaha between himself and his wife. The wife 'had acted in a very bizarre manner, inappropriately, angrily, in a rage'. She had pulled off her blouse, pushed her breasts in Jim's face and said, 'You see these? Aren't these better than Sally's?'

The patient said, 'I can see that he is still entangled with her and the divorce isn't happening quickly enough. I just stepped back. Withdrew. I could feel myself doing it'. She explained that she was concerned that Jim would not be available for a committed relationship with her. The analyst asked, 'What about drawing back?'

'Well, maybe it triggered something to do with my anxieties about anger. As he described the extent of his wife's rage it also made me think of how it was with Tom [her ex-husband] and my father. Did I look at him and wonder what instills such a rage in a woman? I am afraid it's a dead end. After he told me about his relationship with his wife, I see that it isn't a done deal. After that I just stepped back. I could feel myself doing it.' While consciously the patient's words 'a dead end' referred to the idea of the relationship with Jim as going nowhere, they convey other unconscious fears: the murderousness of competition with the rageful wife; the end of a relationship between mother and daughter, and/or analyst and patient; or deadened or non-functional genitals.

The analyst observed that it seemed there was anger and jealousy about sex in this story—the wife seemed to be reacting to Sally as a rival and the fireworks had started when the wife found out that her husband was now involved with Sally. This context clearly underlines the data for attributing triangularity to this material. We have two women vying for one man. The patient made it clear that this is connected to her memories of her father.

Such a triangle, a competitively charged dynamic interaction around sex, is a necessary condition for us to assume 'oedipal' meaning to a clinical material. This is to be distinguished from a triangular competition in which siblings vie for attention from and possession of the mother. Goals and level of object relationships are different. The presence of three people is a necessary but not sufficient condition for the attribution of 'oedipal' or Persephonal dynamics.

Sexual relations form the action.

'Hmmm. Now I'm "the other woman". That's interesting. And he really likes me sexually. Sex with Jim is more basic but I couldn't enjoy sex with Jim after I heard what had happened.' That is, out of her anxiety, Sally had to inhibit her sexual desires (literally to deaden her end). The idea that the still legitimate wife of the man she wants would be so angry has evoked her conflicts around being an 'oedipal' victor over her mother—'the other woman'. The analyst said, 'You cannot allow yourself to be the victorious woman'.

Sally mused, 'Maybe, but why? It hits on some of my fantasies? Hmmm. I did send for the new *Joy of sex* book. And before this happened I was kidding around about it with Jim, that we would try it. But does this whole thing move me into Pandora's Box?' We recognize the metaphoric meanings of 'whole thing' and 'box'. She recognizes that she has entered into something forbidden, going after a married man. The genital sexual nature of this material is unmistakable. (Pandora, the first woman, was entrusted with a box she was warned not to open. Disobeying this prohibition out of curiosity, she opened it and out flew all the ills of humanity.) Thus, the session ends on the note of forbidden and punished sexual pleasure.

The following session:

P: I want to go back to yesterday. I felt better after yesterday. I'm not certain exactly why. More understanding which always makes me feel better. The whole issue of being victorious. That really strikes me. Although it is victorious by default. I don't even know her. It's not like I am in a race and she is the opponent.

[Note the defensive negation here. The defensive position is similar to Persephone's being abducted 'against her will' to be queen of her own domain.]

A: Yes, but symbolically it is a victory.

P: Hmmm. And her anger. It's so primitive. I think I've felt that rage myself to the toes, but I didn't ever express it. Yes. What crosses my mind is sexual rage. I remember how bad things were sexually between Tom [her ex- husband] and me ... [She elaborated.] Hearing about Jim's wife's actions scared me. I wish I could have been so outrageous, really, letting Tom know how enraged I was. In my marriage I was so submissive, and took everything on as my fault. What's confusing me is feeling distanced from Jim. Is this him or me?

A: Time will tell about Jim. But certainly it has to do with your feelings.

P: This whole idea of being chosen, being the special one ... He must have sensed that I pulled back. I glommed on to details about him that aren't important, and criticized him to myself, like he is too old for me.

[In reality Jim was a few years older than the patient. This dynamically determined exaggeration reflects the triangular or 'oedipal' meaning of the relationship for Sally]

P: Perhaps that diminished the victory. Oh that's something to ponder. With a victory, part of it feels good, but part of it makes me feel uneasy. It must make me feel uneasy, this idea of victory ... because I'm blanking out.

[Silence.] Victorious over someone. Being chosen. Hmmm. Why do I keep going back to my mother?

In case the analyst did not get it, the patient specified the link with her rival, her mother, and her fears of loss of the object and loss of the love of the object because of her forbidden wishes. And, remember, termination is in the air for this woman, and thus loss of the analytic relationship.

She laughed. 'That's so oedipal! I don't know if I experienced her as being victorious. Maybe it's just a fantasy ... I remember that time when she was with me at the gynecologist's office. When I was having all those problems. Mother bragged about how good her sex life was and how she always had orgasms. So it was in that context when I felt there was something the matter with me sexually, as a woman, anyhow. I could really hate her for that. But she doesn't have a clue. She would be horrified if she knew what she had said hurt me.'

Here, analyst and patient are working through an important dynamic: Sally's conflict about being victorious. Avoiding the intensity of the transference, the patient expressed her experience of the analyst as hurtful in displacement, via the memory of the mother at the gynecologist's office. Moreover, she defensively made the mother and analyst clueless, 'nice', without hostile intent.

And, of course, the patient herself did not acknowledge her own rage and competitiveness, again like Persephone—'Hades made me do it'. The conflict is, as she recognized it herself, 'oedipal'. The analyst felt pleased that the analysis seemed to be progressing. What happened in the next session, however, was very interesting. Manifestly there was a return to themes that had dominated earlier periods of the analysis, concerning preoedipal issues.

The patient arrived at the following session five minutes late, an action that was unusual for her. 'Yucky weather. I had a dream, or some kind of thoughts, while I was asleep. *Someone took me to a cottage in the middle of winter. It was like in the middle of nowhere. The person left. The cabin was primitive. I had no idea of what the place was going to be like, but it was changing. The place wasn't heated. I would have to haul in the wood to heat it. I worried if I would have enough supplies. I was alone, and I thought, What will I do to occupy my time? I thought I could take a walk but I didn't have warm enough clothes. And I had only a few books. Or I would just think. Or I could sleep a lot. But then I realized it was only a week, so then I planted a man therefor myself, magically*, and that was the end.' (Another end.)

'Definitely, the theme is being alone like when I went to the cottage alone last summer, and I didn't like it. Stranded. It is the concern that I have that I won't be in a relationship.' In this material the patient shows fears of loss of a relationship on the heels of being called victorious in a triangular sexual competition. Viewed by itself, without knowing its context, this session could look simply like dyadic separation anxiety. In this sequence, however, the loss of the mother/analyst is a consequence of rivalrous fantasies. Left alone in an unheated cabin without supplies, stranded—a cold lonely existence for the girl who triumphs over her mother.

The patient continued, 'Before the dream I got a call from Jim. He kind of kiddingly said, "The calls I make to you every day are beginning to feel obligatory". But it kind of made me angry. Somewhere in the night I had the thought to myself, 'You have this need to be victorious. The favorite girl'. She elaborated her associations to the cabin with the memory of the unhappy vacation she had taken the summer before. She had gone to a cabin alone, although she had hoped a current boyfriend would have accompanied her. At the time she had been very angry with the analyst and blamed her for her unhappiness.

Somehow she felt that the analysis should have produced results by then, results being equated with her having a good relationship with a man.

She continued, 'Stranded. What I think of is that it's you. Or the process, actually. I've done this—now where am I? This isn't magic. If the cabin is me, then the question is what will I do? How will I function in the cold bad world? I'm alone'. The analyst, not understanding the triangular, competitive nature of this material, fell into the familiar pattern of thinking about the transference in terms of the nurturing mother, and said, 'So you are saying that you feel you are not getting what you want from me'.

'Yes. As I listen to you, I want to cry. People, my parents, never accepted me for what I was. There was always a "Yes, but". Even Jim now says, "Don't get angry", like when I was talking about the broken heater. [The patient feared that the analyst also did not want her to get angry.] So I do feel alone a lot. [She was crying.] You understand me more than anybody, but you can't go with me into the world.'

The wish here is that the analyst would not be angry with her, but rather make the patient feel secure. At the next session she reported another dream, one of a series of dreams with an association of a Cinderella theme. (For example, one portrayed the wish that the analyst be the fairy godmother and help

492

the patient get the prince.) In the dream *there was a voluptuous, brassy blonde.* She associated to this figure as 'the kind of gal who gets the man. Is that the way I see me when I'm pursuing men? I haven't got it exactly together … You seem to have it together. You have a man. You have everything'.

The patient's fantasy about Jim's first wife, who was 'still in the picture', unsettled her completely. The direct competition reawakened humiliating triangular situations in which her father or her former husband did not choose her. This patient came to the commonly held idea that sexuality was the domain of her mother, forbidden to her. To do so threatened to evoke her mother's wrath and to disrupt her continued support and love. Her rage toward the rival was expressed, albeit defensively, and was quickly followed by recollections of miserable times alone. It was the triangulated aspect of her anger at the analyst that had not been recognized the previous summer. Not understood at that time was that in the patient's mind the analyst was deliberately and competitively keeping the patient from having a man of her own. In the current material, family relationships are clearly triangulated: there are repeated references to an older man, and a hated older woman rival who owns the man, and a younger sexually humiliated woman. Her competitive feelings are central.

In the session the analyst's focus on Sally's being victorious was taken as if it were a criticism; a sign in itself of the patient's projected competition with the mother. The patient had experienced the focus on her conflict as a criticism and a threat, and felt hurt by it. She experienced it as a competitive put-down by the analyst/mother. The analyst's own 'oedipal', competitive strivings were probably at play here in her, perhaps, overly zealous interventions. Of course, the patient's fears of being abandoned by the analyst via termination are ever lurking in the background. Part of this woman's conflict in the current treatment was her fantasy that if she found an appropriate man she would lose the analyst and the analysis, as in her dream that ended abruptly when she found the man. Thus, having a man would unconsciously mean the 'dead end', the end of the analytic relationship and, perhaps, the death of the analyst. In this context, the analytic interaction became a repetition of the manner in which her triangular strivings were originally experienced. That is, the patient felt she was told in one way or another, 'Be a good little girl, and leave the domain of erotic heterosexuality to me or you will be abandoned or rejected'.

Another fearful fantasy can be discerned in this material: that of genital damage as punishment for the girl's forbidden, guilt-ridden competitive wishes toward her mother. After talking of her competitive feelings toward the mother, the patient remembers her mother's bragging about orgasms and recounts, in contrast, her own suffering from gynecological difficulties. In this sequence we might infer the patient's sense of genital damage and malfunction as a consequence of her competitive strivings and as punishment from her rivalrous mother. Similarly, the patient's dream of the cold empty cabin may represent her unhappy experience of cold unsatisfied genitals and empty womb, both also punishment for forbidden wishes. As we demonstrated, the patient's repeated phrase 'dead end' also carries this meaning—a dead genital.[2]

In the summer before these sessions, the material centered on separations. The analyst erred by taking the *content* of separation (the patient's feelings of wanting to be nurtured and cared for and her anger and disappointment at being left) as indicative of pre-oedipal separation problems. The analyst had been blind to the underlying competitive and 'oedipal' issues, which might have sharpened her interpretive focus and relieved the patient of her guilt about her anger and competition with the analyst. This anger became projected into fears of abandonment. Here, psychoanalytic theory, as well as an unconscious preference for being the nurturing and giving mother, combined to derail the treatment for some time. The analyst's interpretation with a pre-oedipal dyadic focus clearly had reinforced the patient's notions that competitive feelings were forbidden and to be eradicated. If this were to be the way in which the treatment had terminated, the analysis would have been incomplete.

---

2 We thank Elena Maenpaa Reenkola for these ideas.

Perhaps it need not to be said that the analyst needs to be acquainted with and have worked through her own 'oedipal' desires, competition and angers in order to recognize and to tolerate expression of these feelings in her patients. We acknowledge the difficulty we ourselves have had with such feelings.[3] It is often easier to recognize such countertransferential struggles in someone else. Reanalyses frequently offer glimpses of the enacted countertransferences in previous analytic work. It is not unusual in our experience with reanalyses to discern evidence of 'oedipal' countertransferences in the first analyst, which have encumbered what appeared otherwise to have been beneficial treatments. The following vignette provides such an example.

Ms. A, a talented professional musician, was an only child. She had left a lengthy analysis in which she had come to feel infantilized and stuck. The first analyst, a female, apparently reacted to, but did not analyze, 'oedipal' competitive transference. The early analytic work appeared mutually enjoyable. The patient experienced the analyst as lovingly 're-mothering' her. Ms. A had always felt deprived, devalued and ignored by her parents. Although she felt her mother ignored her, she nonetheless took narcissistic credit for her daughter's accomplishments. The patient had never married and was trying to find a suitable mate.

In her second analysis with a second female analyst, rich triangular material soon emerged. For example, the patient often dreamed and spoke of scenarios that involved triangles—two women and a man. She complained that, in addition to having difficulty finding a mate, her relationships with women had always been a problem. In one session she spoke of her former analyst, Dr. E. She recounted the following occurrence from the previous treatment: She had been complaining to Dr. E about her feeling of being excluded from a party

---

3 Another example of countertransference was an amusing repeated typographic error. Meaning to say the analyst's 'own' competitiveness, and after supposed corrections, we found time and time again 'won' competitiveness in the manuscript.

given by a friend, S, because Ms. A was dating a former boyfriend of S. We suspect that the sense of ownership over sexuality, as with Persephone, still belonged, in the patient's mind, to the rival mother, Demeter, or the girlfriend S.

Subsequently, she told Dr. E that she had decided to go on a short vacation with this man, which precluded attendance at several analytic sessions. Here, again, separation material is intertwined with triangular material. Ms. A spoke of her admiration and attraction for this man. She had been extolling his virtues to Dr. E since she had met him. She felt that Dr. E was annoyed with her. Finally Dr. E blurted out, 'I'm tired of hearing about him. You prefer seeing this guy to me!' With hindsight, Ms. A could see that she had tried to and succeeded in make the analyst jealous by negatively comparing her to this man and choosing him and vacation over analysis.

Retrospectively, the patient mused, 'I think Dr. E was just like my mother. She was insecure. Dr. E expected me to be loyal to her, just like my mother did. I felt that both my mother and Dr. E wanted to thwart my development, were jealous of me and didn't want me to get ahead and get married'. With the word loyalty, Ms. A reminds us of Persephone's balancing act between father and mother. She experienced her analyst and mother as wanting to keep her close, just as Demeter did. The myth portrays the dangers of straying from the mother's side.

She then reported a current dream: 'I had a dream, the first time in years that Dr. E was in my dreams. *I asked her for a name of someone for me to see besides her: a man. She backed away*'. Ms. A associated, 'I always felt that I couldn't love both my mother and my father; it could only be one or the other. And my mother was very jealous'. It should be noted that the patient had spent a lot of time praising and exalting the male analyst of her current boyfriend, in an attempt to make the current analyst jealous, frustrated and guilty, just as she had succeeded in doing with her former analyst, and with her mother. At this point in her treatment, she had finally begun to enjoy satisfactory sexual relations and to talk of her wishes to marry and have children. This dream represented and was interpreted to the patient as a fear that the current analyst would thwart and reject her for finding and loving a man of her own.

In the next session the patient began by saying, 'This is not a complaint about the inconsistency of our recent sessions …' (A defensive negation of the patient's feelings about separations.) The patient was referring to the analyst's two-week vacation, probably represented by the phrase *'she backed away'* in the dream the previous day. The asking for another name in the dream represented a wish for an analyst who was more consistent. What is crucial here is the way that the separation at this time in her analysis is unconsciously interpreted as punishment by the analyst for her getting a man. The feelings about separation seem dyadic but come in relation to triadic conflicts. Then Ms. A went on to talk about familiar 'oedipal' themes, her conflicts of loyalty about her close girlfriend and her new serious boyfriend. Here, once again, she expressed fears that a girlfriend would break off the relationship with her because of her desire to spend time with a boyfriend. The analyst pointed out that, indeed, the patient was afraid to complain because she feared the analyst might break off their relationship. Ms. A corrected the analyst: 'No, it's not that you'll break off with me, but you won't be nice anymore. I feel you are confident with yourself. Dr. E was insecure and jealous and envious. She didn't want me to do that well. I sense you want me to soar, to do well. I think Dr. E was more like my mother and, at that point when she got mad, it really came out. My mother was envious of me'.

Certainly, it was the patient's sense that Dr. E's unconscious, and apparently conflicted, competitiveness with her meant that she could not help the patient with such feelings. Perhaps Dr. E's countertransference contributed to the infantilization, or we might say pre-oedipalization, that the patient experienced within a prolonged analysis. The second analyst's therapeutic zealousness and confidence could contain its own countertransference, that is, competitiveness with the former analyst. The patient may have been experiencing the second analyst as she did her mother treating her as a narcissistic object, working for her own glory, and not really for the patient.

While this vignette concerns a female analyst, this sort of problem occurs with both female and male analysts and their female patients. In this case, the patient's separation fears took the form of fear of the analyst not being 'nice', meaning a withdrawal of affection, nurture or closeness from her. The patient's healthy strivings toward sexuality and maturity were fostered by the achievement of a sense of a safe and stable relationship with a maternal figure: the analyst.

CONCLUSION AND SUMMARY

In this paper, we have presented clinical material to demonstrate that adherence to an erroneously labeled theoretical proposition, combined with a commonly found counter-transference in female analysts with female patients produces a limiting and/or constraining effect upon the otherwise forward progressive movement in an analysis. Such problems are also prevalent in analyses with male analysts and female patients.

We have delineated the contextual clinical clues, which should direct our attention to the triangular separation issues in female development. That is, three figures are involved; competition and sexual desire are in the air.

Generational age differences are apparent. Frequently, the context is an important milestone in the patient's life: marriage, loss of virginity, a new job, going off to school etc. In both of the cases reported here, a new love affair and burgeoning sexuality brought up triangular conflicts. In both clinical cases, intensification of competitiveness and conflicted triangular material were precipitated by actual analytic separations.

In this paper, we have attempted to reconcile contemporary changes in psychoanalytic understandings of female development, particularly in respect to separation issues, with their clinical applications to female patients. We elucidated ways in which changes in theories about women affect technical considerations and interpretive attitudes in the analyses of females by both male and female analysts. Two clinical examples of theoretical preconceptions and countertransference, which led to stalemate or prolonged analyses, were presented. In the first case, the analyst misread separation material as pre- oedipal, and hence missed the competitive, 'oedipal' meanings of the transference. In the second, reanalysis revealed how the first analyst apparently enacted an unrecognized competitive, 'oedipal' countertransference.

A lack of attention to 'oedipal' meanings of separation issues can lead to a suppression or denial of aggressive and sexual strivings and stymie progress in analyses and in our patients' lives. We argue that such an allegiance to erroneous theory and/or individual blind spots have led to the infantilization, pre-oedipalization or cultural stereotyping of females, which constrain the effectiveness of their analyses. We look forward to hearing from our colleagues about their experiences in this area.

REFERENCES

Abelin, E. (1971). *The role of the father in the separation-individuation process. In Separation-individuation,* ed. J McDevitt, C Settlage, New York: Int. Univ. Press, pp. *229–52.*

Bernardez, T. (1987). Gender based countertransference of female therapists in the psychotherapy of women. In *Women, power and therapy, ed.* H Braude, New York: Ha worth Press, pp. *25–39.*

Bernstein, A.E., & Warner ,G.M. (1984). *Women treating women.* New York: Int. Univ. Press.

Bernstein, D. (1991). Gender specific dangers in the female-female dyad in treatment. *Psychoanal. Rev.*78: *37–48.*

——— (1993). *Female identity conflict in clinical practice.* Northvale, NJ: Jason Aronson.

Bigras, J. (1990). Psychoanalysis as incestuous repetition: Some technical considerations. In *Analysis and childhood sexual abuse,* ed. H Levine, Hillsdale, NJ: The Analytic Press, pp. *175–96.*

Birksted-Breen, D. (1996). Unconscious representation of femininity. *J. Amer. Psychoanal. Assn.*44(S): *119–32.*

Broverman, I. et al. (1970). Sex-role stereotypes and clinical judgments of mental health. *J Consulting and Clinical Psychol* 32:*1–7.*

Burch, B. (1997). *Other women.* New York: Columbia Univ. Press.

Butler, S.E., & Zelen, S. (1977). Sexual intimacies between psychotherapists and their patients. *Psychotherapy: Treatment, Research and Practice* 14:*143–5.*

Chasseguet-Smirgel, J. (1984). The femininity of the analyst in professional practice. *Int. J. Psycho-Anal.* 65:*169–78.*

Chodorow, N. (1978). *The reproduction of mothering.* Berkeley: Univ. of California Press.

Dahl, E.K. (1989). Daughters and mothers: Oedipal aspects of the witchmother. *Psychoanal. St. Child* 44:*267–80.*

David, C. (1970). A masculine mythology of femininity. In *Female sexuality,* ed. J Chasseguet-Smirgel, London: Karnac Books, 1992, pp. *47–67.*

Dahlberg. C.C. (1970). Sexual contact between patient and therapist. *Contemp. Psychoanal.*6: *107–24.*

Eisenbud, R. (1986). Lesbian choice: Transferences to theory. In *Psychoanalysis and women: Contemporary reappraisals,* ed. J. Alpert, Hillsdale, NJ: The Analytic Press, pp. *215–33.*

Foley, H.P. (Ed.) (1994). *The home sic hymn to Demeteo.* Princeton, NJ: Princeton University Press

Gabbard, G.O., & Lester EP (1995). *Boundaries and boundary violations in psychoanalysis.* New York: Basic Books.

———— & Wilkinson SM (1996). Nominal gender and gender fluidity in the psychoanalytic situation. *Gender and Psychoanal.*1:463–81.

Gilligan, C. (1982). In a different voice. Cambridge, MA: Harvard Univ. Press.

Goldberger, M., & Evans, D. (1985). On transference manifestations in patients with female analysts. *Int. J. Psycho-Anal* .66:295–305.

———— & Holmes, D.E. (1993). Transferences in male patients with female analysts: An update. *Psychoanal. Inq.*2:173–91.

Grunberger, B. (1980). The oedipal conflicts of the analyst. *Psychoanal. Q.* 49:606–30.

Holtzman, D., & Kulish, N. (1997). *The hymen and the loss of virginity.* Northvale, NJ: Aronson.

———— & Kulish, N. (2000). The femininization of the female oedipal complex, part I: A reconsideration of the significance of separation issues. *J. Amer. Psychoanal. Assn.*48:1413–37.

Kernberg, O. (1995). *Love relations.* New Haven: Yale Univ. Press.

Kestenbaum, C. (1984–5). The public and the private woman. GJ Stein and E Auchincloss, reporters. *Bulln Assoc Psychoanal Med* 24:1–19.

Kulish, N. (1984). The effect of the sex of the analyst on transference: A review of the literature. *Bull. Mennin. Clinic.*48:95–110.

———— (1986). Gender and transference: The screen of the phallic mother. *Int. Rev. Psycho-Anal.*13:393–404.

———— (1989). Gender and transference: Conversations with female analysts. *Psychoanal. Psychol.*6:59–71.

———— & Holtzman, D. (1998). Persephone, the loss of virginity and the female oedipal complex. *Int. J. Psycho-Anal.* 79:57–71.

———— & Mayman, M. (1993). Gender-linked determinants of transference and countertransference in psychoanalytic psychotherapy. *Psychoanal. Inq.*2:286–305.

Kumin, I. (1985–6). Erotic horror: Desire and resistance in the psycho-analytic situation. *Int. J. Psychoanal. Psychother.*11:3–20.

Lasky, R. (1989). Some determinants of the male analyst's capacity to identify with female patients. *Int. J. Psycho-Anal.* 70:*405–18.*

Lerman, H.E. (1982). Special issues for women in psychotherapy. In *The woman patient, Vol. 3: Aggression, adaptations and psychotherapy,* ed. M.T. Notman, C.C. Nadelson, New York: Plenum, pp. *273–86.*

Lerner, H. (1980). Internal prohibitions against female anger. *Am J Psychoanal* 40:*137–48.*

Lester, E. (1990). Gender and identity issues in the analytic process. *Int. J. Psycho-Anal.* 71:*435–44.*

McDougall, J. (1986). Eve's reflection: On the homosexual components of female sexuality. In *S.E* Analytic Press, pp. *213–28.*

Mendell, D. (1993). Supervising female therapists: A comparison of dynamics while treating male and female patients. *Psychoanal. Inq.*13:*270–85.*

Meyers, H. (1986a). How do women treat men? In *The Psychology of Men,* ed. G Fogel et al., New York: Basic Books, pp. *262–76.*

——— (1986b). Analytic work by and with women: The complexity and the challenge. In *Between analyst and patient: S.E* NJ: Analytic Press, pp. *159– 76.*

Moldawsky, S. (1986). When men are therapists to women: Beyond the oedipal pale. In *The psychology of today's woman,* ed. T Bernay, D Cantor, Hills ale, NJ: The Analytic Press, pp. *291–303.*

Myers, M.F. (1982). The professional woman as patient: Are view and an appeal. *Canadian Journal of Psychiatry*27: *236–40.*

Notman, N. (1984–5). The public and the private woman. GJ Stein and E Auchincloss, reporters. *Bulln Assoc Psychoanal Med* 24:*1–19.*

Ogden, T. (1987). The transitional oedipal relationship in female development. *Int. J. Psycho-Anal.* 68:*485–98.*

Person, E, (1983). Women in therapy: Therapist gender as a variable. *Int. Rev. Psycho-Anal.*10: *93–204.*

Raphling, D. Chused J (1988). Transference across gender lines. *J. Amer. Psychoanal. Assn. 36:77–104.*

Reenkola, E.M. (2002). *The veiled female core. New* York: Other Press.

Ruderman, E. (1986). Creative and reparative uses of countertransference by women psychotherapists treating women patients: A clinical research study. In *The psychology of today's woman,* ed. T Bernay, D Cantor, Hillsdale, NJ: The Analytic Press, pp. *339–63.*

Schafer, R. (1974). Problems in Freud's psychology of women. *J. Amer. Psychoanal. Assn. 22:459–85.*

Seiden, A.M. (1976). Overview: Research on the psychology of women II. Women in families, work and psychotherapy. *Am. J. Psychiatry 133:1111–23.*

Wyre, H. & Welles, J. (1989). The maternal erotic transference. *Int. J. Psycho-Anal. 70:673–84.*

CHAPTER 17

Female Exhibitionism: Identification, Competition and Camaraderie

(2012). Int. J. Psychoanal., (93)(2):271–292

With Deanna Holtzman

The ancient figure of Baubo plays a pivotal role in the Greek myth of Demeter and Persephone with an exhibitionistic act that brings Demeter out of her depression. The Baubo episode raises questions about the meaning of female exhibitionism, suggesting divergences from earlier psychoanalytic conceptualizations as either a perversion or a compensation for the lack of a penis. In line with contemporary thinking about primary femininity, such as that of Balsam or Elise, the authors propose a more inclusive understanding of female exhibitionism, which would encompass pleasure in the female body and its sexual and reproductive functions. They argue that female exhibitionism can reflect triangular or "oedipal" scenarios and the need to attract the male, identification with the mother, competition or camaraderie with other women, a sense of power in the female body and its capacities, as well as homoerotic impulses. The authors posit a dual early desire and identification with the mother that underlie and characterize female sexual development. The authors present clinical data from adolescent and adult cases of female exhibitionism which illustrate these Baubo-like aspects and discuss the technical issues that are involved in such cases.

She lifted her skirts and the other woman laughed. Who would believe that a woman's lifting her skirts would bring another woman out of a deep depression? But that is what happens in a pivotal episode of the myth of Persephone. The goddess Demeter, bereft and frantic, is roaming the world in search of her daughter Persephone, who has been abducted to the underworld by her uncle Hades. Disguised as an old woman, Demeter offers herself as a servant to a mortal family to care for their infant boy, Demophoon. "Voiceless with grief" (Foley, 1994, p. 12), Demeter refuses food and drink. An older servant woman, Baubo (also known as Iambe), jests by lifting up her skirt and displaying her genitals to the despondent Demeter. Responding to this gesture, Demeter laughs and is brought out of her depression.

The Baubo episode suggests some divergences from the traditional psychoanalytic view of female exhibitionism as either a perversion or a compensation for a sense of lack. Our literature has been tilted in its emphasis on shame and negative feelings that women and girls have toward their bodies and on cases of women who are dissatisfied with their bodies, long to be boys, or dislike anything 'feminine,' as in Abraham's (1922) 'masculine protest'. However, recent psychoanalytic writings on 'primary femininity' (Balsam, 2008; Elise, 1997; Kulish, 2000, among others) have explored a different idea that female exhibitionism may reflect pleasurable narcissism, pride, and pleasure in the female body. In this paper, we will present clinical data that augments these contemporary views of female exhibitionism and illustrates important additional, developmental interpretations which focus on triangular and homoerotic issues.

Exhibitionism as a concept started out with Krafft-Ebing's (1886) description of a sexual perversion, but later expanded to include other non-pathological behavior. Adopting Krafft-Ebing's view, Webster's (1976) *International Dictionary* defines exhibitionism, male or female, as 'a perversion marked by a tendency to indecent exposure of the person so as to excite or gratify oneself sexually by such exposure' or, secondarily, as 'the act or practice of attracting attention to oneself.' Psychoanalysis has stressed one side of this—the 'indecent' perverse genital display, which has been understood as a defense against castration anxiety. We want to restore balance by emphasizing exhibitionistic behavior meant to elicit positive sexual attention to the body. We regard exhibitionism, in general, as encompassing a broad range of behaviors, from perverse to 'normal' or ordinary, which express varied unconscious and conscious meanings, and are defined by their underlying psychic structures and the social, interpersonal context in which they emerge. We will argue that female exhibitionism can frequently carry the meaning: *Look what I have and value as a female.*

In the triadic persephonal or 'oedipal' phase, female exhibitionism frequently has the function of attracting the father/male (or mother/another female). We have found clinically that female exhibitionism also regularly carries a Baubo-like *female-to-female* aspect in the unconscious or conscious psyche, including an inextricable mix of competition and identification with other women, homosexual interest and a joyful sharing of pleasure. This clinical and developmental picture suggests that the girl simultaneously both identifies with the maternal body and is aroused by it, processes which underlie or accompany her heterosexual interest in the father.

Let us return to the figure of Baubo whose story we take as a metaphor for female exhibitionism. Baubo in her various personae is frequently and widely depicted in ancient art. Freud reproduced one of the famous terracotta figurines of Baubo in the margin of a paper entitled *A mythological parallel to a visual obsession* in the *Standard Edition* (Freud, 1916, p. 338). These typical Baubo figurines are bodies of women with faces on their abdomens. Large heads sit directly on top of the legs, and the lifted dresses frame the faces like rings of hair.

Over the ages the image of Baubo has appeared in inscriptions, poems, figurines, carvings, and rituals (Foley, 1994; Lubell, 1994; Olender, 1990). Her Orphic origins in the 7th century BC precede Greek culture, and have also been documented (Olender, 1990). Baubo-like representations have been discovered carved into the walls of English and Irish churches of the 12th to 14th centuries.

The celebrity of this figure is astonishing, given how it has receded in recent Western culture. Wherever she appeared she was associated with holes, entrances, or caves. The very name 'Baubo' is associated with a Greek noun for body, cavity, womb, vagina or nurse (Lincoln, 1991; Olender, 1990). The artist and classicist Lubell (1994) sees Baubo as representing the strength of the female.

The fascinating figure of Baubo appears in one form or another in all versions of the Persephone myth. The associated gestures ('anasuramai' = lifting the skirt), and/or joking ('aischrologia' = indulging in indecent speech or joking) became important rituals played out by women in the widespread Eleusinian mysteries, which are based on the Persephone myth. Baubo is the iconic representation of pleasure in the female body, a joy in female display, innocent of the later-Judeo/Christian overlay of sin, which accounts for her submersion in modern times. The dramatic effect of Baubo's gesture on Demeter cannot be easily explained by ideas about perversion, castration anxiety, or negative feelings about the female genitals. Rather, Baubo's display of her belly and genitals expresses an unencumbered and uninhibited sense of pleasure and pride in the female genital and its life giving and replenishing powers (Kulish and Holtzman, 2002). The communication between the servant and the goddess is humorous and life affirming. Considerable more recent scholarly work on Baubo (Burkert, 1985) offers confirmatory material for Balsam's (2008) thesis of the communicated pleasures of women – both consciously and/or unconsciously in their child-bearing capacities.

Early psychoanalytic theory had no place for the boisterous female genital pride of the Baubo story. One of the few psychoanalytically oriented explanations of the Baubo episode evokes a traditional view in terms of the concept of penis envy (Arthur, 1994). We suggest alternative explanations. In the context of the Persephone story, Baubo's gestures and jokes offer a life-affirming camaraderie. In essence, she says to Demeter, woman to woman: "There is more to life than loss. Rejoice in your capacity for sexual pleasures, in the possibility of replenishment, and in your fertility. We women share something wonderful." We suggest that permission for, and acknowledgement of, sexual and bodily pleasure by one woman to another is an important message of the Baubo episode. In our experience, unless a girl perceives at some level an implied permission from her mother to be sexual (even if in the future—when you are grown up'), her road to a comfortable and unconflicted sense of agency over her sexuality is very difficult. Baubo's gesture indicates that, even for an aging woman, whose fertility may be over, life and sexuality go on (Stuart, 2009).

We see these kinds of dynamics in contemporary clinical material, and we think that it is unproductively pathologizing to conclude that girls' and women's display of their bodies is an expression of penis envy, in the absence of clinical data that warrant this conclusion.

Similarly, we think that it would be unfortunate to conclude that women's exhibitionistic behavior is always or even typically a symptom of pre-oedipal pathology or perversion, and we will attempt to show that these behaviors can frequently reflect triangular dynamics.

PSYCHOANALYTIC THEORIES OF FEMALE EXHIBITIONISM

In general, Freud positioned exhibitionism in adults as a component of infantile sexuality or as a perversion. In 1900 he categorized typical dreams of nakedness, in which the dreamer feels embarrassment and tries to hide, as exhibition dreams. Childhood events behind such dreams include experiences of being scolded and humiliated for nudity or being sexually stimulated by seeing nude adults. Yet Freud also allowed for the pleasures of exhibitionism. "We can observe how undressing has an intoxicating effect on many children even in their later years, instead of making them feel ashamed ... One can scarcely pass through a country village in our part of the world without meeting some child of two or three who lifts up his little shirt in front of one - in one's honour, perhaps" (Freud, 1900, p. 244). He thought that some dreams of nakedness expressed wishes to return to an early Eden-like time, a 'paradise' in which complete freedom and pleasure reigned. Ferenczi (1910) discussed these in terms of desires to be admired. Like Freud, Ferenczi commented on the general pleasure in nakedness and the desire to use the sexual endowments of the body to attract another.

Freud described exhibitionism as a 'component instinct', an early component of the later sexual function paired with its opposite, scopophilia (Freud, 1905, 1915). But as his theorizing was turning to the effects of the child's discovery of sexual differences at about age 3, Freud (1905, 1914) began to characterize exhibitionism in terms of perversion and female exhibitionism as a defense against the narcissistic wound of not having a penis. He proposed that little girls, unlike little boys whose phallic narcissism focuses on a visible and tangible genital, feel mortification at their lack of a one, and react with a compensatory narcissism that spreads to all other parts of their bodies (Freud, 1905, 1933).

His theory no longer allowed for a girl's feeling 'Look at what I've got and I invite you to like it too,' a delight in her sexual endowment, which, we argue, represents an important aspect in the development of female narcissism. For Freud, such delight could only exist pre-oedipally in very small children without shame. He viewed the exhibition of the genitals by any female over the age of 2 or 3 as a form of the revenge type of the castration complex in women, that is, as an act aimed at magically castrating the male. The aspect of the female genitals to attract and to arouse *pleasurable* desire in the subject and the object is completely disregarded.

Before going further, we will need to specify what we mean by perverse or a perversion, although it is beyond the scope of this paper for a complete review of the contemporary psychoanalytic literature on perversion. There is no simple or agreed-upon definition of perversion (Jacobson, 2003; Tuch, 2010). Perversion can be defined from the descriptive, etiological, characterological, sexual, defensive, clinical, nosological, developmental, or transferential vantage points, each valuable. Freud (1905) posited several criteria for perversion: firstly, as any preponderant, sexual interest in parts of the body other than the genitals or, secondly, as an activity aimed at anything other than heterosexual intercourse. Stein (2005) points out that perversion defined in this way has become a socially, historically, and theologically loaded term. She reminds us, however, that Freud viewed perversion on a continuum with normal sexuality.

Contemporary definitions of perversion have turned away from a sole emphasis on sexuality to stress aggression, narcissism and object relations. Lacan (1966) defines perversion in terms of castration, but in a different sense from Freudas a separation. Goldberg (1995) sees perverse pathology as a failure of internalization and includes in his definition a distorted psychic structure, seen in a split sense of reality, and self. The Novicks (1987, 2004) stress an underlying state of infantile omnipotence and hostility in perversion, as in the use of others to humiliate or be humiliated. Joseph (1971) describes a particular 'perverse relatedness' that appears in the clinical situation, echoed by Etchegoyen (1978) or Richards (2002) who speak of the 'perverse erotization' of the transference.

A common characteristic in almost all definitions of perversion is some sort of distortion or splitting of reality, as, for example, in Chasseguet-Smirgel's (1984) notions of the perverse inability to accept generational and gendered differences or Goldberg's split sense of self. Many retain the necessity of sexualization of behavior, among them descriptions of the perverse erotization of the transference, frequently accompanied by underlying narcissistic structures. Richards (2002, 2003) emphasizes sexual pleasure in the service of aggression and feels that aggression toward the mother underlies female perversions. Almost all include in the clinical picture compulsory behavioral or fantasized scenarios and perverse scripts, either sexual or simply as a means of expressing hostility. Richards (2003) regards perversion "as a range of behaviors, and associated thoughts, feelings, and fantasies, that are felt as compulsions" (p. 1200).

We agree with the stress on aggression, humiliation and dehumanization of the object and early narcissistic problems as intrinsic to the understanding of perversion. Additionally, we would include the notion of some sort of splitting or distortion of reality as a criterion and would retain the idea of a sexualized compulsive component. And like Stein, we would hope to separate the understanding of perversions and perverse behaviors from condemnatory, marginalizing attitudes and indictments of difference. We are in sympathy with Tuch (2010) who warns that: "There is a clear-cut danger in overextending a term to include so wide a variety of phenomena of different phenomena as to render the term conceptually useless" (p. 159).

Until recently, most analysts (Bak, 1953; Fenichel, 1945; Ferenczi, 1919; Greenacre, 1953; Greenspan, 1980; Harnik, 1932; Kernberg, 1991; Zavitzianos, 1971) have followed Freud's ideas about the phallic and perverse meanings of female exhibitionism and have argued that female exhibitionism as a perversion is rare.

Anna Freud (1966) offered a classic example of female exhibitionism in a little girl who compulsively lifted up her skirts to exhibit herself. Anna Freud interpreted this behavior as a need to display the nonexistent organ, the penis: "Her envy and her wish for a penis took the form of a desire to have, like her brothers, something to display" (p. 86). She induced her family to come to admire something that was not there at all: "Come and see what a lot of eggs the hens have laid!" (p. 87). It is possible to postulate more meanings than penis envy for this behavior. In pointing to eggs, the little girl was referring not only to missing male attributes but also to *feminine* ones, that is, the future fecundity that her brothers would never have. Yet Anna Freud made no comment about babies or fertility. Early psychoanalytic theory considered women's reproduction in compensatory terms: baby makes up for an absent penis. Horney (1933) first wrote of the possible pride and pleasure that a female derives from her genitals and capacities for having babies. Contemporary theorists, such as

Balsam (1996) or Tyson (1986) would offer other explanations for the wish for a baby, such as positive identifications with the mother.

Over the years analysts have moved away from the phallic and perverse understandings of female exhibitionism. Edgcumbe and Burgner (1975) differentiated phallic/narcissistic from oedipal manifestations of exhibitionism, depending upon the developmental level of object and self-representations, and suggested that exhibitionism represents a wish to be admired or loved. Similarly, Frankel and Sherick (1979) provided observations of little girls before the age of 3 wanting to be admired, within what they called, but did not define, a 'dominantly feminine disposition.' Tyson (1986), working within a framework of primary femininity, suggested that, in the course of early development, resolution of *rapprochement* conflicts can lead to support for feminine exhibitionistic strivings, independent of castration anxiety.

Broadening the definitions of perversion, some analysts contend that there are female perversions. Kaplan (1991), for example, conceptualized female perversions as attempts to resolve unconscious conflicts around gender: she argued that the term exhibitionism "technically is appropriate only when applied to those rare women who express revenge for their childhood deprivations and humiliations by exhibiting their genitals to non-consenting male victims" (p. 257). Lieberman (2000) viewed female exhibitionism as originating in a deficit in the mother-daughter relationship which affects the consolidation of the body image. Additionally, both Lieberman and Waites (1982) cited general cultural influences on women's comfort or discomfort with exhibiting their bodies. (We will give an example of social influences on female exhibitionism later.) In Tuch's (2010) expanded view of perversion as an attempt to reconcile unacceptable aspects of reality, not driven by castration anxiety alone: "... Perversion, by necessity, would apply equally to men and to women" (p. 91).

Insisting on the use of the body as a central criterion for perversion, Welldon (1988) offered a convincing clinical example of a female perversion of exhibitionism. Her patient compulsively exposed her genitals to certain women, literally flashing and stalking them. Welldon's hypothesis was that the patient was repeating an early trauma to ensure a new maternal authority figure would not sexually abuse her as her mother had. We wonder if the opposite was also true: namely, that the patient's behavior was an invitation to once again be abused/ fondled by a maternal figure.

We are strongly in accord with Ross's (1990) argument that intense exhibitionistic urges in women are not usually explained by penis envy, but rather reflect an unconscious wish to attract the father. Kernberg (1991) agreed that female exhibitionism is a plea for sexual affirmation from father (p. 351) and asserted that psychoanalytic interpretations of female exhibitionism as a reaction formation to penis envy need to be amended to incorporate more recent ideas about female development. We argue that the woman's act of exhibiting the self can also represent turning passive into active – an attempt to stimulate the other, based on early experiences of being sexually stimulated by the father (or the mother).

The two contemporary psychoanalysts who have made the most significant contributions to the understanding of female exhibitionism are Balsam and Elise. Balsam (2003, 2008) stressed the central importance and meaning of the female body in all stages of female development. She argued that psychoanalysis has under-appreciated the importance of the woman's body and its pleasures. Her explanation of female exhibitionism places special emphasis on childbearing capacities and meanings. She suggests a normative spectrum for pleasurably active sex seeking and pleasurable procreative desire and fantasy that is present in a female's use and display of her body. Our own clinical observation offers an opportunity for further elaborations of Balsam's ideas.

Elise (2008) also has given an extensive and inventive discussion of female exhibitionism. She maintained that girls' overt genital exhibitionism (and boys') is quashed by parental discomfort, and is internalized as shame and inhibition of exhibitionistic wishes. Such shame becomes attached to forbidden incestuous desires and to fantasies of inadequacy and defeat in the triangular drama.

Elise defined genital narcissism in women as primary and the inhibition of exhibitionism as defense; she does not view exhibitionism as a defense against a narcissistic wound of lack. She argued that, without positive imagery of the female body with which she can identify, a woman struggles to be able to voice and take agency over sexual desire. Like Balsam and Elise, Marcus (2004) emphasized the special role of the mother in promoting the girl's comfort in her sexuality and pride and pleasure in her body. (Compare this idea with that of Benjamin [1988] who argued, more skeptically, that, since the mother is not generally available in our society as a model for the daughter in developing agency over her own sexuality, the girl sees the father as subject, and mother as object of sexual desire.)

CLINICAL EXAMPLES

Sexting and Peggy

Peggy, a 15-year-old adolescent, came to treatment because she was not getting along with her mother's boyfriend and was feeling insecure at school. Peggy's parents had been divorced since she was 10, and she lived with her attractive mother who was, according to her, preoccupied and permissive. Her father, who resided in another state, was characterized by Peggy as more strict and demanding. Peggy attended a competitive and demanding private high school for girls. She acted as if "everything was cool," not wanting to admit to strong feelings or talk about her vulnerabilities and insecurities. While she did talk vaguely about "boyfriends" and how other girls were "sluts," she did not at first bring up her own sexual feelings or behaviors. Some months into the treatment, however, the analyst received a frantic telephone call from Peggy, who confessed that she had done "a stupid thing." She had e-mailed a video of herself to a boy who had moved out of state, in which she, nude, exposed her genitals and masturbated. The boy had called Peggy to let her know that his father had seen the pictures and "freaked out." Apparently, this 'sexting', as it is called, was rampant at the girls' school she attended.

Peggy was frightened about the consequences of this internet display, and about it being discovered by her family. Listening to this, the analyst was not surprised, but felt both empathetic with Peggy and concerned about her poor judgment. The analyst advised Peggy to tell her mother what she had done, which she did. The mother then called the boy's father and calmed him down. Peggy was surprised by her mother's support and understanding, and felt closer to her because of this. On the other hand, she was very frightened that her own father would hear of this and see the pictures. We suspect that this fear most likely overlaid the wish that she could get her distant father to pay attention to her, to her body and to her sexual desirability.

When Peggy came in for subsequent sessions, she was able to talk more about her own sexuality. The analyst felt that Peggy moved closer to her as she had with her mother. The analyst was able to address the girl's shame and her previous difficulties in owning her sexual feelings. Peggy said that she done the e-mailing because she wanted boys to like her and felt badly that she didn't have a special boyfriend. She said that she felt that she was pretty and felt good about her slender and athletic body. But she was jealous of the popular girls in her school and was especially upset since her best girlfriend had found a boyfriend and was no longer interested in her.

In this brief clinical example, we see evidence of triadic dynamics. Peggy's jealousy of her friend paralleled her unconscious jealousy of her mother, who also had a "boyfriend of her own," with whom Peggy did not get along. Undoubtedly Peggy also was jealous of the attention that the girlfriend and, behind this, the mother were giving to a boyfriend. Peggy did not act or seem ashamed of her body; consciously she thought that this exposure would be inviting, enticing, and stimulating to those who saw it, in particular the males (boyfriend/father/stepfather) for whose affection she longed. Even though the girl appears needy and insecure, her plea for attention does not seem to us to fall readily into traditional or contemporary definition of perversion. That is, it was neither a compulsory accompaniment for sexual pleasure, nor a display of infantile omnipotence and hostility. On the other hand, Peggy's display may have been unconsciously intended to shock and disturb her absent father and certainly ended up hurting herself. Thus, it could also be considered as bordering on the 'perverse'. Plausibly Peggy's behavior could also be seen as a counter-phobic response to an underlying, unconscious sense of shame. 'Sexting' or 'sex-texting' has become very common societal phenomenon with today's adolescents (Goodstein, 2007; Morris, 2011; CBS News, 2009). This phenomenon exemplifies how cultural factors influence the 'normality' of exhibitionism so that the parameters of permissible behavior vary by time and place. Nevertheless, female genital exhibitionism in sexting seems to be less an expression of penis envy rather than a way to appeal to peers and to be seen as 'hot' and sexy. Whether or not such a widespread phenomenon could be considered perverse is an open question. More detailed psychoanalytic data from such cases than we have available to us at this point might help to answer this question. In a recent article, (Lemma, 2010) observed that the use of cyberspace can become a psychic refuse for adolescents struggling with the challenges of integrating the reality and meaning of their changing sexual bodies into their images of themselves.

The movie *Babel* reflects the commonality of and changing mores about exhibitionistic behavior in adolescence in a poignant series of scenes in which a teen-aged Japanese girl is desperately trying to get a male's attention—to have a boyfriend like the other girls. Wearing no underwear, she lifts her skirt and exposes her genitals to try to entice a teenaged boy in a restaurant. Again, exhibitionism is a means towards an erotic relationship. Clumsy and sad it may be, but it still represents the use of the body in general, and the genitals in particular, as a 'come-on'.

The dynamics in both of these adolescent situations can be understood—at least in part - in terms of triadic/'oedipal' (what we call Persephonal) scenarios. In the first, Peggy is jealous of her girlfriend and her mother, and she feels excluded by both her mother and her father. Identified with her mother, she wants her own boyfriend. She picks someone who, in his geographical distance, is unconsciously related to her father. In *Babel* the girl wants to be valued among her friends, and, as we learn as the film unfolds, she wants the love of someone like her father, if not her father. Although there are complicated issues in these two examples of exclusion and jealousy, the explanation of the female exhibitionism cannot readily be understood simply as extreme or simply 'perverse.' The girls thought that the way to get attention from a male was through their genitals. Whatever personality problems that are reflected in either of these exhibitionistic acts, the genitals seem to be valued and their exposure used as a method to attract positive attention. Such acts can plausibly be interpreted as pleas for sexual affirmation and erotic interest from a father/ male and to be seen as 'hot' and not 'prude' in the contemporary adolescent culture.

Analytic Case: Ms. A

The following is process material from an analytic case, in which memories of Baubo-like gestures of exhibitionism during childhood re-emerged in the context of an intense on-going triangular or 'Persephonal' transference. In this series of five sessions with a heterosexual woman, heterosexual and homosexual fantasies arose and alternated. In comparison to the case of Peggy, which may include some perverse features, we consider this woman's exhibitionism as an indication of her positive feelings about her body and its attracting and attractive potentialities.

An attractive woman in her early 40s, Ms. A sought treatment because she was depressed and felt stuck in a very troubled marriage which had become completely non-sexual. She had been married for 20 years and had four children. She thought that she had made a terrible mistake by marrying her husband, a successful physician. Ms. A wanted a divorce but she was fearful about taking that step. A lawyer, she had an unrewarding position with a governmental agency in which she felt as unappreciated and stuck as she did in her marriage.

Ms. A was the eldest of three girls and had always been considered "the pretty one." She perceived her mother as intelligent but very unattractive. She remembered times when she felt special and loved by her father, but lamented that he loved her mother more—"after all, he gave her those babies." Sexual development came relatively early for Ms. A; her menses began at 11. She reported the following behavior in early adolescence at about age of 12: she would stand at the window and lift her blouse to show her breasts. She loved that the neighborhood boys would stand outside to look. She was afraid of being caught but she felt tremendously excited and filled with a sense of glee. She recalled feeling that she had a wonderful athletic body and that she was happy to have it. Her favorite aunt had validated that feeling by predicting that she would marry early and well because of her good looks. Ms. A felt she was always able to attract and please men. The power of her body was used to compete with other women and to attract males.

The following material comes from the third year of her analysis. The earlier analytic work had focused on Ms. A's troubled marriage. She and the analyst had come to understand the conflicted reasons that she had picked her husband, who not incidentally had the same first name as her father. Her husband was, and always had been, passionless and not very sexual -the opposite of Ms. A. Thus, her choice seemed to be a defense against her fears of her own intense sexuality, and a punishment for her unconscious incestuous wishes and strong sexual interests. She spoke of all her prior sexuality as "promiscuous" and "naughty". By this point in the analysis, Ms. A had divorced her husband and was doing some dating. The analysis had deepened and sexually-tinged and more openly competitive fantasies about the analyst were entering the transference. The analyst's strategy was to allow these fantasies to emerge more fully by closely following the patient's anxieties around them and the transference/countertransference.

Immediately following a two-week vacation of the analyst, Ms. A's appearance and first words were dramatic. She arrived at her session wearing a fashionable short skirt with high-heeled boots. To the analyst's inner consternation, she reported that she had had unprotected sex during the last several weeks with a man who had just told her that he had herpes. At some level, the patient at this point must have realized the dangerous nature of her sexual behavior and unconsciously inferred the analyst's concerns/disapproval. Musing about her relationship with her mother and her sexuality, Ms. A said: "I felt mother disapproved of me being a feminine girl … really being cute and attracting the interest of men and boys. I remember being rejected by all the girls because I showed my underpants to the boys in the schoolyard when I was about 9 and that gave me a lot of attention. I would raise my skirt and they would look and ask me to do it again. I loved doing it."

Patient: To my mom anything sexual was bad and she would disapprove. It [sex] was a deep dark secret—she didn't want me to be doing what she was doing. She thought that I was naughty and shameful, and my thought was when I did it with my boyfriend: 'Screw her'—am free to do what I want to do.' I thought: 'I'm not supposed to do that, not supposed to think about it: little girls are not supposed to have anything to do with anything like that.' The thing was it was really for adults—it was seen as dangerous.

At this point the analyst noted to herself the double meaning of 'screw' and was aware of a growing feeling of concern for Ms. A's unprotected sex.

Analyst: You are trying to demonstrate to yourself and me that sex is indeed dangerous, and arranging it so that you might be punished now

*with herpes. You invite me to be critical of your sexuality as your mother
had been. My absence added to your feeling unprotected.*

P: My mother wanted to thwart me.

A: And you think I do too?

*Ms. A said that she actually had experienced retaliation from her
mother who would hold things against her and try to shame her.*

A: How do you imagine I might retaliate against you now?

*P: You would be cold and uncaring and try to thwart whatever I
want to do.*

*At this time the patient had anxiously applied for a top management
position at work and was being considered for advancement in her job.*

*P: [Musing] Maybe that also has to do with the competitive thing
with you if I'm thinking of moving ahead. You'll try to squash me. You'll
be threatened by me. You won't want me to shine. It would diminish you.*

A: How would it diminish me?

*P: I'm not sure. Part of it is in relationship to a man. I am now seeing
many men. But you are not negative. It feels kind. It upsets me. You're
nice to me.*

Here the analyst was thinking that the patient was upset because the reality was
not what she imagined, yet at the same time this made her feel closer to her.
This is perhaps a moment as described by Chused (1996) - of psychic change
resulting from the disconfirmation of the transference.

In the transference, the patient seems to feel that the analyst will be threatened by the patient's desire to be as or more successful and sexual as she perceives her analyst. We see this as an example of a typical triadic conflict in
the girl who feels sexuality is the mother's domain from which she is to be
excluded. The patient repeatedly indicates that females did not like her sexuality—the other little girls, her mother and the analyst. The childhood feelings
of guilt-ridden sexuality and the memory of raising her skirt now emerge in

an adult version in her dress and her acting out an adult sexual danger (unprotected sex) with men. We read the patient's tone and language (such as calling herself "naughty") as a link from the present to earlier childhood notions of sexuality and her attendant guilt. These competitive dynamics are repeated as the session progresses.

The revival of primal scene feelings of exclusion seems to have emerged in reaction to the analyst's vacation. Typically, in the past, whenever the analyst left, Ms. A would bring up feelings of exclusion and jealousy and openly expressed fantasies about the analyst "going off" with her husband. The memory of the Baubo skirt-raising gesture re-emerged in this context. We speculate that this memory came up here to defend against feeling excluded and rejected by the analyst's absence. The memory may have been reparative just as the behavior was in the first place, finding a way, in identification with her mother and her analyst, to try to be competitive and victorious. On the other hand, it could be reasoned that the memory of the raising of the skirt here arose in reaction to separation, not as a competitive gesture, but as a developmentally earlier expression of a little girl's proven way to get some attention and feel better.

In the next sessions Ms. A continued with similar themes. She returned to feelings of exclusion and being on the outside, which were interpreted by the analyst in terms of primal scene, that is, being left out by the analyst's being away. In response, the patient reported her first sexual intercourse, how wonderful and exciting it was: "I don't think his mother liked me. She didn't like that her Jewish son would have a girlfriend, let alone a Catholic one. And his mother didn't like sexual stuff." Here, the analyst was thinking that another mother figure disapproves of her sexuality. After a pause, the patient said: "Mother made me feel like a bad seed. I wanted to be the most special child to my mother although I fantasized I was to my father. But the most problem to them was that I was interested in boys."

The analyst questioned herself here. She wondered silently: 'What have I done that is making the patient feel this way, so judged, so bad, here now?'

P: *[After an extended silence] I do feel guilty if I look better than you.*
A: *Why?*
P: *You'd be angry. [Ms. A recalled how she was cute and popular and mother was fat and angry.] I tried very much to outshine all of the other girls in the family and, if I did, that made me feel guilty and frightened. I was not like my mother, but I was like her. I think she felt threatened by it.*
A: *What was she threatened by?*
P: *That I was bad and naughty. I wanted attention. I was coquettish, cute and spunky. The attention felt awful and wonderful at the same time. I felt demeaned by it a little that I got the attention by being cute and sexy—felt powerful that I could get attention… In a way I really was victorious but concerned: What if I am better than you? Cuter than you?*

At this point the analyst internally scanned her awareness for envious feelings. She knew she felt pleased as a mother would with a daughter who felt good about herself, but also acknowledged that she was envious of the patient's youth and good looks.

P: *At times, I tried to minimize the victoriousness with my mother. [The analyst mused to herself about how the patient had always been under-achieving.] I remember that when I was little I was afraid at the same time I wanted her to go away. Then who would take care of all of us? …I was smart enough to get good grades. You and I share so much in common—we work; we like clothes. The whole thing about it is scary.*
A: *What's so scary?*
P: *I don't know what was scary … I remember that my father said: 'Girls don't go to college—they get married and have kids.'*
A: *[Remembering how the patient earlier in the hour had expressed her anxiety about bettering the analyst, summed up:] I think you are scared that I will be angry at your ambition and talent and looks and that I*

would abandon you if you pursued all that you would like for yourself—
and you are afraid that you want to do better than me.
P: Can there only be one winner? Can only one woman be the beautiful
one? [The patient then became tearful and quiet, and murmured:] All
of this is too difficult. I always felt alone as a child.

We assume that this material, the exhibitionistic behaviors and associations, are triangular in nature. For example, Ms. A keeps bringing up father as she discusses what is going between her and mother or her and the analyst.

Moreover, the analyst's competitive feelings can be taken as a strong clue of the competitive nature of the transference/countertransference at that moment. The patient's statement that she wanted her mother "to go, but then who would take care of us" seems to capture what we have termed the core Persephonal/triadic conflict for a girl: How to keep her mother and compete with her at the same time.

In the next session Ms. A talked about how her parents argued. Then she described her mother's curfew and other rules, which existed —in her mind— to prevent her from having a boy/man or sexual contact.

P: I was aware of sexuality and competing with my mother. I can do what
you can do. When I was 15, I was having intercourse. I wanted to know
that some boy would really care for and about me ... I was in love ...
It was fun even though scary - exposing yourself to danger. The analyst
thought, but did not say, in order not to interrupt the patient's flow of
associations: 'which you are repeating now by having unprotected sex.'
P: I remember a friend's father had Playboy magazines in his basement
we were about 9 years old. We would sneak and look at them—just
breasts in those days. We were afraid we would get caught so we would
whisper. It was all female—sounds homosexual? With my girlfriend look-
ing at naked women together—it was exciting and confusing. We would

play lots of imaginary games, hopscotch and dolls and pretend we were going out on dates. And pretend a boy would call - dressing, showering, what to wear—-trying to look beautiful for men—a Barbie doll life. I wanted to be attractive and to have a girlfriend to be chummy with. It was very hard to share a girlfriend with someone else. I was hurt if a girlfriend pulled away from me to someone else. You went away and I have to share you.

A: And that hurts your feelings. It feels to you as if I am pulling away when you long to be close. That feels 'homosexual' and so you also try to get yourself punished for those feelings.

We wonder whether this patient may be describing here some homosexual origins of heterosexual longings. We note the sequence of the associations: first, adolescent sex with her boyfriend, then back in time to being with another female excited by breasts in pictures, and then moving directly into desires of being attractive to males in a 'Barbie doll' world. We have come to think that this is a core dynamic in the development of girls' sexuality. The homoerotic excitement for the mother as object is simultaneous with an identification with that sexual body to attract the male like mother does. On the other hand, the patient is describing a typical instance of camaraderie between herself and her girlfriend, as they play, share exciting experiences, and practice at being grownup women.

The following is a dream from the next session, which seems to illustrate these conflicted homoerotic fantasies. Ms. A paused briefly and commented on what the analyst was wearing.

P: I'm uncomfortable about noticing.

A: That must bring up comparisons to you.

Ms. A then reported a dream: *I am in bed with a beautiful woman with dark hair and gorgeous eyes. Beautiful and feminine.* It didn't look like me and it didn't look like you. I didn't notice the breasts on the body in the dream. She associated then to a girl friend whose body reminded her of the body in the dream. She remembered that her mother had said: "Boy, that girl is beautiful."

> *P: I used to think my body was straight. I think my body is changing. I seem to be becoming more feminine. I notice you have curves too—if this had to do with your body, I would be very uncomfortable.*
> *A: I wonder why it would make you so uncomfortable to be noticing my body?*
> *P: That's too homosexual … Ah, maybe my breasts and body are better than yours. But the most negative feeling is being the outsider. That makes me think of being outside the bedroom.*

In this hour the patient goes from a disavowed desire, to attraction, to comparison and competition, to fear of abandonment. The patient seems to be struggling with what would make her the most desirable to the analyst -being a boy or an attractive girl. Ms. A had in the past described this 'outsider feeling' of a primal scene experience, in which she had heard and glimpsed her parents having sex. Perhaps, the patient's observations of the analyst's body in addition to the analyst's absence re-evoked these primal scene experiences of exclusion. Conflicts around gender and oscillations of desires and identifications that are evident in this material are often a result of being privy to that scene. However oscillating the identifications are, the patient directed attention to the triadic nature of the looking at and the competition with the analyst. Note here that the analyst, still fixed on the competitive nature of the previous material, at first interpreted the patient's need to look at her body and clothing in competitive, comparative terms and not in scopophilic terms. Fortunately, however, the patient herself brought the analyst to the truly charged aspect of the looking its homoerotic meaning.

The patient began the next session by reporting two more dreams. In the first dream, *her knees are stuck together as she is driving, which prevents her from getting to the accelerator or the brakes. There is a priest, 'Father McGowan', next to her.* In the second dream, *she is wearing a fur jacket and matching fur gloves. She has long brown hair. She sees a long-haired deer that matches the coat and the gloves. She sees smaller deer and thinks they are beautiful.*

Her associations led to the following material. She elaborated that in the dream *there was absolute terror that she couldn't control the car.* "I can't have sex if my knees are stuck together," Ms. A remarked. She guiltily admitted that she was attracted to Father McGowan, her parish priest, an attraction she felt was "naughty and dangerous," because he seemed interested in her and because such an attraction was "taboo".

P: *Knees together ... I remember when my mother would sit down, she should have put her knees together but she didn't. She would sit with her legs apart. She was careless. The dark pubic hair showed. I found it curious—she wore a garter belt—it must have been sexy to my dad. I am afraid to know that as a little child I must have been attracted to my mother, although today I find mother's body fat and unattractive. I was maybe aroused in her presence. And all of that makes me feel as if I am crazy. I don't want to look at it. Maybe I do.*

[She continued.] The animals make me think of impulses—ferociousness—if you dress like them - they will think you are one of them. [She commented that she owned a fur coat but was not in favor of killing animals to adorn oneself.] You, [she said to the analyst] I notice, have a lot of clothes—different colors and styles - interesting. I like them. I like to dress well. My mother didn't have a sense of style and dressed repulsively. And maybe being aroused is repulsive—animal-like.

[The long straight brown hair reminded her of a girl in middle school.] I wanted to see her breasts. She was very large-breasted —flamboyant—I think she liked her breasts. When she would undress, I saw they were big. Mine are round and small. I like them now. When I was little, maybe I thought they were too small. [The analyst chose to interpret the homosexual theme in the transference:] You are afraid I will find your sexual interest in me as repulsive and animalistic.

[Ms. A confirmed this interpretation with a seemingly cryptic comment made in a fearful anxious manner:] I want a guarantee!

A: A guarantee of what?
P: That you won't throw me out or tell me I'm too kooky.

The analyst was surprised at the intensity of this fear at this juncture.

These two dreams and their associations seem to express triadic hetero-sexual desires towards the forbidden father/priest, and competitive, rivalrous and erotic feelings toward the mother/analyst. There are fears of her out-of-control sexuality, the dangerous consequences of ferocious aggressiveness, and disavowed wishes to stand-out, or 'out-dress' others. These fears of being out of control and ferocious aggressiveness could be understood in terms of their preoedipal precursors and influences. In addition, we see evidence in this material of an important accompaniment of sexual arousal—a conflict-ed, ever-present erotic interest in the mother intertwined with identification with her. The words "I don't want to look at it. Maybe I do" refer not just to the conflict of looking into herself, but, more to the point, to looking at her mother's body. These disavowed desires toward a woman's body are stimulated by current feelings in the transference. Yet all of this occurs in the context of aroused erotic feelings toward Father McGowan, the forbidden male, like the father who belongs to the mother.

The references to the primal scene from which she was excluded give further evidence of the triadic dynamics of this exhibitionistic material. Blum (1979) suggests that the over-stimulated oedipal child, exposed to the primal scene, is likely to feel passionate jealousy, betrayal, and rage, as well as guilt over forbidden gratification. He links exhibitionistic tendencies in adults to such early exposure.

As in all these sessions, exhibitionistic material abounds, inextricably woven with homoerotic and competitive themes. We are convinced that the exhibitionistic desire here reflects both identification with an exhibitionistic mother and a conflicted desire both to attract her and to be her. For Ms. A, forbidden desire and competition bring fear of punishment and abandonment by the mother.

The central transference can be described as a maternal, triadic, and competitive one in which homoerotic origins of her sexuality were also active. The analyst's reactions in the countertransference were also maternal, such the desire to support and to protect a daughter, along with occasional stirrings of competitive feelings. However, it is possible that in current revival of the exhibitionistic behavior from the patient's childhood and adolescence, in an unrecognized transference, the analyst could also have become the male object of the patient's desire—that is, the male object of the exhibitionism. At this point in the analysis, the analyst was focused on the competition and exhibitionism in the transference, and did not focus on direct aggression, which was evident in the content of the last two dreams. Alternate interpretations would target the possible aggressive and phallic meanings of the patient's exhibitionistic behavior—her need for control and power.

In summary, Ms. A felt good about her body and liked the way it looked and felt, but had conflicts about her sexuality. She was caught up in Persephonal/triadic competition and had worries about the intensity of her sexual impulses. Her acts of childhood exhibitionism—the expressions of Baubo-like skirt and shirt-lifting—expressed competitive fantasies concerning other females and wishes to attract and exert power over males. We do not feel that these desires and behaviors to attract boys and men constituted perverse behavior. Rather, they seem to carry a playful pleasurable aspect. In the course of her analysis, her residual guilt over her exhibitionism, and its triadic (and phallic) meanings were better understood so that Ms. A felt more comfortable in using her sexual body within a meaningful adult sexual relationship. Her exhibitionism, as with most patients, was a complex compromise of female triadic (Persephonal) homosexual and heterosexual, narcissistic, and phallic fantasies.

DISCUSSION

Until recently, exhibitionistic women have been viewed in the psychoanalytic literature in one of two ways, both pejorative: either as seductive sirens or as examples of 'masculine protest' (Abraham, 1922), full of castrating hatred. In contrast, in our clinical work, triangular, Persephonal female exhibitionism has more positive, 'Baubo-like' aspects, including the girl's identification with a sexual, desirable and desiring mother, with whom there is a shared knowledge and pleasure in their female bodies. A reference to the mother is present, alive in the transference either as an expression of camaraderie, a plea for approval, permission for sexual expression, a manifestation of competition as a rival, or a homoerotic gesture. We have seen the theme of camaraderie, which was not as prominent in the clinical examples we have included in this paper, more clearly in many other cases. In the longer analytic case we have presented, exhibitionism represented homoerotic interest in the mother's body and a means of attracting the mother, as well as competitive strivings with her for a male's attention.

Female exhibitionism may have different meanings if directed toward a male versus a female figure. Toward a female, it seems to carry the meanings we have outlined of camaraderie and shared pleasures, as well as expressing motives of competitive display and homoerotic enticement. In the literature, writers such as Lieberman (2000) and Welldon (1988) describe more perverse instances of female exhibitionism that seem to be aimed at repairing a more disturbed early relationship with the mother. Towards a male, it of course entails sexual enticement as well as wishes for power and control. Within the treatment setting it can be difficult to tease apart these meanings since the analyst can take on male and female aspects unconsciously in a patient's mind. Whether the intended object is male or female, however, there are clearcut cases that fit the traditional explanations of a perverse act aimed at humiliating the other and/or a compensating for shame about the body.

Identification and Arousal

We find that a girl's comparison of her body with her mother's combines two distinct and important aspects: firstly, identification, both with the mother's body and with its capacity to arouse others and, secondly, *sexual arousal by the mother's body.* That is to say, the mother's body becomes both object of identification and object of sexual desire. This identification should not be mislabeled as one of early merger, but is based on the knowledge of a similar body and shared experience. Wells and Wrye (1991) have written about the encompassing 'maternal erotic transference', which has its roots in early sensual bodily interactions between mother and child, and includes the more differentiated triadic homoerotic phase transference. We find in our adult cases that there is an oscillation between heterosexual and homosexual impulses and fantasies, and we speculate that this reflects a similar developmental phenomenon in the triadic phase. Many writers, such as Deutsch (1932), Chodorow (1978), Burch (1992) and Suchet (1995), posit an oscillation between father and mother - a 'bisexual relational triangle' as comprising the usual oedipal configuration for girls. *In our patients, who are heterosexual, as with Ms. A, we always find an accompanying component of homoerotic arousal, however subtle.* We think this regular occurrence of homoerotic arousal is an interesting finding, and we wonder if it can be attributed to the fact that our experience occurs within a female-to-female dyad. However, in supervision and consultation, we have observed that, when male analysts work with female patients, there is often a triadic picture of a heated heterosexual transference around the figure of the analyst, with a homoerotic/identificatory figure, apparent in extra-analytic material or life.

Pleasure in the Female Body

Clinically, many female patients describe being pleased with their bodies, enjoying their partners' admiration of them, and liking sex. Their treatments do not necessarily focus on conflicts around their bodies and are not caught up in problems around exposing or exhibiting their bodies at appropriate times. On the other hand, we are all too familiar with cases of women who *do* have significant conflicts around displaying their bodies. The underlying sources for their sense of shame and inferiority about their bodies, such as 'penis envy', negative feelings about being a female or sexual trauma have been well documented in psychoanalytic theory. In previous work, we have elaborated two factors contributing to inhibitions about the body that have received insufficient attention: firstly, triadic/Persephonal conflicts in which conflicted incestuous fantasies lead to the denial of genital and bodily pleasure, similar to those cases described by Elise (2008) and, secondly, unfavorable competitive comparisons of their bodies with those of other females, especially their mothers (Kulish and Holtzman, 2008).

Competition with Mother Stemming from the Triadic Phase

Our examples demonstrate another neglected aspect of female exhibitionism competition with mother stemming from the triadic phase. When the girl reaches adolescence, she may indeed feel ready to take on the competition with her mother and display her new-found mature sexuality. Appreciation of and pleasure in her body, which now often compares more favorably to the mother's, may set the stage for competitive exhibitionism. The exhibitionism of Ms. A and Peggy was aimed, at least in part, at luring the father away from the mother. Such competitive exhibitionism is often experienced in the female-to-female therapeutic dyad but has rarely been documented in the literature. An exception appears in Balsam (2008), however. She describes a case in which vivid and charged needs to be admired and watched by the analyst appeared in the transference. She writes that the patient, a young student "was excited to display herself to both her mother in the past and me in the present, even if old guilts and anxieties about competing with her adoring and punitive mother image would emerge" (p. 109). Bodily display can also be aimed at winning the mother away from the father, as demonstrated clearly by Ms. A. Anger and competition between women, which do not overtly appear in the Baubo episode, make up a latent theme in the Demeter myth as a whole, which we have described elsewhere (Kulish and Holtzman, 2008).

ADDITIONAL CLINICAL CONSIDERATIONS

Within the therapeutic setting, female exhibitionism is evidenced by an increased focus on the appearance of the body, its display and the attention it attracts. Somehow or other, the patient draws attention to her body, in her apparel, in her stance, in her dreams, in her associations. In turn, the female analyst may become aware of, or self-conscious about, her appearance. With a male analyst, the female patient will usually display some form of exhibitionis-tic desire over time, in which her body or dress become the center of attention. Countertransferences to this emergence may produce a stereotyped reaction, that is, the male analyst may label the behavior negatively, as a way of handling his fear of his own conscious or unconscious arousal.

For example, one attractive patient in a second analysis with a female analyst reported that her previous male analyst had spoken in a disapproving manner about a somewhat sheer skirt: "You know, if you stand in the light, one can see through your skirt." She felt chastised and humiliated. In retro-spect, it seemed to her that he was disapproving and hyper-attentive to any nuance of alluring feminine display. Hopefully, this disapproving paternal response by male analysts to allure of the female body is not currently a common one. Our point, however, is that, for both male and female analysts, the patient's competitiveness or wish to be desired and/or admired physical-ly can be disquieting. Countertransferences along these lines can be easily overlooked or rationalized.

When we miss the simple idea that a patient may take pleasure in her female body, we miss a clinical opportunity. One child analyst in training was writing up a case report of her work with a 4 year-old girl. After the report was written, she suddenly remembered to her amazement that she had totally forgotten about an important event in the later stages of the treatment, when the little girl was expressing her affection toward her more and more openly. The girl had suddenly lifted her dress and pulled down her tights to expose her genitalia. Taken aback, all the analyst had thought to say was something like: "Girls can be curious and worried about their bodies." It did not occur to her at the time also to suggest that girls can want to show their genitals and have them be admired and thought special. Later, the analyst realized that her own anxieties had been evoked, and that she had had no theoretical place into which to fit the incident. She did not realize the possible Baubo meanings here—ca-maraderie and pleasure in the body, shared with another female. We suggest that another missed element might have been the little girl's homoerotically tinged, positive gesture of affection for her female analyst.

SUMMARY

In closing, our wish is for a more inclusive picture of female development. In particular we are expanding upon the original classical understanding of female exhibitionism as essentially negative, perverse and/or phallic. We elaborate aspects of female exhibitionism as components of a healthy narcissism, not unduly defensive or conflicted and that express a desire to allure and to attract. Healthy female exhibitionism includes a desire to attract the other and a positive pride in the female body and genitals. It expresses both hetero and homoerotic desire: I, like my mother, can attract a man with my female body and I like my mother's body. We hope that drawing attention to the positive side of female narcissism and exhibitionism will help to balance the psychoanalytic story, which until recently has focused on the negative. This view of female exhibitionism amplifies the picture of the triadic Persephonal period and its related conflicts. Baubo's joyful skirt lifting as a remedy for Demeter's depression has served as a metaphor for these ideas.

REFERENCES

Abraham K (1922). Manifestations of the female castration complex. *Int J Psychoanal*3:1–29.

Arthur, M. (1994). Politics and pomegranates: An interpretation of the Homeric hymn to Demeter. In: Foley HP, editor. *The Homeric hymn to Demeter*, 214–42. Princeton, NJ: Princeton UP.

Bak, R.C. (1953). Fetishism. *J Am Psychoanal Assoc*1:285–98.

Balsam, R. (1996). The pregnant mother and the body image of the daughter. *J Am Psychoanal Assoc*44S:*401–27*.

——— (2003). The vanished pregnant body in psychoanalytic developmental theory. *J Am Psychoanal Assoc*51:*1153–79*.

——— (2008). Women showing off: notes on female exhibitionism. *J Am Psychoanal Assoc*56:*99–121*.

Benjamin, J. (1988). *The bonds of love*. New York, NY: Pantheon.

Blum, H.P. (1979). On the concept and consequences of the primal scene. *Psychoanal Q*48:*27–49*.

Burch, B. (1992). *On intimate terms: The psychology of difference in lesbian relationships*. Urbana, IL: U Illinois Press.

Burkert, W. (1985). *Structure and history in Greek mythology and ritual*. Berkeley, CA: U California Press, 1979.

CBS News (2009). "Sexting" shockingly common among teens, [accessed 19 Dec. 2011]. Available from: http://www.cbsnews.com/stories/2009/01/15/national/main4723161.shtml.

Chasseguet-Smirgel, J. (1984). *Creativity and perversion*. New York, NY: Norton.

Chodorow, N. (1978). *The reproduction of mothering: Psychoanalysis and the sociology of gender*. Berkeley, CA: U California Press.

Chused, J.F. (1996). The therapeutic action of psychoanalysis: Abstinence and informative experiences. *J Am Psychoanal Assoc*44:*1047–71*.

Deutsch, H. (1932). On female homosexuality. *Psychoanal Q*1:*484–510*.

Edgcumbe, R., & Burgner, M. (1975). The phallic-narcissistic phase: A differentiation between pre-oedipal and oedipal aspects of phallic development. *Psychoanal Stud Child*30:*161–80*.

Elise, D. (1997). Primary femininity, bisexuality, and the female ego ideal: A reexamination of female developmental theory. *Psychoanal Q*66:*489–517*.

——— (2008). Sex and shame: The inhibition of female desires. *J Am Psychoanal Assoc*56:*73–98*.

Etchegoyen, R.H. (1978). Some thoughts on transference perversion. *Int J Psychoanal*59:*45–53*.

Fenichel, O. (1945). *The psychoanalytic theory of neurosis.* New York, NY: Norton.

Ferenczi S (1910). *The psychological analysis of dreams.* Contributions to psychoanalysis, *94–131*. Boston, MA: Gorham Press, 1916.

——— (1919). Nakedness as a means for inspiring terror. In: *Further contributions to the theory and technique of psychoanalysis.* London: Hogarth, 1950, *329–32*.

Foley, H.P. (1994). *The Homeric hymn to Demeter. Princeton*, NJ: Princeton UP.

Frankel, S., & Sherick, I. (1979). Observations of the emerging sexual identity of three and four-year old children: With emphasis on female sexual identity. *Int Rev Psychoanal*6:*287–310*.

Freud, A. (1966). The ego and the mechanisms of defence. In: The writings of Anna Freud, vol. 2, *3–191*. New York, NY: International UP.

Freud S (1900) The interpretation of dreams. *S.E.* 4, 5.

——— (1905). Three essays on sexuality.*S.E.*7, *130–243*.

——— (1914). On narcissism: An introduction.*S.E.*14, *73–102*.

——— (1915). Instincts and their vicissitudes. *S.E* 14, *111–40*.

——— 1916). A mythological parallel to a visual obsession. *S.E* 14, *337–8*.

——— (1933). On femininity. *S.E* 22, *112–35*.

Goldberg, A. (1995). *The problem of perversion.* New Haven, CT: Yale UP.

Goodstein, A. (2007). What teens and tweens are really doing online. *Totally Wired.* Available from: http://totallywired.ypulse.com/archives/2007/02/the_new_generation_gap_require.php

Greenacre, P. (1953). Certain relationships between fetishism and the faulty development of the body image. *Psychoanal Stud Child*8:*79–98*.

Greenspan, S. (1980). Analysis of a five-and-a-half-year-old girl: Indications for a dyadic-phallic phase of development. *J Am Psychoanal Assoc*28:*575–604*.

Harnik, E.J. (1932). Pleasure in disguise, the need for decoration, and the sense of beauty. *Psychoanal Q*1:*216–64.*

Horney, K. (1933). The denial of the vagina. *Int J Psychoanal*14:*57–70.*

Jacobson, L. (2003). On the use of 'sexual addiction': The case for 'perversion'. *Contemp Psychoanal*39:*333–62.*

Joseph, B. (1971). A clinical contribution to the analysis of a perversion. *Int J Psychoanal*5:*50–65.*

Kaplan, L.J. (1991). Female perversions. New York, NY: Doubleday.

Kernberg, O. (1991). Sadomasochism, sexual excitement, and perversion. *J Am Psychoanal Assoc*39:*333–62.*

Krafft-Ebing, R. von (1886). *Psychopathia sexualis.* New York, NY: Bantam, 1965.

Kulish, N. (2000). Primary femininity: Clinical advances and theoretical ambiguities. *J Am Psychoanal Assoc*48:*1355–79.*

——— Holtzman D (2002). Baubo: Rediscovering women's pleasures. In: Alizade AM, editor. *The embodied female, 109–19.* London: Karnac.

——— Holtzman D (2008). *A story of her own: The female Oedipus complex reexamined and renamed.* Lanham, MD: Aronson.

Lacan, J. (1966). *Ecrits.* Paris: Seuil.

Lemma, A. (2010). An order of pure decision: Growing up in a virtual world and the adolescent's experience of being-in-a body. *J Am Psychoanal Assoc*58: *691–714.*

Lieberman, J.S. (2000). *Body talk.* Northvale, NJ: Aronson.

Lincoln, B. (1991). *Emerging from the chrysalis.* New York, NY: Oxford UP.

Lubell, W.M. (1994). *The metamorphosis of Baubo.* Nashville, TN: Vanderbilt UP.

Marcus, B.F. (2004). Female passion and the matrix of mother, daughter, and body: Vicissitudes of the maternal transference in the working through of sexual inhibitions. *Psychoanal Inq*24:*680–712.*

Morris, A. (2011). They know what boys want. *New York Magazine*, 7 February, *31–6.*

Novick, J., Novick KK (2004). The superego and the two-system model. *Psychoanal Inq*24:*232–56.*

Novick, K.K., Novick, J. (1987). The essence of masochism. *Psychoanal Stud Child*42:*353–84.*

Olender, M. (1990). Aspects of Baubo. In: Halperin DM, Winkler JJ, Zeitlin FI, editors. *Before sexuality, 83–118.* Princeton, NJ: Princeton UP.

Richards, A.K. (2002). Sadomasochistic perversion and the analytic situation. *J Clin Psychoanal*11:*359–77.*

——— (2003). A fresh look at perversion. *J Am Psychoanal Assoc*51: *1199–218.*

Ross, J.M. (1990). *The eye of the beholder: On the developmental dialogue of fathers and daughters.* In: Nemiroff R, Calarusso C, editors. New dimensions in adult development, *47–72.* New York, NY: Basic Books.

Stein, R. (2005). Why perversion? 'False love' and the perverse pact *Int J Psychoanal*86:*775–99.*

Stuart, J. (2009). A story of her own: The female Oedipus complex reexamined and renamed. *Int J Psychoanal*90:*1207–11.*

Suchet, M. (1995). Having it both ways. In: Glassgold JM, lasenza S, editors. *Lesbians and psychoanalysis: Revolutions in theory and practice.* New York, NY: The Free Press.

Tuch, R. (2010). Murder on the mind: Tyrannical power and other points along the perverse spectrum. *Int J Psychoanal*91:*141–62.*

Tyson, P. (1986). Female psychological development. *Annu Psychoanal*4: *357–73.*

Waites, E. (1982). Fixing women: Devaluation, idealization, and the female fetish. *J Am Psychoanal Assoc*30:*435–9.*

Webster's (1976). *Third international dictionary.* Springfield, MA: Merriam.

Welldon E.V. (1988). *Mother madonna whore.* New York, NY: Guilford.

Welles, J.K., & Wrye, H.K. (1991). The maternal erotic countertransference. *Int J Psychoanal72:93–106.*

Zavitzianos, G. (1971). Fetishism and exhibitionism in the female and their relationship to psychopathy and kleptomania. *Int J Psychoanal52:297–305.*

www.ingramcontent.com/pod-product-compliance
Lightning Source LLC
Chambersburg PA
CBHW062109020426
42335CB00013B/898